English Renaissance Drama
and the Specter of Spain

English Renaissance Drama and the Specter of Spain

Ethnopoetics and Empire

Eric J. Griffin

PENN

UNIVERSITY OF PENNSYLVANIA PRESS

PHILADELPHIA

Published by
University of Pennsylvania Press
Philadelphia, Pennsylvania 19104-4112

Printed in the United States of America on acid-free paper
10 9 8 7 6 5 4 3 2 1

Library of Congress Cataloging-in-Publication Data

Griffin, Eric J.
   English Renaissance drama and the specter of Spain : ethnopoetics and empire / Eric J. Griffin.
   p. cm.
   Includes bibliographical references and index.
   ISBN 978-0-8122-4170-9 (alk. paper)
   1. English drama—Early modern and Elizabethan, 1500–1600—History and criticism. 2. English drama—17th century—History and criticism. 3. Spain—In literature. 4. National characteristics, Spanish, in literature. 5. Spain—Foreign public opinion, British—History. 6. Public opinion—Great Britain—History. 7. Great Britain—Relations—Spain. 8. Spain—Relations—Great Britain. 9. Shakespeare, William, 1564–1616—Knowledge—Spain. I. Title.
   PR658.P65G75 2009
   822'.30935846—dc22   2009005893

For my mother,
in memory of my father

The past is full of life, eager to irritate us, provoke and insult us, tempt us to destroy or repaint it.
  —Milan Kundera, *The Book of Laughter and Forgetting*

CONTENTS

ILLUSTRATIONS

Introduction

The Specter of Spain

> And thries hadde she been at Jerusalem;
> She hadde passed many a straunge strem;
> At Rome she hadde been, and at Boloigne,
> In Galice at Seint-Jame, and at Coloigne.
> —Geoffrey Chaucer, *The Canterbury Tales*, c. 1390

> *Queen Gertrude.* How now, Ophelia?
> *Ophelia. (sings)* How should I your true love know
> From another one?—
> By his cockle hat and staff,
> And by his sandal shoon.
> *Queen Gertrude.* Alas, sweet lady, what imports this song?
> —William Shakespeare, *Hamlet*, c. 1600

THE REMARKABLE LITERARY florescence we associate with the English Renaissance is exactly contemporary with England's protracted conflict with the Spanish Empire, an epoch that saw the emerging Protestant nation's traditional ally transformed as an archetypical adversary. And yet "the specter of Spain" rarely figures in our discussions of the drama long regarded as the period's crowning aesthetic achievement. This book will raise the Spanish specter in order to discover the role played by the drama in the production and dissemination of anti-Spanish sentiment during this troubled historical conjuncture. I maintain here that within the field of early modern studies, discussions of national identity have too often failed to register—for reasons I also explore—the set of international relationships that loomed largest in the minds of the early modern English themselves, those connecting England with the nations of Iberia.

The book's argument unfolds in three ways. First and most evidently, it demonstrates that the anti-Spanish discourse known as the Black Legend of Spanish Cruelty—which "ethnopoetically" *made* or *marked* Iberians as essentially "other"—was far more pervasive in early modern English public culture, and more important to England's emerging sense of nationhood, than we have tended to recognize. I show that the influence of Black Legend discourse (the presence of which has been only casually observed in relation to Renaissance drama) extends even to plays as canonical and thoroughly studied as Thomas Kyd's *Spanish Tragedy*, Christopher Marlowe's *Jew of Malta*, and William Shakespeare's *Merchant of Venice* and *Othello*, texts that remain central to both our curriculum and our critical discourse.

Second, I contend that we see on the stage a pattern observable elsewhere in the early modern English "precursor" public sphere: in the plays, as in the religiopolitical publications that circulated during the 1580s and 1590s, may be detected a movement away from arguments grounded in concerns of *ethos* and toward perspectives valorizing constructions of *ethnos*. While the former recognize shared or coeval relationships between peoples who, though temporarily at odds, hold out at least the possibility of compromise or reconciliation, the latter bridge residual and emerging conceptions of racial difference in order to dichotomize a Spanish other as essentially incompatible with an emerging sense of English nationality.[1]

Finally, I argue that even in the face of their intense international conflict, despite the hardening Hispanophobic positions advocated by Elizabethan elites and their apologists, and in spite of the way their story has been told and retold down the centuries, the specter of Spain—a figure I employ in order to evoke the range of historical and cultural connections that linked the peoples of the British Isles and the Iberian Peninsula even during the period of their most storied antagonisms—continued to permeate English culture in ways the Anglo-American world has largely forgotten. As I will show, powerfully redolent traces of this interrelationship remain readily observable. We can discern these traces most obviously in the many expressions of imperial envy we hear in early modern England's colonial discourses; but we may also hear them during long-cherished moments of theater. Oddly enough, despite centuries of repetition, rehearsal, and performance, a number of these—such as Ophelia's mournful hope that she will recognize her true love "By his cockle hat and staff," or Othello's determined summoning of his "sword of Spain"—have passed by without generating substantial critical comment.

While the obsessive (if understandable) desire of the English to counter Hapsburg hegemony with innovative foreign policy strategies suggests the most obvious dimension of the Spanish specter, this cultural formation looms over many more fields of endeavor than England's return to Mediterranean adventuring or its attempts to establish New World colonies.[2] If we imagine an island people linked to a totality of Iberian influences—a set of associations that, although never fully recoverable, are at once religious and political, material and philosophical, genealogical and dynastic, geographic and cultural— we soon discover ourselves amid a nexus of relationships and connections that predated, permeated, and survived the period we have circumscribed as England's "Renaissance." At some moments clearly manifest, at others barely visible, often contextually assumed to be waiting just offstage, the specter of Spain was ever present in early modern England, often providing a crucial third term in the nation's negotiations with its neighbors, potential allies, or trading partners, and of course, its enemies.

As the historical durability of the Black Legend attests, the purveyors of Hispanophobia were ultimately successful in their efforts to dichotomize the people of Spain. And yet, its rampant Hispanophobia notwithstanding, Renaissance England simultaneously inclined toward Hispanophilia. Residual notions of Anglo-Spanish complementarity—the inheritance of several centuries' worth of prior cultural exchange and interaction—could not easily be overturned; and Iberia's continuing accomplishments, especially, though not exclusively, in imperial and colonial matters, generated substantial admiration and imitation, even among those who were most emphatically opposed to Spanish policy—a phenomenon the book also seeks to recover.

The Burden of Comedy

But this recovery will not be easy. In order to convey a sense of the kind of burden (and the burden of kind) under which a discussion such as this must labor, I offer the following story:

> Elizabeth was twenty and five years old when she began to reign, and she reigned over England forty and four years. . . .
>
> And she was endowed with wisdom from above . . . she chose unto herself wise and able ministers . . . and governed her kingdom with power and great glory.
>
> The sea also was subject unto her, and she reigned on the ocean

with a mighty hand. Her admirals compassed the world about, and brought her home treasures from the uttermost parts of the earth. The glory of England she advanced to its height, and . . . her love was fixed on the happiness of her people, and would not be divided.

The era of learning was also in her reign, and the genius of wit shone bright in the land. Spenser and Shakespeare, Verulam and Sidney, Raleigh and Drake adorned her court, and made her reign immortal.

And woe unto you, Spaniards; woe unto you, ye haughty usurpers of the American seas; for at the lightning of her eyes ye were destroyed, and at the breath of her mouth ye were scattered abroad; she came upon your Armada as a whirlwind, and as a tempest of thunder she overwhelmed you in the sea.

Wisdom and strength were in her right hand, and in her left were glory and wealth.

She spake, and it was war; she waved her hand, and the nations dwelt in peace.

Her ministers were just, her counselors were sage; her captains were bold. . . .

Now the rest of the acts of queen Elizabeth, and all the glorious things that she did, are they not written in the books of the chronicles of England?

And Elizabeth slept with her fathers, and she was a virgin; she tasted not of man, neither subjected she herself unto him all the days of her life.

And she was buried in the chapel of King Henry the seventh, and James of Scotland reigned in her stead.

And Jamie thought himself a bonny king, and a mickle wise mon. Howbeit he was a fool and a pedant.[3]

Although this essentializing invocation of "Spanish haughtiness" pales in comparison to some of the constructions of Hispanicity that follow, these rhetorical constructions exemplify "ethnopoetics."[4] Their most recent reinscription may be among the most widely disseminated. Responding to the Spanish ambassador's warning that "there is a wind coming that will sweep away [her] pride," Cate Blanchett, reprising her Oscar-winning role of 1998 in *Elizabeth: The Golden Years* (2007), declares, "I too can command the wind, sir." Virtually replicating the commonplaces we have just read, Blanchett's Elizabeth threatens: "I have a hurricane in me; it will strip Spain bare if you dare to try me."[5]

It would be difficult to conceive of a story more familiar. From the moment of its earliest narrations, its attractions have been found irresistible, especially among those born into the national cultures that constitute "Greater Britain."[6] Our collective familiarity is doubtless attributable to a considerable amount of received knowledge: we have not forgotten the romance of Elizabeth Tudor and her court, the legendary intrigues of which have so often been the stuff of popular history, fiction, and film; we recall the central place in this world of our English Renaissance writers; we remember as pivotal the 1588 victory over England's "traditional enemy," which secured the nation and gave birth to its empire. When our native speech is English, we imbibe these cultural memories with language itself.

Thereby hangs my tale. For the narrative quoted above does not come from a writer of the sixteenth or early seventeenth century, some half-remembered contemporary of Drake or Raleigh or Bacon who might have had some personal experience of the world it represents. This selection from *The Chronicle of the Kings of England* is a virtual recollection that comes via the eighteenth-century pen (and press) of Robert Dodsley, the publisher, playwright, and poet who was also one of the principal inventors of the dramatic canon that remains a cornerstone of literary study.[7] Yet so much inside Dodsley's narrative loop do we remain that only the odd shift of voice with which he ethnopoetically marks the ascension of James I (and signals that the reign of the Stuarts will consist of another story altogether) estranges us. As strange, I think, is the fact that, despite the more than two and a half centuries that lie between us and the composition of this biblically affected prose, Dodsley's parable reveals the metanarrative around which our literary and historical traditions have often remained structured.

Although we might find its equivalent in many places, Dodsley's most obvious precedent is the "official" one, a version of which is preserved in William Camden's *History of the Most Renowned and Victorious Princess Elizabeth, Late Queen of England* (1615). The story Camden relates is as attractive as the young Elizabeth herself: "She being now 25 years of age," he writes, "and taught by Experience and Adversity, (the most effectuall and powerfull Masters)," the queen "had gathered Wisdom above her age: the first proof whereof she gave in chusing her Counsellours."[8] Elizabeth then "applied her first Care . . . to the restoring of the Protestant religion, which both by her Instruction from her tender years, and by her own Judgement, she verily perswaded her self to be most true, and consonant to the Sacred Scriptures, and the sincerity of the Primitive Church" (6). Camden describes how Europe's most eligible princess entertained the amorous "King Philip," whose untoward advances "she putteth off by little and little, with a most modest answer, and honest and maidenly shamefec'dness, but in very deed out of scruple and conscience" (13). He recalls that with the help of her devoted courtiers, who had "declaimed against the Spaniards as a People puffed up with Pride," the humble young monarch, "being a virgin of most mild disposition" (13), began to grow "most adverse to this Marriage" and "thought nothing more pleasing to God . . . [than] to put off the importunate Suitor" (14). Soon her government had called for "an Act . . . restoring the Crown of England to its former Jurisdiction in matters Ecclesiastical: to wit, by renewing the Laws of Henry the Eighth against the See of Rome, and of Edward the Sixth for the Protestants, which laws were repealed by Queen Mary" (19). With "the Protestant Religion being now by Authority of Parliament established," Elizabeth resolved "to hold an even course in her whole life and all her actions" and took for her Motto, "SEMPER EADEM, that is, ALWAYS THE SAME." Through this highly ceremonial act, the English estates had been reconciled, and "the rest of [Elizabeth's] Counsels consisted in these points: That she might carefully provide for the Safety of her People: for (as she often had in her mouth) that the Commonwealth might ever be in Safety, she was never without Care: And that she might Purchase herself Love amongst her Subjects, amongst her Enemies Fear, and Glory amongst all Men" (35–36).

From the spirit of Camden's history Dodsley had departed nary a jot. His primary improvisations, though he was hardly the first to emphasize the themes, were to bring the writers of the age within the circle of Elizabethan elites (which is not surprising, considering the range of literary occupations upon which his own livelihood depended), and to heap "woe" upon the nation whom Camden had seen as "a People puffed up with Pride," and whose failed invasion, Philip II's Enterprise of England, Elizabeth had set upon as "a tempest of thunder." Virtually summoning the famous *Armada Portrait* of George Gower, the iconic representation that has so often served as a metonym for the signal event, Dodsley's rhetorical construction clearly reproduces the authorized "Story of England."

More than thirty-five years ago Hayden White showed us that history emplotted as "comedy," no less than a drama staging "a movement from one kind of society to another," tends to hold out hope "for the temporary triumph of man over his world by the prospect of occasional *reconciliations* of the forces at play in the natural and social worlds."[9] In such narratives, "the condition of society is represented as being purer, saner, and healthier as a result of the conflict among seemingly inalterably opposed elements in the world," which "are revealed to be, in the long run, harmonizable with one another, unified, at one with themselves and others."[10] It has long been recognized that the view of Elizabethan history Dodsley reinscribes, the one his epoch inherits from Camden's, draws heavily on the literary conventions of courtly romance and romantic comedy. The purest expressions of this tendency may be found, of course, in the pastoral and romantic epic of Edmund Spenser, the sonnet sequences produced by courtiers like Philip Sidney, Michael Drayton, Walter Raleigh, and others, and most especially and influentially, in the history plays and comedies of William Shakespeare, which achieve resolution by fulfilling the endless courtship ritual that the Virgin Queen herself declined to consummate.[11]

As evidenced in Camden's works and in any number of contemporary aesthetic productions (which inspired, in turn, countless subsequent rewritings), a "world picture" became the unquestioned master plot of Elizabethan society. But as White cautioned, we should recognize that the values of an earlier period are not those that tend to matter most in the narrative reconstruction of the past. Rather, he writes, "It is the *value* accorded to the current social establishment . . . that accounts for . . . different conceptions of both the *form* of historical evolution and the *form* that historical knowledge must take."[12] Comic form, especially the form of Shakespearean comedy, requires an obstacle, some tired tradition or agency that its youthful protagonists must overcome if their society, like the one over which Portia presides in *The Merchant of Venice*, is to achieve its "natural" state of unification and harmony.[13] If the "truth" of Elizabethan history has been most commonly reinscribed in terms of the generic conventions and rhetorical operations we associate with the comic kind, this historiographical inclination may be traced to the generation of Kyd, Marlowe, and Shakespeare. To the extent that we have valorized their outward-looking view as natural, we have allowed to remain undisclosed the emerging attitudes toward ethnicity and "race" to which their vision had begun to incline.

Ethnicity and Race

In his study of the history of the idea of race in the West, Ivan Hannaford observed, "Dynastic ambitions and religious issues were of such great consequence [in the sixteenth century] that there was little room for the growth of a conscious idea of race as we understand it today."[14] Thus Hannaford was led to argue that in the writings of John Foxe and the "early volumes of Richard Hakluyt," as in the polemics of Bartolomé de Las Casas, we see "very little movement from the basic notion of a Greco-Roman political order in the Aristotelian and Ciceronian sense" (183). But this discussion of "thought before race" broke off with Hakluyt's written accounts of the "voyages to Guinea in the 1560s and to North America in the 1570s" (183), before leaping ahead a hundred years to consider the period from 1684 to 1815, "when major writers dealt explicitly with race as an organizing idea and came to understand it as an ethnic grouping rather than as a race and order" (187). Perhaps by virtue of the fact that Hannaford took the high road through philosophy, religion, political and natural science, rather than consulting the more public discourses of early modern nationalism, the essentialist spirit of the Black Legend eluded his view. In any case, it was precisely the linkage of dynastic ambitions and religious issues with newly inflected discourses of otherness that provided the conditions from which more recognizably modern racial categories would emerge.

And this early modern discourse hardly appears to have been "unconscious." Indeed, many of the period's plays, including *The Jew of Malta*, *The Merchant of Venice*, and *Othello*, have in common with the most virulent Black Legend polemics the fact that we find in them a discourse of Hispanicity that is clearly racialized—which is to say that in its "mature" form, *la leyenda negra* is very much a discourse of color. As one Black Legend polemicist delighted in pointing out, "The *Mores* in eight monthes conquered *Spaine* . . . and . . . the *Spaniards* were eight hundred years before they recovered that losse: during which time, we must not thinke that the *Negroes* sent for women out of *Aphrick*."[15] Here the rhetorical force of "blackness," to borrow Kim Hall's formulation, "draws power from England's ongoing negotiations of African difference and from the implied color comparison therein."[16] During the hundred years Hannaford's history elides, religious controversies and dynastic conflicts of the kind that moved Foxe and Hakluyt had combined with incipient racialist thought to a devastating international effect. It is not difficult to imagine how in this cultural climate the white/black opposition that would be staged so infamously with the performance of Thomas Middleton's *A Game at Chess* (1624) took on a vividly racialist charge.

Reflecting on the influence of James Shapiro's important *Shakespeare and the Jews* (1996), Jonathan Burton has observed that, while the premise that "the English turned to Jewish questions in order to answer English ones" has been instructive, "Shapiro sometimes fails to acknowledge ways in which other racialized outsiders also functioned 'as answers' to 'English questions' often in complex relation to each other."[17] Shapiro's study itself, while noting that "in the wake of the Spanish and Portuguese Inquisitions, the Protestant Reformation, and the expansion of English overseas travel and trade, the question of who was a Jew began to be asked with greater frequency and, on occasion, urgency,"[18] reveals numerous Spanish connections to Jewish communities, such as to the Marrano communities harboring in the Protestant North and to the Sephardic exiles of Italy, North Africa, and the eastern Mediterranean. Alongside Shapiro's work, Burton's own *Traffic and Turning: Islam and English Drama, 1579–1624* (2005), Daniel Vitkus's *Turning Turk: English Theater and the Multicultural Mediterranean, 1570–1630* (2003), and Nabil Matar's *Britain and Barbary, 1589–1689* (2005) have recently demonstrated that when we look at the arc of Anglo-Turkish and Anglo-Moorish aspiration and policy, emblematized especially by "the negotiations and collusions that took place between Queen Elizabeth and Mulay Ahmad al-Mansur,"[19] we find ourselves in the presence of Anglo-Islamic triangulations intended to confront the involved parties' anxieties regarding the expansionist aims of Spain. In other words, the "English questions" posed in complex relation to all of these "racialized outsiders"—Jews, Turks, and Moors—often point in the direction of Spanish answers.

I am not attempting to argue that the English, like the people of most nations, were not prone to feeling fearful of outsiders.[20] But I do not believe that the evidence suggests that the people of England were any more "naturally" xenophobic than their neighbors; it may indicate, however, that they were "guided" into thinking in terms of essentializing categories. It was the period from 1588 until the moment of James I's ascension that saw Spain become "Hispanized" (if I can summon an Elizabethan coining). This word initially tended *not* to refer to Spanish ethnicity in any essential way; rather, it meant "to make Spanish" or "to imbue with Spanish ideas." As such, it connoted a kind of popular Hispanophilia, a taste for "things Spanish" or following the "Spanish fashion."[21] In the context of England's late sixteenth-century Spanish troubles, to be Hispanized implied one's sympathy toward Philip II's policies and came to suggest, most especially, an identification with Roman Catholic universality over and against Protestant particularism. But the word and its various cognates gained their full persuasive force only when they began to acquire the racialist tinge of color in the post-Armada years.

As Protestant claims to English governmental institutions and cultural life were legitimated, the religious traditions, imperial obligations, dynastic inheritances, and colonizing projects of Catholic Spain (along with "native" Roman Catholic pretensions) were demonized, delegitimized, and deposed. Within the canon of our Renaissance drama, as in the corpus of extant print matter from various discursive genres, we can view the special role the Black Legend played in the forging of a new "fictive ethnicity" for Spain during this early moment of national becoming, even as it simultaneously helped to consolidate the interests of an English national culture struggling to define itself.[22] This was the cultural work accomplished by the marking of Spanish ethnicity and the Hispanization of Spain. Perhaps never has a collective propaganda campaign been so successful: not only in the short run but also over the *longue durée*.

Winding through this book, then, is an argument about incipient racism. Although it is often claimed that to speak of "race" in the early modern period is to indulge in anachronism—indeed, I once tended toward this view—my exploration of Black Legend discourse has convinced me that a racialism prefiguring that which would prove so influential in later periods was already emerging in the late sixteenth century. I have come to believe, with Shapiro, that "to write about nation and race in the sixteenth century independent of each other (and of theological paradigms) is to underestimate how racialized nationalism was, and how nationalized racial thinking was, at this time."[23] But a substantial strain of this racialism arises within a cultural sphere in which we have not commonly looked for it, the sphere of Anglo-Spanish relations.

This is not to say that we are in the presence of modern racist discourse. As Arthur Little has observed, "race" in the early modern era "works less as a stable identity category than as a semiotic field, one as infinitely varying as the cultural discourses constituting what we have come to identify as the early modern era or Renaissance."[24] In Black Legend texts, as elsewhere in early modern discourses that strain in their efforts to categorize difference, "depictions of race can draw from mythology, the Bible, the voices of classical authorities, the humors, physiognomy, and . . . cultural location and habits" (2). But during the "golden age" of *la leyenda negra*, the period between the Armada crisis and the Stuart succession, not only does proximity to and relationship with Africa become an index of Hispanicity, "Africa" begins to signify in such a way as to play into the conjuncture's growing obsession with miscegenation.

It has been argued that modern European miscegenation anxieties begin in Spain.[25] The *pureza de sangre*, or "purity of blood," with which the Spanish Inquisition famously concerned itself certainly did take root there. And yet the tendency to identify modern racism's roots in Iberia may itself be a Black Legend inheritance. For to ascribe Spanish origins to such a pernicious phenomenon as the racist "structure of feeling"[26] is to locate a cultural impulse solely in others, when, like so many inquisitional practices—prejudgment, incarceration, extortion, execution, ethnocentrism, xenophobia—it may have been far more widespread. As a number of important studies have shown, early modern England harbored miscegenation anxieties of its own. And while English polemicists, preachers, and politicians could denigrate Spain by pointing to its "mixed" origins, they could also propose "Spanish" solutions to their own "racial" problems. Thus Elizabeth Tudor, during what was perhaps the most Hispanophobic moment in English history, would replicate the quintessentially Iberian sin of expulsion by deporting the "Negroes and Blackamoors" residing in the realm,[27] even as her polemicists and propagandists were vilifying Spain for the same sort of policy.

As Sujeta Iyengar has shown, "blackness," far from existing as a hermetic category, could signify in literary contexts in ways that "entangle with variable concepts of skin color and emergent racial distinctions."[28] Prior to the institutionalization of scientific racism, as Kim Hall reminds us, "black" could be a trope "applied not only to dark-skinned Africans but to Native Americans, Indians and even Irish and Welsh as groups that needed to be marked as other."[29] Such "color comparison" becomes relevant in this discussion for a number of reasons, not least because many of England's negotiations with difference are mediated by its associations and antagonisms with the nations of Iberia, which, in fact, become the first of the modern era to articulate, encode, and institutionalize the differences that other European nations will adapt and adopt to their own needs until, ultimately, later centuries grant them "scientific" basis.[30]

Although at times the Black Legend appears to concern literal or bodily blackness, because in early modernity the word "race" signified in such variable and problematic ways[31]—as Imtiaz Habib recognizes, "to the Elizabethans the word more often than not meant lineage rather than physical or cultural difference"[32]—I appeal here to "ethnos," which I derive from the root of the somewhat less emotionally charged term "ethnicity." I find this differentiation useful in describing the processes of national individuation in the period because, as Stuart Hall suggests, "The term 'ethnicity' acknowledges the place of history, language and culture in the construction of subjectivity and identity, as well as the fact that all discourse is placed, positioned, situated, and all knowledge contextual. Representation is possible only because enunciation is always produced within codes which have a history, a position within the discursive formations of a particular space and time."[33] It is the processual nature of this "coding" that will be of particular interest to this study. I suggest that the "situatedness" of Hispanophobia, coming as it does at this early moment of national definition (not only in England but also in France, the Netherlands, and elsewhere)—aided and abetted by the development of print mediation—renders Black Legend discourse an important field of investigation.

Like "race," "ethnicity" comes to us replete with its own slippery meanings and quite troublesome (and troubling) history. And like "racial," "ethnic" did not acquire its modern sense, "pertaining to race; peculiar to a race or nation;" or "designating a racial or other group within a larger system," until a later historical conjuncture.[34] As John Minsheu noted in his *Dictionarie in Spanish and English* (1599), "an Ethnick" designated "a heathen," "gentile," or "pagan," "one that knoweth not God."[35] This significance is important because in early modernity to name another "pagan" was to render that other not fully human. More threatening than the "barbarian" of classical distinction, the pagan existed in Christian terms among the "fallen," reprobate, or Antichristian—which was precisely how the warring tribes of Christendom each named the other during the European Reformation. In the early years of Elizabeth's reign, the preface to the English translation of Gonsalvius Montanus's widely known *Discovery and Playne Declaration of the subtill and sundry practices of the Holy Inquisition of Spayne* (1568), used the term in this way, noting that the institution was established to triumph "over Paynims and Ethnickes"[36] (a "Spanish" dichotomization to which the text's translator did not object). The English reformer John Foxe, more troubled by the institution's "ceremonial pomp" and "barbarous abuses" (of Protestants) than with its persecution of "Jews" (for whom he expressed little sympathy), seems to have held a similar view.[37]

In the interest of clarity, then, I will follow this line of "reasoning": "ethnicity" will be conceptualized here as the construction of *others*, whereas "nationality," with its accentuation of the internal consanguinity valued by institutions such as the Inquisition, will refer to the tendency of peoples toward *self*-identification.[38] I will also push beyond much recent discussion of ethnicity and race by emphasizing the religious implications of ethnos as constructed by English Protestants. By discovering the pagan nature of Iberian Catholicism, Protestant biblicists were able to reconstruct the Spanish Christian as no longer Christian at all. By 1580, the Black Legend discourses of the north had begun to link the pagan quality of Iberian faith with particular racial (that is, genealogical) antecedents that were seen to constitute a distinct Spanish ethnicity.

Hispanophobia

For a number of historically specific reasons, then, one *otherness* was impressed most profoundly upon the English imagination, the otherness of imperial

Spain. But unlike the unknown, or barely known, others of, say, Africa or the East and West Indies, the culture groups of Iberia were not mysterious peoples about whom English playwrights could only hazard imaginative constructions. To the contrary, England knew "the Spains" extremely well. Indeed, their aristocratic, military, clerical, scholastic, and merchant classes had been on intimate terms for centuries, possessing a shared history of intermarriage and commerce, crusade and pilgrimage, technological and intellectual exchange. Rarely in human history have two cultures that shared so much dropped so far and so rapidly in mutual esteem as did the national cultures of England and Spain.

The discursive processes that helped to precipitate this decline and fall have not often come under scrutiny. But the *representation* of Hispanicity in English public culture, including the *repetition* of anti-Hispanic typologies in popular drama, played a significant role in the astonishingly rapid dissemination of the anti-Spanish discourse we have come to know as the Black Legend of Spanish Cruelty. If there were a dozen public theaters in London, each capable of admitting as many as 1,500 or more audience members per show, up to 25,000 people per week may have attended performances.[39] These venues would thus have provided an experiential community surpassed only by required church attendance. While I am not suggesting that the stage operated primarily as an ideological platform for the Elizabethan regime, highly placed government officials recognized the theater's potential for furthering their own aims as well as for inspiring resistance to their policies. So it is not surprising that they would encourage the harnessing of its energies. However, if the theater served the aims of the state, it probably did so in ways that were often as tacit or consensual as they were coerced. For as anthropologist William Beeman suggests, "Theater does more than engage participants in the immediate context of the theatrical event. It evokes and solidifies a network of social and cognitive relationships existing in a triangular relationship between performer, spectator, and the world at large."[40] Feeling the pressures of their historical moment, with its military conscriptions, refugee movements, dearth, and rumor, Elizabethans would have turned to the theater not only for entertainment or relief but also to help them, as a community, to make sense of the times in which they lived, to interpret the challenges their world presented, and to understand the nature of the enemies they faced. In the process, the Elizabethan theater played a substantial role in conveying to the English a sense of who "the Spaniard" was, in convincing them of his designs on their nation, and in inculcating Black Legend assumptions as representing historical truth.

Margaret Greer, Walter Mignolo, and Maureen Quilligan have gone a long way toward redressing the relative paucity of critical inquiry with respect to the Black Legend. Their recent collection *Rereading the Black Legend: The Discourses of Religious and Racial Difference in the Renaissance Empires* (2007) contains a number of essays that situate Hispanophobic discourse in a global and comparative context. Still, like much earlier scholarship, this work is often primarily descriptive. Although the study acknowledges that the Black Legend precipitated "a racism that was subtended by religious differences and that not only helped to structure the imperial programs of sixteenth-century western European societies but also continued to structure western Europe's thinking into the time of Emmanuel Kant" (1), it does not go far enough toward describing the character of these religious differences.[41] It was, I will argue, the "form and pressure" of English Protestantism, to borrow a construction voiced by Hamlet, and the pressure that this ideology exerted on any number of cultural forms—including, of course, dramatic ones—that endowed the Black Legend with both its contemporary rhetorical effectiveness and its astonishingly long afterlife.

In order to discover the contours of these important religious differences, I add in this book to the critical discussion of the relationship between the Black Legend and early modern discourses of ethnicity and race an intensified interpretive dimension that marries methodological approaches that literary studies and cultural anthropology hold in common. While I will argue that *la leyenda negra* remains, to borrow M. M. Bakhtin's formulation, a phenomenally identifiable "speech genre,"[42] I recognize that its detection has often been complicated by the messiness of early modern national and ethnic identifications. As several recent studies have shown, a number of inherited frameworks for describing ethnic, national, and racial groupings competed for dominance in early modernity.[43] The period's anti-Spanish "ethnologists"—mostly northern Protestants, although writers from rival Roman Catholic nations also participated in Hispanophobic inscription—tended to employ genealogical, geographic, and humoral categories, which they drew from a primordial stew of biblical and classical sources. The Elizabethan polemicists, propagandists, and playwrights of the 1580s and 1590s annexed to these typologies more current historical anecdotes and exempla in order to derive an array of stereotypes that coalesced to constitute the Black Legend.

To survey these Hispanophobic discourses is to recognize that by the 1590s a new set of "rules" had begun to govern the public representation of Spanish nationality. Through the era's rapidly expanding print media, Black Legend typologies became so widely disseminated that they came to constitute a sign system pointing indexically to a specific ethnonational referent. In semiotic terms, we might say that the indices of Hispanicity became increasingly *overcoded*.[44] The incessant repetition of these commonplaces—which remain readily identifiable to the trained ear and therefore quite accessible to analysis—created, if I can employ an anachronistic metaphor for a moment, a kind of "feedback loop" that functioned to valorize an emerging ethos of religiopolitical and ethnic homogeneity. This semiotic overcoding occurred in any number of public venues and discursive domains. Evidence of the process lies principally in the polemics and treatises, sermons and commentaries, broadsides and ballads that were rushed into publication by printers working on both sides of the confessional divide, as well as in extant government documents. The most casual examination of these "leftovers" from the Reformation print wars leaves the impression that scholarship has underestimated the extent of the Black Legend's dissemination and the pervasiveness of its influence.[45]

Although the broad dissemination of *la leyenda negra* has become somewhat axiomatic, especially among Hispanists and Latin Americanists, in the many decades since Julián Juderías drew attention to its enduring presence, advancing scholarship has continued to probe its origins, to draw its representational contours more sharply, and to explain its broader cultural effects.[46] David J. Weber's explanation may be the most usefully succinct. The Black Legend, he writes, is "the inherited . . . view that Spaniards were unusually cruel, avaricious, treacherous, fanatical, superstitious, cowardly, corrupt, decadent, indolent, and authoritarian."[47] Observing that this "Hispanophobia" had "deep roots in Europe," Weber notes that the perception "reached full flower in the sixteenth century among Protestants in northern Europe, where it had taken the form of propaganda against Spain's militant Catholicism and its highly successful imperialism, and it had continued to flourish in the earliest English-language histories of Spain's North American provinces" (336). Helpful as this formulation is, however, it does not tell us much about *process*. More than simply identifying the presence of this propagandistic discourse and observing its pervasiveness, I am concerned with *how* the "white" proponents of this discourse were so successful in fashioning an opponent that is so manifestly their "black" opposite.

To take one example of this ethnopoetic fashioning, *A Pageant of Spanish Humours* (London, 1599), a pamphlet "translated out of Dutche" and printed by stationer and propagandist John Wolfe, declared that "Truth intending to travel triumphantly, the worldes circumference, doth by her true recording trumpe, blazon the severall and sundry natural humours of a Spanish

Signior, as the limitation of time will permit her."[48] What followed was a list of sixteen "true" aphorisms, glossed in such a way that "the kinds and qualities of a Signior of Spaine" were "naturally described and lively portrayed" (A2). By focusing on the gap between Signior's public and private faces—he is "an Angel in the Church" and a "Divel in his lodging"—the *Pageant* discovers "the Spaniard" as, among other things, "A Foxe to deceive Women," "Avaritious," "Ambitious," "Bloodthirstie and tyrannous," "Greedie of revenge," and "Faithlesse and perjourous," before proclaiming it "A miserable estate to be under a Signior's subjection" (A2v). This particular tract, which enumerates the defining characteristics of the Black Legend precisely as Weber describes them, had a long, international shelf-life, appearing in French translation as late as 1608, in spite of Henri IV's reembrace of Roman Catholicism and France's participation, after 1598, in the Treaty of Vervins and a general Pax Hispanica.[49]

This seems to have been a pattern of distribution repeated numerous times. Originating in the Low Countries, *A Pageant of Spanish Humours*, like many artifacts of the Hispanophobic genre, circulated throughout the Protestant north, disseminating propagandistic typologies that were never quite dislodged. "[The Spaniard] is never glutted with blood," the pamphlet declares, "he farre surpasses *Pharoah* in cruelty, *Herod* in tyrannie, and *Antiochus* in bloodthirstiness. It is inough," it continues, "yea too much knowne in our Netherlands, and not only in *Europe, Asia* and *Affrica*, but also in the farthest part of *America*, whereby he sheweth himselfe to bee sprung from the cruell *Goths* and blood-thirstie *Wandals* [sic]" (B3). Spanish "cruelty," "bloodthirstiness," and "tyranny"—more extreme than the brutality of Pharaoh, Herod, and Antiochus of antiquity, and that of the Goths and Vandals of more recent historical memory— were being felt in every corner of the globe: from Europe, Asia, and Africa to the "farthest part of *America*."

An overarching concern of my book will thus be to observe how these Hispanophobic commonplaces were promoted. Although it is true that occasional expressions of anti-Spanish sentiment can be heard in the discourses of earlier decades, the number of publications bearing imprints from the 1580s and 1590s suggests that by the late sixteenth century Black Legend typologies were becoming so thoroughly codified that Protestant nationalists could deploy them as a virtual Hispanophobic catechism. In the face of the threat posed after 1580 by a unified Iberia, English writers and adventurers—much in the manner of their contemporaries in France, the Low Countries, and Spanish-dominated Italy, with whom they shared similar resentments and nationalist aspirations—unleashed an onslaught of demonizing rhetoric from which the

English- and Spanish-speaking worlds have never fully recovered. Going far beyond the discursive assaults one rival might be expected to direct toward another, the purpose of these texts was the propagation of anti-Hispanic attitudes among a public increasingly immersed in Protestant biblicism, whose perceptions regarding the Iberian nations with whom England had a long tradition of mutual exchange were now in flux. It should not surprise us that these cultural energies registered in the period's drama, which drew freely from the print trade in order to craft the ethnic identity of England's Iberian imperial rivals and to inculcate attitudes favorable to the political interests of the Elizabethan state.

Hispanophilia

And yet, within the network of relationships and connections that linked England with Spain we may observe a profound ambivalence. For there was a reverse side to the Hispanophobic coin. Throughout this period of European national consolidation, the specter of Spain could loom as positively as it could negatively. Even Protestant England could express rank Hispanophobia in one breath and effusive Hispanophilia in the next. Ben Jonson may have best expressed the tendency:

> Ask from your courtier, to your inns-of-court man,
> To your mere milliner; they will tell you all,
> Your Spanish jennet is the best horse; your Spanish
> Stoup is the best garb: your Spanish beard
> Is the best cut; your Spanish ruffs are the best
> Wear; your Spanish pavanne the best dance;
> Your Spanish titillation in a glove
> The best perfume; and for your Spanish pike,
> And Spanish blade, let your poor Captain speak. (4.4.7–15)[50]

Even granting Jonson's satirical slant, in this passage from *The Alchemist* (1610) we see Hispanophobia and Hispanophilia walking hand in hand. While complicating the anti-Hispanism characteristic of so much contemporary religiopolitical discourse, the dramatization reveals how admiration and attraction could mix with resentment and fear, as the things that came by way of Iberia—the finest horses, articles of clothing, hairstyles, entertainments, and toiletries—were often judged superior to their native counterparts and therefore valued as marks of status. As Fernand Braudel reminded us, obsession with "the Spanish fashion" was continent-wide during the sixteenth century, "a sign of the political preponderance of the Catholic King's 'world-wide' empire";[51] we should not, therefore, be surprised to find this aspect of the Spanish specter, often betrayed by an immodest, if understandable, covetousness, inhabiting early modern England. While Jonson pokes fun at England's taste for things foreign, much as Shakespeare had done in his somewhat earlier comedy, *The Merchant of Venice* (c. 1596–97), his humor assumes a deadly serious tone when his lines turn to the technology of warfare, emblematized by the Spanish pikes and blades of which many a "poor [English] Captaine [could surely] speak." While Iberian accomplishments, then, were often read by Protestant ideologues in Black Legend terms—that is, as signs of Spanish tyranny, cruelty, and irreligion—they could as readily be viewed as manifesting the Spanish monarchy's divine favor. For any nation-state seeking similar national cohesion and imperial reward, Spain continued to represent an example worthy of emulation.

To observe sixteenth-century England in relationship to Spain is to recognize that the obsessions attributed to the Spanish national temper prove to be more the province of their common European history than we have often been willing to admit. As early modern subjects of various nations engaged in acts of "cultural mimesis" in situations of encounter and exchange that were often without unambiguous precedent, these nation writers drew on a common store of classical and biblical models in an effort to negotiate them. However, as Barbara Fuchs points out, "mimetic mirrorings among emerging early modern nations challenge the process of individuation by which those nations attempt to become fully consolidated states with an exceptional claim to imperial destiny," for "[i]mitation compromises the narratives of national distinction by emphasizing inconvenient similarities and shared heritages."[52]

Though increasingly exceptionalist in its outlook, early modern England presented no exception to this pattern. Far earlier than their neighbors, the Spanish and Portuguese had to confront "modern" problems such as transoceanic exploration, long-distance communication and supply, the prospect of internal threats posed by an ethnically and religiously diverse population, how best to incorporate immigrant and refugee groups, what moral and legal obligations the empire owed colonized peoples and slaves, and so on. A number of the choices the Spanish made in their attempts to address these issues did prove, to borrow Las Casas's term, "devastating." But this should not lead us to ascribe to Spain any essential ethos attributable to a particular "nationality." For historically speaking, cultural hyperbole such as that in which texts like *A Pageant of Spanish Humours* indulged—projected upon the peoples of Iberia by competitor states that lagged nearly a century behind them in the era of European colonial expansion—often worked to provide a moralistic smokescreen behind which imperial rivals of a quite similar temper could operate with relative impunity.[53] This was certainly the case for the English, who would go so far as to consider "Spanish" solutions to their own internal problems—a pattern mirrored (as I demonstrate in Chapters 4 and 5), in the drama of Marlowe and Shakespeare.

"Renaissance" England

As I explore some of the complexities and contradictions that characterized Anglo-Spanish relations in early modernity, I also put into question the notion that this era represented England's "rebirth" (over and against an innately different late fifteenth or early or mid-sixteenth-century experience). I do so because the term "Renaissance"—like so many of the categories we inherit—comes down to us wearing a conceptual heritage that masks as much as it reveals. Concerns about periodization and tradition will thus surface at a number of junctures in this book. By problematizing this literary-historical signpost I do not seek some orientation toward history and textuality "truer" than that of the many studies that have viewed the English achievement in relation to the broader European (or a more narrowly Italian) epoch of cultural florescence, nor do I aim to construe from Elizabethan art "the particular Spirit" of the English people.[54]

However, since the era of Hippolyte Taine's *Histoire de la littérature anglaise* (1863), our discipline has tended to embrace a conception of the later sixteenth century that mirrors the historical structure posited in Jacob Burckhardt's *Civilization of the Renaissance in Italy* (1860). For England, as in Italy during the epoch of Michelangelo, Leonardo, and Machiavelli, "a new fact appears" in the Elizabethan period, "the State as the outcome of reflection and calculation—the State as work of art," a structure that provided an atmosphere in which "people were forced to know the inward resources of their own nature."[55] Imagining just this sort of cultural apotheosis (Hayden White's sense of comic "harmony" is once again apropos), a long tradition of historical criticism (which had internalized this nineteenth-century model) neglected important international and temporal linkages in favor of describing a totalizing Elizabethan "achievement" or "world picture."[56] Against this sort of coherent whole, my book attempts to figure an English nation very much in *process*, a cultural system in which the "residual" and "emergent" are, to adapt Raymond Williams, "significant both in themselves and in what they reveal of the characteristics" of the epochal view we have regarded as "dominant."[57] In addition, to characterize the Elizabethan moment as England's "Renaissance" is to invoke a broadly humanist interpretive tradition (a worthy yet often obfuscating inheritance), when the English poetics of the late sixteenth century were commonly as nationalist in orientation as they were classicist. Perhaps more properly, Tudor England's humanism tended to be filtered by, and subordinated to, its nationalism. England's ethnopoetic discourses reveal much about the character of this nationalism, particularly insofar as that character can be divined from the various representational modes via which the Elizabethans conceived and promoted their vision of the state.

Temporal prejudices have thus joined disciplinary ones as we have periodized away connections that for contemporaries would have been patent. In no field of early modern English culture are the hazards of periodization more apparent than in the field of Anglo-Spanish relations. The sixteenth century alone saw two Anglo-Spanish dynastic unions, and several proposals for a Spanish succession came with the unavoidable conclusion that the Tudor line would remain without an heir. The royal houses of England and Spain had earlier benefited from a number of important dynastic marriages, including those arranged for Edward I and John of Gaunt. When James I proposed a Spanish match for his son Charles, he sought a return to the status quo ante—and not to promote an "unnatural" union as his and Spain's detractors so effectively argued. Although much of this book's focus will be on drama produced during the last two decades of Elizabeth Tudor's reign, it will also reach back to the years prior to the English Reformation in order to recover memories of an international relationship that held much more in common than it did in contrast, and remained relatively unblemished by religious and ethnic division. Insofar as it is possible, I want to imagine a sense of what the possibilities for Anglo-Spanish relationships might have been before the Whiggish teleology we have often taken for granted emerged as one of history's givens.

I noted a moment ago that in *Hamlet*, when Ophelia sings that she will know her true love "By his cockle hat and staff / and sandal shoon" (4.5.25–26), she pictures him in the traditional habit of the returning Santiago pilgrim.[58] The first epigraph to this Introduction recalls an earlier literary example. In *The Canterbury Tales* we find the Wife of Bath counting among her prior pilgrimages one to "Galice at Sainte Jame" (General Prologue: 466). Thus arises, from what are probably the two most canonical texts in English literature, the specter of an England linked to Spain as a site of intercultural ritual and shared belief. And yet, because we have been culturally conditioned to read Chaucer and Shakespeare as standing for either "timeless art" or "English genius," interconnections such as these have been allowed to remain largely latent. For the thousands of English men and women whose transnational longings had led them over many generations to make the pilgrimage to Santiago de Compostela alongside the faithful of all nations, the Spanish specter would have beckoned positively—as indeed it did for the English "fugitives" of the Elizabethan era.

Loose though "medieval" and "Renaissance" texts often play with history, they also mark moments of profound intercultural significance. When we cease replaying the comic (and temporal) isolation of our nationalist (and disciplinary) forebears, features such as these begin to emerge, not only within literary texts, but from any number of discursive fields. To reanimate these relationships and connections is to circumvent the anachronistic insularity we inherit from previous generations, and to reinvigorate them for more globally attuned audiences in the present day.

No Island Is an Island

It will be clear to most readers that *English Renaissance Drama and the Specter of Spain* shares a number of affinities, both political and methodological, with the New Historicist movement of the 1980s and 1990s. But like a number of scholars who came into the profession in its wake, I began to sense that as much as some New Historicist criticism spoke of crossing borders and as committed as many of its practitioners were to unmasking the apparatuses of ideology, New Historicist critical methodologies—like those of the older historicisms they claimed to be interrogating and displacing—often failed to envision a time when the boundaries between nations were substantially different from what they were in modernity.[59]

As the twenty-first century began, the institutionalized study of literature was still manifesting what Roland Greene dubbed "an almost superstitious obeisance to the category of the national."[60] Our historicizing practices often reproduced a critical discourse in which "the nations" of Europe—frozen synchronically at the moment of their early modern birth—rarely figured in relationship to each other. To the extent that the New Historicists viewed Europe's nascent national cultures as discrete "self-contained wholes"—rather than porous "arrays of intersections"[61]—they tended to forgo the "horizontal relationships and connections" that might also be drawn upon "the planes of History."[62]

By foregrounding the transnational or cosmopolitan potential of the past, a new generation of critics has been pushing beyond the national borders that remained a feature of New Historicist criticism. A productive framing of this trend, as Barbara Fuchs has suggested, might be "Imperium Studies." To invoke *imperium* "is to call attention to the term's inherent polysemy," denoting "both internal control of a polity and external expansion beyond that polity's original boundaries."[63] Such a view alerts us to "to the continuities and interdependence between the formation of early modern nations and their imperial aspirations. And by underscoring the connection between internal sovereignty and external expansion, it constantly challenges the inevitability of those nations, thereby correcting our post-facto view of nationhood" (73). This positioning ought to be of particular utility to those of us concerned with examining the "ambivalence and contradiction" that characterized the global rivalry in which England and Spain were caught up during the sixteenth and seventeenth centuries.[64] For in a pattern shortly to be followed by early modernity's other emerging nation-states, the Spanish were first to face the problems generated by simultaneous internal consolidation and outward expansion.[65] At the same time, to think in terms of imperium is to recognize that the empires of early modernity were not exclusively, perhaps not even primarily, European.[66]

Engaging these concerns, my book joins a growing body of scholarship that imagines a literary and cultural conversation that was as global in early modernity as it is today. Recognizing, as Giles Gunn observed in a special issue of *PMLA* devoted to "Globalizing Literary Studies," that national and temporal "loosenings" have begun slowly to transform our field,[67] I take the view that, especially where literary and cultural relations between early modern England and Spain are concerned, much scholarship has failed to move beyond the literary-historical deep structures that have burdened literary studies for generations. Although it remains possible to construct genealogies, whether broadly cultural or more narrowly literary, in such a way as to show that nations possessed individual "souls," to foreground multiple external connections is to see that no national culture is insular (however much some may express a desire for insularity), not even England's. "No island is an island," as Carlo Ginsburg so incisively puts it.[68] And as Stephen Greenblatt reminds us, "A vital global cultural discourse is ancient; only the increasingly settled and bureaucratized nature of academic institutions in the nineteenth and early twentieth centuries, conjoined with a nasty intensification of ethnocentrism, racism, and nationalism produced the illusion of sedentary, indigenous literary cultures making sporadic and half-hearted ventures towards the margins."[69] In early modernity there remained in place visible, prominent, and extremely influential traditions that enable us to inscribe genealogies far more international than the tired lineages that have so commonly been invoked as indices of group identity.

When we recognize how thoroughly inherited senses of what it means to be "English" or "Spanish" have overdetermined our thinking, we begin to understand that while the literary traditions of Europe's nations may be seen to draw from various "native" traditions, they draw equally from centuries of shared cultural heritage. To borrow a formulation from Clifford Geertz, one of the New Historicism's most generative influences, the boundaries of any single European society (or language) were permeated with "socially established structures of meaning"[70] that announce linkages between Europe's various peoples (as well as groups lying beyond the boundaries of Renaissance studies as traditionally conceived), even as, historically, they provided material that could be manipulated in order to function as indicators of group identity.

Retaining the interpretive aims articulated by Geertz, my approach thus seeks to extend the New Historicism's anthropological turn. But I also adapt more recently articulated ethnographic practices.[71] While attending to the local perspectives of English Protestant nationalism, by situating texts in ways that move cultural intersections into the foreground, I also emphasize the international relationships and connections that were a prominent feature of early modern culture. While it may appear to some that my interpretations strain the limits of verbal and/or semiotic polysemy, they do not indulge radical indeterminacy. With James Clifford, I believe that "whereas the free play of readings may in theory be infinite, there are, at any historical moment, a limited range of canonical and emergent allegories available to the competent reader (the reader whose interpretation will be deemed plausible by a specific community). These structures of meaning are historically bounded and coercive. There is, in practice," then, "no 'free play.' "[72] Or as Geertz once put it, "Societies, like lives, contain their own interpretations."[73] And while there is, as I have mentioned, a sense in which I view my book as an act of recovery, I also recognize that my reading of early modern culture allegorizes concerns forced on me by my own historicity. The issues that I bring to the fore—the dangerous dance of ethnocentrism and xenophobia, the desire for cultural reform, the exigencies of commercial interest, problems of immigration and exile, the manipulation of national and religious feelings via various print and performance media—are all features of my own historical moment. And so readers will observe here the play of similitude among signs of difference.

Chapter 1 begins the work of surveying the Anglo-Spanish world of the early sixteenth century. As I chart the gradual dissolution of relations between England and Spain as the Reformation progresses, I also interrogate the popular view that the two nations were "traditional" or "natural" enemies. Considering the historiographic fate of Katherine of Aragon, and situating the Black Legend in relation to its "white" opposite, I observe how *ethical* objections to Spain's imperial practices—which England attempted in many ways to emulate—gradually came to be characterized in Protestant discourse as the inevitable result of Spain's *ethnic* heritage. Chapter 2 then shows how this discourse moves onstage during the period immediately following the Armada crisis in the early Hispanophobic productions of George Peele, Robert Wilson, and Robert Greene.

While distancing *The Spanish Tragedy* from a tradition of criticism that has cast the play in Black Legend terms, Chapter 3 demonstrates that Kyd largely avoids the ethnic demonization characteristic of Hispanophobic discourse (though it does admit that later adaptations draw his drama toward this end). Contextualizing the play in relation to Philip II's 1580 assumption of the Portuguese throne, I show how Kyd's prophetic subtext dramatizes the apocalyptic vision of English Protestant nation-writers like Foxe and Hakluyt even as its heroine, Bel-imperia, while fictively recalling the dubious morality conferred retrospectively on England's historical Spanish princesses, bodies forth multivocally both the seductive attractions of empire and the ethos of the transnational dynastic system that made the unification of "the Spains" possible.

Chapter 4 situates Christopher Marlowe's *Jew of Malta* within the world of London's late sixteenth-century immigrant culture. While examining the relationship of the play to the "Dutch Church Libel," the notoriously inflammatory document whose posting led to the arrest of both Marlowe and his associate Kyd, the chapter counters a received tradition that has seen the English as "naturally" xenophobic. In order to suggest that English animus toward outsiders was being fueled by radical Protestant polemicists, even as the Crown's official policy advertised openness to "strangers," I explore here the period's Machiavellian discourses. Arguing that *The Jew of Malta* stages a cacophony of ethnicity that itself plays a role in the production of popular Hispanophobia and its related anti-Semitism, I suggest also that Marlowe offers a "Spanish" solution to England's ethnic unrest via his play's appeal to a key Hapsburg ally, the powerful "Fernese" family of Parma and Piacenza. As important, by way of his central character Barabbas, Marlowe links Jewish Diaspora culture with the language of the Spanish Empire in order to embody Black Legend perceptions of essential Spanish otherness. Hyperbolically combining the excesses of Roman Catholic, Jewish, and Moorish culture, Marlowe's representation paves the way for the subsequent overcoding of Hispanic ethnicity evident in later English drama.

Chapter 5, the first of two chapters on Shakespeare, suggests that *The Merchant of Venice*, even if it does not invoke Spain as explicitly, may be among the most profound realizations of early modern English Hispanophobia. I argue that the presence in the play of Shylock, Arragon, and Morocco (characters all implicitly linked to Spain), in conjunction with the child whom Launcelot conceives with an unseen Moorish lover and Jessica's embrace of Christian society via her husband Lorenzo, suggests the limits of Elizabethan tolerance for ethnic admixture. Situating the drama in relation to a range of contemporary nationalist and colonialist discourses, I show that the society Portia authorizes in act 5 mirrors an English desire to be cleansed of undesirable ethnic elements while retaining the economic bounty their presence makes available. It is a denouement consonant, I maintain, not only with the ethnic purging associated with Inquisitional Spain but also with the "white" Anglo-Saxon derivation that historiographers as potentially opposed as the Protestant William Camden and the Catholic recusant Richard Verstegen are beginning to imagine for England.

Finally, Chapter 6 situates *Othello* at the moment of James I's unification of the British Crowns and the new empire's entry into Philip III's Pax Hispanica. I argue that no play embodies the popular Hispanophobia of the Elizabethan years more fully than Shakespeare's second Venetian drama, which also resists the Spanish policies of the new Scottish sovereign. Even as it incorporates material from the poet-king's "Lepanto," *Othello* plays upon England's long heritage of involvement with Iberia—including a tradition of shared reverence for Santiago Matamoros, Saint James the Moor-killer (whose neglected kinship with the villain Iago is central to both the play's thematics and its tragicomic structure)—while also working to undermine, in the manner of so many Black Legend publications, that common heritage as "unnatural."

In my attempt to approach early modern dramatic productions in ways that are both sensitive to historical difference and cognizant of historical continuity, I have often been troubled by what I have observed in them. Ethnic division, religious intolerance, economic disparity, and cycles of violence and reprisal much in the vein of those we have experienced in the late twentieth and early twenty-first centuries were as much a feature of England's Renaissance as the rebirth of knowledge, the birth of a nation, the discovery of new worlds, and the creation of timeless art. But I have also found that an ethnopoetic focus can offer several pedagogical and critical advantages. Drawing out the diversity of the past makes it possible to read these four-hundred-year-old texts in ways that cease projecting upon them continuities and stabilities that were simply not there. At the same time, to tack back and forth between the local and the global, the national and the international, is to engage even the most canonical texts in ways that avoid both the dry rehearsal of universal themes and the particularistic yearnings that sometimes define the field so narrowly as to shut out all but initiates. If we are ever to forge a future upon which all peoples have a purchase, we must make room for them in the past we hold in common, however troubled (and troublesome) that past remains.

CHAPTER ONE

From Ethos to Ethnos

S. Ant. Where England?
S. Dro. I looked for the chalky cliffs, but I could
   find no whiteness in them. . . .
S. Ant. Where Spain?
S. Dro. Faith, I saw it not; but I felt it hot in
   her breath.
S. Ant. Where America, the Indies?
S. Dro. O, sir, upon her nose, all o'er embellish'd
   with rubies, carbuncles, sapphires, declining their rich
   aspect to the hot breath of Spain. . . .
S. Ant. Where stood Belgia, the Netherlands?
S. Dro. O, sir, I did not look so low.
   —William Shakespeare, *The Comedy of Errors*, c. 1588–93

Ignatius. Game? What game?
Error. The noblest game of all, a game at chess
   Betwixt our side and the White House, the men set
   In their just order ready to go to it.
   —Thomas Middleton, *A Game at Chess*, 1624

WHEN JAMES ANTHONY Froude closed his twelve-volume *History of England from the Fall of Wolsey to the Defeat of the Spanish Armada* (1862–70) with the signal event of 1588, he gave the English-speaking world what may be the fullest realization of the Whig view of the literary-historical period traditionally framed as the English Renaissance. Of his decision to emphasize the episode commemorated in his title as more pivotal than any other, Froude wrote, "Chess players, when they have brought their game to a point at which the result can be foreseen with certainty, regard their contest as ended, and sweep the pieces from the board."[1] This interpretation was not particularly original; Froude reproduced the mythology the Whigs of the eighteenth century had favored before him, just as Interregnum, Jacobean, and Elizabethan historiographers had seen "God's obvious design" at work in history earlier still.[2] As for Froude's metaphor, it was one that had been most notoriously employed in Thomas Middleton's *Game at Chess* (1624), the controversial performance of which had caused an international incident leading to the playwright's incarceration.[3] Through his "art," Middleton had made an unambiguous political statement about the inadvisability of an Anglo-Spanish dynastic union by reminding audiences first of Spain's Jesuitical devotion to the prospect of "universal monarchy" (1.1.51) and then of "the fired ships" that had "severed the fleet / in '88" (3.1.186–87). Whereas Middleton constructed a match that, again, "since '88" (4.4.6) had remained without a final move (which the playwright sought to provide), for Froude the evident checkmate had given birth to the modern English nation: after "the Armada" England was free, in the phrase Richard Helgerson has made current, "to write" itself.[4]

A tacit, uncritical acceptance of this inherited view, in the academy as in public culture more generally, has tended to mask much of the complexity, ambivalence, and contradiction that characterized Anglo-Hispanic cultural relations during the early modern period. Among analysts of English literature and culture, antipathy toward "the Spaniard" is typically explained either in terms of some vaguely remembered sense of Spain as England's "traditional enemy," or by appeal to the "natural" xenophobia of an island people. Generally speaking, we have internalized a "primordialist" perception of the Anglo-Spanish conflict of the sixteenth century, which takes as its grounding principle the view that "ethnic communities and nations are 'natural,' that they are part of the natural order, just like speech or physiognomy."[5] As a result, we have commonly failed to consider the various ways these two emerging nation-states participated together in a larger cultural system.[6] Even when we have been willing to grant that the process of becoming national was far more contested than the Whigs allowed, our narratives have tended to share with theirs the reemplotment of England's history as mainly an *internal* becoming.[7]

But it is often the case, as Walker Connor has suggested, that "a group of people must know ethnically what they *are not* before they can know what they *are*."[8] Any number of textual productions from the late sixteenth and early seventeenth centuries make evident that, from among the range of possible "nots," not-Welshness, not-Scottishness, not-Irishness, and certainly not-Frenchness contributed to the realization of a sense of nationality among the people of early modern England. But while "the French fetish," as Deanne Williams has shown, would retain the allure of "Romance" throughout the Elizabethan years, as indeed it would throughout the Stuart period, the possibility of another "Spanish match" would become forever foreclosed.[9]

As Shakespeare's *Life of Henry V* (1599) demonstrates, in spite of their storied antagonisms it was becoming increasingly plausible to imagine a kind of national unity among the peoples of early modern Britain. English Gower, Welsh Fluellen, Scottish Jamy, and Irish MacMorris could, in spite of "national" differences in language and culture, together accomplish great deeds.[10] And there is room enough in Shakespeare's imperial vision for the French, who can, as King Charles and his peers are made to see in the play, share in England's greatness, provided they recognize the legitimacy of her Continental claims. The English lesson given Princess Catherine by the not-so-rough-tongued Harry suggests the renewal of a historic kinship of peoples separated by language, geography, and custom, but not so different in essence.

The English and the Spanish, too, shared blood and history. But no such familial rapprochement would be thinkable to the people of England, as James I would discover when he attempted to arrange the marriage to which Middleton so strenuously objected. By the time the House of Stuart ascended the English throne, a uniquely powerful and culturally distinct essentialism had come to stand in the way. For a number of historically specific reasons, it was "not-Spanishness"—or rather, an ideologically motivated "forging" of what it meant to be *ethnically* Spanish—that for several centuries gave the English their surest sense of national identity.

Froude's gamesmanship notwithstanding, the outpouring of printed materials from the 1590s that treated Iberian themes suggests that, far from declining, England's anxieties about the Spanish threat *increased* substantially after the Armada crisis. During this conjuncture—the very period that saw the great florescence of English drama—differences that for several hundred years had been seen in both Britain and Iberia in terms of cultural complementarity became *marked* in England with the inherent and insurmountable ethnic incompatibilities we now associate with the Black Legend of Spanish Cruelty.

In order to sketch the developing context in which the ethnic marking of the Spaniard took shape,[11] we need first to observe some of the ways in which earlier religiopolitical discourses were superseded by newly inflected constructions of ethnicity and "race." For to survey these Hispanophobic discourses is, on the one hand, to recognize that we have neglected several important structural features of the early modern "literary" (or "precursor") public sphere;[12] on the other, it is to make visible the cultural work accomplished via England's ethnicizing constructions of Spain.

Katherine Unparagoned

To my mind, no historical actor proves a more appropriate figure through which we may observe the complexities and ambivalences of Anglo-Spanish cultural relations during the early modern period than Katherine of Aragon. Although the facts of her life have inherent interest—Ferdinand and Isabella, Spain's Most Catholic Monarchs were her parents; she was the wife first of Arthur Tudor and then of his younger brother Henry VIII; as queen of England she became friend and confidant to Thomas More, patron to Erasmus, and mother of "Bloody Mary"—Katherine of Aragon is important in the present context because she came to England during an era in which European aspirations toward nationhood were just beginning to take shape. Further, the cultural space she occupied—between Britain and Iberia, between England's Catholic traditions and its Protestant Reformation, between an empire's universal aspirations and the particularist desires of a single nation—makes Katherine a valuable subject today, just as it made her a valued intermediary during the late fifteenth and early sixteenth centuries. But rather than focusing upon the details of Katherine's biography, let us briefly consider her life in relation to some of the historical forces that brought her to England, especially those that propelled the European dynastic system. As we do so, let us observe the way Katherine has been made to function in relation to the discursive practices—the "ethnopoetics"—that during the course of the sixteenth century began to animate a view of her that still colors cultural memory.

Imagining "Katherine of Aragon" as more a *site* than a historical figure in the usual sense of the word, let us write her name, Katherine with a "K," in the anglicized style she preferred. For this child of the Castilian Isabella and the Aragonese Ferdinand was named for one of her *English* forebears, Katherine of Lancaster, daughter of John of Gaunt.[13] We should emphasize this lineage because when "Katherine" is invoked in later representations, she often comes to stand synecdochically for the special "darkness" of her native land.

By way of demonstrating how the historical role scripted for Katherine by later revisionists has influenced popular perception of her, let us turn to a representation from the very early sixteenth century. After she had lived in England for about four years, the nineteen-year-old princess sat for the Flemish portrait painter, Michael Sittow (Figure 1). To a certain degree Sittow painted Katherine as a cultural ideal: her fair skin, Madonna-like brow, gold-highlighted hair, and dutifully lowered blue-gray eyes embody feminine humility and princely grace. The attire chosen for the sitting is richly elegant and yet, especially when compared with the "magnificence" represented in so many royal portraits, it also reflects the modesty that contemporaries identified as a feature of Katherine's personality.

Though the painting appears to portray Princess Katherine more or less realistically, like the representations of Elizabeth Tudor that have received so much critical commentary, the meaning of Sittow's portrait does not lie in its verisimilitude. Katherine's iconography speaks volumes about the aspirations of the dynastic cultures her marriage was intended to reunite. Her necklace intertwines her initial, "K," with the red and white roses of the House of Tudor. Around her cowl we find embroidered Katherine's personal emblem, the pomegranate by which John Skelton invoked her, at once a fertility symbol, its many seeds representing the generations of princes who are to be the fruit of Anglo-Hispanic union, and the symbol of the Kingdom of Granada, where, when Katherine was seven years old, she had witnessed the culmination of the Iberian *reconquista*.[14] Along the neckline of her gown are sewn the cockleshells of Santiago de Compostela, simultaneously representing Saint James, who had interceded so many times in behalf of Christian Spain during its long struggle against the Moors, and the Galician pilgrimage route that had linked Britain with Iberia for nearly half a millennium. Together, Katherine's various emblems predict a future of cultural complementarity and international harmony.[15] But they also evoke a past in which England and Spain participated together in ways that later nationalist traditions have obscured. Against later essentializations, it is possible to view Katherine as embodying a productive dynamic of cultural cross-pollination and hybridity, the exchange of commerce, art, and ideas, the challenging of gender and ethnic stereotypes, and the possibilities of openness.[16]

The cultural currents that bought Katherine to England in the late fifteenth century remain visible in one of the earliest histories of Protestant England, *The Union of the Two Noble Illustre Famelies of Lancastre & York, Beeing Long In Continual Discension for the Croune of this Noble Realm . . . Beginnyng at the Tyme of Kyng Henry the Fowerth, the First Auctor of this Division, and so succesively proceadyng to the Reigne of the High and Prudent Prince Kyng Henry the Eight, the Undubitate Flower and Very Heire of Bothe the Said Linages* (1542).

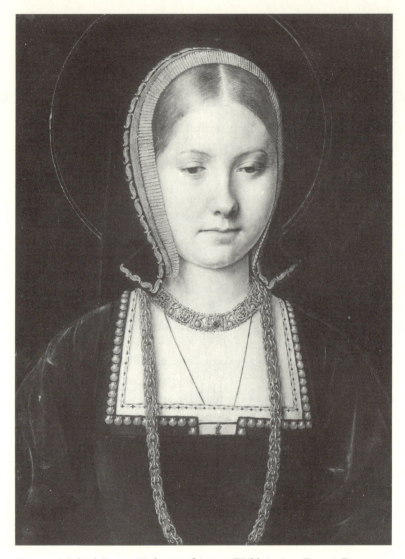

Figure 1. Michael Sittow, *Katherine of Aragon* ("Bildnis einer Furstein"), 1505. Courtesy of Kunsthistorisches Museum, Vienna.

If there is one thing that can be quickly gained from visiting this text, better known as *Hall's Chronicle*, it is a sense of the interconnectedness of late medieval dynastic culture. As Edward Hall set down his story of the apotheosis of the House of Tudor from among the intrigues of England's "native" barons and the wrangling of the Scottish, the Welsh, and the French, he also preserved textual traces that have much to yield concerning the religiopolitical inclinations of pre-Reformation Europe's ruling families: their aspirations, their disputes, their collaborations, and their mobility.

A particular moment from 1492, the sixth year of the reign of Henry VII, is worth a visit: "Saynct James, saynct James, saynct James, Castil, Castil, Castil, Granado, Granado: By high and mighty power, Lord Fernando and Elizabeth, kynge and quene of Spayne, have wonne fro[m] the Infideles and Moores, the cytie and realme of Granado, through the help of our lorde God and the most glorious virgyn his mother, and the verteous apostle saynct James, and the holy father Innocent the VIII, together with the aide & souccours of y great prelates, knyghtes and other gentlemen borne, & commons of their realms and countreys."[17] The inclusion of this commemoration suggests that chronicler Hall, in spite of his participation in the Protestant movement that was coursing through his homeland, still recognized that the signal event of Spanish history also represented a great moment in the history of England. While this early modern triumph, along with the others of 1492, has from a postmodern point of view come to be regarded as the culmination of a somewhat dubious battle, it symbolized for pre-Reformation Europe a "victory obtyaned . . . to the glory of God, and to the publique wealth of all Christianitie" (519–20). And so the good news of the completion of the *reconquista*, a centuries-long project in which English knights participated alongside brethren in arms from throughout Christendom, was publicly lauded in England by Lord Chancellor John Morton, archbishop of Canterbury. Since the reconquest had been simultaneously an international and an English triumph, Henry VIII, in the second year of his reign, would find it both honorable and expedient to send a contingent under Lords Darcie, Grey, Guyldeforde, Weston, Broune, and Sydney to aid his father-in-law Ferdinand in the maintenance of the Iberian peace.[18]

I do not offer this anecdote in order to praise the militarism that characterized early modern religiopolitical culture. Rather, I want to underscore how interconnected Britain and Iberia had been prior to the Reformation as a result of their mutual participation in a religiopolitical and dynastic system that was transnational. In the wake of several hundred years of nation-centered history we tend to forget this interconnection, just as we forget that for much of the thirteenth, fourteenth, and fifteenth centuries "England" and "Spain" shared a common frontier, where the shifting boundaries of Brittany, Navarre, Aragon, and France converged (Figure 2).[19] Indeed, for missionaries, pilgrims, and crusaders (religious and secular alike), to travel across "national" borders was often to undertake a work conceived as much in support of the larger

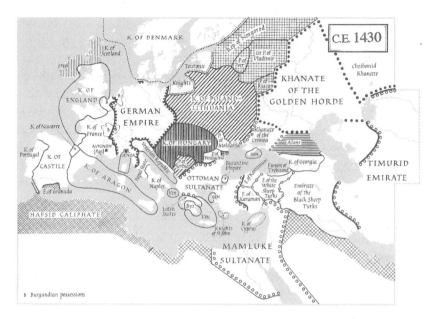

Figure 2. Europe in the age of Henry V and Henry VI, c. 1430. Note the fluid borders of England, France, Castile, Navarre, and Aragon. From *The Penguin Atlas of Medieval History* © Colin McEvedy, 1961, 1992. Reproduced by permission of Penguin Books Ltd.

corporate community as in the interest of any individual nation-state. The cockleshells bordering Katherine's gown provide visible signs of this kind of devotion, as do the extant spiritual autobiographies that describe participation in the pilgrimage culture Chaucer represented, recalling arduous journeys to places like Jerusalem, Rome, and Santiago de Compostela.[20]

Writing at a time before the Hispanization of Spain had been accomplished, Hall rendered these Anglo-Spanish involvements (his Protestantism notwithstanding) without projecting on them a negative valence; they were simply a fact of England's international commitment. Nor did he see such cooperation as representing an unnatural entanglement with a "foreign" nation. The important other in this instance was Islamic. At this early moment in English Protestant history, Hall still considered this historic commitment to a common Christian ethos worth remembering.

Saving in Spain and Portugal

Viewing Katherine of Aragon from the perspective of the post-Marian years, John Foxe casts a far different light on the years of her reign. Although the Black Legend had begun to darken Anglo-Spanish relations during the period in which Foxe attained his widest readership, his *Acts and Monuments* declines to essentialize Katherine by reason of her ethnicity. Rather, as his narrative introduces us to Katherine in middle age, Foxe concentrates his rhetorical energies in an effort to discredit the institutions that had authorized her marriage in the first place.

To listen to Foxe's account of "the first occasion and beginning" of England's "public reformation" (5:45), the proceedings so often represented in the discourses of English national ascendancy, is to hear emerging a telling play of contraries. Opposing a morally motivated Henry VIII, who appeals in all humility both to scripture and "to all the most famous universities abroad," we find a self-serving clergy, who, "understanding the king's case and request," refuses to "define in the case" because it fears "what might follow after, if learning and Scripture here take place against the authority of their dispensations" (5:53–54); countering a Solomon-like spiritual leader concerned primarily for the pastoral well-being of his commonwealth there sits a papacy whose objective is to maintain "the keys" of its own power (5:46–47); facing an English king seeking nothing more than a legitimate succession for his realm stands a Holy Roman Emperor so ambitious for power that he is willing to flirt with an incestuous arrangement abhorrent even to his own subjects; in opposition to Henry's bigamous Spanish wife and his unmarriageable "bastard" daughter, we see a new royal marriage, "established, approved, and ratified for good and consonant to the laws of Almighty God" (5:60), to "the most virtuous and noble [English] lady Anne Bullen" (5:61). Contemplating this theater of opposites, Foxe presents Henry VIII as a conscience-torn man whose formidable powers of self-reflection have led him to realize that, "saving in Spain and Portugal, it hath not been seen, that one man hath married two sisters, the one being carnally known before: but the brother to marry the brother's wife, was so abhorred amongst all nations, that I never heard that any Christian so did, but myself" (5:61).

By supplying the negative precedent of the marriage of Afonso V of Portugal (1432–81)—who, after the death of his first wife, had married Juana, the daughter and namesake of his own sister and Henry IV of Castile[21]—Foxe follows in the tracks of Henry's litigators, who attempted to construct as an unethical Iberian practice the matrimonial maneuvering toward which all of

the dynastic houses of Europe inclined. The litigators' assertions brim with
unintended ironies. First among them is the fact that Henry's advisers had already gone so far as to propose a marriage between his own bastard son, Henry
Fitzroy, duke of Richmond, and Fitzroy's half-sister, Mary (the daughter of
Henry and Katherine), that would ensure a truly Tudor heir.[22] And second,
according to both canon law and the logic of the crown's suit, the king and the
two Bullen sisters were already "family" in the same triangular way that it was
being argued that Henry, his brother Arthur, and Katherine had been related.
For Anne Bullen's sister, Mary, had been Henry's mistress.[23]

My point in revisiting this royal divorce is not to revive a scholastic dis-
putation after half a millennium. It cannot be our concern whether Henry's brother Arthur "knew" Katherine—"which thing," as Hall records, "she
clearly denied" (5:51)—or whether sores of conscience vexed Henry's mind for
reasons more carnal than Foxe cared to admit;[24] nor should we let ourselves be
tempted to judge the conjugal (or libidinal) habits of a culture so distant from
our own. More relevant here is the recognition that Foxe, positioned at a very
different historical node from that of the lovers and legates of Henry's reign,
reconstructed Katherine's position from the vantage point of the Elizabethan
years. For in his representation of the Tudor-Aragon divorce, his own era's
investments in Anglo-Hispanic affairs betray themselves. "By these premises,"
writes Foxe,

> it is sufficient to judge and understand what the whole occasion was,
> that brought this marriage first into doubt, so that there needeth not
> any further declaration in words upon this matter. But this one thing I
> will say, if I might be so bold to speak what I think . . . that the stay of
> this marriage was taken in good time, and without the singular favour of
> God's providence. For if *that one child, coming of this foresaid marriage,*
> *did so greatly endanger this whole realm of England to be entangled with the*
> *Spanish nation,* that if God's mighty hand had not been betwixt, God
> only knoweth what misery might have ensued: what peril then should
> thereby have followed, if, in the continuance of this marriage, more issue
> had sprung thereof! (5:50, my italics)

Clearly, the Protestant martyrologist had visited the sins of the daughter upon
the mother, back-shadowing the events of the Marian and early Elizabethan
years onto those of the 1520s and 1530s.[25] As surely as present values shape
my narrative's relation to the past, it was the second Anglo-Spanish dynastic
union in Foxe's lifetime (and perhaps the possibility of a third) that burdened

his history: the real concern of the *Acts and Monuments* was with the marriage of Mary Tudor, the daughter of Katherine of Aragon and Henry VIII of England, with Katherine's grandnephew, Philip of Hapsburg, son of Holy Roman Emperor Charles V and Isabel of Portugal.

Chained to the altar of every parish church, and made available for perusal in public places throughout England, Foxe's assessment of where "the Lord" stood upon Henry's "Great Matter" entered the public record.[26] By compressing Katherine's twenty-five years at the center of Tudor culture within the providential "coming in of queen Anne" and the christening of "the high and mighty princess of England Elizabeth,"[27] Foxe erases every trace of the cultural interchange that had characterized the years of Katherine's courtship and reign.[28] What we cannot hear in these passages from the *Acts and Monuments*, however, is the Black Legend of Spanish Cruelty. As the exilic experience of the first generation of England's Protestants had been one of "close association and cooperation" with "scholars from all over the Protestant world,"[29] the ideological position sketched in the *Book of Martyrs* remained just internationalist enough for it to embrace Iberian martyrs and reformers alongside English ones—witness the "Table of Certain Martyrs, who, for the cause of Religion, suffered in Spain" (4:447). Distrustful though Foxe was of the Spanish monarchy, and much though his remarks (detached from their original contextual mooring) may have contributed historically to the dissemination of anti-Hispanic sentiment, he argued against Spain's policies on grounds of *ethos*.[30] It was the adept maneuvering of the Spanish monarchy within the imperial dynastic system, coupled with the "unbiblical" support provided Spain by the institutions of Roman Catholic culture, that Foxe objected to—he did not implicate Katherine of Aragon in his nation's difficulties on the basis of her ethnicity. The English nation would not be so kind to all of its Spanish queens, as we will see when we turn to its Renaissance drama.

Satan Loosed Out

"Communication," writes Johannes Fabian, "is ultimately about creating shared time"—that is, "for human communication to occur, coevalness has to be *created*."[31] In the course of discussing "separating and distancing in colonialist praxis" (27), Fabian considers the difference that characterized post-Enlightenment (or perhaps as properly, post-Reformation) temporality relative to medieval temporality. In essence, this difference constituted a break from "a conception of time/space in terms of a history of salvation to one that ultimately resulted in the secularization of Time as natural history" (27). Whereas secular time is linear, evolutionist and exclusionary, "in the medieval paradigm the Time of Salvation was conceived as inclusive or incorporative" (26). Medieval others, "pagans and infidels (rather than savages and primitives)" were thus "viewed as candidates for salvation" (26). "Coevalness" is precisely what texts like the *Acts and Monuments* removed from England's relationship with traditional European Christianity, even as, after the death of the Protestant Edward VI, the royal houses of England and Spain attempted to restore it with the marriage of Mary Tudor and Philip of Hapsburg.

Contra the numberless histories that Whiggishly construct England's mid-century re-Catholicization as an unnatural importation, it may have been that "the broad majority of the nation accepted and welcomed the return of traditional religion."[32] Some who had vigorously backed the Henrician and Edwardian regimes looked forward to being welcomed back into the corporate body of the Roman faith. Among those who reversed themselves was John Elder, a Scot who, with the ascension of Mary Tudor, "looked forward to the return of the true, Catholic, religion to 'this moste noble and holy yle of Britayn'"; like many who had lately been Protestant, Elder celebrated the marriage of Queen Mary to Prince Philip, "a ruler for whom God had foreordained a worldwide empire" and who was bound to "enriche the empyre of Englande."[33]

Elder was not alone in his expectation of enrichment. In the half-century since Katherine's arrival in England, the wealth Spain had drawn from the New World had become legendary. The possibility of another Anglo-Hispanic dynastic association meant legal (if severely mediated) access to the vast territories ceded to Spain by the papacy. Looking westward, Richard Eden commemorated the Tudor-Hapsburg wedding of state with the gift of his translation of Peter Martyr's encyclopedic *Decades of the New World* (1555).[34] In spite of the charges of Turk-like cruelty being leveled at roughly the same moment by Bartolomé de Las Casas, whose public disputations with Juan Ginés de Sepulveda in the early 1550s were reexamining the legality of the conquest itself, there appeared to be no stopping the Spanish colonial behemoth. Nor did many in England seem to be concerned with the status of the Indians in the New World, as the English stood to gain much from renewing the dynastic ties that had been severed during the reign of Henry VIII.

Along with its more commonly remembered church history, Foxe's *Acts and Monuments* records a number of anecdotes from the period of Philip's tenure as England's king consort that reveal the more hopeful expectations for the Spanish alliance harbored by men like Eden and Elder. One of these events announces the extremes to which the Spanish Hapsburgs were willing to go in their attempt to restore a measure of coevalness to the intercultural field. "On the Tuesday following," writes Foxe, "being the 2d of October, twenty carts came from Westminster, laden (as it was noised) with gold and silver, and certain of the guard with them through the city to the Tower, and there it was received by a Spaniard, who was the king's treasurer, and had custody of it within the Tower. It was matted about with mats, and mailed in little bundles about two feet long, and almost half a foot thick; and in every cart were six of those bundles. What it was indeed, God knoweth; for it is to us uncertain" (6:560). Foxe's twenty carts do indeed seem to have been carrying Spanish bullion. And this shipment was followed by a second, reputed to have been so great that it required "nearly a hundred horses" to draw the two wagons in which it was hauled.[35] Just as it was hoped, mineral wealth had begun to flow from America to England. In spite of the Spanish Crown's financial overextension, Philip had been directed, as David Loades points out, to make public display of these assets by distributing "pensions and gifts with a generous hand."[36] It seems that "more than 15,000 ducats [went] to the privy councilors who had attended the marriage and as much again to courtiers and gentlemen" (158). Although the terms of Philip's marriage to Mary Tudor "neither crowned him, nor granted him any English patrimony" (158), these rituals were an attempt to parade the positive implications of an international relationship restored to its pre-Reformation condition.

In spite of these rites of complemetarity, Foxe preferred to mark moments of Anglo-Spanish communication with ironic asides, like the artfully disingenuous "What it was indeed, God knoweth," that accompanied his recollection of Philip's monetary transfer. Contrary to the views expressed by men like Elder and Eden, Foxe offered the perspectives of Protestants like the younger Thomas Wyatt, who had participated in the "campaign of vilification" that had gone on from "the autumn of 1553," creating "an atmosphere of suspicion in which even the most exemplary behavior [of the Spaniards] had been misrepresented."[37] Certainly these interpolations, like those that treat the "Form and Manner of the execrable Inquisition of Spain" (4:451), would have evoked powerful nationalist feelings among Foxe's readership.[38] But it was the removal of "shared time" in Foxe's book that cleaved a once and future chasm between Protestant England and Catholic Spain.

As Richard Helgerson has keenly observed, sometime between the 1563 edition of the *Acts and Monuments*, in which Foxe's dating of the years since "the loosing out of Satan" conformed to the interpretation of the Apocalypse accepted by the Geneva exegetes, and the edition of 1570, Foxe tampered with the Reformed religion's eschatological clock. Deciding that Satan had not after all been "bound" at the time of the Resurrection, as the traditional view had insisted, he put Satan's binding at "the end of the ten persecutions of the primitive church."[39] This revision changed the timing of Satan's "release" to coincide with the "persecution [that] began to rage again in the fourteenth century" (262). As Helgerson recognizes, "the change in Foxe's dating of the thousand-year binding of Satan increases the contribution of England to the history of the true church," for this modification made the "earthly instrument of Satan's binding" the emperor Constantine, "a Briton by birth and education," while the "first victims of Satan's loosing" were now "the English followers of Wycliffe" (263)—a typology Whig historians continued to reinscribe well into the nineteenth century.

Foxe's temporal machinations and the "national election" they imply had grave implications where the coevalness of Britain and Iberia was concerned. For if traditional Christian temporality viewed the "pagan world" as "always *already* marked for salvation," the Calvinistic theology favored by the Elizabethan Reformers fixed *before time itself* the number to whom salvation was available.[40] Thus, in contradistinction to the nearly infinite communion of souls who might make up the corporate body of Christ in Roman Catholic universalist theology, the number marked for saving grace became extremely limited. This limitation grew all the more severe when a particular nation came to deem itself nationally elect. To the degree that the English Reformers constructed London as a "New Jerusalem," they also rewrote the significance of Rome, moving it from Christianity's spatial and temporal center to the pagan periphery. Rome as the Holy City thus underwent a process of inversion whereby it became transformed into a type of "Babel," or "Babylon." It was not that salvation became impossible for the Catholics now judged to be inhabiting the pagan world: witness again the testimony of "Divers good men and martyrs of Spain" (4:451) within Foxe's representation of the international struggle for reform. However, what was possible in theory became, in the practice of those invested in the election of a particular nation, highly unlikely. Rather than being viewed as potential converts, Roman Catholics were *prejudged* as agents of Babylon or Antichrist. Through the antithetical rhetoric employed by Reformation writers like Foxe (and the propagandists and playwrights who would follow him), whose persuasive force depended upon precisely this kind of conceptual (or more properly, *figural*) inversion, an othering much like that which Fabian describes for later colonialist contexts was quite guiltlessly accomplished.

Perhaps the most potent example of this distancing process can be found in the portions of Foxe's history of the Marian regime that were directed at the

English subjects Foxe is in the process of Hispanizing: that is, "such as seemed in England to carry Spanish hearts in English bodies" (6:580). Describing the occasion of the royal marriage on Saint James's Day, July 25, 1554, Foxe emphasized that the book of James had been the subject of archpapist Stephen Gardiner's sermon on "true teaching" immediately following the royal honeymoon.[41] He recalled that on September 30, Bishop Gardiner, "his long declaration . . . speaking very much of love and charity . . . had occasion, upon St. James's words, to speak of the true teachers, and of the false teachers; saying, that all the preachers in Edward's time, preached nothing but voluptuousness, and filthy and blasphemous lies: affirming their doctrine to be that false doctrine whereof St. James speaketh" (6:559). Whereas Gardiner argued that the Edwardian Reformers had erected a "false doctrine" that ran counter to the apostle's instruction that "faith, *if it hath not works*, is dead" (James 2:17, my italics)—an insistent repudiation of the Protestant *solo fides* formula—Foxe attempted to show that Philip's arrival, his marriage to Mary, and their Catholic restoration had erased the advances of the Edwardian church, suggesting that the "true" doctrine of faith had been supplanted once more with its Roman Catholic antithesis, the "false" doctrine of works.[42] Encouraged by the incendiary rhetoric of England's "hot-gospelling" preachers, many Protestants came to internalize the view that justification as traditionally conceived was now the "Devil's Faith."[43] And as important, an antithetical understanding of the idolatrous nature of "this covenant of works"—on which the meaning of the faith had been built in Iberia with no less than the aid and intercession of Spain's patron saint, James the Greater, "brother of Christ"—became a key mechanism through which the notion of a redemptive English "national covenant" was "clarified and reinforced."[44] Soon enough, these inversive perspectives found their way onto the stage.

When we set Foxe's types and tropes in relation to his adjustment of the sacred clock, the anti-Hispanic thrust of the *Acts and Monuments* comes powerfully into relief. While Spain did not descend so far in his esteem that it wore the "more than Turkish cruelty" epithet of later sixteenth-century propaganda, Foxe went to some length to construct the Iberian kingdom's ethos of works as the most Antichristian in Christendom. Whereas in Katherine of Aragon's day the stars Arcturus and Hesperus—as England and Spain were figured in the pageant that had welcomed Katherine to England[45]—could revolve harmoniously in the same heaven, the firmament in Foxe's model became the province of a particular nation and its coreligionist allies. Because relations between Protestant England and Catholic Spain were no longer felt to occur on the same temporal plane, having been prefigured instead within the arc of sacred history as revealed in the Apocalypse of Saint John—the foregone conclusion of which had been written before time itself (as well as for all time)—real international dialogue hardly remained possible. For though Foxe wrote of a church that was "universal and sparsely through all countries dilated" (1:5), he was Janus-faced when it came to the relationship of his own nation to the Protestant movement. The body of believers may have been dilated throughout the earth, but his England was the David who would lead them.

Guiding Culture

In its struggle toward self-constitution, Protestant England sought to translate itself not only via nativist readings of biblical precedents like those Foxe depended upon; it also looked to contemporaries whose achievements had outstripped its own. By virtually any measure imaginable—wealth, power, influence, dynastic connection, colonial expansiveness, international prestige—none had achieved more than Spain had. Thus, in order to inspire in Elizabeth a similar devotion to England's nascent colonial efforts, a confirmed "Anti-Spaniard" like Richard Hakluyt could in one breath appeal to the example of Isabella of Castile, who "laied her owne Jewells to gage for money to furnishe out Columbus . . . [which] the Princes of the [Protestant] Relligion (among which her majestie ys principall) oughte the rather to take in hande," while propagating Black Legend infamy in another, constructing "the Spaniarde" as "the scourge of the world . . . Ravisher of virgins and wives."[46]

While it is understandable that an advocate of colonial expansion like Hakluyt would turn an envious eye toward Iberia, Hispanophilic imitation could, somewhat more surprisingly, extend to internal affairs as well.[47] As Lord Burghley himself instructed Elizabeth, the Spanish Empire had been able to achieve so much "precisely because it allow[ed] only one religion, and if she desire[d] the same kind of greatness for her own country, she must do the same."[48] Largely in an attempt to fulfill this end—the establishment of a sovereign empire of church and state—an ideologically Protestant ruling body took an increasingly active role in the manipulation of Elizabethan public discourse in an effort to cultivate, among other things, sympathy for its own policies, heightened feelings of nationalism, and antipathy toward all things Roman Catholic.[49] The cultural management provided by these political elites was, of course, partial, uneven, and more successful in some fields than others. In the area of foreign relations, as work by Lisa Ferraro Parmelee and Denis Woodfield has shown, Burghley, Francis Walsingham, and their confederates were indeed able to put together a network of hack writers, translators, and printers who aided them in their project "to enlighten the English reading public as to the nefarious activities of the Spanish,"[50] whose machinations they believed to be a primary cause of Europe's religiopolitical ills.

Recent reflection on early modern "publicity" has cautioned against the wholesale importation of Jürgen Habermas's model as described in his highly influential *Structural Transformation of the Public Sphere: An Inquiry into a Category of Bourgeois Society*. In an era during which, as A. E. B. Coldiron points out, "the refusal of an oath of loyalty, or the praying of an incorrect prayer, or the publication of a pamphlet could be grounds for investigation, imprisonment, or execution"[51]—an issue of direct concern for a playwright like Middleton, as it had been for Kyd and Marlowe before him—Habermasian "openness" can hardly have been a constituent feature of public life. Many cultural constraints would have to be shed before anything resembling a "republic of letters" could emerge. So distinct was this "public sphere of early print" from the imaginative space Habermas articulated that, as Joseph Loewenstein and Paul Stephens suggest, we must articulate the contours of "a whole pragmatic sphere of action" that included "printers and translators . . . apprentices, journeymen, other workers, the gear and machinery they used, the spaces they inhabited, their techniques, and the institutions and practices" that connected them.[52]

In his classic study of Golden Age Spain, *Culture of the Baroque: Analysis of a Historical Structure*, José Antonio Maravall posited a set of structural relationships quite different from Habermas's model. Maravall argued that a culture enters its "baroque" phase when a "conservative" ruling class imbued with a "consciousness of crisis" begins to "guide" a growing urban populace within a "conflictive" social climate through the workings of a "mass media" mobilized in the service of an increasingly absolutist state.[53] If we bracket off the strains of his thought that (after Jacob Burckhardt and Heinrich Wölfflin) prompted him to abstract a unique period mentality from the epoch's literary and visual productions, and if we recognize the caveat that a totalizing religious ideology such as that which became dominant in Spain never acquired such hegemonic status in England, the emphasis Maravall's model places on print, theatrical, and visual mediation is worth considering in relation to the slightly earlier English case.[54]

Although it may seem at first glance an act of historical violence to yoke the early modern English experience with a model describing the society of its "opposite," Inquisition Spain, by the 1590s there seems to have emerged in England a set of relationships that had much more in common with Maravall's guiding culture than the one Habermas saw cultivating "Enlightenment" a century later. While it may be true that England never quite attained the kind of "theater state" that John Beverley, adapting Clifford Geertz, associates with Counter-Reformation Spain, it was not for lack of trying.[55] As Burghley's Hispanophilic meditation on Spanish "greatness" suggests, the impulse toward this level of social control was certainly present. And the desire to harness the subversive potential of print mediation, or, when possible, to turn the new technology—along with such media as authorized portraiture, progresses, pageants, proclamations, public executions, sermons, and homilies—for the aims of the state must have been irresistible.

The Mirror of Spanish Tyranny

While the pervasiveness of Black Legend discourse in England has become somewhat axiomatic, we have not commonly reflected on the imperial ideology that the Protestant writers who marketed it to such great effect sought to displace. Because, as Walter Mignolo has shown, the Black Legend is a conceptual frame concerned with "internal imperial difference,"[56] only when we situate the discourse of Hispanophobia in relation to its opposite, the "gilded" legend of Spain's imperial election,[57] do we gain a sense of the Black Legend's rhetorical power. Although condemnations of Spain's reputedly inordinate greed had been circulating with reports of New World encounters since as early as the work Richard Eden had presented to Mary and Philip in 1555, Peter Martyr's *De Orve Nobo Decades* (1516), during much of the sixteenth century concerns regarding the ethical implications of Spanish colonial activities tended to recede before an appreciation of the magnitude of the conquest itself.[58] The acknowledged odds and unprecedented circumstances over which the conquistadores prevailed were seen to have required extreme methods. The Hispanophile Eden had gone so far as to argue that "the Spaniardes as the ministers of grace and liberite [had] browght unto these new [Amerindian] gentiles the victorie of Chrystes death whereby they beinge subdued with the worldely sworde, are nowe made free from the bondage of Sathans tyrannie, by the myghty poure of this triumphante [Spanish] victourer."[59]

Alejo Fernández's painting *The Virgin of the Navigators* (c. 1535) may be the fullest expression of the ideology reinscribed by Eden, which the Protestant polemicists of the later sixteenth century would counter so militantly with their inversive polemics (Figure 3). In Fernández's representation Columbus, Magellan, Cortéz, and the celebrated mariners who had embarked under the flag of Aragon and Castile-Leon congregate around an immense figure of the Madonna.[60] While the shadowy shapes of Amerindians gather near—brought from "pagan" darkness to the light of Christianity by the navigators who have set sail in her holy name—the *Santa María* straddles the seas, uniting the continents. In the view of the Roman Church, it was the enlargement of Christendom through the conversion of millions of Indian souls that most glorified Spain. While the accomplishments of men like Cortéz, Pizarro, and Balboa, in combination with the seemingly endless shipments of bullion sent homeward from the American mines, were seen to confirm heavenly favor, the extension of the boundaries of Christendom—with Spain adding vast territories in America even as Portugal established new colonies in Africa and Asia—provided the most visible and unambiguous evidence that the Almighty had elected the nations of Iberia for his special work.[61] Gold, riches, and the expansion of the empire's boundless New World dominions were but the earthly signs of the blessings gained through Iberia's propagation of *la Santa Fé*, which was seen to offset the loss of so many Christian souls, first to Islam and later to Protestant heresy.

My appeal to this Catholic theological ideal, the *immensum imperii corpus*, is not intended to revivify the "White Legend" of Spain's apologists any more than I want to reinscribe the black one that has so colored Anglo-American historical thought.[62] Nor do I want to minimize the international complexity of the early modern colonial dynamic. But to position this ideology in relation to *la leyenda negra* is to recognize that whereas critiques of Spain had been more commonly framed in terms of Spanish ambition, Carolingian or Philippine hubris, or "pagan" Roman Catholic error, after 1588 the focus of this new strain of international polemic was increasingly on Spain's ethnic difference.

Produced in the context of William of Orange's dynastic struggle with Philip II (over the northern kingdoms the Spanish king had inherited through his father, Charles V), the widely circulated *Apology or Defense, of the Most Noble Prince William . . . Against the Proclamation and Edict Published by the King of Spaine* (1580) seems to have laid the foundations for a discourse that provided England with the major indices of the Spaniard's ethnicity, even as it altered Anglo-Protestant perceptions of what it meant to be ethnically Spanish for centuries to come. While drawing upon two newly translated Dutch editions of Bartolomé de Las Casas's *Brevissima relación de la destruyción de las yndias* (1552), one of which had received the inflammatory new title *The Mirror of Spanish Tyranny, in which are Told the Murderous, Scandalous, and Horrible Deeds Which the Spaniards Have Perpetrated in the Indies*, Orange's *Apology*, published in the Low Countries no less than seventeen times before 1600, made explicit, among other horrors, a connection between Spanish

Figure 3. Alejo Fernández, *The Virgin of the Navigators*, c. 1535, perhaps the fullest expression of the Spanish Hapsburgs' ethos of empire. Courtesy of El Ayuntamiento de Sevilla. Copyright © Patrimonio Nacional.

colonizing practices in the New World and the atrocities his own subjects had been experiencing under the Hapsburg yoke.[63] More significantly, Orange and his coreligionists added a discursive formation clearly *not* present in Las Casas, which located the root of this cruelty in Spain's ethnicity. "I will no more wonder," writes William, "at that which all the worlde beleeveth, to witte, that the greatest parte of the Spanyardes, and especially those, that coounte themselves Noble men, are of the blood of the Moores and Jews, who also keepe this virtue of their Auncestors, who solde for readie money downe tolde, the life of our Saviour, which thing also, maketh me to take patientlie this injurie layde upon me."[64] Beginning with a question of ethos, the potentially negotiable matter of his "injurie" (the Hapsburg rejection of his "nation's" secession), the prince of Nassau's rhetoric slides rapidly into ethnic essentialization: the "mixed blood" of Iberian culture becomes a sign of both the religious and the racial "corruption" from which Orange entreated the United Provinces to extricate themselves.[65]

We can read in this discourse what may be observed in any number of plays, a distinct shift from the discourse of religiopolitical ethos to a dichotomizing rhetoric that adds a strongly essentialist view of the ethnic features that define Hispanicity. Once Europe's militant Protestant nationalists had begun to recognize the "educational" value of the *Brevissima relación*—especially when Las Casas was used to amplify certain gruesomely triumphalist passages in the widely reprinted accounts of Cortéz and Gómara (which described the Mexican conquest), or León and Zárate (which recounted the conquest of Peru)—they never ceased exploiting it.[66] Certainly other texts were important to the dissemination of *la leyenda negra*: key contributors were Girolamo Benzoni's *History of the New World* (1565), *The discourse of the history of Florida, containing the treason of the Spaniards, against the subjects of the king, in the year 1565* (1566), written by Anthony Le Challeux, a survivor of the punitive attack on the Huguenot colony at Fort Caroline, and Gonsalvius Montanus's *Discovery and Playne Declaration of the sundry and subtill practices of the Holy Inquisition of Spayne* (which had appeared in English translation by 1568).[67] But, in combination with the racializing strategies employed by William of Orange and his followers, it was the language and imagery of Las Casas—who claimed that the American "destruction" had been "carried out with but one aim: to extract gold from the Indians"[68]—that would surface again and again in the most potent anti-Spanish diatribes.[69]

I would not go so far as to suggest, with Thomas Scanlan, that the 1583 publication of Las Casas's *Brevissima relación* as *The Spanish Colonie, or briefe chronicle of the acts and gestes of the Spaniardes* (1583) marks a "starting-point" for the "study of English colonial writing" because it "demonstrates the extent to which England's colonial project was born, at least in part, out of a conscious desire to compete with its Catholic rivals (especially Spain) for power and prestige on the world stage."[70] England's Hispanophilic inclinations remained far too vital during this early colonial moment, and although the English had learned from their privateering ventures how much was to be gained from New World enterprise, their imperial eyes were at this point focused much closer to home. But Scanlan is right to suggest that we can discern in these adaptations of Las Casas that the English were straining in their emerging discourses of nationhood to articulate some sense of being "not-Spanish."[71] Indeed, the preface to *The Spanish Colonie*—a text published by Foxe's collaborator John Day in the same year that their final, expanded fourth edition of the *Acts and Monuments* was printed[72]—picked up on Orange's ethnic typologies by introducing the behavior of the Spanish in the New World as flowing from their "firste fathers the Gothes" and "their second progenitors the Saracens."[73] The text's translator offered this genealogical gesture in the spirit of national awakening so that the Low Countries might "beholde as it were in a picture or table, what they are like to be at, when through their rec[k]lessness, quarrels, controversies, and partialities themselves have opened the way to *such an enemie*" (q2a, my italics). Examples of this new discursive knot, which tangled earlier religiopolitical discourses—especially those of Protestant national election (whether Dutch, Huguenot French, or homegrown English)[74]—with this newly inflected language of ethnicity appeared only rarely in England prior to the Armada. We can locate them in Hakluyt's unpublished 1584 manifesto, *A Discourse of Western Planting*, which quotes directly from the Las Casas material Englished just the previous year; but at this juncture, the argument from ethnos was neither dominant nor officially authorized.[75]

　　In the texts printed *after* 1588, however, we begin to hear repeatedly a discourse that hits all of the notes sounded in Orange's *Apology*. Perhaps inspired by the success of Nassau's widely circulated exhortations, English Protestant polemicists began to play the Spanish "race card" over and over again. As it had been in the Netherlands, the public sphere in England was now flooded with essentializing typologies that marked the Spaniard as cruel, duplicitous, arrogant, bestial, hypocritical, over-sexed, Antichristian, and ethnic. When we unravel the strands of English public discourse that construct Hispanicity in this manner, we begin to get a clearer, if also more disturbing, glimpse of the imaginative universe within which the early modern English nation-state took shape, as well as the place of Spain in England's national consciousness and on its Renaissance stages.

CHAPTER TWO

A Long and Lively Antithesis

Preachers, Printers, & Players . . . *be set up of God, as a triple bul-*
warke agynst the triple crown of the Pope, to bring him down.
    —John Foxe, *Acts and Monuments,* 1570

In breefe, such is this comparison that if some Rhetoritian would employ
his eloquence in framing of a long and lively Antithesis, he could not in
the world find a subject more sortable to his purpose then the comparing
of our conditions with those of this mongrell generation.
    . . . *I would say more, were it not for displeasing of the delicate*
sort: and we have here set the Spaniardes on stage . . . to furnish our
selves with laughter at their charges. And I pray you what man is there
so melancholy, that could forbeare laughter.
    —Robert Ashley, *A Comparison of the English and Spanish*
    Nation, 1589

JOHN FOXE DID not live to experience the full pressure of the crisis mentality that permeated his nation during the final decade and a half of Tudor reign. Having died in 1587, when the Armada's approach remained yet a rumor, he did not witness the variety of ways in which the reformation of national memory that constituted his life's work would be effected. While it is true that Foxe had believed that "the Lord began to work for his Church, not with sword and target . . . but with printing, writing and reading . . . so that either the pope must abolish knowledge and printing or printing at length will root him out,"[1] and although he would certainly have been acquainted with the accounts of Spain's "More than Turkish Cruelty" his coreligionists were about to publish—in John Day, Foxe and the Englished Las Casas of *The Spanish Colonie* shared the same printer, after all—his great martyrology ultimately declined the path of ethnos. But the discourses of kind that eventually combine to other Spain will go a long way toward completing the nationalistic revisionism to which the *Acts and Monuments* contributed.

The volume of anti-Spanish material that appeared in England from the late 1580s through the end of Elizabeth's reign, much of it imported from France and the Low Countries with the Crown's authorization and approval, suggests a high level of cultural guidance on the part of key conservative elites with whom Foxe had been well acquainted.[2] What these Hispanophobic texts (which were of inestimable propaganda value to the Protestant nationalist cause) make astonishingly clear is the fact that authors and translators high and low were being actively encouraged to participate in the state-sponsored production of pro-English, militantly Protestant, and violently anti-Spanish propaganda. Indeed, so successfully disseminated were these Hispanophobic typologies that, by means of their incessant repetition, they have echoed down the centuries as a "truth" of history. Influential though it may have been, however, this print propaganda may have been neither the most direct nor the most effective means though which Black Legend "patriotism" entered English public memory. As it quite literally "set the Spaniardes" on stage, to borrow a figure from Robert Ashley's contemporary *Comparison of the English and Spanish Nation* (1589), England's Renaissance drama delighted audiences even as it inculcated the Hispanophobic attitudes their government was working so hard to foster.

The Sinking of Spain

Although the era's propagandist polemics and pamphlets provide the most obvious index of Elizabethan Hispanophobia, the constitutive features of the Black Legend, including the racializing of Spain and the erasure of Anglo-Spanish complementarity, are more readily activated by several dramas of the immediate post-Armada period. George Peele's *Famous Chronicle of king Edward the first, sirnamed Edward Longshankes, with his return from the holy land* (1593), probably first performed in 1590–91, may be taken as emblematic.

At a late moment in Peele's play we encounter two members of the English royal house, Queen Elinor and Princess Jone—historically, the women are Eleanor of Castile and Joan of Acre, the wife and the daughter of Edward I

(Edward Longshanks, reigned 1272–1307)—making their way across "Charing greene." Having been witness in a prior scene to the brutal murder of London Maris, the Lord Mayor's wife—carried out at Elinor's command and with her personal direction—we find the queen and her daughter transported from the play's initial location in Wales, where the homicide had been committed, to a pastoral setting near London. Here, the princess confronts her mother with the crime. In a hyperbolic attempt to deny any connection with the murder Elinor blasphemes, "Gape earth and swallow me, and let my soule / Sincke down to Hell if I were Autor of / The womans Tragedy" (18.2197–98).[3] "Sincke" Elinor does. Quite literally, she is swallowed by the mold the two are traversing, which, following her descent, "is new closed up again" (18.2201).

It is not difficult to imagine how such an incident might have been staged—the boy actor playing Jone affecting disbelief while the one personating the queen dropped lithely beneath the boards. We can also imagine how Elizabethan theatergoers might have been awed at Elinor's "rising," which occurs several scenes later, as they observed the marvelous reappearance of the "Queene who suncke this daie on Charing greene" (20.2280). Soon they would have seen an amazed Elinor, fearing death's onset and proclaiming that she must "bewaile her sinfull life" (20.2289), beg the humble potter's wife who has rescued the queen for safe conduct to her husband Edward's court. In a scene much like the one Shakespeare composed ten years later for *Measure for Measure*, they would have looked on while Elinor is shriven by none other than Longshankes himself. Having heard report of his wife's "sincking," Edward offers to "take the swete confession of [his] Nell" (21.2334) and "be ghostlie Father" (21.2353) to her. As she unburdened herself, audiences would have heard the dying Elinor reveal not only that she had committed incest with Edward's brother, Edmund, "Uppon [her] bridal couch and by [her own] concent" (23.2476), but that Princess Jone had been a bastard "baslie borne, begotten of a Frier" (23.2494).

The Famous Chronicle embodies several of the ways in which the Black Legend could be written across the broader field of English culture at a moment during which the outcome of the Anglo-Spanish conflict was far from certain. By resurrecting a historical actor of Spanish ancestry, Peele recalls a long tradition of Anglo-Hispanic interrelation and alliance. By representing an Elinor whose sexual proclivities, like those attributed to Katherine of Aragon and the Iberian nobles whose close consanguinity so troubled Henry VIII in Foxe's *Acts and Monuments*, bring shame upon the English royal house, Peele calls into question the legitimacy of a reign three hundred years in the past. Casting Eleanor as a villainess capable of unspeakable cruelty and immorality, his play rewrites English history in order to evidence essential otherness, inherent cultural incompatibility, and the dangerous marital politics that were so "typical" of "the Spaniard."[4]

I do not suggest here that Peele's contribution is unique. Rather, it was becoming fairly common practice for English playwrights, in the manner of the day's Protestant propagandists, to recall actors and events from an internationalist Roman Catholic past in order to rewrite their significance for a nationalistic, post-Reformation present. It was a rare anti-Spanish diatribe that did not include some variation on this theme, just as it was a rare Roman Catholic apologetic that did not perform the reverse by appealing to the shared traditions of the earlier age. The importance of Peele's effort lies in what it reveals of the revisionist process.

Raphael Holinshed had entered the more familiar assessment of the life of Eleanor of Castile in the obituary included in his *Chronicles of England, Scotland and Ireland* (1587):

> In the nineteenth yeare of king Edward queen Elianor king Edwards wife died upon saint Andrews eeven at Herdebie . . . neere to Lincolne, the kinge being as then on his waie towards the borders of Scotland: but having now lost the iewel which he most esteemed, he returned towards London to accompanie the corps unto Westminster, where it was buried. . . . She was a godlie and modest princesse, full of pitie, and one that shewed much favor to the English nation, readie to releeve everie mans greefe that sustained wrong and to make them friends that were at discord, so farre as in hir laie. In everie towne and place, where the corps rested by the waie, the king caused a crosse of cunning workmanship to be erected in remembrance of hir, and in the same was a picture of hir ingraven. Two of the like crosses were set up at London, one at Charing and the other at Westcheape. Moreover he gave in almes every Wednesday wheresoever he went, pence a peece, to all such poore folk as came to demand the same.[5]

To Holinshed's memorial we can add the legend, reinscribed in William Camden's 1586 *Britannia*, that honored Eleanor for having saved Edward's life, when, during their Holy Land Crusade of 1270–72, he had been wounded by a Saracen adversary's poisoned blade: "What then can be more rare than this woman's expression of love? Or what can be more admirable? The tongue of a wife, anointed (if I may say so) with duty and love to her husband, draws from her beloved those poisons which could not be drawn by the most approv'd

Physician; and what many and most exquisite medicines could not do, is effected purely by the love of a wife."[6] Between these two influential Elizabethan historiographers, we glimpse a fairly complete picture of the Eleanor of famous memory.

Over and against this popular Eleanor, Peele performs Spanish otherness by deploying a cast of characters that bear scant resemblance to the figures represented in the historical accounts available to the Elizabethans. That he departs from sources like Holinshed and Camden in highly significant ways is signaled by the second of the play's subtitles. As printed by Abell Jeffes in 1593, the copy advertises the inclusion of "the sincking of Queene Elinor, who sunck at Charingcrosse, and rose again at Pottershith, now named Queenehith." Peele's redundancy, "the *sincking* of Queene Elinor, who *sunck*," lays claim to the public memorial to Eleanor's reign remarked by Holinshed, a reconstruction of which today marks the entry to Charing Cross station. By way of this cultural landmark (which would have been known to anyone in his audience), Peele rewrites the historical significance of this public monument to Anglo-Spanish cooperation. One of twelve Gothic structures erected posthumously by Edward I to honor Eleanor of Castile's memory, the cross at Charing, like the one at nearby Westcheap, had stood for three centuries as a monument to one of the "chariest" queens to grace the English monarchy. We might go so far as to say that Charing Cross stood as a memorial to cultural as well as conjugal complementarity.[7] In *The Famous Chronicle*, a very different meaning accrues to Eleanor's English sojourn, to her Iberian heritage, and to the site of her famous monument. Peele's Elinor returns to England from Edward's crusade only to reveal the markers of Hispanicity propagandistically ascribed to the Spaniard, circa 1590. Sharing a private moment with her daughter Jone in the play's opening scene, Edward's Castilian consort preens,

> Now Elinor, now Englands lovely Queene,
> Bethinke thee of the greatnes of thy state:
> And how to beare thy selfe with royaltie,
> Above the other Queenes of Christendome,
> That Spaine reaping renowne by Elinor,
> And Elinor adding renowne to Spaine,
> Britaine may her Magnificence admire. (1.229–35)

Although warned by her half-English daughter that "The people of this land are men of warre, / The women courteous, milde, and deboniare" (1.247–48, and so she ought not to "gin swell with pride" (1.251), Elinor remains intransigent, displaying the hubris so commonly associated with the Spanish Hapsburgs of the sixteenth century. "Indeed we count them headstrong Englishmen," she continues, "But we shall hold them in a Spanish yoake, / And make them know their lord and sovereign" (1.256–58). Against Castilian luxury and pomp, the play's warlike Englishmen and mild English maids outshine Elinor's "Magnificence." Concerned primarily with enhancing the reputation of her native nation, and evidently accustomed to a tyrannous (and quite un-English) exercise of royal prerogative, Elinor must be schooled in the "milder" ethos of Edward's England. And of course Elinor's desire to make the English wear "a Spanish yoake" resonates within the Armada context in ways it could not possibly have done in earlier centuries. Prior to the divorce of Katherine of Aragon, England had tended far more often toward Spanish alliances than Spanish antagonisms.

Surveying the episodes that feature Queen Elinor, we find Peele's character gradually manifesting the interior corruption and disturbing tendency toward brutality that will ultimately bring on the rebuke symbolized by her "sincking." Scene 6 finds Elinor arriving in Wales, where the English face a resistance movement mounted by the rebel Lluellen. At her entrance, we observe "Queene Elinor in her litter borne by foure Negro Mores" (stage direction at 6.1015). Much in the manner of the notorious *Coppie of the Anti-Spaniard* (1590)—like many Black Legend polemics, imported from France by the London printer John Wolfe—which ethnopoetically characterized Spain as a "Mauritanian race" of "Negroes" who had "intreate[d] the Indians with all unchristian humanitie,"[8] Peele plays antithetically upon a kind and quality associated with concurrent modes of Spanish self-representation. For even as it gloried in the achievement of its *reconquista*, sixteenth-century Iberian culture had begun to manifest a significant strain of "maurophilia." As Barbara Fuchs has shown, "if Spain's self-representation continually invokes Moorish culture, in both a domestic and international context, when other nations rehearse Spain's maurophilia they often transform it into an essentialized discourse of racism and xenophobia that negates Spain's place within Europe."[9] While figuring Iberia's geographical proximity to and historical connection with Africa, *The Famous History* simultaneously evokes its "mongrel generation," as Ashley's *Comparison* described Iberia's racial heritage and the Spanish Empire's "typical" enslavement of its colonial subjects.

Peele's scene also sets up a dramatically central meeting between Longshanks and four Welsh barons invited to witness the naming of Edward's newborn as the first "Prince of wales by Cambrias full consent" (10.1510).[10] In this representation of the younger Edward's christening, *The Famous Chronicle* takes yet another Hispanophobic turn. For when "the foure Barrons of Wales" enter to swear fealty to the new prince, Elinor insults them by rejecting "the Mantle of fries" (stage direction at 10.1565) that they have ceremoniously presented to the king's namesake. Offended that her son should be offered such a common garment for his christening gown, she prefers one that "will make him shine like the sonne, and perfume the streets where he comes" (10.1601–2). As Longshankes reproves Elinor yet again for her excessive "Spanish pride," his ire is softened by the "lookes" and "sweetness" that are soon revealed to be masking darker impulses. Elinor then asks a boon, to which Edward immediately accedes: "What wants my Queene to perfecte her content[?]" (10.1633). The Welshman "Rice ap Meredith" reads aloud the "Queenes request":

> Then shall my wordes make many a bosom bleede.
> . . . .
> The pride of Englishmens long haire,
> Is more then Englands Queene can beare:
> Womens right breast cut them off al,
> And let the great tree perish with the small. (10.1642–48)

By resourcefully countering that the king and queen themselves should be the first to endure the punishment she has prescribed for England's nobles, Edward, characterizing his wife's demand as a "Spanish fitte" (10.1639), circumvents the carnage to which he has unwittingly agreed.

With Elinor's demand for blood has come a further revelation of the brutality Edward immediately associates with his wife's nationality. London Maris, nurse to the young prince Edward and the one character who openly speaks the "truth" of her mistress's evil, pays the price for the discovery. In order "to purge [her] melancholly, / And be revenged upon this London Dame" (15.2072–73), Elinor orders her waiting maid Katherina to "binde [Maris] in the chaire," "draw forth her brest / And let the Serpent sucke his fill" (15.2092–95), committing the murder mentioned a moment ago. Whereas tradition had it that England's Spanish queen had heroically saved her husband's life, in Peele's representation the historical Eleanor's virtue becomes the fictional Elinor's vice. In an obvious inversion of popular memory, Eleanor of Castile becomes her antithesis—a dispenser of death rather than a legendary healer.

Queen Elenor's Confession

The Hispanophobic material from which *The Famous Chronicle* draws does not come by way of any of the era's "official" historiographers; instead, Peele appears to have imported Eleanor's crimes by way of two popular ballads, "The Lamentable fall of Queene Elenor" and "Queene Elenor's Confession," the origins and printing histories of which are uncertain. Although the extant copy of "The Lamentable fall" dates from circa 1600, and "Elenor's Confession" from even later—suggesting at least the possibility that the ballads could have drawn from *Edward I* and not the other way round—their convergence in Peele's play is unquestionable. In the former, we find not merely Elenor's "vain desire" but also her request to "the king, that ev'ry man / That ware long lockes of hair, / Might then be cut and polled all," her order "That ev'ry womankind should have / Their right breast cut away," and the murder of the Lord Mayor's lady by setting "two snakes unto her breast, / that suck'd away her blood." Elinor's response to the accusation that had she committed the crime, "She wish'd the ground might open wide," is identical, as is her fate. And in what must have struck contemporary audiences as delicious irony, for it was to be sung to the tune of "Gentle and corteous," the ballad, like Peele's play, concludes "at Charing-cross she sunk / Into the ground," only to rise and confess "the lady's blood. . . . / And likewise how that by a fryar / She had a base-born child."[11]

The role played by "Queene Elenor's Confession" in Peele's revision is also significant. From this ballad Peele takes the episode in which Elinor is shriven by her husband. "To a pleasant new tune," the ballad reports, "The king pulled off his fryars coate, / And appeared all in redde; / She shrieked, and cryd, and wrung her hands, / And sayd she was betrayed."[12] What is most interesting with respect to this interpolated material, however, is that the subject of "Queene Elenor's Confession" is not an incident in the lives of Edward I and Eleanor of Castile; rather, the ballad from which Peele draws represents an episode from the legendarily turbulent marriage of Henry II and Eleanor of Aquitaine. The conflation of the two ballad texts suggests that as Peele merges these anecdotes about the reigns of two very different Eleanors, he is thinking far more typologically than historically. This sort of typological collation appears to have become, as we will see in the chapters that follow, a fairly common representational strategy. Peele's aim being to show the ill effects of a foreign queen on the English body politic, one Eleanor was apparently as useful as another.

Although it would certainly be possible to find antecedents for the sort of depravity attributed to Eleanor of Castile in other kinds of sources, from 1580s onward "damnable deeds" such as these are most commonly attributed in English religiopolitical discourse to "the cursed Spaniard."[13] Elinor prescribes the very sort of "strange cruelties" ascribed to Spain in virulent Black Legend polemics such as *A Pageant of Spanish Humours*. Indeed, the discourse of Hispanophobia lends considerable significance to the more sexualized aspects of Elinor's sinking. For we often find accusations of depravity such as Elinor's mobilized in Protestant anti-Spanish polemic, whether in William of Orange's insinuation that Philip II had committed incest with his daughter the Spanish Infanta or in lurid accounts of the sexual brutality of Spanish soldiery.[14] Like much of the Hispanophobic discourse of the 1590s, Peele's incorporation of contemporary ballad material reaches beyond the proscriptions of Las Casas—whose condemnations of his nation's colonizing ethos were never essentialized as indices of "race"—and toward the emergent view of Spain's essentially tainted ethnicity.

The dramatic license Peele takes made for the sort of sensational theater that the Elizabethans found irresistible, and in spite of its clumsy dramaturgy and structural inconsistencies the play seems to have attracted audiences in print as in performance.[15] But what is perhaps most significant about *The Famous Chronicle* is the way its representation of Eleanor of Castile rewrites her story in terms of the religiopolitics of post-Reformation England. By portraying Eleanor's progeny as "basely born" Peele does more, however, than desacralize England's Roman Catholic past. As an important progenitor of the House of Lancaster, Edward's heirs would advance a number of legitimate claims on the English throne. As Margaret Aston has shown, Peele's play delegitimizes these claims by revealing the "bastardy" of Lancastrian origins.[16] At the moment of *Edward I*'s production, several suits were being made in behalf of a Spanish succession based on the legitimacy of their lineal connections to the House of Lancaster, a concern that will lend considerable significance to our discussion of Christopher Marlowe's *Jew of Malta*.

I do not mean to suggest that the historical Eleanor of Castile would have been as blameless as she was portrayed to have been by the cultish promoters of the English monarchy. There is some chronicle evidence, to which Peele may also have had access, of resistance to some of her policies, objection to some of her methods, and resentment of her foreign roots.[17] It has also been alleged that, shortly before her death in 1290, Eleanor influenced her husband Edward's decision to expel the Jews from England (though coming, as it does, fully two hundred years prior to Spain's expulsions, to perceive in the act an Iberian influence may itself suggest a Black Legend inheritance).[18] But whereas from the thirteenth century on she had most often been described as "a pious, modest and merciful lady, a lover of all English people and a support for the whole realm,"[19] Peele's Elinor is made to bear the entire weight of the Black Legend. The topoi of Spanish ambition and pride (as exemplified by her attitudes toward the "baseness" of Wales and its people), spiritual and physical depravity (as suggested by the "whoredome" of her incestuous sexual relations with members of the clergy and her husband's family), a racialist identification of Spain with its "African" past (as emblematized by the "Negro Mores" who carry Elinor in the "luxury" of her sedan), and a characteristically "Spanish" taste for cruelty (as borne out by the bloody punishments and poisoning she devises for England's political body) all coalesce to shape her as a figure of English Protestantism's antithesis, imperial Spain. At the same time, Peele's ethnopoesis participates in a nationalistic remapping of the English landscape that dichotomizes away all signs of earlier international complementarity. Via *The Famous Chronicle*'s argument the significance of a centuries-old architectural landmark is rewritten; no longer a remembrance of the "chary" Anglo-Spanish queen, it is now a sign of essential Spanish depravity. The play's revelation is that it had been only as a result of Eleanor's redemption by an English monarch (whose memorialization had visited on her the undeserved honor of covering her many faults) that the twelve famous monuments dotting the English landscape from Lincolnshire down to London had been allowed to signify positive cultural value.

If, as Mary Douglas suggests, among the "kinds of social pollution" are threats of "danger pressing on external boundaries" and "danger from internal contradiction,"[20] the Leviticus-inspired arguments made by Protestants on behalf of the English monarchy seem to betray both of these "dangers." If Henry VIII's marriage to Katherine of Aragon had defiled the English monarchy, it had done so as a result of England's "entanglement" with a nation whose ethos of dynastic extension was also its own. In order to mask an internal contradiction the Henrican regime was not prepared to confront, it was now alleged that the seeds of that defilement had been sown in an earlier Spanish match that had been its type. Whereas the contingencies of dynastic connection had once been negotiated in relation to a common ethos, they were now being construed as signs of a crisis of ethnos. If the monument at Charing Cross had honored the memory of a virtuous Spanish queen, that virtue was now discovered to be a lie.

Lords of Spain

If Peele's Hispanophobic orchestrations are somewhat obscured by our historical (and disciplinary) distance from the thirteenth-century events he represents, *The Three Lords and Three Ladies of London* (1590), an early city-comedy
by the Puritan playwright Robert Wilson, a member of Leicester's company,
embodies far more obviously the popular commonplaces that were coming
to be associated with the Spaniard in England's Black Legend pamphlets.[21]
Remembered today primarily for *The Three Ladies of London* (c. 1584)—a play
that prefigures the multicultural Mediterranean of *The Merchant of Venice*[22]—
Wilson also turned his dramatic energies toward Spain. In the later *Three Lords
and Three Ladies of London* he dramatizes three villainous "Lords of Spaine,"
Ambition, Pride, and Tyranny, each personated in a manner reminiscent of
the Vice figures of an earlier age. The Spanish nobles are soon joined onstage
by their similarly contemptible pages, Shame, Treachery, and Terror who arrive intent on besting "Los Luteranos Angleses" and, just as significantly, eager
to possess their women, a motivation evoking the lurid acts recounted in any
number of the Black Legend tracts that had come to England via the Low
Countries.

Clearly providing a dramatic accompaniment to the era's political warn-
ings, the constellation of these allegorical stick figures in Wilson's comedy also
indicates how widely disseminated such commonplaces were becoming during the immediate post-Armada period. Not only does *The Three Lords* deliver
an officially authorized caution to a popular audience—however attractive
Spanish appearances may seem, they are not to be trusted—it also illustrates
vividly how the allegorical mode we tend to associate more with medieval
dramaturgy remained a viable poetic.[23] Wilson's recourse to this sort of naive
allegory marks his play as more akin to political cartooning than the polyse-
mantic fusion of image and theme we typically associate with the Renaissance
dramatic achievement.[24] But its most interesting feature may be a brief moment that allows us to glimpse the way that content from one medium, in
this case a printed account of an English privateering raid on the West Indies,
could migrate to another.

When Shame, Treachery, and Terror stumble onto the stage in *The Three
Lords*, they bear a shield emblazoned *Non sufficit orbis*, "The world is not
enough,"[25] a motto with which Philip II had augmented the Spanish Hapsburgs' traditional *Plus ultra*, "Yet still further," following the 1580 unification
of the Iberian Crowns. Wilson's display of Spanish arms reveals the not-so-
hidden motive behind Spain's imperial project. This was, in effect, the same

strategy employed by Richard Field—the English printer whose involvement in the propaganda wars seems to have been eclipsed only by the notorious John Wolfe[26]—when he emphasized the discovery of Philip's device with the publication of *A Summarie and True Discourse of Sir Frances Drake's West Indian Voyage* (London, 1589). Later reprinted by Richard Hakluyt, the episode recounts the reaction of several English seamen to the recently enhanced Hapsburg arms, which they had encountered during their ransacking of the Spanish governor's mansion in Santo Domingo: "Wherein upon one of the walles, right over against you as you enter the sayd place, so as your eye can not escape the sight of it, there is described & painted in a very large Scutchion, the armes of the king of Spaine & in the lower part of the said Scutchion, containing in it the whole circuit of the sea and the earth, whereupon is a horse standing on his hinder part within the globe, and the other fore part without the globe, lifted up as it were to leape, with a scroll painted in his mouth, wherein was written these wordes in Latin NON SVFFICIT ORBIS: which is as much to say, the world sufficeth not" (245). As told by Thomas Cates in the published version, Drake's crewmen reacted to Philip's motto with the expected mix of English understatement and martial bravado. As the account recalls, "By some of our companie it was told [to the Spaniards that] if the Queene of England would resolutely prosecute the warres against the king of Spaine, he should be forced to lay aside that proude and unreasonable reaching of his, for he should finde more then inough to do, to keep that which he had alreadie, as by the present example of their lost towne that might for a beginning preceave well inough."[27] The Field narrative absolves the English of any of the ethical implications of their piracy, which is recast as a response to the "proude and unreasonable reaching" of the Spanish king. Wilson's play goes Field's propagandistic discovery one further, deploying the Spanish king's coat of arms not merely as a token of Spanish imperial hubris but, quite as significantly, as a figure of essential Spanish depravity: it is, after all, the flower of English womanhood that the Spaniards desire in *The Three Lords and Three Ladies*, almost as much as they desire Indian gold.

While the broad humor of Wilson's comedy hardly resembles the complex engagement with the imperial ethos we will soon encounter in *The Spanish Tragedy*, it has in common with Kyd's drama the impulse to play allegorically upon the topoi of pride and ambition so commonly linked in Hispanophobic discourse with the excessive sexual appetites that Protestants were projecting upon the Spaniard. But although *The Three Lords and Three Ladies* clearly sounds the notes typical of Hispanophobia, it does not deploy the Black Legend in its most "mature" form. For like Foxe, and as we will also see, like Kyd,

Wilson declines the linkage of racial and religious elements that will make the discourse of ethnos such an effective (and affective) propaganda apparatus over the course of so many centuries. In terms of its contribution to our understanding of the strategies common to the discourse of Hispanophobia, however, Wilson's play is important in relation to what it reveals about *process*. As "news from the front" makes its way into the public sphere of early print, it circulates from one discursive genre to another. As it does so, the "original" or "official" significance of Spain's colonial mission is emptied out and reconstituted as low dramatic humor. In much the same manner as we saw material from popular ballads surface in Peele's play, within a year of their instantiation in Field's narrative encounter, Philip's motto and device have moved across linguistic and cultural boundaries. A material product of Spanish imperial culture thus becomes a sign that, when subjected to generic modulation and consequent repetition, gets reconstrued in order to signify ethnopoetically (that is, as an essential quality of Spain's national character). It is a procedure Protestant apologists, propagandists, and poets repeated time and again with any number of Spanish cultural artifacts. Without respect to any occasional audience or purpose, words and images, signs and symbols, pass from one discursive location to another. In the process, such markers acquire iconic significance; drained of intention and probity, they now signify essential Hispanophobic excess.

The Spanish Masquerado

If the post-1588 propaganda campaign changed popular perceptions regarding the relationship between Hispanicity and Englishness, this alteration in the public mind may be most accessible to us through the work of Robert Greene. Like his contemporary George Peele, Greene had represented Elinor of Castile in his *Honorable History of Friar Bacon and Friar Bungay* (c. 1589), a play we have long regarded as canonical. But unlike Peele, he had done so in a way that resisted the argument from ethnos.

As in his slightly earlier *Alphonsus, King of Arragon* (c. 1587), Greene presented in *Friar Bacon* a largely sympathetic, perhaps even Hispanophilic, characterization.[28] *Alphonsus* did stage otherness, via the attractions of a subjected Turk and the revelation of Mohamet as false prophet.[29] But the other of *Alphonsus* is the pre-Reformation other of *Hall's Chronicle*, and its hero is more exemplary Christian king than exotic foreigner. By conflating the deeds of Alfonso V of Aragon and I of Naples (1416–58) and his type, "El Batallador" (the Battler) Alfonso I of Aragon and Navarre (1104–34), Greene seems primarily interested drawing from a shared European past in order to construct an essentially comic protagonist destined for the inevitable marriage. Like *Friar Bacon*, which explores class values that the English and Spanish monarchies of the play seem largely to share (as did the historical Eleanor and Edward), *Alphonsus* seems unconcerned with promoting anti-Spanish sentiment.

It is true that *Friar Bacon* does emphasize a difference in status between Elinor and Margaret the Keeper's daughter, the younger Edward's first love and an authentically "English" beauty. But Greene resists the temptation to ethnicize England's future queen. Interests of state recommend Edward's marriage to Elinor, and so the union with Castile is made. In the arrangement, Margaret of Fressingfield is matched with a lord of appropriate rank so that she too may grace the royal household, predicting a future of complementarity within the multinational court. Indeed, with Longshankes's father Henry III having praised the Castilian princess on her arrival as "the lovely Elinor, / Who dared for Edward's sake cut through the seas" (4.9–10), and with Edward gushing over her as "one that overmatcheth Venus in her shape" (9.185), Elinor becomes the maternal source from which will flow the greatness of the English monarchy. With Friar Bacon proclaiming "that this royal marriage / Portends such bliss unto this matchless realm" (16.38–39), King Henry demands of the repentant necromancer, "What strange event shall happen to this land, / Or what shall grow from Edward and his queen?" (16.41–42). Prophesying that, after a period in which "Mars shall be master of the field" (16.50), "Diana's rose" will grow from the Edward-Elinor tree and thereby enable England to glory "over all the West" (16.77), Greene could hardly be accused of promoting Hispanopobia.

In *The Spanish Masquerado* (1589), however, a production clearly penned in the wake of the Armada scare (and obviously intended to exploit the emotional temper of that troubled moment), we find Greene working in another register altogether. If *Alphonsus* and *Friar Bacon* represented anything like Greene's previous views on England and Spain's shared past, his experience of crisis had apparently transformed them. For in the masque he dedicated that year to "the Right Worshipfull M. Hugh Ofley, Sherrife of the Citie of London," we find Greene prefiguring dramatically the ethnopoetic mode we have seen his associate Peele deploy in *The Famous Chronicle of Edward the first*.

Once again, a subtitle tells the tale. *The Spanish Masquerado* advertises that "under a pleasant devise" will be "discovered effectuallie, in certain breefe sentences and Mottos, the pride and insolencie of the Spanish estate: with the disgrace conceived by their losse, and the dismayed confusion of their troubled thoughtes."[30] What follows is a relatively standard, albeit imaginatively dramatized, rehearsal of Spanish "errors," each of which are trumped by some commonplace of England's recent victory at sea. In his address *"To the Gentlemen Readers,"* Greene acknowledges that "Hitherto . . . I have writte of loves," but that "now least I might be thought to tie my selfe wholly to amorous conceites, I have adventured to discover my conscience in Religion" (A3). To this end, Greene's pageant opens with a satirical representation of the pope. "Since sinceritie in Religion and humilitie, were put into exile," argues the masque, "and [since] mens traditions . . . [had been] pride-erected as pillers of the church" so "that from feeders of the flocke" the Catholic clergy "have . . . proved ravening Wolves, and Subverters of Christ and his doctrine," exchanging the "humble puritie of Christes Disciples" for "extreme covetousness," "open Simony," "Whoredomes," "Sodomie," "palpable and grosse heresies" (B1r).

Greene's entertainment then compresses into a few lines an orthodox Church of England perspective on the Reformation, suggesting that his rehearsal has as much to do with performing public consciousness as with discovering his individual "conscience." Describing the faults of "this Monster, the Antechrist [*sic*] the Pope" while proclaiming the virtues of "Henrie the eight, king of England, who seeing the abominatiō of that proud Antechrist . . . pulled down their sumptuous buildings . . . subverted their estate" and "for blind Papistrie gave us the light of the Gospell" (B2–B3r), Greene turns his pen on "The rest of the rascal Rable of the Romish Church, as Monkes, Friars, and dirging Priestes . . . sitting banqueting with the fair Nunnes, having store of daintie Cates and wines before them, stall-fed with ease and gluttony, grone out of their fat panches this passion."[31] Greene's representation gives flesh to the Protestant anticlericalism that suffuses the *Acts and Monuments*, his morally bankrupt friars, like those we met in Peele's *Edward I*, evoking the luxury, decadence, and depravity his "masquerado" will reveal as constitutive of the Iberian Empire.

When Greene's masque turns finally to his Spanish protagonists, we meet none other than "Phillip king of Spaine, attired like an Hermite . . . riding towards the Church on his Mule, attended on onely with . . . his slaves that are Moores" (B3). A figure reminiscent of Spenser's Archimago, the Philip of *The Spanish Masquerado* has been "housed from his infancie in the darke and obscure dungeon of Papistry." He "therefore" takes "the Pope for Peter's successor" and so "suffereth himselfe to be led and ruled by this man of Sin" that he is inspired to gather "a great Armado" of "Shippes huge and monstrous," manned by the "chosen Cavaliers of Spaine, Portugall, Italie and other Provinces" (B3–B4v).

While rehearsing favorite Protestant topoi related to Roman Catholicism's emphasis on justification by "Works"—such as overdependence on a corrupt clergy, obsessive devotion to saints, and excessive cruelty in conquest—Greene appropriates the Hispanophobic discourse enabled by the publication of Las Casas's discoveries. "Like brute beasts," the Spanish "caused the Indians to be hunted with dogs, some to be torne with horses, some to have their hands cut off, and so many Massaquers as greeveth any good minde to report" (E2v–E2). Like Peele's *Edward I*, Greene's masque goes beyond Las Casas to join the physical hue of Philip's "Moores" with the spiritual darkness of Spain's Roman Catholic faith. An ethnopoetic of color thus merges with the web of Las Casian commonplaces to which this faith was now increasingly linked, giving the Black Legend the added rhetorical force its promoters would find so religiopolitically persuasive. In the manner of the polemicist Edward Daunce, whose *Brief Discourse of the Spanish State* (1590) begged his English readership to consider that "the *Mores* in eight monthes conquered *Spaine* . . . and . . . the *Spaniards* were eight hundred years before they recovered that losse: during which time, we must not thinke that the *Negroes* sent for women out of *Aphrick*,"[32] Greene's Spaniards, like Peele's, are subjected to the new poetics of racialization. Alongside Daunce's polemic, the two dramatic productions reveal, to adapt Kim Hall, how Black Legend Hispanophobia "draws power from England's ongoing negotiations of African difference and from the implied color comparison therein."[33]

What is especially significant about *The Spanish Masquerado* is the fact that Greene designed it (though we do not know that the masque was actually performed) as a pageant for the city of London. Even in its printed form—as a public review of England's relationship to and participation in the Reformation chronicled by writers like Foxe and Camden, a rehearsal of the recent Armada crisis endowing that event with an officially authorized interpretation and revelation of the ethnic nature of England's Spanish adversary—Greene's masque endows relatively recent phenomena with a primordial character. Modeling a microcosm of England as reconceptualized by the Reformers against a world inherently more complex and multivocal than their binary thinking could allow, Greene condenses the indeterminate signs of the "lived-in world" so as to signify an unambiguous English solidarity.[34] Further, by publishing his *Masquerado*, Greene casts his pageant as an act of public religious profession. Quite in line with the rhetoric of election articulated by England's Protestant leadership, his dramatic intervention couples the notion that a "mercifull God" had made their island "like Eden, a second Paradise" (G4), with a view of Spain as England's theological, ethical, and ethnic opposite.

In Greene's 1589 production we find Foxe's "Preachers, Printers, & Players" formulation realized as public spectacle. Like any number of the aesthetic productions of this historical moment, Greene's *Spanish Masquerado*, like Peele's *Famous Chronicle*, guides English audience members *away* from a shared, international, and potentially "golden" past—which Roman Catholic contemporaries like William Allen, Robert Persons, William Weston, Henry Garnet, John Gerard, and others were successfully reviving in order to promote reconciliation with England's traditional faith—and *toward* a present (and future) built upon new, *national* traditions. These *English* traditions virtually required—in combination with the investiture of the monarchy with quasi-divine status and the creation of institutions and rituals that could fill the void left by the wholesale evacuation of Roman Catholic customs and infrastructures—an experience of otherness. If a people cannot know what they are until they know what they are not, it was the Spaniard, by virtue of his religious and ethnic difference, who could provide the otherness against which England was to measure its emerging sense of national self.[35] Is it reasonable to assume that the argument from ethnos as given flesh in Greene's masque and Peele's history play did not undergird at least some portion of the dramatic achievement we associate with the English Renaissance? Can we ignore the possibility that Reformation England's desire for "purity"—which partook of a broader cultural obsession with purities such as those of faith, tradition, and lineage—was in some strong sense related not merely to its Protestant doctrine but also to its consciousness of being literally "whiter" than its Hispanic adversary?

As if taking their cue from Robert Ashley, whose *Comparison of the English and Spanish Nation* had suggested the potential of "framing of a long and lively Antithesis" by dichotomizing England and Spain, *The Famous Chronicle of Edward I*, *The Three Lords and Three Ladies of London*, and *The Spanish Masquerado* actively intervene in the evolving and intensely conflicted relationship between the emerging nations of Britain and Iberia. The rhetorical strategies these dramatic representations employ—the antithetical logic of which turns white to black by rewriting virtually every index of Spanish identity as the ethnic opposite of everything essentially English—exemplify the range of tropes and figures that constitute the Black Legend, even as they demonstrate how the raw material of Hispanophobia could circulate within the public sphere of early print among virtually any of the available discursive genres.

While productions like Peele's, Wilson's, and Greene's played an important part in shaping what will constitute the specter of Spain in the minds of generations of Protestants to come, they do not record, nor do they transmit, a sense of the complexity, ambivalence, or profundity that characterized the historical relationship that continued to connect the cultures of the British Isles with those of the Iberian Peninsula. While they too may resort at times to Hispanophobic stereotyping, the plays of Kyd, Marlowe, and Shakespeare do probe, and in ways far less reductive than we have thus far encountered, the complex web of interconnections and relationships that constituted the early modern Anglo-Hispanic nexus. Having partaken sufficiently of the discourse of Hispanophobia as deployed in its basest forms, we are now in the position to discern this important difference. And so we may turn to that seminal drama of the English Renaissance, *The Spanish Tragedy* of Thomas Kyd.

CHAPTER THREE

Thomas Kyd's Tragedy of "the Spains"

For heresie and Schisme, were the Greeke Emperours *discharged, and* the Empire thereby trāslated *to the Germans . . . now our holy father* Sixtus the fifte . . . *therefore hathe specially intreated* Philip the highe and mightie Kinge Catholike of Spaine . . . *for his singular love to-wardes that nation whereof by marriage of* Holie Queene Marie *of blessed memorie he was once king, for the olde love and league betwixt said cuntrie and the house of Burgogne, for the infinite injuries and dis-honours done to his maiestie and people by* Elizabethe, *and to conclude for his speciall pietie and zeale towards Gods house and the see Apos-tolicke . . . wold take upon him in the name of God almighty, this sacred and glorious enterprise.*
    —William Allen, "Englishman," 1588

Declare among the nations, and publish it, and set up a standart, proclaim it and *conceale it not: say, Babel is taken, Bel is confounded, Merodach is broken down: her idoles are confounded* and *their images are burnt in pieces.*
    —Jeremiah 50:2, Geneva translation

For an Historiographer discourseth of affayres orderly as they were done, accounting as well the times and the actions, but a Poet thrusteth into the middest, even where it most concerneth him, and there recoursing to thinges forepaste, and divining of things to come, maketh a pleasing Analysis of all.
    —Edmund Spenser to Walter Raleigh, 23 January 1589

PHILIP II'S ASSUMPTION of the Portuguese throne in 1580 sent shockwaves through a Europe embroiled in a military and ideological struggle that would not exhaust itself until well into the next century. Suddenly, the balance of power had swung, perhaps decisively, in the direction of the Spanish Haps-burgs and their allies. The English and the French especially feared what a united Iberia might be able to accomplish, which accounts for their unchar-acteristic cooperation in the attempt to prop up the "native" pretender, Dom Antonio of Avis, the Prior of Crato, in his rather futile attempts to claim the Portuguese crown for himself.[1]

The annexation of Portugal and its overseas possessions to the Spanish Empire in 1580 precipitated something on the order of a structural shift. "For the sudden extension of Philip's realms," as Fernand Braudel wrote, "raised the question of control of the Atlantic. Whether consciously or unconsciously, Philip's composite empire by force of circumstance became centered on the Atlantic, that vital sea connecting his many dominions, the base of the claims to what was known even in Philip II's lifetime, as his 'Universal Monarchy.'"[2] In the face of this strategic windfall—brought on by the death of the Portu-guese king Sebastian I in the Battle of the Three Kings, famously memorial-ized by George Peele in *The Battell of Alcazar* (c. 1589)[3]—the public sphere of early print swelled with equal parts envy and dread at the prospect of an Iberia unified as the empire of "the Spains," even as the promoters of the Black Legend began to construct Portugal as yet another victim of Spanish tyranny. In Iberia, of course, the prospect of unification signified quite differently. As Fray Hernando del Castillo had counseled Philip II, "Uniting the kingdoms of Portugal and Castile will make Your Majesty the greatest king in the world . . . because if the Romans were able to rule the world simply by ruling the Medi-terranean, what of the man who rules the Atlantic and Pacific oceans, since they surround the world? . . . The gain or loss [of Portugal] will mean the gain or loss of the world."[4] It is in this milieu that we should place *The Spanish Tragedy*, probably the first English drama to face the Portuguese incorporation head on and to grapple with its historical complexity.[5] Absent this cultural development, neither the "glorious enterprise," as the Hispanized Cardinal William Allen dubbed the Armada crusade, nor Thomas Kyd's singular drama would have been thinkable.[6] Like the signal event of 1588 itself, the problems Kyd stages are the consequence of an encompassing cultural watershed.

When we approach *The Spanish Tragedy* in a manner less dependent upon our often anachronistic sense of how fully the national cultures of early mo-dernity had constituted themselves[7]—that is, *internationally*—it seems clear that the play neither alludes specifically to contemporary events nor simply parrots, in the manner, say, of Greene's *Renegado*, the orthodoxies of Elizabethan Protestantism.[8] For the structures of meaning Kyd mobilizes are at the time of his writing quite well established, at once a common inheritance of all early modern Europe *and* the discursive raw materials to which each of its emerging national cultures could resort in their attempts to construct difference. By mobilizing these cultural codes Kyd is thus able to play upon the discursive resources that England, Spain, and Portugal hold in common, and, by way of a number of manifestly English rhetorical operations, transform them in service of his own monarchy's imperial vision.

Acknowledging that no appeal to "culture" can ever hope to bridge all of *The Spanish Tragedy*'s formal discontinuities (or its ideological fault lines), any more than archival research can recover some singular originary meaning, this chapter offers a much more expansive sense of context for the play than we have commonly allowed. At the same time, it reanimates a web of significance that extends well beyond the boundaries of both the text itself and the individual "nations" Kyd labors to represent in order to consider how it was that the nations of Iberia were drawn together in the late sixteenth century as the first truly global empire.[9] Kyd focuses his argument on the international dimension of this cultural crisis, much like his Spanish contemporaries Luis de Góngora (1561–1627), who wrote the famous *Oda a la Armada Invencible* (1588) in commemoration of the Enterprise of England, Lope de Vega (1562–1635), who would conceive *La Dragontea* (1595), a lengthy mock epic treating Spain's final victory over "El Dragon," the infamous pirate Francis Drake, and Miguel Cervantes, whose somewhat later novella *La Española Inglesa* (1613) pictured English corsairs raiding the Iberian coast.[10] But rather than sinking into the dichotomizing Black Legend rhetoric characteristic of so many of his countrymen, Kyd explores instead the religiopolitical system through which imperial Spain was constituted. Thus the playwright is able to look beyond surface events, "thrusting into the middest" in order to confront the very idea of empire itself, a notion his great tragedy explores allegorically and in relation to the corrupting influence of the imperialist Roman Catholic ethos on Iberian society.

To strike at the heart of the matter, *The Spanish Tragedy* displaces the *literal* events of the 1580s in order to project them *literarily* into a mythic space at once past and future: in Edmund Spenser's contemporary prescript, by "recoursing to thinges forepaste, and divining of thinges to come," Kyd places himself at a critical remove from the ethnopoesis of his contemporaries, standing back to observe the structural upheaval that was shaking European culture at the moment of his writing, before making "a pleasing Analysis of all." In order to render Kyd's thematics visible, however, we will need to "open" the name Bel-imperia (much in the way a contemporary hermeneutist might have opened this sign). For to trace the relation of this explicitly allegorical figure to the two highly public traditions of empire that prevail during the early modern period—one a Latin inheritance, the other a Hebrew—is to revivify a neglected interpretive matrix that may have given birth to much of *The Spanish Tragedy*'s meaning.[11]

Translating Empire

As the highly symbolic and multivocal name worn by its central character proclaims, *The Spanish Tragedy* comes to us cast in terms of empire. To invoke this religiopolitical problem—which Henry VIII had forced upon England during the 1530s, and which his doctrinally orthodox daughter Mary, along with her Spanish husband Philip and their English Catholic counselors, had tried in the 1550s to reverse—is to recognize that the argument of Kyd's play turns upon a principal crux of Reformation culture, the "implicit trend towards the sovereignty of State over the Church."[12] But unlike the many treatises, polemics, and correspondences of the era that betray the political uncertainties and religious anxieties generated by the Portuguese succession, Kyd's play mediates these occurrences by endowing them with positive historical meaning. His largely fictive argument, though vaguely allusive, does not draw attention to "the facts" of history so much as it tries post facto to make sense of the cultural reordering that is still very much in process at the time of the play's production.

For it is quite clearly a postunification Iberia into which we are thrust in *The Spanish Tragedy*; Kyd's is a tragedy of "the Spains"—as the Iberian kingdoms collectively construct themselves after 1580—in which the new imperial arrangement is already in place.[13] Portugal is not ruled by a Portuguese king in the play, and, contrary to what an audience of the 1580s or 1590s might have had reason to expect, a native pretender does not wait in the wings. What must be stressed at the outset, then, is that the difficulties we see staged in Kyd's opening scenes are at once international and *internal*. And within the Spains of the play conflict centers around one character—that figure of empire, Bel-imperia herself.

A number of *The Spanish Tragedy*'s commentators have recognized that the play stages an act of Providence—a *translatio imperii*—pointing toward "the emergence of England as the new Empire."[14] As Eugene Hill has shown,

Kyd could not have appropriated more fitting models through which to stage this providential translation than the prophetic Virgilian mode, which his play inverts as a kind of "counter-Aeneid," and the tragic Senecan style, which he uses to evoke a "nightmarish" political realm reminiscent of Nero's Rome.[15] But precisely how Bel-imperia figures in this Senecan and Virgilian scheme remains a problem. Hill writes that "what that somewhat tarnished Spanish virgin . . . represents—the glory of Empire—will be transmitted to another and truer imperial virgin. I mean to Elizabeth, who from captive Princess (the parallel with Bel-imperia's plight is, I think, intended) had become an adept juggler of suitors, a skillful wielder of Empire. Elizabeth will rule on an island at the end of the world, an island which her countrymen—following an ancient tradition—identified with the Elysian fields. And that, of course, was the destination of Aeneas, which he reaches at the center of Virgil's poem. The depths of Kydian implication are Spenserian indeed."[16]

I believe that Hill is right to invoke Spenser. But while it seems evident that Elizabethan theatergoers would feel urged to compare their own princess with Bel-imperia, we should not rush too quickly toward this positive identification. As William Empson stressed (and Hill may sense this too, because he reads Bel-imperia as "somewhat tarnished"), it is also quite probable that they would "be rather shocked by her because it is clear that she goes to bed with her lovers (among the first words of the play are 'In secret I possessed a worthy dame')."[17] Unlike Elizabeth Tudor—or more to the point, unlike the official image so artfully disseminated by the Elizabethan regime and like the Spanish queens of England's Protestant revisionists—Bel-imperia seems too fraught with imperfections to make this identification so easy.[18] In other words, although the role she assumes in the play's final masque does help Hieronimo stage his valiant act of revenge, the "facts" of Bel-imperia's previous life appear far from chaste—as Empson also underscored, she "hath practised the French" (4.2.177) with Dons Andrea and Horatio.

However interesting these details of Bel-imperia's private life may be, we should refrain from speaking of this character as though required to regard her solely according to the demands of verisimilitude (that is, as a princess in a literal or historical sense). Instead, let us begin to unwind the fabric of quite public meaning that her name surely invites us to trace. When we put slightly more pressure on Bel-imperia—casting her both more allegorically and in concert with the typologizing habits of Reformation (and Counter-Reformation) culture—Kyd's imperial princess begins to assume a much more multidimensional and culturally relevant shape. By mobilizing the name Bel-imperia, Kyd "shadows"—with a multivocality much in line with that we have more commonly associated with his fellow Merchant Taylors' alumnus—a "dark conceit" that "beareth two persons."[19] Indeed, *The Spanish Tragedy*'s imperial princess has much in common with a character like Spenser's Duessa, whose "seeming glorious show" could bewitch "all men's sight."[20] For though we may presume her beautiful, alluring, and perhaps victimized, and though she does represent, in a strong sense, the beauty or "glory of Empire"[21] (traits that could equally describe Duessa), we should also recognize that there is something terrible about her beauty.

This is, of course, the point, and any attempt to make Bel-imperia stand for simply "beauty," "glory," or "Elizabeth" reduces her interpretive richness. For while we can read Bel-imperia's name after *bella*, we can also read it as though derived from *bellum*, suggesting her relation to "war." We are after all, from the play's prologue forward, in *Bell*ona's domain "where lovers live, [with] bloody martialists" (1.1.61).[22] And contrary to what Andrea, "who for his love tried fortune of the wars, / and by war's fortune sought both love and life" (1.1.39–40), boasts in the prologue, the real issue in the play may be not so much the fact that he once possessed Bel-imperia but the fact that he is possessed by her—as are all of Kyd's other Dons in turn: Horatio, Balthazar, and even Hieronimo. But while a foreshadowing such as "Then thus begin our wars" (2.4.35)—coming as it does from a character about to be brutally slain—may be suggestive, the more Protestant members of his audience would have known far in advance of this allusion that there is something perilous, duplicitous, seductive, and false about Bel-imperia's charms.

In the years since S. F. Johnson showed *The Spanish Tragedy*'s relation to the apocalyptic poetics of Bale and Foxe and other mid-sixteenth-century Protestant ideologues, it has been amply demonstrated that Kyd employs a symbolic vocabulary derived from Daniel and Revelation, which posits Spain as the "new Babylon" within the received apocalyptic typology of the Calvinist tradition.[23] This exegetical approach furnishes a provocative counterpoint to Hill's resuscitation of the play's Senecan and Virgilian interpolations, which do indeed, as Nashe recognized, ride uneasily with their biblical counterparts, because they effectively "thrust Elysium into Hell."[24] However, the implications of how this collision of Latin with Hebrew works in relation to "Bel-imperia," the figure upon whom *both* of these typological traditions converge, have remained undeveloped. It is in relation to the coming together of these Latin and Hebrew codes that we should think of Spenser and the Protestant allegorical tradition that his poetical "histories" attempt to realize.[25] If we subordinate the Latinate resonances of the sign "Bel-imperia" to the equally resonant tones of English Protestant reformism, we can begin to grasp the name's profound allegorical fullness. For even as "Bel" resounds with "beauty" and "war," it also strikes a far more apocalyptic note, ringing in a more culturally relevant biblical seductress (and surely Bel-imperia—again like Spenser's Duessa, who barely stops to grieve for one lover before attaching herself to another—is as much seductress as seduced).[26] As we are instructed "Against idolaters" in the Geneva Bible (or in any number of like-minded Elizabethan sermons and commentaries), "Bel" is one of "the chiefe idoles of Babylon."[27]

Bel-imperia is thus a double: the roots of her name are both Latinate and Hebrew.[28] And as Kyd dramatizes a string of incidents (the outcome of which is anything but *bella*), the play unfolds, in Maureen Quilligan's formulation, "a series of running commentaries, related to one another on the most literal of verbal levels,"[29] each implied by the various significations of "Bel" as they converge within the intersections of the play's various interpretive "pretexts": Virgilian epic, Senecan tragedy, and, quite as important, the Protestantized biblical master-narrative to which the play subordinates these Virgilian and Senecan elements.[30] In other words, if we attend to the allegorical "thickness" of "Bel," we soon hear that this sign is not merely a univocal signifier of "beauty" but a highly multivocal sign that comes to us "saturated with meaning."[31] For when Kyd puns the Latinate "Bel" against its biblical homonyms, the effect is to extend a "verbal echo" that plays against the various senses of their common sound. This allegorizing strategy does indeed thrust Elysium into hell by collating it within the already written of the Almighty's (that is, English Protestantism's) apocalyptic plan.[32] As it brings together these Latin and Hebrew codes, *The Spanish Tragedy* dramatizes how an exterior "that conquers kings" (3.10.88) may harbor an unchaste, seductive, and insatiable essence, an essence that all of the play's Dons—Balthazar, the succeeding hope of Portugal, and Andrea and Horatio of Castile before him—must find irresistible, because it has been providentially foreordained.[33]

Babylonian Captivity

If Kyd seems to go against his age by forgoing stereotypical Spanish cruelty and granting most of his Dons a nobility they seldom attain in the religio-political discourse of the Protestant north, he goes yet more against the representational status quo in his portrayal of "the Portingale." We encounter in the play no "daring race" of Lusitanians, "bolder in enterprise than any the world has yet seen,"[34] of the kind that one of early modernity's most successful Virgilian imitators, Luis Vaz De Camões, presents when constructing

Portugal's place in the pantheon of nations in *The Lusiads* (1572). Kyd's Portuguese do not seem to be awaiting a signal to rise against Spanish tyranny as the Elizabethan government had been assured they would, nor do we find, as in Hakluyt's correspondence with Walsingham, a "poor King" like Dom Antonio, accompanied by a dwindling retinue that "still hang[s] upon" him.[35] And while the play, much in the manner of George Whetstone's *English Myrror* (1586), which observed "The calamitie, and servile bondage of Portugall, under the government of Phillip king of Castile,"[36] does in fact mark the loss of both Portugal's national sovereignty and its colonial possessions—"For as we now are," observes Kyd's Castilian king, "so sometimes were these, / Kings and commanders of the western Indies" (3.14.6–7)—it does not lament its crushing failure to regain them.

Like Cervantes's roughly contemporary drama *The Siege of Numancia* (1580)—which prophesies the greatness of a Hispanic empire restored to its ancient unity by "el segundo Felipo sin segundo" (the "unrivaled" or "peerless" Philip II)[37]—*The Spanish Tragedy* accepts the Portuguese incorporation as an act of historical completion. But whereas Cervantes, who maps the consolidation of the peninsula by putting these words into the mouth of an allegorical figure of the river Duero, also complicates the imperial process by registering the painful loss of Numantine cultural identity, Kyd seems not to mourn his Portingales' loss of sovereignty.[38] In what is perhaps a tacit recognition of Philip's dynastic claim, and of the illegitimacy of Dom Antonio's, Kyd's tragedy locates Portugal's aspirations to legitimacy in marriage with Bel-imperia and in submission to the Crown of Castile.

The importance of this point cannot be overemphasized. Although it is composed at the very historical moment during which Dom Antonio is soliciting the French and English to mount an enterprise that might help him regain his kingdom's sovereignty, *The Spanish Tragedy* orients us quite differently toward Portugal. None of Kyd's major Portuguese characters—neither the groveling, tribute-hoarding viceroy nor the double-dealing Villuppo—inspires admiration or sympathy. When we meet Prince Balthazar—the Janus-faced heir apparent who will conspire with Bel-imperia's Machiavellian brother Lorenzo in the murder of Horatio—we find him first "insulting over" the fallen Andrea and "Breath[ing] out proud vaunts" (1.2.73–74), in recompense for which he is by Horatio "straight . . . beaten from his horse" (1.2.79). Politicly admitting the thoroughness of defeat, and his father's "late offense," Balthazar quickly learns to relish his Spanish captivity, as "guest" to Lorenzo, with whom he shares a like "estate" (1.2.186) (that is, rank and social class), and brother in arms to Horatio, "whom he admire[s] and love[s] for chivalry"

(1.2.194).[39] Soon we find him "plead[ing] for favour at [Bel-imperia's] hands" (1.4.70) and praising the "pleasing servitude" of the captivity in which his "freedom is enthralled" (1.4.81–83). The prince's imperial "seduction," mediated of course by the Janus-faced go-between, brother Lorenzo, is signaled by the Petrarchan cliché of his lover's complaint:

> Yes, to your gracious self must I complain,
> In whose fair answer lies my remedy,
> On whose perfection all my thoughts attend,
> On whose aspect mine eyes find beauty's bower,
> In whose translucent breast my heart is lodged. (1.4.93–97)

In stark contrast with the beaten but unbowed nationalists of the era's anti-Spanish political propaganda, so driven by imperial ambition—and so seduced by imperial charms—are Kyd's "Portingales" that they are yet more corruptible than his "Spaniards." In point of fact, virtually no ideological difference separates the Castilian and Portuguese "nationalities" represented within the play. What draws these erstwhile opponents to both the battlefield and the bed is their mutual admiration for Bel-imperia, the beautiful, war-inspiring, idol of empire.[40] As Bel-imperia coyly "lets fall her glove," which "Horatio coming out, takes up" (stage direction at 1.4.100), both Horatio's fate and Balthazar's meaning in the play are sealed. For the typological continuum that yokes Babylon with Philip II, the Spains, and Bel-imperia, the figure of empire, also implicates the prince of Portugal in *The Spanish Tragedy*'s allegorical exploration of the imperial ethos.

We often tend, in English Renaissance studies, to emphasize the "England is Israel" topos of Tudor and Stuart historical thought without recalling that in Christian exegesis "Israel" more traditionally represents an example to "the nations," a type of "every-nation" gone astray.[41] Our error of enthusiasm may help to account for the many interpretations that recognize mainly the English nation in *The Spanish Tragedy*'s apocalyptic stew, or read Bel-imperia and Hieronimo as representatives of English justice.[42] But in Kyd's play it is Portugal that functions as an Israel by providing the negative example of a nation given over to the worship of the golden calf of empire. This typology provides a key to the actions of our duplicitous Portuguese prince, for Balthazar—a variant of *Bel*teshazzar—derives from the same biblical root as the name of Kyd's Spanish princess. It is, we should recall, the appellation given to Daniel in his Babylonian captivity by both Nebuchadnezzar, king of Babel, and Ashpenaz, his master of eunuchs. The Calvinist exegetes of early modern England teach that the names given to the Israelites by their Babylonian masters represented "a great tentation and a signe of servitude, which they were not able to resist."[43] The reformers also believe that it "was a great griefe to Daniel not only to have his name changed, but to be called by the name of [Bel] a vile idole."[44] In addition, and according to a related tradition, they suggest that Daniel's Babylonian name also signifies "he that storeth riches," or "keeper of the treasure"[45] (it is, we should recall, the withholding of riches that occasions the battle with which the play begins and in which Balthazar kills Don Andrea of Spain). Read in concert with "Bel-imperia," then, the name of Kyd's Portuguese prince extends multivocally from an inclination toward servitude to these double "tentations": covetousness, and an attraction or devotion to idols.

If there is a master sin in early modernity, a catch-all that seems to define irrevocably the otherness of religious practices different from those of one's own culture, it is surely idolatry.[46] No accusation gets bandied about so often by polemicists on either side of the Reformation divide. In England and the Protestant north the militant Catholicism of the Spains, once a devotion so exemplary as to be emulated and partaken of throughout Christendom, is judged to be riddled with idolatrous practices and therefore to be resisted at all cost—even as a native Roman Catholic like William Allen admonishes his English compatriots to oppose the royal cult that fashions Elizabeth "a verie nationall idol."[47] By taking up this primal error, the problem of idolatry, Kyd explores its relation to the ethos of the most successful imperial project of his time, the global empire of the Spains—"Baal," in the typology current in the Protestant discourse of the day[48]—against which hopeful English Protestants believe themselves to be pitted in a struggle the result of which has been providentially foreordained.

The Romish Whore

Just when the consolidation of the Crowns of Portugal and Castile is being read prophetically in Hispano-Catholic thought, Kyd too renders the event as apocalyptic. But while Hapsburg enthusiasts read the event as a confirmation of Philip II's election as the "Last World Emperor," who will, after he has "defeated the heretic and unified the hemispheres in the Christian faith under his rule,"[49] bring in an era of universal monarchy and millennial peace culminating in the return of Christ, *The Spanish Tragedy* interprets the Iberian unification as the ideological reverse of the Hapsburgs' hubristic prophecy.

Read via the apocalyptic logic of the Protestantized book of Daniel, the Portuguese falling off—which sets the play on the path toward its climactic Babel-like bloodbath—is necessary to the fulfillment of a historical plan that will bring in *not* the peace of Christ under a Hapsburg heir to imperial Rome but a quite different historical epoch, that of independent national churches and sovereign nations (with England, if its people prove worthy, reserving a chosen place among them) not answerable to universal Roman aspirations.[50]

So when the Castilian king proclaims the dawn of a new era, "Now, lordings, fall to. Spain is Portugal, / And Portugal is Spain" (1.4.132–33), his chiastic recognition chimes the Protestant apocalyptic clock by effectively asserting the historical necessity of the Iberian unification for the realization of Europe's further reformation. And by representing a Spanish society that disavows a marital union between Bel-imperia and at least two native sons (while sanctioning an ill-gotten international proposal), Kyd's godly drama delights in discovering the method behind the madness of imperial dynasty building.[51] In the process, his "doctrine by ensample," to borrow another of Spenser's suggestive formulations, instructs that only a system of governance which guards national sovereignty may hope to preclude the inevitable internal ruptures born of idolatrous devotion to the illusory attractions of transnational imperial dynasticism. This is the lesson that *The Spanish Tragedy*'s Portuguese must, through the experience of their imperial seduction, learn for themselves. The fictional viceroy's recognition in the last line of the play proper, that "Spain hath no refuge for a Portingale" (4.4.217)—a moralizing aphorism that valorizes national difference in a manner found nowhere else in the play—affirms that he has learned what the nobility of the historical Portugal failed to see: that a nation's affairs are best conducted in the interest of sovereignty rather than in pursuit of the seductive glory of empire.

Thus we should not read the cycle of attraction and desire that draws *The Spanish Tragedy*'s male characters—Castilians and Portuguese alike—to the allegorical figure of Bel-imperia in terms of the merely sexual, just as we should not read Elizabeth's "virginity" (or a Spanish queen's lack thereof) as emblematic of mere physical chastity. These desires are the symptoms of a deeper, more serious kind of wantonness. For what represents *pietas* in the Spains—where the Hapsburgs adopt an iconography of Aeneas-like piety in order to advertise their strict adherence to the orthodox religious practices demanded by the Counter-Reformation church—may be figured in the Protestant north as a visible sign of the irremediable "promiscuity" of the "Romish Whore." As militant proponents of Catholic orthodoxy, it is the Spanish who become in Protestant discourse the Babylonian exemplars of those idolatrous practices, or "papisticall supersticions and abuses," which, as they become subsumed within a general argument against "Workes," are seen to encompass everything from bell-ringing, to the ceremony of the Latin mass, to almsgiving, to the veneration of saints and relics, to the singing of dirges—all of which, while resonating within the world of Kyd's play, remain vital, authorized rituals of *la Santa Fé*.[52] In order to reprobate the promiscuous excesses of this "irreligion," England's practical preachers commonly mobilize the sexual metaphorics of the biblical text itself: "Idolatrie is most fitly compared in the scripture unto adulterie," writes the Cambridge-trained John Knewstub, "and the Idolaters called whoores, because as whoores admitte unto their love others than their owne husbandes, so Idolaters, and the false worshippers of God, reserve not their faith and confidence unto the Lord alone."[53] It is an orientation toward doctrine given bodily form in *The Spanish Tragedy*.

We can now begin to audit the truly Spenserian richness of the play—whose characters are historical only insofar as they live in mythic, apocalyptic, or typological time. By reading *The Spanish Tragedy* in such a way as to discover its relation to the biblicism to which Kyd—in the manner of so many the Protestant nation writers of his generation[54]—subordinates his classical borrowings, we can hear how the play's orchestration of Latin and Judeo-Christian codes represents an Iberia which is hubristically torn by its attraction to the beautiful idol of empire, and which is bound, as a result of its promiscuous ambitions toward her, to go down—as had its "type," the Old Testament Babel—to the confusion that inevitably will come to reign within.

Washed with Blood

"Religion is sociologically interesting," writes Clifford Geertz, "not because, as vulgar positivism would have it, it describes the social order (which, insofar as it does, it does not only very obliquely but very incompletely), but because, like environment, political power, wealth, jural obligation, personal affection, and a sense of beauty, it shapes it."[55] Nowhere, perhaps, can the shaping potency of early modern Hispano-Catholicism—and its difference vis-à-vis the *soli Deo gloria* pretensions of English Protestantism—be seen more clearly than in the exhortation drafted by the Duke of Medina Sidonia, commander of the Armada, as the Enterprise of England prepares to sail. The duke's speech is worth quoting at length, not because it alludes to any event mysteriously represented in *The Spanish Tragedy*, but because of the ethos—the "set of moods and motivations"[56]—its theological orientation reveals:

> The saints of heaven will go in company with us, and especially the holy patrons of Spain and, indeed, those of England, who are persecuted by the heretics and cry aloud to God for vengeance, will come out to join and help us, and those who gave their lives to establish the holy faith in that land and washed it with their blood. We shall find waiting for us there the help of the Blessed John Fisher, Cardinal-bishop of Rochester, of Thomas More, John Forrest and innumerable saintly Carthusians, Franciscans and other religious, whose blood was cruelly spilt by King Henry and who call on God to avenge them in the land which they died. There shall we be helped by Edmund Campion, Ralph Sherwin, Alexander Briant, Thomas Cotton and many other reverend priests, servants of Our Lord, whom Elizabeth has torn to pieces with ferocious cruelty and nicely calculated tortures. With us will be the blessed and guiltless Mary, Queen of Scotland . . . coming fresh from her sacrifice.[57]

Comforting his troops in the company of the saints, whom the Enterprise aspires both to represent and to appease, Medina Sedonia puts supreme among their collective motivation a desire to become agents of God's "vengeance." Urging his international company "to avenge" the guiltless victims of the English schism, he affirms their service not to the Spanish nation but to a much larger community of believers, the *immensum imperii corpus.*[58] The cooperative acts of this body—which inclusively admits a number of beatified Englishmen and women (those so demonized in the histories of the Protestant reformers) whose devotion to the faith they place above loyalty to the nation—represent for him a kind of Old Testament "sacrifice" of "blood." Further, the duke characterizes the Enterprise as both a continuation of the work these saintly individuals have begun (the establishment of "the holy faith" in England) and an offering from "us" (the living) to "them" (the dead), "whose blood was cruelly spilt." In this logic of propitiation—the effective opposite of "faith only" Protestantism—valiant acts of sacrifice enable the saints' continuing communion with, and intervention on behalf of, the body of earthly believers who hope one day, should their works prove sufficient in God's sight, to join their "company." In other words, through human efficacy—which provides visible evidence of the faith upon which God's grace depends—the equilibrium of the heavenly scales remains assured.

It is at the moment during which England is attempting to write a different ethos for itself that this theology of propitiation—the active seeking of heavenly favor or appeasement—comes to play an increasingly vital role in shaping the social order of Catholic Iberia. For "the sixteenth century," as

Carlos Eire has reminded us, "marked the beginning of a 'golden age of purgatory' in Spain."[59] The same had been true, of course, in the re-Catholicized England of the Marian years: as the villain of the *Acts and Monuments,* archpapist Bishop Stephen Gardiner writes (apparently bringing the Latin term into the vulgar), "Withe . . . sacrifices God is made favorable, or God is propitiate, if we shall make new Englishe."[60] As *The Spanish Tragedy* builds to its act 4 climax—with Bel-imperia browbeating the "unkind father" (4.1.7) Hieronimo into the recognition "that heaven applies our drift, / And all the saints do sit soliciting / For vengeance on those cursèd murders" (4.1.32–34)—this theological orientation moves to center stage. For when Hieronimo ceremoniously presents the bloody handkerchief—which he preserved in act 2, scene 5, even as he honored his son by "say[ing] his dirge" (2.5.66) in solemn Latin—he reveals a memorial that has become charged with the kind of agency attributable to a sacred relic.[61] "And here behold this bloody handkerchief," he says,

> Which at Horatio's death I weeping dipped
> Within the river of his bleeding wounds;
> It as *propitious,* see, I have reserved,
> And never hath it left my bloody heart,
> Soliciting remembrance of my vow
> With these, O these accursèd murderers,
> Which, now performed, my heart is satisfied. (4.4.122–29, my italics)

By embracing the strategy that Bel-imperia advocates, becoming at once ambitious to appease the saints through sacrifice and to avenge his personal loss—rather than following his initial (and, from a Protestant nationalist perspective, appropriate) impulse to "plain me to my lord the king . . . for justice" (3.7.69–70)—Hieronimo guarantees the bloodbath that closes the tragedy. But, since it is the empire he serves that (in the play) "reck[s] no laws that meditate revenge" (1.3.48), we must reemphasize that it is not Hieronimo's action itself that is to blame for the carnage. Rather, it is the prevailing ethos of the society in which his valiant act is carried out—the theological *system* that shapes, supports, and sustains the Roman Catholic social order from which Protestant England has so recently withdrawn—that determines its meaning:[62] the ethos that demands that God's vengeance be carried out by his servants on earth in behalf of those who have gone before.

The Spanish Tragedy's explicit invocation of the doctrine of propitiation returns us to one of the interpretive problems that has most bothered us about the play, just as it seems to have bothered Nashe. This is the difficulty of

Hieronimo's "justice"—in Frank Ardolino's phrase, "the paradox of his being rewarded and his enemies punished in the classical underworld."[63] While it is true that the underworld of the play's prologue and epilogue is "classical," it is the *pagan* quality of Kyd's hellish Elysium that should draw our attention. It is for souls in the "underworld" of purgatory that propitiation is most concerned, a recognition that does much to answer several of the apparent paradoxes that unsettle the play's opening and closing scenes. For what Kyd must be straining here to represent are "the paradoxes" that Protestants, John Foxe among them, identify as the "fantasies of the later church of Rome concerning purgatory."[64] To recognize this feature of early modern religious culture is to go a long way toward solving both this long-standing hermeneutic enigma and the play's advertised "mystery" (1.1.90).

As William Allen taught in his first widely circulated apology, *A Defense and Declaration of the Catholicke Churches Doctrine, touching Purgatory, and prayers for the soules departed* (1565), "There be some, which after their death may have absolution of their lighter offenses, in debt whereof they passed out of this life . . . through the prayers and almes of their friends."[65] In *The Spanish Tragedy*'s opening scene we learn that just such an act has been performed "By Don Horatio, our Knight Marshall's son," in the play's prehistory. It is Horatio's administration of these "funerals and obsequies" (1.1.25–26) that enables his fallen compatriot Don Andrea to pass over Avernus and enter the Virgilian underworld in which the play begins and ends. Once there, Andrea is allowed to wind his way "to Pluto's court" so that Proserpine might intercede by awakening sleeping Revenge to the play's action. But what inspires Proserpine "to smile," and so pleases Pluto that he seals (in the manner of a pope) Don Andrea's doom "with a kiss," is that which has already inspired Minos to issue Don Andrea's passport: "'This Knight,' quoth he, 'both lived and died in love, / And for his love tried fortune of the wars, / And by war's fortune lost both love and life'" (1.1.38–40). As Minos recognizes, Don Andrea has risked everything for love. The object of this love, of course, has been Belimperia, the embodiment of empire. The valiant acts of war Andrea carried out in her service earn him, in turn, the right to perform his own acts of intercession: as we see in the play's epilogue, Don Andrea is given permission to "consort" with his "friends in pleasing sort," taking pleasure in the knowledge that Revenge will hale his enemies "down to deepest hell" (4.5.15, 27).

Whatever relative peace Hieronimo, Horatio, and the others seem to attain in the play's Virgilian denouement, we should note that the afterlife we see represented there hardly resembles, even from a Catholic perspective, a place of everlasting bliss. Rather, it has much in common with the "prison house" of the elder Hamlet in a play that more famously takes up the revenge problem: in Roman Catholic theology (as in Shakespeare's later tragedy) even when one attains its upper, "Elysian" levels, purgatory remains a place where the soul remains aware of its distance from God.[66] That a contemporary like Nashe would object to such a representation of the afterlife as Kyd stages may be a sign of the shaping power of the religiopolitical ideology of the English state religion. For the official doctrinal position on propitiation and mediation is from the time of the Elizabethan settlement manifestly Protestant, asserting that "the end of [Christ's] coming"—which had "quenched and appeased the wrath of his father"—was "to fulfill the Law . . . to reconcile us in the body of his flesh, to dissolve the workes of the devill, last of all, to become a propitiation for our sinnes."[67] If we look closely at the pagan rewards of *The Spanish Tragedy's* more "virtuous" characters—which include an eternity for Horatio of "never-dying wars" and Isabella's "train / Where pity weeps but never feeleth pain" (4.5.19–21)—we can see that not even Bel-imperia's "joys" and Hieronimo's orphic "pleasure" (21–24) measure up to the heavenly bliss that English Protestantism assures its elect, who through their faith are to receive for "eternal days" the "glory" of "his heavenly kingdome," there "to raigne with him," in the refrain of the Elizabethan church's official Christmas sermon, "not for a time, but for ever."[68]

The Spanish Tragedy's relation to the raw material of this propitiation controversy is further underscored by the fact that we do not have to delve very deeply into the larger context out of which this discourse emerges to find that Catholic arguments from tradition are grounded in the teachings of Hieronimo's namesake, Saincte Hierome, traditionally revered as the translator whose *Biblia Vulgata* had brought the light of the Word to Christendom, who grants that certain "privileges do serve for few" to lessen purgatory's pains.[69] According to Protestant polemicists like Foxe, these privileges, which reduce the purgatorial period before "the mercy of God doth translate [the deceased] to heavenly bliss," are the basis of the *system* of "Helps and releases . . . pope's pardons and indulgences, sacrifice of the altar, dirges and trentals, prayer, fasting . . . alms and charitable deeds of the living, in satisfying God's justice for them, etc.,"[70] on which the temporal authority of the Roman Church rests. Further, it is indeed the Catholic proclivity to thrust Elysium into hell that provides early modern Protestantism with some of the more forceful rhetoric it employs in order to unmask the pagan inheritance of the Romish theological system. As John Vernon argues, "I thynke [that] this is the privilege, that is described in the Aneides of Virgile, which the Sibylle speaking to Aeneas doeth reherce."[71] As Vernon discovers, this system rewards Catholics "for their

valiāt actes and lyfe most commendable . . . [according to] Thys . . . privilege
of [the] good doctour [Hierome]," adding "it was easy for Jupiter too obteyne
that thinge of his brother Pluto, unto whome, certayne aunciente writers have
attributed the keyes of all the infernall regions, and so paynted with keyes in
his hādes as a Pope."[72] It is, then, as a Virgilian underworld ruled by Pluto
as by a pope that Protestants construct purgatory, a place of "Heathenishe
superstition and Idolatrie."[73] *The Spanish Tragedy*'s "originality" lies not in
Kyd's "thrusting Elysium into Hell"; rather, Kyd's innovation is to translate
the topos for the stage by bodying it forth dramatically.[74] For though he may
render it idiosyncratically, Kyd thrusts us into precisely the kind of Virgilian
afterlife that the reformers of his day characterize as "pagan." In its discovery
of propitiation, *The Spanish Tragedy* reproduces the doctrinal orientation that
is at the moment of its production shaping the new social order of the sovereign English Empire—with its sole head, propitator. and mediator—a theology advanced not merely in the polemics of hot-gospellers like Vernon and
Foxe but in the approved homilies of the Elizabethan church as well.

This England Is an Empire

If Kyd's translation of empire stages a counter-*Aeneid*, and our discovery of
The Spanish Tragedy's logic of propitiation would seem to affirm that it does,
it is "counter" in relation to the Hapsburg ideology that provides the sixteenth
century's most successful appropriation of that Virgilian iconographic tradition. For it is indeed the exemplary piety of Aeneas that the iconography of
Philip II is designed to promulgate—an image that attracts Catholic apologists like William Allen, who proclaims the Castilian king's "speciall pietie and
zeale towards Gods house and the See Apostolike"[75] even as he explains the
imperial translation to his English audience. But the *Aeneid* is not the only
originary myth mobilized by the Spanish Hapsburgs. Their global imperium
(like England's national sovereignty) must also be legitimated by the authority
of a scriptural genealogy that "christens" its Roman roots. Along with Philip's
Solomon-like prudence, it is the book of Daniel that provides the Hapsburgs
with their link to the timeless authority of the Hebrews. In the culminating
vision of Daniel 2, "the Dream of the Four Kingdomes," it is written: "And
in the days of these kings, shall the God of heaven set up a kingdom, which
shall never be destroyed: and this kingdome shall not be given to another
people, but it shall break and destroy all these kingdomes, and it shall stand
for ever."[76] While Christian exegetes since Augustine had identified this final

world kingdom with Rome, imperial panegyrists, Thomas Campanella among them, begin to claim that it is the Spanish Hapsburgs, as the heirs of Augustus, who have been chosen "to be the agents of the final unification of the world."[77] This is the exemplary *translatio imperii* of the early modern period: from Troy to Rome via the line of Aeneas, from Rome to the Spanish Hapsburgs by way of the line of Augustus—with the mediation and authorization of the Hebrew prophet himself (Figure 4).[78]

What Kyd's biblical and classical medley also allegorizes, then, is a collision of two of the dominant imperial ideologies of the day: "empire" understood in its relation to sovereignty, the rights which accrue to the leader of a particular nation, or people, and synonymous with the term *status*, or state (the sense in which the term is used in the oft-celebrated phrase of Henry VIII's 1533 Act in Restraint of Appeals: "This Realm of England is an Empire"); and "empire" as transnational imperium,[79] understood as seeking, in Cardinal Allen's phrase, "the unit[i]e of Gods universall Churche."[80] The *translatio imperii* implied in *The Spanish Tragedy* suggests another kind of translation: a shift from the transnational or universal imperial model advocated by the Hapsburgs and the

Figure 4. The prophet Daniel explains the *translatio imperii* to Charles V. Dedicated to Charles's son, the future Philip II. Jorg Breu the Younger, "The Prophecy of Daniel." In *La historia del origen y sucesión de los Reinos e Imperios desde Noe hasta Carlos V*, vol. 1, fol. 27v. of *Origen de la Nobleza*, 1547–48. Escorial MS 28.I.11. Copyright © Patrimonio Nacional.

Roman Church, which the play represents as covetous, amoral, and unwork-able, to the less internationally ambitious and (presumably) less corruptible sovereign state that England, along with the United Provinces and several of the nations held "captive" within the transnational "Babylonian" system, is struggling to realize in the late sixteenth century.

But if the Spains of *The Spanish Tragedy* represent an imperial Babylon, what can we say of England's role in the drama? The simple answer is that England exists as the implied theatrical audience, the one that will behold the play's "mystery." But England also exists onstage, in Hieronimo's act 1 and act 4 entertainments. While the question of audience is perhaps the most impor-tant single consideration for any reading that attempts to recover something of the play's contemporary rhetorical force, let us set this issue aside for a mo-ment in order to take up the question of England's role in the play itself. In the comic history of Hieronimo's act 1 dumb show, Kyd introduces three English knights and three Iberian kings: two Portuguese and a Spaniard.[81] The scene's first action, as Hieronimo glosses it, represents "Robert, Earl of Gloucester,"

> Who, when King Stephen bore sway in Albion,
> Arrived with five and twenty thousand men
> In Portingale, and by success of war
> Enforced the King, then but a Saracen,
> To bear the yoke of the English monarchy. (1.4.142–46)

It is not clear how Kyd comes by the cultural knowledge his interlude puts to use. Whatever its source, this allusion to the siege of Lisbon embroiders the 1147 event considerably; contra the play's imaginative anecdote, the seige did *not* end in the vassalage of Portugal to King Stephen (reigned 1135–54) and the English monarchy.[82] Historically inaccurate though it may be, however, the brief scene is quite suggestive in terms of what it reveals about the past, pres-ent, and *future* of Anglo-Spanish cultural relations.[83]

The particulars of the battle, during which the combined forces of Chris-tendom wrested Lisbon from the "Saracen," are less important than what the play's representation does with them, and what is most significant about Kyd's improvisation is that it elevates England's role in the ongoing trans-national project that was the Iberian *reconquista*—realized only in 1492, less than a hundred years prior to the tragedy's composition. In the play's provi-dential calculus, Gloucester's "English" victory provides a foundational cor-nerstone of the towering Spanish Empire. According to this logic, England's agency in the recovery of the Spains for Christendom is a matter of historical necessity: in order that its Babel-like destruction may be enacted when the propitious moment arrives, the Empire's ancient Roman wholeness must first be restored. Though it might seem a trifling consolation from a nationalistic perspective, there *is* something in the anecdote to make the Portingale's "late discomfort seem the less" (1.4.149): to owe tribute to a Christian king in a unified Iberia—surrendering national sovereignty to the greater glory of the Empire—is a far more desirable end than to be ruled by "a Saracen" (a fate that even so Protestant a writer as John Foxe cannot wish upon the Spains).[84] It is when we factor in the tales of Hieronimo's second and third knights, however, that the logic of Kyd's somewhat strained history lesson becomes yet more clear. For alongside Robert of Gloucester, Kyd places Edmund of Langley, Duke of York, and John of Gaunt, Duke of Lancaster, patriarchs of the two houses from which the English monarchy descends.[85] Surely, it is here that Kyd's play, however dumbly, portends the "future": for the *translatio imperii* we see in the making is prefigured by the appearance of these highly significant Tudor forebears.

It is the "third and last" of the interlude's episodes—that in which "a valiant Englishman, / Brave John of Gaunt, the Duke of Lancaster . . . with a puissant army came to Spain, / and took our King of Castile prisoner" (1.4.161–67)—that deserves special notice, "not least" because Hieronimo himself gives it emphasis, but also because John of Gaunt's Iberian adventuring was much celebrated in Kyd's day.[86] So highly regarded is the event that it is even represented in one of the standard Latin grammar-school histories of the Elizabethan era, Christopher Ocland's *The Valiant Actes And victorious Battailes of the English Nation*.[87] In the version Englished by John Sharrock in 1585, Gaunt "himself" explains the significance of his Spanish mission to the young Richard II:

> Whilst uncle to your maiestie, and princes offspring, I,
> Beholde my spouse in wedlocke bandes conioyned, of Hispanig land,
> Her fathers onely heir, by force the Spaniard to withstand,
> And barre from Kingdomes rich, which publike lawes her gives as due.

To which Richard responds:

> Goe with good luck unto the land which floud Iberus streames
> Doe famous make, and what as dower unto thy wife pertaines,
> By custome due, which Nations all have eerst allowed for right,
> If that the Spaniard wil not yeeld, that stoutly win in fight.[88]

The exchange between King Richard and his uncle testifies to the intense cultural anxiety that Europe's received system of dynastic inheritance could often generate, especially when a claim is made by right of matrilineal descent—a matter of tremendous import in the play. *The Spanish Tragedy*'s action, after all, turns upon the expressed desire "To knit a sure, inexplicable bond / Of kingly love and everlasting league / Betwixt the crowns of Spain and Portingale" (3.12.46–48) by the marriage of the niece of the apparently childless king of Castile with Balthazar, "the only hope of [the Portuguese] successive line" (3.1.14). At precisely the historical conjuncture in question, similar succession problems had already engendered tremendous difficulties within the royal houses of the nations Kyd's play represents. Indeed, in the absence of a legitimate "native son," dynastic chaos had ensued: in the British Isles, England and Spain together had experienced the brief Lady Jane Grey debacle and the somewhat more lengthy reign of Mary Tudor and Philip of Hapsburg, while in Iberia, Philip's claim to Portugal had come as a result of that throne's lack of a direct heir.[89]

As significantly, what *The Spanish Tragedy*'s historical dumb show and Ocland's *Valiant Actes* both seem to recognize is that Gaunt's intervention in Spain—like Philip's Portuguese intervention and his attempted Enterprise of England—represents not merely an act justifiable according to historical precedent but also an acceptable use of military force. The thematic and formal relevance of Kyd's Gaunt anecdote to the argument of the play as a whole deserves emphasis.[90] For when the Portuguese ambassador observes, "This is an argument for our viceroy, / That Spain may not insult for her success, / Since English warriors likewise conquered Spain, / And made them bow their knees to Albion" (1.4.168–71), the play registers a recognition that the Duke of Lancaster's Iberian adventuring was, as *The Valiant Actes* affirms, as much about *marital* maneuvering of the kind that the Hapsburgs had so perfected—John of Gaunt had succeeded in wedding daughters to the heirs of both Portugal and Spain, even as he claimed the Spanish Crown for himself through his own marriage to Constance of Castile—as it was about *martial* conquest.[91] Gaunt's success on the conjugal front, as we will see, does much to trouble the question of the Elizabethan succession. But in the terms through which Ocland's contemporary history frames the problem, what the ambassador's observation implies is that Kyd's fictional Castilian king—having enforced "custome" with arms ("in fight"), and having had his claim affirmed by the victory God has granted him—conducts himself quite properly and in accord with the "publike lawes" of the received dynastic system. In other words, Castile has waged a "just war." For as in Ocland's imagined exchange between Gaunt and Richard II, each of *The Spanish Tragedy*'s armed encounters—England's with Portugal and Spain, Portugal's with the Saracen, and Castile's with the Portuguese—constitute in early modern political theory an instance of the *jus belli*, according to which, like Philip's Enterprise of England, war may be lawfully carried out in defense of the faith, to redress national injuries, or to enforce rightful claims of inheritance.[92] What may be most significant about Kyd's incorporation of the play's three English conquests, however, is that these events function not as a criticism of the Spanish themselves but as yet another way to expose the flaws of the traditional imperial *system* in which all of these polities are embroiled. It is the combination of religion, custom, and law that can justify the intervention of foreign princes in the affairs of individual *nations* in order to maintain an expansionist transnational empire that comes under scrutiny in *The Spanish Tragedy*; just as, in the providential reasoning of English Protestantism, it is the idolatrous Roman Catholic *system* that generates the spiritual error of the "pagans" who live according to its propitiatory logic.

The object, then, of Kyd's allegory of imperial idolatry, and of the play's *translatio imperii*, is to valorize and advocate the more local ideology of empire to which Tudor monarchs from Henry VIII, to Edward VI, to Elizabeth I (the notable exception being, of course, the "Spanish Tudor," Mary), cling precariously in the face of the continuing expansion of the dynastic system that opposes them—a system that realizes new, global proportions with the unification of the Spains in 1580. It is between the national/sovereign and imperial/universal poles of this structure that the allegorical oscillation of the sign "Bel" freezes long enough for an audience to fix Elizabeth Tudor's place in relation to *The Spanish Tragedy*. For when, in order to carry out her role in Heironimo's act of revenge, the fictional Bel-imperia is urged to assume a virtue she does not have, attiring herself as "Phoebe, Flora, or the Huntress" (4.1.148), we can momentarily behold the difference between the Spanish princess on stage and the royal actress in whose image she is (for the moment) dramaturgically clothed. These three epithets, three of Elizabeth's most widely circulated ceremonial personae—Phoebe-like beauty and light, Flora-like fertility and renewal, Diana-like resolution and chastity[93]—set off a chain of pretextual resonances that discovers the font from which the "true" (from an English Protestant perspective) glory of empire springs.[94] The valiant act of Elizabeth's militant chastity (a chastity the play's princess has clearly forgone)—which enables the life-giving, realm-enriching fertility celebrated in so many of her own policy statements and the countless encomia of her subjects—opposes the barrenness and death that are the fruits of Bel-imperia's vulnerable promiscuity.[95]

For by staging a Spanish princess who is at once Elizabeth's mirror image and her ineffectual opposite, Kyd, no less than his more famous contemporary, Spenser, writes not only his own (and his audience's) subjection to the empire of England but also that empire's difference (whether real or imagined) in relation to the universalist ethos of the Empire of the Spains. And as it rehearses both the mystery and the difference of Elizabeth's power, *The Spanish Tragedy* also allows us to observe the formation of a number of the discursive modes and rhetorical strategies through which that power is, by Elizabethan Protestants, written into English culture.[96]

Los Jerónimos

If the outcome of *The Spanish Tragedy* ultimately rests upon English Protestantism's orientation toward those doctrinal impurities that support early modern Europe's imperial religiopolitical system, and I think that the startling number of resonances that pervade these contemporary discourses suggests that it must, we cannot but find it disconcerting that Kyd's protagonist, Hieronimo, bears a name so sacred—literally, *hieros nym*, the sacred name. This fact alone demands exegetical attention.[97] And if such traditional habits of devotion as the idolatrous invocation and propitiation of "dead saints"—"causes" that criticism has largely neglected in its focus on the symptom of revenge—are characterized in Protestant discourse as among those pagan impurities that came into the faith as a result of the Latin corruption of the primitive church, it is surely significant that the name of *The Spanish Tragedy*'s "hero" also resounds with that of one of the church's principal Latinizers, Saincte Hierome,[98] whose theology plays so crucial a role in these disputes. Indeed, Hieronimo comes to Kyd's play freighted with a thousand years of Christian cultural significance. Although recent scholarship has recognized this, bringing much of the following "data" to bear on Kyd's protagonist, it has been less successful in suggesting how *The Spanish Tragedy* transforms the meaning of his highly significant name. In order to weigh the function of "Hieronimo" within the world of the play, let us explore the fullness of this sign in an openly allegorical and polysemous spirit, tracing not merely its signifying role within the world of sixteenth-century England but also its relation to the larger, pan-national culture in which it plays a vital, public role.[99]

If Hieronimo, who embraces a propitiatory solution to his ethical dilemma after he is seduced into Bel-imperia's way of thinking, represents traditional Catholic religion in any way, it is a strange Christianity he practices—for the dark ritual he composes in order to exact his revenge runs afoul of both the Levitical letter of the Old Law and the charitable spirit of the New. Indeed, just as *The Spanish Tragedy*'s representation of a pagan afterlife communes with the Protestant refutations of the doctrine of propitiation, so does its representation of Hieronimo's chief work, his final courtly entertainment—which "incorporates many of the elements of the [actual] Roman Mass as constructed by its Protestant detractors"[100]—play into this Protestant discourse of discovery.

Huston Diehl has provided a window into the cultural field of which Kyd's final bloodletting partakes, observing that "by mystifying and privileging spectacle and displaying 'real' bodies and blood, 'Soliman and Perseda' manifests the very qualities of the Roman Mass that the Calvinist reformers condemn when they complain that 'of the sacrament' the Papists 'make an idol; of commemoration make adoration; instead of receiving make a deceiving; in place of showing forth Christ's death, make new oblations of his death.'"[101] This is to say that the Roman Catholic sacrament of the Eucharist is *not*, as the reformers argue it ought to be, a ceremony commemorative of Christ's sacrifice; rather, it is an idolatrous Work, a ritual sacrifice, an act of propitiation of the kind authorized by Saint Jerome.[102]

What is more, Hieronimo's pattern of behavior in *The Spanish Tragedy* seems the very mirror of the bereaved father in another text often mobilized by England's Protestant reformers in their condemnations of the idolatrous nature of Roman Catholic tradition. While casting Hieronimo's tragedy-within-the-tragedy in terms of the archetypal Old Testament idolaters of Babylon, Kyd also amplifies this typology by answering it with its Apocryphal correlative from the book of Wisdom, which contains a discussion of the origins of idolatry that complements the iconophobic arguments drawn from the canonical books of Law and Prophecy and remains a key text for early modern purifiers of doctrine. Even in William Allen's Douai translation, with its more sympathetic leanings toward *simulacra*, a believer could be instructed that "the beginning of fornication is the devising of idols: and the invention of them is the corruption of life." The believer would read that "a father being afflicted with bitter grief, made to himself the image of his son who was quickly taken away: and him who had then died as a man, he began now to worship as a god, and appointed him rites and sacrifices."[103] And certainly the more scripturally oriented among Kyd's audience would know—as they watched Hieronimo honor Horatio "as a god" and hear him pronounce over his son's body a solemn Latin incantation—that such "diriges" are yet another pagan sacrifice discovered by English gospellers, who find no precedent for their practice in the Book. Perhaps not surprisingly, it is, as Cardinal Allen confirms, upon the authority of "S. Hyerom" that "diriges" remain justified by canon law and thus propitatorily acceptable to God.[104]

But *The Spanish Tragedy's* exploration of the societal effects of false doctrine would not be complete if its apocalyptic scriptural journey did not incorporate the appropriate New Testament anti-types as well. In order to see what use Kyd's play makes of the originary moment of the New Dispensation, when the Word becomes revealed to "the nations," let us turn to chapter two of the book of "Actes" (the title of which becomes a kind of Protestant code word for historiographers as various as Foxe and Ocland). As recorded by Saint Luke, "when the Day of Pentecost was come" and the apostles "were all with one accord in one place,"

> 2 And suddenly there came a sound from heaven, as of a rushing and mightie wind, and it filled all the house where they sate.
>
> 3 And there appeared unto them cloven tongues, like fire, and it sate upon each of them.
>
> 4 And they were all filled with the holy Ghost, & began to speake with other tongues as the Spirit gave them utterance.[105]

The Geneva translation recommends that this "extraordinarie and necessarie gift of tongues" reverses by spiritual means the confusion of Babel in order that the Word may be disseminated to "every nation under heaven."[106] But it can be readily seen, I think, that Hieronimo's valiant acts parody those of Saint Luke's spiritually motivated evangelists by effectively inverting their outcome.

Whereas in the historical Pentecost "the holy Ghoste governed [the believer's] tongues" in order "to bring men to salvation by faith,"[107] when Hieronimo demands that each of his actors "must act his part / In unknown languages" (4.1.172–73), he plays at the role assumed by the "holy Ghost" in the book of Acts, inverting a work of the spirit by transforming the gift of tongues into an idolatrous human invention. Further, the action of Hieronimo's drama does not reverse the effects of Babel; rather, it reproduces them. Filled with the vengeful spirit of the Old Law, his actors do not receive the good news of salvation; as the play's epilogue bears out, they are condemned instead to an eternity characterized by purgatorial absence from the Father. As the sacred name is profaned, with its bearer literally (and literarily) taking on the Antichristian mantle of "the Turk," as well as the "Scourge-of-God" role Christendom has long accorded the agents of Islam,[108] the representatives of each nation who constitute the audience of Hieronimo's play (Castile, Portugal, and by implication England) are not granted a moment of international harmony in the holy city; rather, they are thrown into a "divinely" orchestrated discord in its figural opposite, the imperial Spanish Babylon. With each link of the play's apocalyptic chain in place, we can now grasp the providentially "comic" element of Kyd's tragedy of the Spains. Though the play's Spanish Empire burns itself out, from its ashes rise sovereign nations. For the onstage deaths generate the rebirth of backsliding Portugal, and, for the benefit of those offstage, agency (as it was in the historical dumb show of act 1) is once again accorded to England—this time not by way of the English *sword* but by means of its Christologically metaphoric equivalent, the English *word*: the tongue of the New Jerusalem into which the play's confusion of languages is translated "for the easier understanding to every public reader" (stage direction, 4.4.10) during *The Spanish Tragedy*'s climactic bloodletting.

So while we may for analytical purposes privilege the play's Virgilian and Senecan modes, or foreground its Danielic and Apocryphal strains, we must also factor the Acts of the Apostles into Kyd's apocalyptic formula as its prophetic capstone.[109] For when in act 4 Hieronimo's players talk in tongues, Kyd's culminating invocation of the English vulgar foregrounds yet again the way *The Spanish Tragedy* functions, and a number of its commentators have recognized this, as a *translatio imperii studii*—a "historical rearticulation of privileged cultural models."[110] How utterly appropriate it is that in Kyd's historical rearticulation the namesake of the original cultural translator of the Roman Church should orchestrate the play's continuously replicating pattern of *inversio*—for like the Hieronimo of *The Spanish Tragedy*, Saint Jerome had been given the gift of tongues.[111] And since, in the logic of national election, the historical Hieronimo's accomplishment, the Latin Vulgate, had been usurped in the service of an idolatrous transnational Empire, how fitting it is that, his role as translator complete and the Word transmitted to the English vulgar, the fictional Hieronmio's tongue should be literally cloven as his diabolized gift for language is revoked in a final, willful (albeit valiant) act.[112] For in his ambition to appease the saints and revenge his son, Kyd's Hieronimo usurps the power of the Almighty in more ways than one. As "actor" and "author" of the vengeful "Soliman and Perseda" he confuses his civil office, as earthly magistrate or "Knight Marshall of Spain," with his aspirations to heavenly judgment: demanding "blood for blood" in the propitious spirit of the Old Law, he effectively negates the New Dispensation that would have him temper the law with charity.[113]

There remains at least one more web of significance that strangely entangles Kyd's Hieronimo. Los Jerónimos, who in early modernity become famous for their generous acts of almsgiving, are the religious order most favored by the Spanish Hapsburgs. When Charles V abdicated in 1555, he entrusted himself to the care of the Hieronymites at Yuste, with whom he ended his days. When Charles's son, Philip II, builds his magnificently austere palace/mausoleum, El Escorial—he dedicates the edifice to San Lorenzo, or Saint Lawrence, upon whose day in 1557 he had won, as Philip, king of *England*, his most impressive military victory. Philip thus endows the Hieronymites, into whose care he commends not only the tombs of the past and future kings of Spain, but also the immense reliquary of some 6000 items he has collected to be housed there. Among the most cherished, and certainly the most famous of the relics Philip obtains is the preserved head of San Jerónimo, Saint Jerome.[114] The Hieronymites, however, may have owed the enthusiastic support of the "Spanish" Hapsburgs to that dynasty's Portuguese line. For since 1497 the order had tended—at the behest of the family of Isabel of Portugal, Charles's wife and Philip's mother—the mausoleum of the Portuguese kings at Belem.[115]

In any event, the fact that Hieronimo presides over the dead bodies of the royal lines of both Spain and Portugal—in the play and in actuality—is surely no coincidence. While certainly Kyd could not have had such a catalogue as we have been constructing at hand when he sat down to write his play, he would not have needed one as an inhabitant of a culture that, whether locally Protestant or universally Catholic, valued its imperial Roman cultural and linguistic roots even as it subordinated them to its Judeo-Christian religious inheritance, and ordered time according to saints' days and martyrdoms. For if "societies, like lives, contain their own interpretations,"[116] *The Spanish Tragedy* can engender this astonishingly multivocal string of ironies because, like the sign "Hieronimo," it is deeply embedded in a society whose traditions both link and oppose Protestant England and Roman Catholic Spain—two nations which read the present in terms of a mythic past and an apocalyptic future that have long since determined its meaning—two "empires" strung together by a web of significance that in early modernity entangled all European culture as well as the expansive colonial field on which it was realizing its designs.

"Roderigo, Ho!"

As we reflect upon the "mystery" of Thomas Kyd's play, we can now recognize that this "tragedy" of the Empire of the Spains discovers the promiscuous ethos of the idolatrous system that continued to challenge the legitimacy of his own nation's developing religiopolitical culture. As it does so, *The Spanish*

Tragedy announces biblically authorized national sovereignty as the less adulterous form of empire. By plugging into a received apocalyptic continuum incorporating figural elements from the Old Testament books of history and prophecy, the Apocrypha, and the New Testament, Kyd effectively stages both imperial translation and national election through his inclusion of Iberian events within the backward projection and forward trajectory of English history. As his highly multivocal allegory probes the theological orientation that maintains the universal monarchy against which the emerging national cultures of early modernity both model and measure themselves, the position he dramatizes, like that of the Protestant reformers who seek to redirect contemporary religious practices, is unequivocal in its condemnation of the spiritual whoredom of Romish Works. While revealing the temptations of traditional Catholic internationalism and reaffirming the Protestant national sovereignty into which English culture had been plunged during Henry VIII's reign, Edward VI's minority, and Elizabeth's settlement, Kyd draws from, participates in, and improvises upon an historiographic formation best exemplified in the writings of Foxe, Hakluyt, Spenser, and the nation-writers who are their contemporaries.

But the real richness of *The Spanish Tragedy*, in contrast with the many propagandistic productions of the day that simply recycle the range of available anti-Spanish stereotypes, stems from its manifest reluctance to sink to an easy rhetoric that would cast the play's argument in terms of an essentially corrupt ethnos. Kyd's quarrel, it seems, is not so much with the Spains themselves as with an ethos that would seek by force to halt the self-determining course his own nation is attempting to set for itself and thereby bring it back within the universalist fold. In this, at least, his tragedy remains catholic. The same cannot be said of the texts of Kyd's play that will be amended by subsequent "cowriters," who will find the demonizing rhetoric of ethnos irresistible.

In the editions of *The Spanish Tragedy* published after 1598, those that include the famous "painter scene" sometimes attributed to Ben Jonson, we find intercalated a different sort of Spanish specter. It is commonly argued that the new lines function as group in such a way as to intensify the inordinate grief Hieronimo feels over the loss of his son, Horatio.[117] "Ay me," says Isabella in the first emendation, "he raves" (2.5.8). Although we cannot say with certainly precisely when they began to be performed, the amendments do more than merely amplify Hieronimo's agitation. With the introduction of the clownish Pedro and Jaques, Kyd's drama begins to list more toward the tragicomic mode characteristic of the later revenge plays that *The Spanish Tragedy* inspired. While these new characters contribute a farcical element not audible in the original, the revised script takes on an entirely new humor via their presence. For with Pedro and Jaques looking on, and in throes of an intensified "madness," Hieronimo swears two previously unglossed, yet ethnopoetically revealing oaths.[118] First, and rather unaccountably, he utters "Roderigo, ho!" (2.5.52), and then a few lines later, at Pedro's recognition of Horatio's lifeless body, Hieronimo declares, "Ha, ha, Saint James, but this doth make me laugh, / That there are more deluded than myself" (2.5.70–71). Somewhat inexplicably, these alterations register nowhere in our critical commentary—yet the addition of these lines constitutes a significant cultural act.[119]

For with these invocations the play's revisers have inserted a scene that finds Kyd's Knight Marshall, in his "delusion," calling down two of the most highly recognizable icons associated with the culture of Iberian Catholicism. Tracing the web of significance suggested by the highly evocative "Roderigo," we find the sign extending multivocally to any number of cherished Spanish icons, from Saint Rudericus the martyr of Cordoba, to Rodrigo the last of Spain's Visigothic kings, to the Christian name of "Ruy" Díaz, or El Cid, the epic hero of the *reconquista*. Construing its significance more locally, it may also point to Rodrigo Lopez, the infamous *marrano* physician who had been executed in 1594 for his alleged employment by Philip II in a plot to poison Elizabeth I. While these "Roderigo" associations all produce powerful Spanish connections, Hieronimo's second invocation, "Saint James," plays yet more assuredly upon Spanish custom, calling down James the Greater, Santiago Matamoros, Spain's storied patron saint, whose many interventions against the infidel had gained him international recognition as the "slayer of Moors." The assignation of these widely acknowledged cultural icons in a play about Spain cannot have been arbitrary. Kyd's amenders meant these allusions to be recognized, and they meant them to do cultural work.

In the amended *Spanish Tragedy* we find Hieronimo behaving quite in the spirit of Greene's *Spanish Masquerado*. While "accounting their Saint of *Compostella* with the pagan idols," Greene constructed a "Nobilitie of Spaine grieved at the dishonour of their shameful return" from the Armada misadventure. Their remedy is to "vow a general Pilgrimage to S. James of Compostella, in hope of his aide for revenge" (Dv). Rather than acting decisively, the Spanish Knight Marshall, like Greene's grieving "Nobilitie of Spaine," withdraws to call on the Spanish patron saint before summoning the painter who will fashion him a "pagan" memorial image. In conjunction with his oath to "Roderigo," Hieronimo's invocation of Saint James—a cultural practice that Greene believed "to deserve this mocke" (D2v)—points assuredly toward Spain's ethnic past.

What might have occasioned such ideologically pointed revisions? What could an argument from ethnos add to a play that had already exposed so eloquently the motivating humors of the imperial ethos? As the struggle with the Empire of the Spanish Hapsburgs wore on, and as the policies of Elizabeth's government, which had been framed so attractively in a context of crisis, came under increasing scrutiny, the English political situation appears to have required a far less ambiguous poetic than *The Spanish Tragedy* had initially employed. In spite of their own Hispanophilic inclinations, with English Jesuits and their devotees becoming more sophisticated in their efforts to avoid discovery and attract converts,[120] with Lancastrian apologists legitimizing the suits of a number of Spanish candidates for the Elizabethan succession, supporters of the Elizabethan regime seem to have seen the utility in magnifying English difference. And so attacks on Spain increasingly came to be framed in ways that belittled, demonized, and *ethnicized* all things Spanish. A decade after the Armada, England's ethnopoetics had become so overcoded that the mere mention of a name could synecdochically evoke an entire Hispanophobic sign system. Shortly after the ascension of James I, William Shakespeare will improvise a yet more significant (and more deviously playful) variation on this semiotic coding. For in *Othello* (1603–4), Roderigo and Sant-Iago will again come together on stage—this time, as the agents of the Venetian Moor's tragedy.

CHAPTER FOUR

Marlowe Among the Machevills

*But so truly he loveth, imbraceth, and nourisheth the Gospell, as he
burneth and bannisheth out of his territories, infinite swarmes of rich*
Jewes, *sworne enemies to the Gospel.*
    *. . . so he loveth, imbraceth, and nourisheth the Gospel, that he
maketh his* Jesuits, *and Shavelings forget all Gospel, and mangleth, and
massacreth all true professors of the Gospel.*
      —G.B., *A Fig for the Spaniard, or Spanish Spirits,* 1591, 1592

Ye strangers yt doe inhabite in this lande
Note this same writing doe it understand
Conceit it well for savegard of your lyves
Your goods, your children, & your dearest wives
Your Machiavellian Marchant spoyles the state,
Your usery doth leave us all for deade
Your Artifex, & craftsmen works our fate,
And like the Jewes, you eat us up as bread.
      —"A Libell, fixte upon the French Church Wall," 1593

Marano. A Jew, an Infidell, a renagado, a nickname for a Spaniard.
      —John Florio, *A World of Wordes,* 1598

NO OTHER ELIZABETHAN play explores and exploits English attitudes toward ethnic outsiders so thoroughly as *The famouse tragedie of the Riche Jewe of
Malta* (c. 1589–91).[1] Projecting England's nascent colonialist and mercantilist

desires into the Mediterranean, Marlowe unfolds a tableau of early modern anxieties concerning the reflexive effects of empire's outward energies on the inner lives of its subjects. By embodying contemporary fears about "impurities" of ethos and ethnos, his representation draws upon a range of contemporary discourses in order to picture a Maltese community that resembles Elizabethan England as much as it does the island evoked in its title.

The various rhetorics of nationhood and ethnicity in which Marlowe's play partakes enable us, in turn, to audit some of the ways in which international history could be enlisted in the service of nationalist aims. As he plays upon England's figural identification with the island of Malta, Marlowe's typological orchestration looks toward a vision of community solidarity by offering a brutally nationalistic perspective on the exercise of force. At the same time, *The Jew of Malta* demonstrates how ambiguous signs of ethnicity may be remade in such a way as to signify absolute and irredeemable otherness. Raising a Spanish specter that is at once religiopolitical, geographic, economic, and linguistic, the play's argument expresses a worldview as supportive of the darker inclinations of early modern statecraft as it was potentially devastating to those unlucky enough to find themselves on the receiving end of power.

If Kyd's generative tragedy declines the low road of essentialization, Marlowe's generically mixed drama revels in ethnopoesis. Given the kind of "humour" in which Marlowe indulges—in essence, a humor of *kind*—it is not surprising that audiences have found the play increasingly difficult to abide. T. S. Eliot may have accurately expressed the nature of the gap between modern and Elizabethan tastes. Betraying, as it does, a "terribly serious, even savage comic humour," Eliot concluded that we should read *The Jew of Malta* "not as a tragedy, or as a 'tragedy of blood,' but as a farce."[2] To rehearse Marlowe's drama in this register is to enter the confused, disturbing, and often contradictory climate in which English nationhood was shaped; it is also to explain something of the playwright's power to command contemporary audiences.

Strangers

Christopher Marlowe unleashed *The Jew of Malta* upon a community of theatergoers whose attitudes toward London's growing immigrant community were characterized by profound ambivalences and anxieties. Oscillating between sympathetic identification and outright contempt, English men and women were discomfited by the presence of "strangers" in their midst, even when they understood why they ought to be offering support.

As the 1590s unfolded, England began to experience a time of dearth and high unemployment, which brought many "foreigners" (that is, native inhabitants of distant English shires) to an already crowded London in search of relief. Once there, they jostled with émigrés who were busily establishing an economic block of their own. Shopkeepers especially complained that London's resident aliens had been "illegally trading in the retail of foreign goods."[3] It was a situation fraught with difficulty, all the more so because the Elizabethans had come to rely on their stranger community, to whom they often turned for assistance, whether in the form of financial backing, technical know-how, or troop levies.[4] Uneasiness about the strangers was magnified by rumor of the intrigues in which some were alleged to be involved, which brought to a boil all manner of resentment, suspicion, and intolerance. To make matters worse, the Elizabethans were deeply anxious over the crisis of succession that would come with the inevitable passing of their aging queen and the impending installation of a new and probably "foreign" dynasty. Aware of these internal trends, and trying to meet the external commitments required by the ongoing war with the Spanish, Elizabeth's government struggled to maintain an uneasy equilibrium in which citizens and denizens might continue to coexist.[5] Into this tense setting was thrust the rough-versed proclamation we have come to know as "The Dutch Church Libel," the inflammatory document that brought about the arrest of both Marlowe and his associate Thomas Kyd.[6]

Addressed to "Ye strangers yt doe inhabite this in lande," the posted handbill (the surviving copy of which, labeled "A Libell, fixte upon the French Church Wall. Anno 1593," was discovered by Arthur Freeman in 1971) was clearly intended to unsettle.[7] The document provides an inventory of ethnocentric attitudes and grievances, a number of which are worth exploring in the present context. And while it may suggest something of "the always latent xenophobia among commoners" usually thought to have been a feature of Elizabethan society,[8] what seems most estranging about the document is that it expresses virtually no sympathy for London's strangers as Protestant coreligionists.[9] Far more disruptively than the contemporary *Booke of Thomas More* (1592–95), the censored Anthony Munday play whose characters curse, in the passages attributed to Shakespeare, the "infection" of "these bastards of dung" in one breath before reversing themselves to proclaim "Let's do as we may be / done by" in another,[10] the Dutch Church Libel communicates bald resentment with regard to Elizabethan participation in Continental "nation-building," objecting

And our pore [English] soules, are cleane thrust out of dore
And to the warres sent abroad to rome,
To fight it out for Fraunce and Belgia,
And dy like dogges as sacrifice for you. (lines 31–34)

Foremost among the grievances expressed by the writers of the Libel is that
they see London's émigrés as performing as "intelligencers to the state &
crowne" while in their "hartes" they "doe wish an alteracion" (lines 15–16).
The implication is patent: the outsiders are suspected of double-dealing, du-
plicitously supplying the Crown with intelligence even as they desire a change
of government.

As significantly, the document points out that it is their "counterfeiteing
[of] religion" that has enabled the "flight" of these immigrants to England
from foreign shores (line 42). The broadside thus begs a question about which
religion its authors imagined was being counterfeited. Since the document
had been nailed to the wall of a nonconformist Protestant congregation, was it
primarily their loyalty to the English national church (and thus to the English
nation) that was being called into doubt? Or, as suggested by the context the
document itself creates, was it the strangers' Protestantism that was suspect?
Were the members of the congregation accused of not being Protestants at all?
If they were in fact secret Roman Catholics, in "thrall" to "coyne" and "in-
fected" with "Spanish gold" (lines 43–45), then they were using membership
in the "Dutch Church" as a cover.

In spite of its writers' attempt to divide England according to a native/
stranger opposition, among the things that the Dutch Church Libel also
betrays is the impossibility of doing so, circa 1593. Though we have often
thought of island England as relatively insulated from Continental troubles,
the Libel suggests quite clearly that its borders were as porous as those of other
nations—all the more so in the years during which the Dutch Revolt and the
French Wars of Religion sent refugees streaming toward its shores.[11] But what
makes the insider/outsider dichotomy posited in the Dutch Libel all the more
problematic is that the strangers crisis seems not to have been generated so
much by the presence of exiled European nationals in London as by the rising tide of *English* outsiders making their way to the city. It was as much an
influx of "returning soldiers, unemployed labourers, 'masterless men and vaga-
bonds'" who were flocking "to the capital in search of food, work or relief"
that was overtaxing the city's "institutions, the hospitals, markets, and system
of poor relief," as it was an invasion of alien "newcomers."[12]

And among these Elizabethan subjects were some who regarded England as no merry "Faery land." Jarring as we may find a revelation like Richard Hakluyt's that a number of English merchants were "drawn to mislike" their English queen and her religion,[13] the assize files of Essex county—a traditional hotbed of English Puritanism—reveal yet more estranging sentiments surfacing among England's tradesman, laborers, and indigents. Among the oppositional voices of Smithfield—a township immortalized in the *Acts and Monuments* as a site of Bloody Mary's burnings—an anonymous weaver declared in 1585 that "King Philip was a father to England, and did better love an Englishman than the Queen's Majesty, for that he would give them drink and clothes."[14] A year later a Coggeshall laborer named William Metcalfe proclaimed "this world will be in a better case shortly," for "the King of Spain, with the noble Earl of Westmoreland, with Norton and six of his sons of noble birth, are come into England with others, and with fifteen or twenty thousand Englishmen" (60). Perhaps more telling may be comments gathered from detainees in Navestock, where, in 1590, two years *after* England's "deliverance," masterless men swore, "with most horrible oaths," that "if they were with the King of Spain, they should not be so used, with whom a great number of good fellows of their quality was" (61). And in 1591, a year that saw an expansion of Black Legend publication, a laborer of Great Wendon named John Feltwell voiced his disgust at England's social ills, as well as a willingness at least to consider doing something about it: "The Queen [is] but a woman," he said, "and ruled by noblemen, and the noblemen and gentlemen [are] all one . . . so that poor men . . . get nothing among them. . . . We shall never have a merry world while the Queen liveth; but [if] we had but one that would rise, I would be the next, or else I would that the Spaniards would come in that we may have some sport" (61).

And there were those who were driven to do more than complain. Significant numbers of "fugitives" were fleeing their homeland for Catholic-controlled kingdoms on the Continent. Some took up residence at English colleges at Rouen or Rome, or at those founded in Spain by Philip II.[15] By 1595, Lewis Lewkenor's *Discourse of the Usage of the English Fugitives, by the Spaniard*, would implore "all the young gentlemen of our Nation" to "beholde the spots & errours of theyr conceyved fancies" and avoid "the service of the Spanish king."[16] "How can you indure to thirst after the destruction of so sweete a countrie, in which you received your being, & that gave you nirture being yong?" asked Lewkenor. In place of a reply, he opposed "the comfortable freedom" (D3v) of England's religion, "learned . . . of the ancient Christians in the primitive church" (F2v), to that of Spain, "a nation not yet fully an hundred yeeres since wholie they received Christianitie," whose people "yet are in their heartes a great number of them, Pagans and Moores." Joining ranks with England's Black Legend polemecists Lewkenor argued that Spain's essential "Paganisme" was observable in the "tyrrany, blasphemy, sodomy, cruelty, murther, adultery, and other abominations sufficiently discover[ed]" (E4r). Once again English Protestantism's paganizing formula is patent. But here it walks hand in hand with color association via Spain's historical connection with the "Moores." Appeals to ethnos like Lewkenor's not withstanding, English Catholics continued to seek refuge abroad.[17] Men like William Stanley and Rowland York had gone so far as to take up arms against the nation that had given them "nirture"; others would stand in wait, privately hoping for another Spanish succession in place of the Stuart ascendancy.[18] And so the traffic in refugees moved across the Channel in both directions. To its credit, the regime saw clearly that it could not allow the blame for its ills to fall on its immigrant community—which must have accounted for the severity of its response to the Dutch Libel's posting.

The scandal surrounding the Dutch Church Libel thus reveals a number of social pressures that by the early 1590s were swelling Elizabethan society nearly to the point of rupture. Without commending the violent sentiments it expresses, we can grant that the document may have voiced several legitimate grievances. For while it was probable that most of the foreigners who sought sanctuary deserved English sympathies, some of the charges the Libel levies may have been accurate. Among the refugees were undoubtedly some who played all sides against the others, putting personal gain ahead of any group allegiance, working both in behalf of the state and against it. A significant number of the newcomers, not only those from Spain and Portugal proper, but also those from the Low Countries (historically, the Spanish Netherlands), would have brought with them "intelligence" on which several concerned governments would have been all too willing to capitalize, even if it required that they practice double- or triple-dealing in order to do so.

Most jarring from a literary-historical perspective is the fact that the Dutch Libel engineered associations with issues of manifest contemporary importance as they had been represented in Marlowe's plays. The gesture suggests more than theatrical flourish. Between its threat of an English slaughter to answer the "paris massacre" (line 40), which recalls Marlowe's representation of the dark Saint Bartholomew's Day incident thought by Protestants to have been the ultimate application of "policy," and its astonishing conclusion, which warns that "our swords are whet" as "per Tamberlaine" (lines 52–53), the discursive parallels between the Marlovian texts and the issues that surface in the Libel reveal that its writers (and presumably its audiences) were acquainted enough with the plays to interpret them in terms of their relevance to current social conditions. Those who posted the Libel wanted to appropriate both Marlowe's rhetorical force and his popularity; they borrowed from his plays because they were certain that their borrowings would be recognized.[19]

Where the Dutch Libel seems most deliberately calculated to inflame local passions is in its "discovery" of alien involvement in the spheres of business and politics. In England and Spain, as elsewhere in the early modern world, and the Libel underscores this, communities of strangers were offered special incentives and tax breaks in order that they might more readily establish themselves within local economies. The stranger community stands accused of exploiting this advantage by harboring "Machiavellian Marchant[s]" who employ dubious or unethical business practices. Specifically, they engage in "usury" and "ingross[ing]," which enable them, "like the Jewes," to "eate us [that is, London's 'native' population] up as bread" (lines 6–9), even as their sheltering by the Crown allows these outsiders to live in England "farre better then at [their own] native home" (line 30).

As in *The Jew of Malta*, perhaps *because* of *The Jew of Malta*—which was probably written in the wake of the Armada and then revived in 1592[20]—the Dutch Church Libel slides Machiavellianism and Jewishness one into the other in ways for which there seems no other obvious precedent. Further, the connections the document makes with the plays suggest that Marlowe had tapped into profound sources of collective anxiety toward which the audiences of the late 1580s and early 1590s felt an urgent attraction. Among Marlowe's plays it is especially in *The Jew of Malta* that we find the playwright embodying a set of postures clearly apposite with the confluence of stranger groups and paranoid xenophobia given off in the Libel. As important was the certainty that those who posted the Libel saw in its references to Marlowe's plays a guarantee of both public and government recognition.

Enter Machevill

The plight of England's émigrés was ameliorated by the fact that the Elizabethans had good reasons for exploiting their strangers for political ends. The queen's government was quick to recognize their continuing ideological use, so Elizabeth's "gracious" reception of refugees became a constant trope of contemporary propaganda.

A typical rehearsal of England's "official" (or at least its public) attitude toward refugees and exiles was deployed in *A Fig for the Spaniard, or Spanish*

Spirits, a government-sponsored publication issued in 1591 and again in 1592 (Figure 5). In many ways an exemplary Black Legend tract, the tone of *A Fig for the Spaniard* is by turns humorously scornful, dismissively reductive, and aggressively taunting. While claiming the moral high ground of a Protestant orientation toward religion and politics, the polemic caricatures Spanish foreign and domestic policies, and Roman Catholic institutions, even as they are measured against the "purity" of Elizabethan motives and the English national religion. While "giving the fig" to Spain's religiopolitical leadership, the pamphlet welcomes outsiders "for Christes sake" to the "happie Realme, where mercie breareth swaie" (sig. A5v).

A Fig for the Spaniard was given a royal imprimatur at the printing house of John Wolfe, one of London's most active and controversial stationers. While issuing a range of more literary titles from English writers such

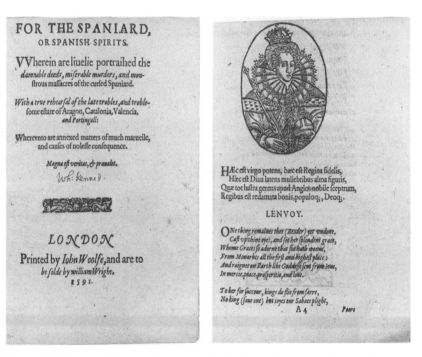

Figure 5. Title page and envoy from *A Fig for the Spaniard, or Spanish Spirits* (the first line is no longer extant in this copy), from the printing house of the Elizabethan propagandist and "Machiavel" John Wolfe. At right, notice the authorizing image of the queen, with the directive "Cast up thine eyes, and see her resplendent grace" in the second line of the English text. Reproduced by permission of the Folger Shakespeare Library, Washington, D.C.

as Thomas Watson, John Lyly, Robert Greene, and Edmund Spenser, as well as foreign language editions of Pietro Aretino, Torquato Tasso, Guillaume Du Bartas—and, most significantly in this context, the major works of Niccolò Machiavelli—Wolfe began after 1588 surreptitiously publishing selected titles from the Roman Church's Index of prohibited books for both domestic and foreign consumption.[21] He also started to specialize in news reports and polemics imported from France and the United Provinces. Ranging in length from exhaustive treatises and disputations to mere pamphlets, many of these betray a marked anti-Spanish orientation.[22]

The role Wolfe played in the Elizabethan print wars led contemporaries to associate him with Machiavelli, and not primarily because he had published the Florentine's work. As early as 1582, fellow printer Christopher Parker had urged Wolfe to "leave [his] Machiavellian devices, and conceit of [his] foreign wit" and "deal like an honest man"; by 1588 the anonymous writer of the Marprelate tracts named him "John Wolfe alias Machivill, Beadle of the Stationers."[23] Sometime between the two incidents Wolfe, having left unfulfilled an apprenticeship at the printing house of John Day (whose notable titles, as we have seen, included the *Book of Martyrs* and *The Spanish Colonie*), returned from travels on the Continent to insinuate himself into the world of government printing and censorship. Having been named Stationers' beadle by the mid-1580s, Wolfe included among his duties "police functions" such as defending patent holders, serving warrants on suspected encroachers, and prosecuting infringers.[24]

The rhetorical strategies Wolfe deployed in *A Fig for the Spaniard* and publications of its ilk did not go unremarked by Catholic contemporaries. In *A Declaration of the True Causes of the Great Troubles Presupposed to be Intended Against the Realm of England* (1592), the recusant Richard Verstegen laid much of the blame for England's religiopolitical strife at the feet of "M. Cecill"—that is, William Cecil—one of whose stratagems, "practized out of Machiavill," was "divulging núbers of false and defamatory libels" which justify their "habite" of failing to differentiate "betwene lying, and telling truth . . . because they tend unto the furtherance of the pretended Gospell."[25] At the forefront of these "libellers," who had "transported them[selves] into such a fervour of folly, that they imagyne all Christendome . . . without any question to the contrary bothe to knowe & acknowledge, *John Calvyns* exposition of the Gospell (as it is understood in England) to be the very Gospell of Christ," Verstegen placed the "*fig giver*," "Woolf"—to whom his *Declaration* bids "*A fig to the figmonger*."[26] Elizabeth may have declared a disinclination to look into men's consciences, but her network of propagandists, and this is especially true of Wolfe, always wrote in support of "conformity to English laws and traditions of the English Church."[27]

Among the things that may be regarded as "Machiavellian" about *A Fig for the Spaniard*—if the notion that "a Prince ought alwaies to nourish some enemy against himself" that "he may be accounted the more mighty"[28] derives from Machiavelli—is that it "livelie portraihed the damnable deeds, miserable murders, and monstrous massacres of the cursed Spaniard" in order to promote saber-rattling nationalism in one breath and the offer of safe haven in another. The encomium to Elizabeth Tudor that prefaced Wolfe's "true rehearsal of the late trobles" emblematized the public face of Crown policy:

> To her for succour, kings so flie from farre,
> No king (save one) but joyes our Sabaes plight,
> Poore strangers from their soyles expeld by warre,
> For Christes sake, find favor in her sight:
> From North, from South, from East, and from the West.
> To her they come, and heere they finde a rest. (A4–Bv)

Making a very public offering of "succour," *A Fig* names "the Romish monster, that monstrous feend of hell," as the prime mover of Europe's intestine troubles. Warning of "Hypocrites [who] in Fryers habites lurke, / That rapines, rapes, treasons, guyles, murders worke" (Bv), the pamphlet promotes the militant anti-Catholicism we have already seen dramatized by Wolfe's associates Peele and Greene, and which so often figured in Protestant polemic. In its darkly farcical way, *The Jew of Malta* also plays upon these Reformation commonplaces. In scenes such as that in which his "Fryar" lusts after the beautiful Abigall—grieving that she will "dye a Christian" and "a Virgin too" (3.4.40–41)—Marlowe taps this vein of Protestant hyperbole.

As did many of the Black Legend tracts of the 1580s and 1590s, which often translated Huguenot propaganda into terms applicable to the English situation,[29] *A Fig for the Spaniard* drew parallels between the troubles being experienced by the French monarchy and those that might erupt in England should religiopolitical heterogeneity prevail over unity of faith. It has long been recognized that Marlowe cribbed freely from these sources in composing *The Massacre at Paris*.[30] While I do not mean to suggest that he employed precisely the same strategy in *The Jew of Malta*, the play clearly mobilizes discourses characteristic of these polemics and suggests Marlowe's willingness to exploit the emotions such rhetorics were calculated to move. As the Dutch Church Libel implies, a key French text—of which both *The Jew of Malta* and *The Massacre at Paris* partake—is *The Anti-Machiavel* (Paris, 1576), by the Huguenot polemicist Innocent Gentillet (c. 1535–95).

If there is a sense in which we can ascribe to "Machevill" the worldview Barabbas incarnates, it is via popular misconceptions about Machiavelli's political theories as disseminated by writers such as Gentillet. Englished as early as 1577 by Simon Patericke, *The Anti-Machiavel* gave voice to popular fears about the implications of such "godless" machinations as the Florentine was seen to promote.[31] Whereas the princes discussed in the actual treatises of Machiavelli tend to focus on political acumen and military accomplishment, the primary concern of Gentillet's Machiavellians is to "gather 'great heapes of money' and collect 'riches and heapes of the treasure of the Realme, whilst it is in trouble and confusion.'"[32] For Gentillet, this was the Machiavellianism evident in the acts of the Duke of Guise and Catherine de Medici. It is also the Machiavellianism represented in *The Massacre at Paris*: "The Mother Queene workes wonders for my sake," says Guise in Marlowe's play, "And in my love entombes the hope of Fraunce: / Rifling the bowels of her treasurie, / To supply my wants and necessitie" (2.133–36); and, it is precisely the sort of greed with which we have seen the Dutch Church Libel charge the "Machiavellian Marchant[s]" of England's stranger community.

Like the unscrupulous businessmen who prey upon Londoners in the Dutch Libel, Barabbas of Malta appears to act solely out of the basest self-interest. The approach to "policy" Barabbas enacts throughout the play is nowhere summed up more succinctly than in act 5. After he has been awarded Malta's governorship, Marlowe's character reveals,

> Thus, loving neither, will I live with both,
> Making a profit of my policy,
> And he from whom my most advantage comes
> Shall be my friend.
> This is the life we Jews are used to lead,
> And reasons, too, for Christians do the like. (5.3.111–16)

In Barabbas's deeply cynical vision, "policy" and "profit" court each other—a philosophy he claims to have learned from "Christians." In the Machiavellianism described by Gentillet—emphasizing such tactics as "not keep[ing] . . . faith, when the observation thereof is hurtful," developing "a turning and winding wit, with art and practice made fit to be cruel & unfaithful," and cultivating a "mind disposed to turn after every wind and variation of fortune"[33]— we see the sort of improvisation Barabbas pulls off again and again, always in the interest of "advantage." Acknowledging that "Crownes come either by succession, / Or urg'd by force," that "nothing violent / . . . can be permanent," Barabbas claims to prefer the "peaceful rule" of "Christian Kings" who "thirst so much for Principality" (1.1.131–35). Entertaining no remorse for any of his deeds, no matter how horrific they might be, by act 5 Barabbas will have responded by committing the ultimate act of duplicity, "turning Turk."[34] Whether Malta lies under Christian or Turkish rule is incidental, so long as the profits roll in. As they are for the Machevills of the Dutch Libel, Barabbas's political and commercial interests are identical and inseparable.

To set *The Jew of Malta* and the Dutch Libel among the Huguenot pamphlets that men like Wolfe so effectively adapted to support the English Crown is perhaps to glimpse, contra official proclamations of welcome, an unintended reaction to the Crown's own propaganda campaign. Overblown remarks by European contemporaries, such as that famously voiced by a Venetian traveler, who claimed that the English "are great lovers of themselves, and of everything belonging to them; they think that there are no other men than themselves, and no other world but England,"[35] have led us to focus repeatedly on England's "natural" dislike of outsiders. But as Andrew Pettegree has cautioned, "How endemic and how widespread this hostility was has been subject of little detailed examination; it can too lightly be assumed that xenophobia was a national characteristic in the sixteenth century."[36] Granted, it could be so for propagandistic reasons, but William Cecil's infamous *Politick Discourse*, printed by Wolfe in 1589, quoted a prominent Frenchman in order to emphasize the contrary. The Vidâme of Chartres had purportedly declared "that if there were any Nation in Christendome, more liberall and courteous towarde strangers, than Englishmen are, he was contented to be registered among such as speake unadvisedly of things they know not."[37] Via printers like Wolfe, the Elizabethan government was in a strong sense "guiding" the nation (unevenly, of course, and toward not-quite-predictable ends) toward xenophobic attitudes by means of a propaganda campaign that advocated, somewhat paradoxically, both feelings of "merciful" openness toward refugees *and* virulent anti-Catholicism, which it often linked to an anti-Semitic Hispanophobia.

Part and parcel of this government strategy was the propagation of an intense fear of "impure" ethnic and racial influences. With their stick-figure friars, ruthless Jews, and Spaniards crueler than "the Turk," England's government-employed propagandists evoked an undifferentiated otherness upon which they could rely to produce knee-jerk fears of religious and ethnic outsiders. During an era in which English Catholics were risking exile, imprisonment, torture, and execution in order to maintain their links with the traditional faith, ridicule and scorn of the sort in which Wolfe and Cecil indulged were among the most effective rhetorical weapons mobilized against Catholic efforts, as potent in demeaning Romish doctrine as in Hispanizing the Crown's political opposition. Whatever the Crown's advertised position, its actual policies were fraught with inconsistencies and contradictions that often left immigrants feeling misled and English nationals feeling betrayed. As the Dutch Church Libel and other expressions of popular resistance make clear, there were among the English those who were not so disposed as the queen's government (and the more "liberall" of her subjects) to extend "favor" and "rest" to "Poore strangers." *The Jew of Malta* exploited these nativist sentiments more completely than any previous Elizabethan play.

"In Typo"

Complicating *The Jew of Malta*'s relation to the lived history of the 1590s is the fact that Marlowe appears at first glance to set his play in the past, during the era of Malta's celebrated resistance to the invading Ottoman Turks. As the 1588 Armada crisis was to England, so was this storied siege of 1565 to the community of Malta. In each instance an island culture, home to various and occasionally competing ethnic, immigrant, and interest groups, was forced to respond to an external threat, achieving in the process a heightened sense of collective consciousness.[38] Beyond producing feelings of solidarity, both events would provide discursive raw material from which narratives of English and Maltese identity would be written and rewritten for centuries.

It is, of course, anachronistic to invoke the English example ahead of the Maltese; the siege of Malta preceded the Enterprise of England by more than two decades. But for the early moderns, chronology was often not the first historiographical priority. What mattered most was historical *type*. Although their confessional orientations differed considerably, the English tended to notice similitude with regard to the island community of Malta. When their Mediterranean complement came under siege in 1565, England sent no "temporal relief." But recognizing that it had been in "Malta (in old time called *Melite*, where S. Paul arrived when he was sent to Rome)," Elizabeth authorized "spiritual aid" with the publication of a "Form of Common Prayer," which was read throughout the nation in order "to excite all godly people to pray unto God for the delivery of those Christians that are now invaded by the Turk."[39] With the breaking of the 1565 siege, another official prayer was issued, this one a thanksgiving "for the delivery of the Isle of Malta for the invasion and long siege thereof by the great army of Turks both by sea and land."[40] Inspired, perhaps, by proclamations such as these, the situational identification between the English and the Maltese—which would culminate with the presentation of the George Cross to the people of Malta in commemoration of their collective heroism in resisting the Axis powers during World War II—may have begun at this moment. Although Maltese policies, as Hakluyt would complain, could sometimes frustrate English designs in the Mediterranean, island England often saw island Malta as a figure of itself. This is certainly how the Maltese setting functions in Marlowe's play.

An audience steeped in more than two more decades of Protestant biblicism, however, could not but have recognized the gap between the ethos moving Barabbas and the teachings of Saint Paul, the historical Jew whom they would have associated with the island, and whose language of belief energized their own religious profession. In Barabbas's materialistic discovery of "poverty" and the "fruits" of "faith" (1.1.15–16), his reflection on "faith," "profession," and "conscience" (1.1.115–19)—perhaps especially in his perverse invocation of "*Corpo di dio*" (1.2.90) and subsequent reduction of the book of Job to a story about "his wealth" (1.2.181)—they would have seen, well in advance of the revelation, "I will show myself to have more of the Serpent then the Dove" (2.3.36–37), that an inversion of Christian figural tradition overdetermines the significance of Marlowe's protagonist.[41] At the same time, Marlowe's characterization plays into public paranoia regarding England's strangers, whose acceptance *and* rejection the English government seems simultaneously to have been promoting. Audiences would have heard in Barabbas's speech, emanating as it does from the mouth of a Spanish speaker, a difference of ethnos as well. And by placing his Jew—whose name Barabbas must surely have called to mind the New Testament oath, "His blood be on us, and on our children" (Matthew 27:25)—on an island at once the outpost of the church militant, the historical refuge of Saint Paul, and the figural equivalent of Protestant England, Marlowe plays upon local fears of irredeemable religious and cultural difference.

By the time Marlowe laid dramatic claim to the island, the famous Knights of Malta, known officially as the Order of Saint John of Jerusalem and colloquially as the Hospitallers, had been established there for more than half a century. In 1530, Emperor Charles V—by right of his grandfather Ferdinand's conquest of Sicily—had been in the position to donate Malta as the order's new base following its 1523 expulsion from Rhodes. The move is said to have rung in the order's "Spanish period."[42] With the normalization of relations between England and Spain after the passing of Henry VIII and his yet more Protestant son Edward VI—whose wholesale dissolution of Catholic institutions such as the Military Orders Reginald Cardinal Pole believed "closely expresse[d] the kingdom of Antichrist *in typo*"[43]—Mary Tudor (now married to Ferdinand's great-grandson Philip), issued an edict providing for the reestablishment of the Order of Saint John on English soil. Had the Tudor-Hapsburg union produced an heir, the Tongue of England (Hospitaller chapters were organized by language) might have attained its former prestige. With the ascension of Elizabeth I, however, the English chapter, along with the many Catholic institutions Mary and her Spanish king consort had sought to restore, was once again dissolved. But Elizabeth was of political necessity more accommodating than her father and half-brother had been. So her government remained conciliatory.

Insofar as *The Jew of Malta* recalls any of this history, it does so by appropriating events associated with the Knights of the Order of Saint John in their Mediterranean environs. But Marlowe fuses historical referents in a manner that, as Emily Bartels observes, "builds on the historical base and places Malta in a position of subjugation by re-writing history."[44] Marlowe accomplishes this rewriting by merging features of the 1565 siege with a key episode that actually occurred during the Hospitallers' earlier defeat at Rhodes. His strategy is not an exercise in mere creative anachronism. To the degree that the two events Marlowe draws upon may be viewed as typological instantiations of the Christian struggle against Antichrist, they could be legitimately equated. Although we cannot say precisely where Marlowe derived the cultural and historical knowledge his play mobilizes, two contemporary documents have been put forward as partial sources. The first is contemporary with the 1565 crisis; the second concerns its type, the 1523 siege of Rhodes.[45] Both bear on our discussion in important ways.

In terms that resonate with the heroics celebrated in Elizabeth's "Form of Common Prayer," the account from the 1560s advertises "the goodly vycvorie, wyche the Christenmen, by the favour of God have . . . latlye obtayned, against the Turks."[46] Reversing the Hospitaller defeat at Rhodes, the daring amphibious assault, undertaken by "the ryght noble & worthye . . . don Garcia of Toledo Capitayn General to the King of Spayn,"[47] came to be known as *El Gran Socorro*, the Great Relief. After one thwarted attempt to relieve the besieged defenders, Garcia de Toledo, viceroy of Naples and Knight of the Order of Santiago, conveyed eight thousand "Spanish" troops—actually, his force was made up of Iberians, Italians, and Germans of various national origins—across the gulf from Sicily under cover of darkness. Holding his troops to a silence so complete that his boatswains were not even allowed their whistles, the viceroy disembarked in less than two hours and sailed to pick up a further eight thousand soldiers before the Turks discovered he had been in port. The "miraculous" appearance of Don Garcia's *tercios* (as Spain's famed infantry regiments were known) sowed terror in the Ottoman ranks, and the siege of Malta, which had, as Braudel once noted, "hit Europe like a hurricane," came mercifully to an end.[48] The western thrust of the Ottomans halted, Christendom rejoiced—as it would again in 1571 when the victory at Lepanto arrested Turkish advances in the eastern Mediterranean.[49]

At first glance, this account appears to report an action resembling that staged in *The Jew of Malta*. One important study from the mid-twentieth century interpreted the drama in precisely these terms, going so far as to dub Marlowe's farce "a patriotic play . . . a Christian play . . . the story of Malta's heroic resistance."[50] But how far does this 1565 account really resemble the incident Marlowe dramatizes? The play includes a Spanish force under a character named Del Bosco. But Marlowe's Spaniards are hardly Malta's rescuers. Though their arrival announces Spain's claim of jurisdiction over the isle and rallies the play's knights to battle, as Bartels also reminds us, the Turks of *The Jew of Malta* are "victorious in their siege" (5). Rather than representing an actual historical event, Marlowe explores literarily a history that might have been—perhaps more potently, he poses a history of what yet could be. In other words, Marlowe depicts *a* siege, though not necessarily *the* siege, of Malta.

While the relationship between *The Jew of Malta* and actual Maltese history is thus an oblique one, the resemblance of the play to our second source, an account of the earlier battle at Rhodes, is palpable. In *The begynnynge and foundacyon of the holy hospitall & of the ordre of the knyghtes hospytallers of saynt Johan baptyst of Jerusalem* (1524)[51]—a French history of the order translated a decade before the Act of Supremacy at the instruction of Sir Thomas Docwra, Grand Prior of the English Tongue of the Venerable Hospital of Saint John—we find not only something of *The Jew of Malta*'s spirit, but several of its key details. In Docwra's account of the "mervilleuse & tréscruelle" battle, which had left an anxious Europe stunned at the gathering might of the Ottoman Empire,[52] an English readership that was still very much Roman Catholic would have seen tremendous urgency. It would have understood that Rhodes, as the narrative points out, was in a very real way "the key of Christendome," and the "hope of many poore Christian men" who were "withholden" captive of the "grand Turke."[53]

In the face of another Spanish invasion, it must have been a sense of similitude that moved Hakluyt to publish Prior Docwra's account of the siege at Rhodes among his *Principal Navigations* (1598–1600). As the narrative recollects Sultan Suleiman's resolution to have the island "by treason or by force," it observes that "for the same cause and purpose his father in his dayes had sent a Jewe physician into Rhodes as a spie, to have better knowledge of it: the sayd Solymon was informed that he was there yet, wherefore he sent him worde that he should abide there still for the same cause. . . . And the same Jewe wrote to him . . . under privie wordes, all that was done in Rhodes to give knowledge thereof to the great Turke: and the better to hide his treason, the said Jewe made himself to bee baptized" (3). Apparently, Hakluyt was not the only English writer to have found the account irresistible. One wonders whether he could have had Marlowe in mind when he decided to reprint Docwra's narrative. For clearly these two great contemporaries were intrigued by the same detail. As in *The Jew of Malta*, when the Antichristian Turk and the false Christian besiege the island from without and within, the prospect condenses Europe's worst fears regarding an unholy league between Muslim and Jew. So determined was the Reverend Richard Hakluyt that none among his readership should fail to behold in Rhodes's undoing a type of England's own peril, he could not resist interpreting the incident for native consumption: "Forren physicians," he wrote, "become spies often-times" (3). The allusion Hakluyt's marginal gloss inscribes is patent. He can only have been referring to the infamous royal physician and indicted traitor so often mentioned in connection with Marlowe's play, that hapless Elizabethan Jew, Dr. Roderigo Lopez.

Conversos, Marranos, and Portingales

Circa 1593, there were by official count approximately 4,300 aliens resident in London.[54] It is a significant figure, but not above 4 to 5 percent of the population.[55] Of this group, few would have been actual "Jewes," the identity the Dutch Church Libel invokes by referring to alleged "Jewish" practices, not to an openly Jewish community. But even if the number of Continental émigrés of known Jewish descent in the city would have been small, by the 1590s several among them had risen to obvious prominence. Although these Elizabethan Jews have been the subject of intensive historical research, especially as relates to their disproportionate dramatic representation, scholarship has less often placed these *conversos* (converted Jews) and *marranos* (those who secretly practiced Judaism) among the deeper historical currents that brought them to England from their various homelands.

Marching in step with the 1492 fall of Muslim Granada and Columbus's New World landing came the third "great project" realized in that *annus mirabilis*, the Catholic Kings' expulsion of the unconverted Jews from the Spanish homelands. Though historians disagree widely on the precise number who chose exile over conversion,[56] the impact of the exodus was felt almost immediately from one end of Europe to the other.[57] With the intensification of the Inquisition's activities in Portugal, another wave of immigrants moved toward England and the Low Countries, even as thousands more ventured across the Strait of Gibraltar to Morocco or eastward to Italy, Greece, and the Ottoman territories.[58]

These Portuguese émigrés, many of whom had only recently arrived from Spain, would have had good reason for seeking new lives outside the Spanish Crown's dominions. But we should not fail to recognize the complexity and diversity of the exilic experience. Not all of those who left Iberia were "unconverted," which is to say that not all of the ethnic Jews who chose exile over commitment to their homeland led secret lives in the faith of their forebears. It appears that a significant number of Iberian New Christians had begun to emigrate ahead of the expulsions, either because they could feel the cultural climate growing more oppressive or because they saw more stable economic or social prospects elsewhere. Some recovered their Judaism in exile; some continued to live in their Christian faith.[59]

It is not absolutely clear among which of the aforementioned groups we should place Dr. Roderigo Lopez. And yet whenever questions arise concerning Elizabethan representations of "Jewishness"—especially in connection with Barabbas or Shylock—Lopez, one of England's most prominent *conversos*, emerges as a "model."[60] While the possibility of his having influenced Marlowe's characterization is complicated somewhat by the fact of the playwright's death in May 1593, which occurred more than a year before Lopez's execution,[61] as early as 1584 the libelous *Leicester's Commonwealth*— which names Robert Dudley as England's foremost "Machiavel"—mentioned "Lopez the Jew" (then in the earl's employ), proleptically crediting him with "skill in poisoning."[62] And although it was his involvement in an intrigue involving a plot against Elizabeth (purportedly engineered by Philip II) that earned Lopez lasting fame, long before the scandal broke Gabriel Harvey had written of "Doctor Lopez, the queen's physician," who "is descended from the Jews, but [is] himself a Christian, and [from] Portugal."[63]

Harvey's brief description is worth lingering over, not merely because it reveals imputations concerning Lopez, but also because it conveys an Elizabethan insider's perception of the stranger community to which the doctor belonged. Harvey surmises that although "Dr. Lopus was baptised . . . his baptism was not of the heart," and that "he looked upon his new faith as a help, not to scorning the world, but to gaining something from it."[64] The remark alleges the same sort of "counterfeitinge religion" highlighted in both the Dutch Church Libel and Hakluyt's marginal gloss.[65] It might also put us in mind of the feigned conversions of Marlowe's play. Although a contemporary like Camden would discover layers of humorous irony in the "confession" Lopez purportedly uttered at his execution, that "he loved the queen as well as he loved Jesus Christ," we cannot know for certain that he was a *marrano*, a secret Jew or Judaizer. While undergoing an interrogation that put him at "dyvers tymes upon the racke"[66] Lopez was forced to admit to being "now a false Christian;"[67] but we cannot know that he did not in fact love the queen, or indeed Jesus Christ. The facts of Lopez's heritage do not preclude either of these possibilities. Although his essentialization in a work as dubious as *Leicester's Commonwealth* suggests that certain Elizabethans believed they saw him clearly as "Lopez the Jew," to accept this categorization out of hand is to be tempted by the logic of the stereotype to which Marlowe, Hakluyt, and so many of their contemporaries were drawn.

If an Elizabethan audience winked knowingly, "Lopez," when they met Barabbas *"in his Counting-house, with heapes of gold before him,"*[68] then the doctor had already come to function within his adoptive homeland much in the way Stephen Greenblatt suggests that Marlowe's character functions in the play, as a man accommodated to "an abstract, anti-Semitic fantasy of a Jew's past."[69] As *A Fig for the Spaniard* demonstrates, the Crown itself had recently been perpetuating such fantasies, asserting that "the Spaniard" had burned and banished "out of his territories, *infinite swarms of riche Iewes*, sworne enemies to the Gospel."[70] Certainly, Lopez was pressed to serve as this sort of embodiment subsequent to his trial, when he was labeled "a perjured murdering traitor, and Jewish doctor, worse than Judas himself."[71] But even granting that some contemporaries regarded him in this prejudicial manner prior to his arraignment, Lopez's ethnicity seems not to have presented any impediment to his having established himself in early modern London. Without discounting the role of his own ambition, from what we can gather from contemporary records it was Lopez who was sought out by Englishmen no less highly placed than Leicester, Walsingham, and even the queen herself, as a result of his reputed medical expertise.[72] Upon entering this circle of elites, he sought and was granted an import monopoly on aniseed and sumac—which might well have given London merchants cause to suspect, in the language of the Dutch Church Libel, that he was attempting to "forestall . . . the markets" by practicing "three trades at least."[73] But while his ethnic background and the religion he may or may not have been practicing in secret had been mentioned in order to slur him in particular circumstances, in most contexts, Lopez—who seems to have been relatively successful at publicly anglicizing himself as "Roger"—was primarily identified not as a Jew but as a "Portingale." When we trace the strands of his involvement in the affairs of England's Portuguese community, especially relative to their "king," the exiled Portuguese pretender Dom Antonio, we find that it was Lopez's complicated position relative to his *nationality* that lead him to participate in the conspiracy that was his undoing.

The Anglo-Portuguese intrigues of the late sixteenth century make up a now largely forgotten chapter of European history.[74] In the early 1590s, however, the stakes were quite high for both England and Portugal, and Elizabethans far more highly placed than Roderigo Lopez found the complex problem of Lusitanian nation-building irresistible. While they lacked sufficient resources and will to secure the Portuguese throne since the Terciera debacle of 1583, which saw a joint Anglo-French expedition fail miserably in its attempt to prop up Dom Antonio's dwindling resistance movement, the English had authorized a number of privateering ventures under the Prior of Crato's flag.[75] Although England remained relatively unscathed by the combined Spanish and Portuguese enterprise of 1588, with threats of new Armadas looming Dom Antonio's star began once more to rise. No less important military minds than Sir Francis Drake, the Earl of Essex, and Sir John Norris thought that a Portuguese coup d'état would short-circuit any future Spanish invasions. The results of their adventure, commemorated in George Peele's jingoistic encomium *A Farewell. Entituled to the famous and fortunate Generalls of our English forces: Sir John Norris & Syr Frauncis Drake Knights, and all theyr brave and resolute followers* (1589), would prove disastrous.[76] Ultimately, the affair scuttled Dom Antonio's hopes of repatriation, while also sealing the fates of Lopez and the two "Portingale" conspirators with whom he would be executed.[77]

Although the details of the Lopez case remain interesting in and of themselves, most important in the present context is the way in which the Portuguese doctor's heritage, profession, social status, and linguistic skills combined to place him so advantageously among the various constituencies involved. Lopez seems to have been pulled irresistibly into a political vortex in which he had little choice but to operate as a triple agent. At various times in the employ of three different sovereigns—Elizabeth I, Philip II, and Dom Antonio—Lopez was in a position to pull the purse strings of each. His services to the English Crown included involvement in the underground activities of Cecil, for whom he deciphered and translated Spanish documents.[78] Whether, like many of his countrymen, Lopez had been won over to the party of Philip II, or if, as he claimed in his own defense, he only meant to "cousen the Spaniard, and never thought any hurt against the Queene,"[79] the affair for which we remember him resists the oversimplification to which it has been subjected from virtually the moment the scheme was discovered. While it is possible that, in the manner of the Dutch Church Libel's "Machiavellian Marchant," or indeed of *The Jew of Malta*'s Barabbas, Lopez may have become involved in the scandal simply to enrich himself, a far more compelling motivation may have been that the doctor, along with any number of Portuguese nationals at home and abroad, had come to see that his former homeland's future lay in the hands of the Spanish monarchy, and not in those of Dom Antonio and his allies, whose resistance to Spain had proven so ineffectual. We need also to consider the possibility that, with any number of influential Englishmen, Lopez had come to believe that as Elizabeth's days began to appear numbered—he was, after all, the queen's personal physician—the smart money looked toward the dynasty that would succeed the Tudors in England. Which dynasty that would be was still an open bet.

As they had in the case of the Portuguese succession crisis, when young King Sebastian had died without an heir, the Spanish maintained a significant claim on the English Crown. As the "Hispanized" Jesuit Robert Persons (or Robert Doleman) was arguing during the 1590s, Spain's suit was as reasonable as any of the others being advanced, and more legitimate than most.[80] It was not self-evident that the Stuarts, through James VI of Scotland, ought to be named the next dynasty to inherit the throne. And while we might imagine that Iberians of Jewish descent would have seen the Roman Catholic Hapsburgs as their "natural" adversaries, influential groups in both Portugal and England favored successions linked to the Spanish dynasty above the "native" candidates, Dom Antonio and James VI. So it would indeed have been possible for a man like Lopez to work as an "intelligencer to the state & crowne" while also "wish[ing] an alteracion."[81] An Anglo-Spanish succession would have produced the third such alliance within a century, after all.[82] It is not difficult to imagine that an English resident alien of Iberian ancestry would have seen advantage in another marriage of English and Spanish interests.

When we view the Lopez case from this perspective, it is far less tenable than contemporaries suggested that the doctor's involvement in the murky world of early modern dynastic politics stemmed primarily from his Jewish antecedents; however, we may claim with some reason—and without essentializing Lopez's ethnicity or religion (whichever one he held in his heart)—that he must have become a participant because he was Portuguese. In point

of fact, when Lopez and his confederates were charged, they were held with
Jesuit prisoners implicated in another plot against the Crown, and his "Jewish
origin was not a key element in his prosecution."[83] It was Lopez's *nationality*
that ultimately determined his loyalties. And yet, it cannot be denied that the
doctor's heritage would have put him in a position to avail himself of a set of
economic connections, which he also seems to have chosen to exploit, that
stretched from London, through the Low Countries, to Iberia and Italy, and
across the Mediterranean to Constantinople.[84]

Marlowe does not mention Lopez by name. But *The Jew of Malta* foregrounds the kind of international commercial network in which the doctor
seems to have been attempting to participate. In Barabbas's reflection upon his
Jewishness, Marlowe appears to implicate Lopez's contemporary and London
associate, Dr. Hector Nuñez:

> They say we are a scattered Nation:
> I cannot tell, but we have scrambled up
> More wealth by farre then those that brag of faith.
> There's Kirriah Jairim, the great Jew of Greece,
> Obed in Bairseth, *Nones in Portugal,*
> My selfe in Malta, some in Italy,
> Many in France, and wealthy every one:
> I, wealthier far then any Christian. (1.1.121–28, my italics)

Though the passage, like the play more generally, reinscribes a culturally hyperbolic commonplace about "Jewish" ability to accumulate wealth, it does
not exaggerate the breadth of the commercial system in which "Nones" participated. Displaced ethnic Jews (whether they practiced their inherited faith
or that of their conversion) could exchange information as well as goods
within such a network. An unintended side effect of Spain's ethnonationalist policies—its "scattering" of *marranos, conversos,* and practicing Jews—had
been to widen the "Jewish" web of economic and cultural connections, inspiring and enabling men like Lopez and Nuñez to seek their fortunes beyond
Iberian shores.[85]

The Jews of Marlowe's play—as does the fact of Dr. Lopez's employment
as one of Cecil's Spanish translators—also raise the specter of a fourth Iberian
achievement of 1492, one that would prove as significant in its way as that
year's three more widely heralded events. Even as Columbus was opening the
door to the era of Spain's unprecedented global expansion, the Spanish humanist Antonio de Nebrija had presented the Catholic Kings with a Castilian

grammar. His eloquent prologue, dedicated to Isabella, accurately predicted the linguistic future of the Spanish language. "When your Highness has subjected many barbarous peoples and nations of foreign tongues," he wrote, "they will have to accept the laws which the conqueror imposes on the conquered, and with them our language."[86] Quite consciously, Nebrija sought to give Spain a "perfect instrument of empire."[87] To a certain extent his words proved prophetic. But Nebrija was an advocate of Castilian nationalism and Iberian consolidation as much as he was a proponent of imperial expansion, nor could he have foreseen that whole continents would one day speak the languages of Iberia. Those whom he believed would be required to adopt the Spanish tongue were "the Basques, the Navaresse, the French, the Italians, and all others who have any traffic and communication with Spain."[88]

It is one of the great ironies of history that among the most active and efficient carriers of Spanish language and culture worldwide were those Spain had expelled from its shores.[89] For an ancillary effect of the expulsion of Spain's Jews was the promotion and propagation of the language of their former homeland; its language, Castilian, became a sort of "Jewish" commercial lingua franca even as it was becoming identified as the language of the Hapsburgs' global empire. While evidence of this may be found in any number of discursive fields, John Florio's contemporary dictionary, which records that the designation of nationality, "Spaniard," could also signify "a jew," suggests the extent of the identification. Via this sort of indexical conflation, the Castilian language came to function simultaneously as a sign of Hispanicity *and* an index of Jewishness. To add a further irony, in the demonizing logic of the Black Legend, the Spaniard and the Jew became identified one with the other, even as Spain's religiopolitical institutions sought to undo that geographical, historical, and genealogical identification.

Though it has not often been remarked, something much like the conflation of ethnic and linguistic identity recorded by Florio occurs in *The Jew of Malta*. For in act 2 Barabbas's connection to Spain is revealed though his speech. When Barabbas delivers full lines in Castilian at this significant moment of the play—"*Bien para todos mi ganado no es*" (My gold is not for the good of all) (2.1.39), and "*Hermoso placer de los dineros*" (The beautiful pleasure of money) (2.1.64)[90]—he draws together two prominent features of the era's Hispanophobic discourse: legendary "Spanish" lust for gold, and equally legendary "Jewish" avarice. It is true that Barabbas speaks several languages in the play, notably, mock Italian and faux French. This has been taken, with some historical justification, to suggest the kind of cosmopolitanism sometimes attributed to the "stateless" Jews. But Barabbas's recourse to Castilian feels far more pointed. By putting the Spanish language into his Jew's mouth, Marlowe implies more than mere cosmopolitanism, adeptness at disguise, and linguistic play. Incarnating Hispanophobic notions about the "infinite swarms of riche Iewes" that had been "scattered" from Spain and were now thought to be participating in a covert international commercial network that had been strengthened by their exile, Marlowe's ethnopoesis reveals the avaricious essence at Barabbas's Iberian core.

"Villains Both"

In Marlowe's linkages of ethnicity and economics there is much to trouble a liberal sensibility. In one of its most unsettling scenes, *The Jew of Malta* reveals (however briefly) the dark heart of the early modern capitalist system.[91] As we watch the "Riche Iewe" Barabbas bait Lodowicke with the promise of his daughter, Abigall—who, as the "Diamond" that "Outshines Cinthia's rayes" (2.3.64), is at once the play's most precious commodity and a figure of Elizabethan identification and empathy—we are transported to Malta's notorious slave market, which during the sixteenth century had become an increasing source of the island's wealth.

Announcing rather suddenly, "But now I must be gone to buy a slave" (2.3.96), Barabbas leads the Governor's son Lodowicke to the marketplace where he and the young aristocrat begin to haggle. "What's the price of this slave," Barabbas asks the officer in charge, "two hundred crowns? Do the Turkes weigh so much?" (2.3.98–99). "Ratest thou this Moore but at two hundred plats?" asks Lodowicke. To which Barabbas adds, "Why should this Turke be dearer than that Moore?" (2.3.97–99). Demanding to "see one that's somewhat leaner" (2.3.125), whose worth is set at "An hundred Crownes" (2.3.130), Barabbas tells us in an aside to "*marke him . . . for this is he / That by my helpe shall doe much villainie*" (2.3.132–33). Telegraphing the gulling to come, Barabbas commands: "Come Sirra you are mine. / As for the Diamond it shall be yours" (2.3.134–35). The transaction that purchases Barabbas a partner in crime also seals Lodowicke's fate; Marlowe's "Machievellian marchant" has no intention of giving his diamond of a daughter to the Maltese Christian. Barabbas sees too clearly the advantage Abigall gives him over Lodowicke and his father: "He loves my daughter, and she holds him deare: / But I have sworne to frustrate both their hopes, / And be revenge'd upon the—*Governor*" (2.3.141–43).[92] As representative Maltese citizens, Don Mathias and his mother participate in the objectification of the slave market—the latter announcing,

"This Moore is comeliest," to which the former replies, "No, this is the better, mother, view this well" (2.3.144–45)—we recoil at the play's fetishization
of sexual and racial difference. We glimpse too the engine that drove Maltese
financial solvency.

It was also an economic engine that the English were, with the support of
the Crown, waiting eagerly to adapt to their own circumstances. As Hakluyt
would recall,

> Master John Haukins having made divers voyages to the Iles of the Ca-
> naries, and there by his good and upright dealing being growen in love
> and favour with the people, informed himselfe amongst them by dilli-
> gent inquisition, of the state of the West India, whereof he had received
> some knowledge by the instructions of his father, but increased by the
> same advertments and reports of that people. And being amongst
> other particulars assured, that Negros were very good marchandise in
> Hispaniola, and that store of Negros might easily bee had upon the
> coast of Guinea, resolved himselfe to make triall thereof, and commu-
> nicated that devise with is worshipfull friendes in London: namely with
> Sir Lionell Ducket, sir Thomas Lodge, M. Gunson his father in law, sir
> William Winter, M. Bromfield, and others. All which persons liked so
> well of his intention, that they became liberall contributers and adven-
> turers in the action.[93]

Although, as a result of the strain Hawkins's "third troublesome voyage" of
1567–68 put on Anglo-Hispanic relations,[94] England's full-scale participation
would be forestalled, during the years in which *The Jew of Malta* enjoyed its
first popularity the English coveted access to precisely the sort of slave economy Marlowe dramatizes. Even though some would raise objections on moral
grounds, by and large Hawkins had demonstrated that "prosperous successe
and much gaine" could come of participation in the capture and transatlantic
transport of Africans to the New World. Soon enough, the English would
return with a vengeance to the business of slaving.[95]

Marlowe's representation of the Maltese slave trade does more than reveal
the underpinnings of the labor market on which the early modern economy
was growing increasingly dependent.[96] Barabbas's human purchase adds to
the play the powerful identification of Marlowe's Jew with a Turkish slave
who bears the punningly Moorish name Itha*more*. When Barabbas declares,
"Make account of me /As of thy fellow, we are villains both: / Both circum-
sizèd, we hate Christians both" (2.3.217–18), Marlowe's ethnopoetic gesture

reproduces the essential Iberian consanguinity we see emphasized again and again in Black Legend propaganda. For we often find the Black Legend pamphleteers of the 1580s and 1590s constructing Spain as a land of undifferentiated ethnic otherness. Across the Protestant north, as polemicists improvise upon the theme suggested by William of Orange's assertion that "the greatest parte of the Spanyardes . . . are of the blood of the Moores and Jews," Spain would be cast as a "Marranish nation," their king a "half crowned Jew," a "would yet-be Saracen, a Barbarian, a Jew," who "should so much as dare to think, much lesse to attempt to march and take place before our most Christian kings."[97] Just as the Jew and the Moor share an intimate bond in Barabbas and Ithamore, so could the two be bound together in a public mind shaped by anti-Judaic, anti-Islamic, and Hispanophobic discourses dedicated to the promotion of English nationalism. These publications have in common with *The Jew of Malta* the strategy of playing on (and preying on) contemporary English fears not merely of ethnic and religious difference but also of a "racial" impurity that was constructed as constitutive of the Spanish monarchy and the Iberian people alike. In this discourse, which is far more invested in producing "racial" antitheses than differentiating accurately between peoples, distinctions between ethnonational groups could often slide together.[98]

This ethnopoetic conflation sits uneasily in *The Jew of Malta*, as do a number of issues that arise from Marlowe's choice to project into the island community characters so openly "Jewish" as the ones we encounter in the play.[99] As Cecil Roth observed, although "their history on the island goes back to immemorial antiquity," the "perpetual expulsion" of the Jews from Malta "was formally and solemnly proclaimed" on 18 June 1492, and in spite of the fact that the measure could leave the island of Malta and neighboring Gozzo "dangerously depopulated," the "instructions from Spain were carried out to the letter."[100] Although more recent research suggests that there may have been Jewish residents on the island from time to time, dependent upon the Grand Master's permission and identifiable by the yellow ribbon of identification they were required to wear, the fact that there were so few Jews on Malta renders Marlowe's setting curious from yet another perspective.[101] Subject as it was to the Inquisition, any Jews who found themselves on the island after 1492, and were unable to buy their way clear, would have been welcomed, if not to the ransomer's cell or the auction block, then to an *auto-da-fé*.

To speak of Malta's edict of expulsion is to raise the specter of one of early modern Europe's most notorious institutions, the Spanish Inquisition—an organ conceived as much out of an impulse to ensure social control by mobilizing "popular passions" as to gain funds or impose Christian orthodoxy.[102]

Although *The Jew of Malta* does not specifically mention the Inquisition, several of its practices are suggested in the action Marlowe dramatizes. When, in response to the Turks' threat to call in the ten years tribute owed by the knights, the Governor announces his plan to deal with the crisis, his brief exchange with Barabbas recalls several modes of operation associated with the kind of social control the Inquisition attempted to assert:

> *Barabbas.* Are strangers with your tribute to be tax'd?
> *2. Knight.* Have strangers leave with us to get their wealth?
>   Then let them with us contribute.
> *Barabbas.* How, equally?
> *Governor.* No, Jew, like infidels.
>   For through our sufferance of your hatefull lives,
>   Who stand accursed in the sight of heaven,
>   These taxes and afflictions are beffal'n,
>   And therefore we are determined;
>   Reade there the Articles of our decrees.
> *Reader.* First, the tribute mony of the Turkes shall all be levied
>   Amongst the Jewes, and each of them to pay one half of all his
>   estate.
> *Barabbas.* How, halfe his estate? *I hope you mean not mine.* [*Aside.*]
> *Governor.* Read on.
> *Reader.* Secondly, hee that denies to pay, shall straight become a
>   Christian.
> *Barabbas.* How, a Christian? Hum, what's to be done?
> *Reader.* Lastly, he that denies this, shall absolutely lose all he has.
> (1.2.59–75)

Making an appeal to his "stranger privilege," and mirroring the economic tensions given voice in the Dutch Church Libel, Barabbas attempts to frame his objection in secular, business discourse, momentarily deflecting the demand that is presented to him in religiopolitical terms. Rather than their being assessed simply as "strangers," the Governor declares that Barabbas and his associates are to be taxed "like Infidels," and thus each will be obliged "to pay one half of all his estate."[103] The scene also suggests the formula of coercion and confiscation that could be enacted wherever the Inquisition held sway.

Although we may find this sort of disenfranchisement ethically (and ethnically) problematic, it is not likely that many members of Marlowe's audience would have reacted with similar distaste. If the Libel suggests anything like the level of popular resentment beginning to be felt on the streets of London, it is probable that an audience would have applauded the exactions laid upon the play's Jewish strangers, and reacted similarly to the prospect of their forced conversion. It may be reasonably suspected that many early modern Christians, whether Protestant or Catholic, would have felt that half of one's monetary worth was a small price to pay for eternity. And why shouldn't the Elizabethans of the 1590s have found themselves attracted to the Governor's logic? Was it not preferable in time of crisis "To save the ruine of a multitude: / And better one want for a common good, / Then many perish for a private man" (1.2.97–99), especially when that one man was "A Jewe"?

Like the strangers of the Dutch Church Libel and the "Forren physicians" that Hakluyt regarded with such suspicion, both Barabbas and his daughter Abigall slide easily between religious identities. As they do so, they perform the anxieties of a culture that had experienced within recent memory state-ordered conversions and inquisitional practices levied by both Roman Catholic and Protestant authorities. That Barabbas may so readily and cynically ask Abigail to pose as a convert (1.2.280) suggests how fluid and uncertain religious identity could be during the era of *cuius regio, eius religio*, as well as the absurdity of religiopolitics in an age of Inquisition. If the sort of social engineering that mandated confessional reversal could lead to the "atheism" we associate (rightly or wrongly) with Marlowe, or the wanton duplicity suggested by both the Lopez case and the Dutch Libel, it is not difficult to see how this might have been so. The cycle of pretended conversion and backsliding represented in *The Jew of Malta* may caricature these cultural pressures; but in staging them Marlowe allows us to behold both the problematic nature of faith by decree and the double-dealing such attempts at social control seem to have fostered.

Mysteries of State

The web of ethnic and religiopolitical intrigue Marlowe weaves in *The Jew of Malta* grows yet more expansive when we recognize that Roderigo Lopez's countryman, Dom Antonio, the presumptive heir to the Portuguese throne, was also a Knight of Malta. Although the Dom Antonio saga lies beyond the purview of this study, the presence of this prominent figure at the English court, like the existence of London's vibrant stranger community, suggests yet again the poverty of the insider/outsider opposition around which we have often constructed Elizabethan culture.

That the English would welcome the former prior of the Hospitaller

Convent at Crato reveals another complication in the vexed relationship between the Crown and the Order of Saint John. By granting Dom Antonio residence the English could exploit a high-profile political exile in precisely the manner advertised by *A Fig for the Spaniard*. But his presence also suggested the limits of their actual commitment to deliver aid, for Elizabeth's efforts in support of the Portuguese pretender, like the concessions she made on behalf of England's stranger community, were driven more by expediency than principle. While it would have been possible to view Dom Antonio's English stay as a significant step toward the normalization of relations between the Crown and an institution that once had exerted an important presence on its shores, the role he was moved to play during the last two decades of the sixteenth century may also reflect a shift in the way the Knights of Malta had begun to perceive themselves. For while the prior of Crato was the representative of a group sworn to serve an international ideal, by nationality he was driven to become a militant advocate of Portuguese sovereignty in the face of the Spanish dynasty whose support had ensured his order's existence. In making this choice, he may have been inspired by the historical currents that had washed the Hospitallers' home island in the wake of the 1565 siege.

As Carmel Cassar has written, "Geographically Malta is sufficiently compact to have its own distinct identity. Yet it was only under the rule of the Order of St. John that a 'Maltese' culture came into being."[104] Like Daniel Defoe's "True-born Englishman," who "from a mixture of all kinds began," the Maltese were a people so ethnically mixed that the question of national bloodlines could be approached only ironically.[105] As Bartels writes, "To be 'of Malta' really mean[t] not to be, originally, of Malta," since historically, "before the coming of the knights, the island had been under the rule of Sicily, but it had exchanged hands so frequently (being ruled successively by the Greeks, Carthaginians, Romans, Goths, Arabs, Germans and Spanish) that it had become a multi-national melting pot."[106] It had been "the shared experience of the Siege of 1565" that, much in the manner of England's shared Armada experience, "in the perspective of the *longue durée* appears to have served as a catalyst in the emergence of Maltese ethnic awareness."[107] Yet this may be to construct the birth of Maltese identity too positively. As the English case suggests, the experience of a common threat may as readily usher in isolationist and xenophobic attitudes, all the more so when powerful interests stand to gain from the consolidation of power.

The Jew of Malta seems to recognize the island's incipient nationalism via the conflict between Barabbas and his primary adversary, the Governor, through whom Marlowe explores a mode of "policy" that could insure national integrity—which returns us to the problem of the play's Machiavellianism. For among the interpretive difficulties that have loomed throughout this discussion of *The Jew of Malta* is that concerning the relationship of the prologue delivered by Machevill to the body of the play.[108] Though it is possible that this induction may have been a later addition (and thus not composed by Marlowe himself), Machevill's appearance at the outset serves to contribute a note of seriousness that lifts the drama above the farcical coarseness that characterizes much of its discourse and action. The prologue prods us to think beyond the play's ethnic jokes, bawdiness, and anti-Catholic excess, in order to look for an argument. Even as it suggestively puns Niccolò Machiavelli's surname with "make evil," the play's prologue offers a typology of Machiavellianism from which materializes, as Catherine Minshull has observed, an "image" of "power politics in which conventional religious and moral scruples play little part."[109] Given this characterization, it does indeed seem strange that the play would commence with the introduction of Barabbas, when the figures who precede him are "the Guize," "Caesar," and "the Dracos" (1.1.3, 19, 21). For the behavior of Marlowe's Jew, as Minshull also notes, "diverges widely from the image of Machiavellianism . . . as an art devoted to gaining and maintaining political power" (40), the image suggested by the political types invoked in the play's prologue. If the prologue suggests via historical types how religious and military resources often merge in the exercise of national and imperial aims, the remark of Marlowe's Governor about Barabbas's apparent unconcern for military matters—"Tut, Jew, we know thou art no soldier" (1.2.52)—further underscores the inappropriateness of casting Barabbas as a follower of Machiavelli. The Florentine believed not merely that the "main foundations of every state . . . are good laws and good arms" but also that "where there are good arms, good laws inevitably follow."[110] Although Marlowe's farce may delight in Barabbas's antics, his play valorizes the way of the sounder Machiavel.

Another way to frame all this is to say that Marlowe's play seems to suggest that national solidarity, even in the face of a shared external threat, does not just happen. It requires agency on the part of those in the position to wield power. *The Jew of Malta* explores such agency by staging two kinds of Machiavellianism: one, embodied in Barabbas, seems to "make evil" out of the basest personal impulses; the other, represented by Marlowe's Governor, schemes toward higher political goals. If the sort of realpolitik implied in Marlowe's prologue and detailed in *Il Principe* haunts *The Jew of Malta* as thoroughly as critics have suggested, we ought to recall that, in terms of his capacity to embody religious motivation while capitalizing on the gains of both policy and strategic military action, it was not his Florentine master, Cesare Borgia, who drew Machiavelli's highest praise. Rather, it was their Aragonese contemporary, Ferdinand the Catholic, whom Machiavelli regarded as a master "because from being a weak king he ha[d] risen to being, for fame and glory, the first king of Christendom."[111]

As Ferdinand's various accomplishments have been looming throughout this book, it will be worth lingering over Machiavelli's assessment of the king of Aragon's approach to policy. "If you study his achievements," the theorist wrote,

> you will find that they are magnificent and some of them unparalleled. At the start of his reign he attacked Granada; and this campaign laid the foundation of his power. First, he embarked on it undistracted, and without fear of interference; he used it to engage the energies of the barons of Castile who, as they were giving their minds to the war, had no mind for causing trouble at home. In this way, without their realizing what was happening, he increased his standing and his control over them. He was able to sustain his armies with money from the Church and the people, and, by means of that long war, to lay a good foundation for his standing army, which has subsequently won him renown. In addition, in order to be able to undertake even greater campaigns, still making use of religion, he turned his hand to a pious work of cruelty when he chased out the Moriscos and rid his kingdom of them: there could not have been a more pitiful or striking enterprise. Under the same cloak of religion he assaulted Africa; he started his campaign in Italy; and he has recently attacked France. Thus he has always planned and completed great projects, which have always kept his subjects in a state of suspense and wonder, and intent on their outcome. And his moves have followed closely upon one another in such a way that he has never allowed time and opportunity in between times for people to plot quietly against them.[112]

From his "undistracted" focus to his strategies for engaging "the energies of the barons," to his prescient understanding of the need for a "standing army" and of the utility of keeping his subjects in a "state of suspense and wonder," the reign of Ferdinand the Catholic provides a virtual template for the national consolidation that would become a visible trend among Europe's polities during the years following the Reformation. Among Ferdinand's greatest military accomplishments was his "campaign in Italy," culminating in the conquest of Naples and the Kingdom of the Two Sicilies, through which he acquired Malta[113]—a fitting bookend for his more "pious work of cruelty," the conquest of Granada. If, as Minshull suggests, Marlowe's Governor "resembles Machiavelli's ideal prince in that he seldom allows his mind to stray from military affairs"[114]—as evidenced when he excuses the Maltese tribute as over-due "by reason of the wars that robbed our store" (1.2.48)—we ought to keep the example of Ferdinand in mind. Quite in the spirit of the king who had brought Malta within the Spanish orbit, the play's Governor—much in the politick manner of Ferdinand of Aragon—remedies a political and economic challenge by levying tribute money from the Jews.

And if *The Jew of Malta* opposes these competing notions of Machiavellianism—Gentillet's greed-driven improvisation versus the real-politik actually described in *Il Principe*—we should not fail to consider the typology Marlowe employs when he names his Maltese Governor, the play's ultimate victor over both Jew and Turk. It is doubtful that an early modern could have heard the name "Fernese" and not associated it with one of contemporary Europe's most powerful political dynasties. It was Alexander Farnese (1468–1549) who had assumed the papal crown as Paul III in 1534, only to be faced immediately with the necessity of excommunicating Henry VIII over his unlawful divorce of Katherine of Aragon. It was also through Paul III that the family became rather famously associated with the Order of Saint John,[115] for as pope he had conferred the Priory of Venice on his grandson Ranuccio (1530–65) (Figure 6). By the 1580s the name would have been pregnant with more immediate significance. For Paul III's namesake, and Ferdinand the Catholic's great-great-grandson, Alessandro (or Alexander) Farnese, the Duke of Parma (1545–92), had become the family's most celebrated member (Figure 7). Widely considered the most brilliant military mind of his age, Parma achieved both fame and infamy as Philip II's governor-general of the Netherlands.[116] Responsible for suppressing the Dutch Revolt, Farnese won brilliant military, and, as important, significant diplomatic victories, regaining the southern provinces from William of Orange and maintaining the religio-political division that would eventually emerge as the nation of Belgium. Although attention could sometimes be drawn to his "cruelty," Parma was seen, even by his Protestant adversaries, as "a brave Prince, a great Captaine, beloved of those over whom he commandeth, esteemed of the others . . . who hath used great moderation, and observed his faith to his people."[117] Key in the present context was the way Alexander Farnese had succeeded in achieving his aims. As Garrett Mattingly once observed, "In Parma's hands, the heterogeneous collection of mercenaries which went by the name of the Spanish army developed new potentialities and a new coherence. . . . Formations of different equipment, different organization, different tactics, different tongues, and

Figure 6. Titian, *Ranuccio Farnese,* wearing the mantle of the Knights of Malta, c. 1542. Grandson of Alexander Farnese, Pope Paul III, Ranuccio was named the order's Venetian prior at the age of eleven. Samuel H. Kress Collection. Image courtesy of the Board of Trustees, National Gallery of Art, Washington, D.C.

military traditions, Spaniards, Italians, Germans, Walloons, were welded into a single instrument which was almost a tool of precision."[118]

Over and against the solipsistic greed of Barabbas, then, we ought to regard Fernese as the play's authentic type of "Machevill," whose decisions are made in the interest of heterogeneous Malta's collective good rather than out

ALEXANDER FERNESIVS PARMÆ ET PLACENTIÆ PRINCEPS, GVBERNATOR ET
CAPITANEVS GENERALIS REGIONVM BELGICAR. SVB PHILIPPO.II.HISPA. REGE CATHOLIC.

Harman Muller excud.

Figure 7. Alexander Farnese, prince of Parma and Pacienza, c. 1590, print by
Harmen Jansz Muller (c.1538/9–1617). Appointed governor-general of the
Netherlands by Philip II, Parma was perhaps the greatest military mind of
his age, widely admired by allies and adversaries alike, both for arms and for
policy. Notice the FERNESIUS orthography, with which Marlowe may have
been acquainted. Image research, Corbis Art Source. Courtesy of La Biblioteca
Nacional. Copyright © Patrimonio Nacional.

of his own greed.[119] Hypocritical as we may perceive some of the Governor's actions to be from a Christian idealist perspective, *The Jew of Malta* places a Fernese—and through him, the rather severe approach to policy contemporaries had seen Parma employ so successfully—in a politically favorable light. For when, as a number of the play's commentators have seen, Fernese speaks the language of faith, whether early in the play when he tells Barabbas that "to staine our hands with blood / Is farre from us and our profession" (1.2. 144–45), or in its final lines, when we find him giving "due praise . . . / Neither to Fate nor Fortune, but to Heaven" (5.5.123–24), we see a figure in whom the guile of policy and the brute force of militarism walk together, as they had in Ferdinand the Catholic, beneath "the same cloak of religion."

Still another Fernese troubles *The Jew of Malta*, even as he troubled the Elizabethans. Among the "Spanish" candidates advanced to rule over an England returned to the Roman Catholic faith was Alexander's son, a second Ranuccio (1569–1622) (Figure 8). Ranuccio I of Parma and Piacenza would eventually inherit the Italian lands and titles associated with his family, earning a reputation for "cruelty" with his violent suppression of political opposition. But during the 1580s, when his father Alexander was so effectively pacifying the Netherlands and preparing for an assault on England, Ranuccio (or "Ranutio" in the orthography of Robert Persons), whose claim on the throne of Portugal had been set aside in favor of Philip II's, was, through his Lancastrian descent from John of Gaunt (whose daughter Philippa had married King João I of Portugal), being openly advanced as a candidate appropriate to succeed Elizabeth Tudor.[120] In order to "naturalize" his claim, William Cecil had, according to the Venetian ambassador, gone so far as to send his son Robert to the Low Countries as his personal emissary to Alexander Farnese with the goal of proposing a marriage of state between Ranuccio and Arabella Stuart, a union that would have circumvented the claim of James VI of Scotland while also appeasing the Spanish Hapsburgs.[121] The installation of Ranuccio I of England would have made the House of Parma the dynasty through which the English crown would pass in perpetuity—or for as long as the Farnese family could hold it by force.

Ultimately, Ranuccio's suit would be seen as less than ideal to the Hapburgs, who feared the prospect of an England ruled by a rival so potentially powerful and charismatic, and the claim of the Spanish Infanta, Isabel, was advanced instead. But can the evocation of these contemporary power politicians via Marlowe's invocation of the Farnese dynasty have been arbitrary? With an actual "Fernese" waiting in the wings, would not Marlowe have expected his type to be recognized?

Figure 8. *Ritratto di Ranuccio I Farnese*, attributed to Agostino Carracci (1557–1602). Courtesy of the Ministero per i Beni e le Attività Culturali—Galleria Nazionale di Parma.

"The Virtues of Our Countrymen"

In the end, the argument *The Jew of Malta* rather disjointedly unfolds, like that unmasked in contemporary critiques of English "Machevills" such as Leicester and Cecil, is truly Machiavellian in that it is one that upholds un-wavering national (dare we say rational?) self-interest. In the Malta through which Marlowe figures England, the subordination of external obligations to local political exigencies, the confiscation, conversion, and/or quite literal expulsion of any outsiders who, like the Jew, refuse to submit to the demands of the state, seem to be preconditions for the absolute realization of community sovereignty. The island of Malta is nearly undone by Barabbas's "stranger" chicanery; but Fernese's resourceful recovery and decisive leadership demonstrate that, like historical Machiavellians as various as Ferdinand the Catholic, Henry VIII, William Cecil, the Duke of Parma, and his heir Ranuccio the Cruel, the "sound Machevil" is as adept in the deployment force as in the deception of policy.

By conflating historical events, merging details from Hospitaller sieges of two different eras and exploiting the typological possibilities suggested by the family name of one of early modern Europe's most dominant political dynasties, Marlowe introduces concerns that could not otherwise have been explored. His compression of the histories of Rhodes and Malta suggests not so much disregard for the "facts" of history as an interest in the forces that drive them. This is also, as we will see, a representational strategy that may have been passed on to Shakespeare, who similarly conflates two famous battles for Cyprus in *Othello*. Rejecting the limitations of chronology for the "truer" lessons of typology, the playwright explores present tensions through the repetition and mobilization of historical exempla. It is a poetics of history that is very much of its day, and one that may have been suggested to Marlowe by Kyd's projection of Iberian events into the forward thrust of English history as portrayed in *The Spanish Tragedy*.

As Marlowe's younger contemporary Thomas Heywood (1570–1641) would observe of the English tragedian's practice, "If we represent a foreign history, the subject is so intended that in the lives of Romans, Grecians or others, either the virtues of *our countrymen* are extolled or their vices reproved."[122] If Marlowe wants us to understand his dark farce in terms of the tragic mode he advertises, it is in this sense that we may do so. Marlowe mirrors his own country in the world of his play: *The famouse tragedie of the Riche Jewe of Malta* probes English society at precisely the moment during which it is arriving at a new level of national awareness. Like Marlowe's England, the Malta of the play has been brought together in the face of a threat from without, and guided from within by a cultural elite that has learned to expend no ruth in safeguarding its integrity.

Thus contextualized, Marlowe's play seems to argue that the road to successful rule melds the public profession of spiritual obligation with the uncompromising exercise of power. It further suggests, and this it has in common

with the political polemics entrepreneurs like John Wolfe were busily repro-
ducing, that by utterly dominating a citizenry, while simultaneously offering
the promise of justice and liberty, and ruthlessly subordinating all international
obligation to national exigency, a state—that is, an "empire"—may be most
effectively governed. However arbitrary the establishment and maintenance of
power may appear in a world in which competing nations vie for international
prominence, the way of the Machiavel provides the surest route to survival. It
is the ethos of the nationalist extreme, a political philosophy shorn of external
obligations, judiciously limited, and ever shifting in its global commitments,
that prevails in *The Jew of Malta*.

And insofar as Marlowe's Maltese adopt "Spanish" methods in order
to solve the problems confronting their community—by appropriating the
wealth of the play's Jewish community, threatening forced conversion, and
quite literally expelling Barabbas the Jew—his play indulges yet another fantasy of English nationalism. For in the dynamic we observe between Barabbas,
Ithamore, and Fernese Marlowe stages the ethnic confusion presumed in Black
Legend discourse to lie at the heart of Spain's Mediterranean empire, a dark,
unruly energy that, but for Fernese's uncompromising command, might have
undone the island of Malta. Declining the higher thematics of Kyd's *Spanish
Tragedy*, *The Jew of Malta* leans in the direction of the paranoid vision offered
in xenophobic outbursts like the Dutch Church Libel and the ethnopoetic
hyperbole of *A Fig for the Spaniard*. It is the religiopolitical, and ultimately the
ethnonational, integrity of Malta (read: England) that the play values above
all else—secured by whatever means necessary. In its savage humor *The Jew of
Malta* may be the Renaissance play that reveals how profoundly these ethnop-
olitical anxieties had penetrated English culture. From Marlowe's argument
may have emerged a kind of answer—which was also an answer of kind.

CHAPTER FIVE

Shakespeare's Comical History

Messenger. Your honour's players, hearing your amendment,
   Are come to play a pleasant comedy. . . .
Sly. Marry, . . . Is not a comonty
   A Christmas gambold or a tumbling trick?
Bartholomew. No, my good lord; it is more pleasing stuff.
Sly. What, household stuff?
Bartholomew. It is a kind of history.
   —William Shakespeare, *The Taming of the Shrew*, c. 1593

Enter two old men:
1. Are you then travelling to the temple of *Eliza?*
2. Even to her temple are my feeble limmes travelling. Some cal her
   Pandora: some *Gloriana*, some *Cynthia*: some *Belphebe*, some *As-*
   traea: all by severall names to expresse severall loves: Yet all those
   names make but one celestiall body, as all those loves meete to
   create but one soule.
   —Thomas Dekker, *The Pleasant Comedie of Old Fortunatus*, c.
   1599

IF COMEDY CAN represent a kind of history, history, in turn, may be conceived as a kind of comedy.[1] Although his full title has not generated substantial critical comment, Shakespeare marked *The Comical History of the Merchant of Venice, or Otherwise Called the Jew of Venice* in terms of this generic crossing. In this seminal Elizabethan drama we are led (even as we watch Bassanio being led) to see the condition of the society it represents as being, in Hayden White's phrase, "purer, saner, and healthier," as a result of the onstage conflict we witness;[2] the play's discordant elements, represented most fully by Shylock, Portia's suitors, and Launcelot's Moor, "harmonize" only because they have been emasculated in the courtroom of Venice or excised from the green world of Belmont.[3] Much in the way that Marlowe's Malta is exorcised of its troublesome ethnicities, Shakespeare represents a Venetian social body that will be purged of "foreign spirits" in order to clarify who, finally, has earned admittance into the "gentle" society we sense has been English all along.[4] While *Merchant*'s "festive" structure may indeed produce, as C. L. Barber once suggested, "a heightened awareness of the relation between man and nature,"[5] to the degree that the Elizabethans constructed their state as England's "natural" social and political unit, especially insofar as Elizabeth Tudor was the figure around whom that social order was organized, we might also say that Shakespeare's first Venetian play brings a heightened awareness of the relationship between man, woman, and *nation*.

I argue here that *The Merchant of Venice* participates in the writing of English national identity, a process which involved, in Anthony Smith's formulation, "the reselection, recombination and recodification of previously existing values, symbols, memories and the like, as well as the addition of new cultural elements" by the poets, playwrights, and cultural elites of Shakespeare's generation.[6] By selecting key features from the wealth of flexible iconographic material that had come to be associated with the Elizabethan regime over the course of nearly forty years,[7] the play breathes new life into a tired set of cultural codes in ways that made them applicable and attractive to post-Armada contemporaries whose experience of discord made them deeply desirous of social harmony. Produced as it was at a time of intense national stress, with the Spanish war continuing to drain England's limited resources, a succession crisis looming, and the end of Tudor reign finally in sight, Shakespeare's *Comical History* reselects, recombines, and recodifies—much in the manner that Dekker's contemporary *Comedie of Old Fortunatus* obviously does in my second epigraph above—key elements of the Elizabethan symbolic economy in an effort to satisfy this wish dramatically.

At a moment during which England's promoters of the Black Legend were recombining the markers of religion, "race," and miscegenation that they linked discursively with Spain in order to construct that nation's essential difference, *The Merchant of Venice* transports tensions that Shakespeare's countrymen were themselves beginning to feel into a setting at once English and Italian.[8] As it does so, the play replicates and reveals the structuration upon which the "official story" of Tudor England had already begun to be erected. Manipulating raw material drawn from extant and emergent discourses of race, nationality, and ethnicity, Shakespeare reveals the racialist underpinnings of an inchoate English structure of feeling.[9] At the same time, he discovers how these discourses were being mobilized ethnopoetically in the face of England's ever-widening array of external contacts. More thoroughly than any other drama that I know, *The Comical History of the Merchant of Venice* embodies the ethnonationalist vision the Elizabethans were beginning to imagine for themselves. It is the progress of Shakespeare's play toward its harmoniously discordant finale—which itself embodies a kind of "progress"—that this chapter explores.

"Our Sacred Nation"

Much of the significant criticism of *The Merchant of Venice* has partaken of history as lived and experienced by the Jews of early modern Europe. Important study has opened connections between Shakespeare's play and England's mostly hidden Jewish community, while work on the history of the Jews of Venice and the Jews of North Africa and the Ottoman territories has revealed important connections with the wider Mediterranean. To survey this scholarship is to see that all of these histories—of the Jews of England, of the Jews of Venice, and of the Jews of the Mediterranean region—are linked, both to one another and to the long history of the Jews of Spain.[10]

The travails and travels of early modern Jewry provide a backdrop for this chapter; without their Diaspora there would be no *Merchant of Venice*. But rather than attempting to recover the identities of any "actual" historical actors—men like Roderigo Lopez and Hector Nuñez—who might have served Shakespeare as cultural models, I want instead to examine the relationship between history and comedy as implied by the play's full title. When we examine this particular instantiation of the dramatic genre Shakespeare explored from so many angles during his career, and bring these generic concerns—including the play's formal, symbolic, and rhetorical orchestrations—into relationship with the narrative modes through which the Elizabethans were shaping both the history of their monarch's reign and the "origins" of their nation, it appears evident that Shakespeare participates in a collective historiographical project.

Issues of ethnicity and nationality enter *The Comical History* most emphatically in 1.3, even as we are introduced to Shylock, whose assessment of

Antonio and his "Christian" practices thrusts into the foreground the opposing views of "peoplehood" explored in the play:[11]

> How like a fawning publican he looks.
> I hate him for he is a Christian;
> But more, for that in low simplicity
> He lends out money gratis, and brings down
> The rate of usance here with us in Venice.
> If I can catch him on the hip
> I will feed fat the ancient grudge I bear him.
> He hates our sacred nation, and he rails,
> Even there where merchants most do congregate,
> On me, my bargains, and my well-won thrift—
> Which he calls interest. Cursèd be my tribe
> If I forgive him. (1.3.36–47)

Shylock's aside serves to further the drama's action by condensing into a few lines his prior dealings with Antonio. But his dichotomizing view also reveals a particular understanding of the relationship between nationality, community, commerce, and faith. Comparing Antonio to a "fawning publican"—an imperial tax collector of the ilk the Gospels link with sinners and harlots—Shylock bases the terms of his hatred of Antonio on the fact that, as "a Christian," he is not a member of "my tribe." In the terms of the play's argument, the "problem" with this worldview is that Shylock does not identify himself as belonging to the citizenry of Venice (never mind that Venetian society has withheld the very possibility of full membership). Even though his most famous lines appeal to a common humanity, to read the "Jew of Venice" in conjunction with such a broadly humanistic perspective would be to align him with the Christian universalism it is his function in the play to abhor. For clearly, his "here with us" suggests exclusive membership in a "sacred nation"—which is to say that his primary identification is with a group residing within and yet apart from the society of Venice. As such, he considers himself to owe the Republic minimal or conditional allegiance.

In his appeal to sacred nationalism and tribal lineage, Shylock lays claim to a primordialist vision in which a covenant has been created between a particular people and a God who considers them "chosen." It is an arrangement based at once upon religion, hence its "sacredness," and kinship or heritage, lineal descent within a specific ethnonational community. Having been created by a deity in time immemorial, the pact with Shylock's nation cannot be altered or revoked: it is that it is. His tribe may be tested and tried, exiled or expelled, punished or rewarded, whether in accordance with the whim of an earthly magistrate or by the will of heaven—all possibilities that are implicit in Shylock's recognition, following Jessica's elopement with the Christian Lorenzo, "The curse never fell upon our nation till now—I never felt it till now" (3.1.72–73). But the tribe remains chosen.

As Shylock's relationship to his own people remains constant, so does his orientation toward their scripture. When he praises Portia as a "Daniel" in act 4, he does so because her interpretation of the law appears consonant with this chosenness. As emblematized, however, by his slippery and rather inept use of the story of Jacob and his uncle Laban's sheep to justify the practice of usury, Shylock is shown to be a not particularly skilled or knowledgeable interpreter of sacred history. Antonio's rebuff—"The devil can cite Scripture for his purpose" (1.3.94)—would probably have brought a nod of recognition among audiences catechized in the intense biblicism of English Protestantism. But in Shylock's world Jacob and Laban, like "father Abram" and the prophet Daniel, belong indubitably to "us" and manifestly not to "them"; Shylock is both unwilling to grant and incapable of granting the possibility that a relationship exists between a prophet of his tribe and another people, let alone that the terms of the sacred covenant could have changed.

The difference between Shylock's sacred nationalism and the understanding of nationhood Shakespeare valorizes comes more clearly into focus during the play's movement toward Shylock's courtroom confrontation with Antonio, who recognizes an obligation to the Venetian social contract as crystallized in his famous declaration of what Spenser called Venice's "policie of right":[12]

> The Duke cannot deny the course of law,
> For the commodity that strangers have
> With us in Venice, if it be denied,
> Will impeach the justice of the state,
> Since that the trade and profit of the city
> Consisteth of all nations. (3.3.26–31)

Over and against Shylock's particularist appeal to the sovereignty of ethnos, Antonio values an ethos represented by "the justice of the state." Both characters speak to a relationship between personal profit and the welfare of a larger community. But the argument and form of The Merchant of Venice, mirroring the logic of Christian culture at large, suggest that the terms of community have altered since the "original" covenant was made with the tribes of Israel.

In Antonio's discourse we confront a sense of nationality that extends beyond the domain of any essential chosenness and toward a post-Pentecost conception of "all nations." Such a "Republican" vision is not without its own exceptionalist orientations. But in this view of peoplehood, primacy of blood is displaced by a sense of group membership that becomes in ideal terms a matter of shared values and rational choice. And yet, in the world of the play, it is clear that not all blood is created equal—which leads us to the problem of Portia's suitors.

Foreign Spirits

Because *The Merchant of Venice* is justly notorious for its embodiment of both early modern anti-Semitism and the range of (mis)conceptions early modern Christians harbored with respect to the cultures of Judaism, we sometimes fail to notice that the Jews are not the only ethnic "kind" whose qualities are held up to scrutiny in the play. Long before we meet Shylock Shakespeare has begun to stage the differentiation of Europe's various *nationes* according to their reputed "humours."[13] Thus we hear of a Neapolitan prince who tends toward "coltish" sexual behavior, a County Palatine prone to "unmannerly sadness," an effeminate French lord who barely "pass[es] for a man" while embodying the flaws of "twenty husbands," and a young German of Saxony whose habitual drunkenness makes him "little worse than a man" and "little better than a beast." Closer to home, "the Scottish lord" with "a neighborly charity in him" who had "borrowed a box of the ear of the Englishman" (and whose "surety" rests in the "Frenchman"), presents an ethnopoetic characterization that is relevant to our discussion in several ways, alluding at once to stereotypical Scottish "thrift," the occasional hostility between Scotland and its neighbor to the south, and the series of French alliances through which the Scots attempted to stave off English expansionism. Finally, Shakespeare provides a nationally self-reflexive moment evoking both the somewhat nebulous condition of the English state during the later sixteenth century and the mercantilist energies we associate with the culture that produced our Renaissance drama.[14] For at the end of this list of potential mates we meet "Falconbridge, the young baron of England," who is stereotypically uninstructed and, though "a proper man's picture," so unsure of his own group identity that he has attempted to buy it in Italy, France, Germany, and "everywhere" (1.2.34–83).

Portia's catalogue of suitors puts into play codes at once generic and thematic: lest we forget (as we are likely to do at a number of junctures), the play's central problem will involve discerning which young couples are meant for each other. At the same time, the scene signals that the argument of this particular drama will cast the class- and gender-related themes characteristic of comedy at the intersection of communal identification and ethnic difference. But whereas the groups enumerated in act 1, scene 2, are evoked through the burlesqued winks and nods of Nerissa's reportage,[15] the nations most thoroughly scrutinized in the drama are represented by the two suitors Portia meets in the "flesh," the Princes of Arragon and Morocco, and even more emphatically by her courtroom adversary, Shylock. It cannot by now escape notice that *The Comical History* raises the specter of Spain. For all three of these figures embody spirits that the early moderns associated with Iberia: Catholic Arragon, Moorish Morocco, Jewish Shylock.

When Morocco and Arragon enter the world of Belmont, they arrive, like the strangers we have previously heard described, wearing indices of public meaning in the form of the cultural stereotypes with which (and against which) Shakespeare's representation will play.[16] We have already been prepared for Morocco's arrival: Portia herself draws attention to the prince's color in such a way as to make clear her disinclination to choose him, whether he plays her father's game wisely or not. "If he have the condition of a saint and the complexion of a devil," she says—prefiguring the demonization of the Jew as scripture-citing "devil" we noted a moment ago—"I had rather he should shrive me than wive me" (1.2.109–10). Portia may be momentarily disarmed when Morocco openly confronts the racialist distaste he assumes she must bear toward him: "Mislike me not for my complexion, / The shadowed livery of the burnished sun, / To whom I am a neighbor and near bred" (2.1.1–3). But fortunately (in the play's logic of "race"), by deferring to the terms of her paternal bond, Portia will be relieved of the uncomfortable and uncourtly possibility that the prince might have to endure her essentialist rebuff.[17] Although Morocco provides an impressive résumé, having slain "the Sophy and a Persian prince / That won three fields of Sultan Suleiman" (2.1.25–26), he is no Othello come to woo; or perhaps more to the point, Portia is no Desdemona. For in spite of this Moor's eloquent delivery and valiant acts, he has been found eminently resistible—perhaps because, as Arthur Little has pointed out, the humanism he offers in his initial appeal to blood is more than canceled out by the boast that he has been loved by "The best regarded virgins of [his] clime" (2.1.10).[18] While confirming that, in spite of the fact that he bleeds red, Morocco is really a lascivious Moor beneath the skin, his exchange with Portia also makes explicit the tension between wealth, breeding, and miscegenation that simmers in each of our visits to Belmont, as it does during Shylock's strained parable of Laban's "wooly breeders" and "parti-coloured lambs" (1.3.75–84).[19]

When Morocco returns in act 2, scene 7, only to have Portia make the choice that is as overdetermined by Elizabethan racialism as it is by any source tale that might stand behind Shakespeare's dramatization,[20] we are not any more surprised than she at his proclamation, "A golden mind stoops not to shows of dross. / I'll then nor give nor hazard aught for lead" (2.7.20–21). Yet his somewhat stock response is rendered more interesting when he reads the golden casket's inscription. For as he does so, he situates his marital venture within a context as global as the reach of Antonio's traffic:

> "Who chooseth me shall gain what many men desire."
> Why, that's the lady! All the world desires her.
> For from the four corners of the earth they come
> To kiss this shrine, this mortal breathing saint.
> The Hyrcanian deserts and the vasty wilds
> Of wild Arabia are as thoroughfares now
> For princes to come view fair Portia.
> The watery kingdom, whose ambitious head
> Spits in the face of heaven, is no bar
> To stop the foreign spirits, but they come
> As oe'r a brook to see fair Portia. (2.7.37–48)

To the European pretenders enumerated in act 1, scene 2, we can now add, or so Morocco implies, suitors from the east, beyond the "deserts" of Hyrcania and "the vasty wilds / Of wild Arabia." The sea that lies between Belmont and these princes provides "no bar" to the play's "foreign spirits," who "come / As o'er a brook to see fair Portia." Certainly the reputation for beauty and wealth (or wealth and beauty) that draws these suitors to Portia's salon from "the four corners of the earth" suggests a conventional romantic plot, and to the degree that the play is about the uniting of rich-girl Portia with poor-boy Bassanio, we may view it in relation to this archetype.[21] But the language Morocco employs as he attempts to flatter Portia also recommends more timely historical possibilities.

It has been suggested that Morocco's reference to "The watery kingdom, whose ambitious head / Spits in the face of heaven" is meant to evoke Spain,[22] whose empire had, since the Portuguese incorporation of the early 1580s, become the first in history to touch the seven seas. Though far too much ambiguity attends Shakespeare's figure to claim this unequivocally, the ambition topos we have seen so often in Black Legend discourse does resonate in a way that suggests the global reach of imperial Spain. Indeed, Philip II's possessions—including the Belearics, Sardinia, Sicily, and Naples, as well as the outposts of Tangier, Cueta, Melilla, Oran, and Tunis—would have stood between Morocco and his Venetian enterprise. But whether or not this particular commonplace plays a shaping role in the play's conflict, by placing a Moroccan prince in *The Merchant of Venice* Shakespeare creates an important Spanish connection—especially in conjunction with the subsequent appearances of his rival suitor Arragon and Portia's courtroom adversary Shylock, called "the Jew of Venice" in the play's full title.

Partly because of attempts by the Spanish and their allies (which included polities such as Finale, Genoa, Milan, Mantua, Padua, Parma, the Presidios of Tuscany, and the Austrian Hapsburg dominions) to control land and sea access to Venice and its commercial affiliates, the Elizabethans had been forced to reassess their relationships with the kingdoms of North Africa and the Levant. Although Morocco was among the states it looked to most often in its efforts to circumvent Iberia's dominance of the American and African trades,[23] what may be most suggestive about the scene is that here we find Morocco looking desirously toward England. Just as he is about to try Portia's golden casket, the prince remarks:

> They have in England
> A coin that bears the figure of an angel
> Stamped in gold, but that's insculped upon;
> But here an angel in a golden bed
> Lies all within. Deliver me the key.
> Here do I chose, and thrive as I may. (2.7.55–60)

Surely it is significant that, in a play that foregrounds its Venetian setting as a nexus of international trade, Morocco would single out an English coin as a figure of Portia's beauty. For coinage, among "emblems of difference" including flags, totems, and ritual objects of various kinds, signifies powerfully as an icon of national sovereignty, prestige, and identity.[24] In point of fact, Elizabethan England did mint "A coin that bears the figure of an angel / Stamped in gold," worth ten shillings. But the far more common and desirable late Tudor currency—including the twenty-shilling pound and the thirty-shilling sovereign—displayed the likeness of Elizabeth herself (Figure 9).[25] While Gustav Ungerer has pointed out that there is considerable irony at play in the scene, because these English coins would likely have been minted

Figure 9. Elizabethan gold angel (1582–84), 10s. 0d., and Elizabethan gold pound (1594–96) 20s. 0d. By permission of the Folger Shakespeare Library.

from Moroccan gold[26]—if not from Spanish plunder—Heather Dubrow has drawn our attention to the possibility that "the fear that foreign coinage was contaminating the English system while English coinage was being drained abroad figure the fears of contamination and loss that construct xenophobia."[27] To a certain extent, she observes, "early fears of miscegenation, as well as longer standing fears of class conflict," were "staged in the struggle between 'fine,' or unalloyed, and base coins" (189). Conceived during a time contemporaries identified with "the dearth," a conjuncture in which, as Conrad Fleer has shown, "there was general agreement that the main problem of the English economy was the shortage of money, which seemed to go hand in hand with rising prices,"[28] it seems clear that *Merchant* plays upon these concerns. At once economic *and* ethnic, these tensions may be most expressly embodied in both the longing eye Morocco casts on Portia and his insistence that "A golden mind stoops not for shows of dross" (2.7.20).

But what may be most significant about Morocco's invocation in formal terms is that, much in the manner that the play's catalogue of foreign suitors refracts our attention from Venice back to England, this scene bids us look northward.[29] Here, as throughout the play, the language and symbolic economy Shakespeare selects in constructing Portia are drawn from a well-established repertoire that had been employed throughout the reign of Elizabeth Tudor. As surely as the coinage invoked by Morocco requires us to picture England, Portia and her charmed life at Belmont serve, as Janet Adelman has observed, as the play's "xenophobic stand-in for England with its virgin-queen."[30]

Portia's attractions are especially reminiscent of the younger Elizabeth, whose allures had been blazoned by the generation of writers who preceded Shakespeare, Marlowe, and Kyd. Thomas Dekker's *Old Fortunatus* would soon recall the salad days of England's national Romance, with his two "Old Men" recollecting the "severall names" by which "Eliza" had "expresse[d] severall loves" in "but one celestiall body" (prologue, lines 1–6). Dekker's rather belated evocation of Elizabeth's "severall" guises underscores—much in the manner of ritualistic public presentments such as George Peele's "Decensus Astraeae," which constructed the queen as "Our faire Astraea, our Pandora faire, / Our faire Eliza, or Zabeta faire"[31]—how thoroughly codified these representations had become by the final decade of her reign. Especially suggestive in Peele's encomium is the Pandora figure, an identity that immediately calls to mind Elizabeth's symbolic role as dispenser of gifts, a part analogous to the casket game over which Portia presides in Shakespeare's play.

Attractive as complex allegories such as George Gascoinge's Kenelworth Entertainment were during the reign of Elizabeth I, the cult of Elizabeth's perpetual virginity—most famously developed by Spenser, even as he was struggling to resolve the ethnic impasse presented by Irish manner and custom—acquired still greater cultural resonance as the arguments that she should submit to a marriage of state in order to ensure a native succession lost their relevance.[32] Any number of Elizabethan poets and poetasters continued to partake of this representational wellspring, which had begun to flow even as Elizabeth Tudor ascended the English throne, reselecting and recombining her various icons even as her child-bearing years became a distant memory.[33]

Morocco's pilgrimage to Belmont and his courtly advances upon Portia, whom he had earlier addressed as his "gentle queen" (2.1.12), thus recodify flexible iconographic elements that had by the 1590s become features of the conventional (and by then somewhat tired) encomia offered by the international cast of ambassadors, merchants, and flatterers who for nearly forty years had been drawn to Elizabeth's court as to a site of pilgrimage. From the "virgin hue" (2.7.22) of the silver casket Morocco does not choose, through his observation that "All the world desires her. / From the four corners of the earth they come / To kiss the shrine, this mortal breathing saint" (2.7.38–40), to his reflection upon her as "an angel in a golden bed" lying "within" (2.7.58–59), the whole speech would have been as appropriately addressed to "E-L-I-S-A-B-E-T-H-A R-E-G-I-N-A," after the mode of Sir John Davies's *Astraea* hymns, as to the mistress of Belmont. In point of fact, Davies's eighth hymn so thoroughly mirrors the courtship subplot of Shakespeare's Belmont scenes that it bears quotation:

To All the Princes of Europe

E urope, the earth's sweet Paradise,
L et all thy kings that would be wise,
I n politique devotion;
S ayle hither to observe her eyes,
A nd marke her heavenly motion.
B rave Princes of this civill age,
E nter into this pilgrimage;
T his saint's tongue is an oracle,
H er eye hath made a Prince a page,
A nd works each day a miracle.
R aise but your lookes to her, and see
E ven the true beames of majestie,
G reat Princes, mark her duly;
I f all the world you do survey,
N o forehead spreades so bright a ray,
A nd notes a Prince so truly.[34]

To go a step further, Portia may condense the play's English and Italian interests by embodying a contemporary commonplace that glorified the Venetian city-state in much the manner that the English praised Gloriana: as Lewis Lewkenor would observe in *The Commonwealth and Government of Venice* (1599), "the rest of the whole world honoreth her [Venice] with the name of Virgin, a name though in all places most sacred and venerable, yet in no place more dearly and religiously to be reverenced then with us, who have thence derived our blessednesse."[35]

Surely Shakespeare's Venetian lady recombines these culturally specific metaphorics while encouraging their multivocalic extension. If we imagine a world in which "public passion for interpreting plays and pamphlets in terms of England's embroilment on the Continent was so intense" that a contemporary like Thomas Nashe could "mention *bread* to be taken as referring to *Bred*en in the Netherlands,"[36] the mistress of *Bel*mont begs to be read as a type of *Bel*phoebe. As a multivocal figure she also has much in common with *Bel*-imperia, the imperial "prize" of *The Spanish Tragedy*, and, if we extend the verbal echo into Marlowe's world, she may even recall Malta's *Bella*mira. Such a reading takes us into the dark recesses of Elizabethan allegory, a place we do not commonly expect to find Shakespeare. But if we situate Shakespeare's text squarely within his age, allowing him to sample Elizabethan public discourses even as he transforms them, the figures of Portia-Belmont (or Portia-Venice) and Elizabeth-England begin to flicker with the sort of compound significance we may associate with so may of the era's representations. Though perhaps not in a manner so openly allegorical as Kyd's Spanish princess or Spenser's many-personed heroine, Shakespeare's Venetian lady serves a similarly mul-tivocal function in *The Merchant of Venice*.[37] To the degree that the mistress of Belmont represents the bounty of Venetian Empire *and* the English body politic, she is quite in the mold of Bel-imperia.[38] And in a strong sense, *Portia* is a *port*: like the Rialto itself, she emblematizes the riches "many men desire," even as the green world over which she presides suggests the idyllic world of the Elizabethan court as fashioned by so many of her courtier-poets.

Although he receives less attention than Morocco in Shakespeare's script, Arragon, the final suitor with whom Portia must dispense before she can en-tertain Bassanio, is in some ways represented as more "foreign" than his North African counterpart. Forgoing his predecessor's humanist appeal to "blood" and turning away from the gold "Because [he] will not jump with common spirits / And rank [himself] with the barbarous multitudes," Arragon is drawn irresistibly to the "silver treasure-house" (2.9.51–53). His immediate attraction to the casket suggests the commonplace of Spain's obsessive covetousness of the New World resources upon which its imperial economy depended, as well as the rapid rise of American silver production that was transforming the economy of England as it was the entire global marketplace. Whereas the early phases of Spain's colonial venture had been fueled by much-storied quantities of Aztec and Inca gold, by the last quarter of the sixteenth century the discov-ery of massive silver veins at Zacatecas in Mexico and at Potosí in Peru had changed the hue of the world bullion market.[39]

The presumption that such blessings stemmed from divine sanction of Spain's imperial mission had produced among the Spanish—or so their Eu-ropean competitors argued incessantly—a legendary national overconfidence that often registered among their neighbors as haughtiness. The commonplace is clearly present in Shakespeare's lines:

"Who chooseth me shall get as much as he deserves"—
And well said too, for who shall go about
To cozen fortune, and be honorable
Without the stamp of merit? Let none presume

To wear an undeservèd dignity.
O, that estates, degrees and offices
Were not derived corruptly, and that the clear honour
Were purchased by the merit of the wearer!
How many then should cover that stand bare,
How many be commanded that command?
How much low peasantry would then be gleaned
From the true seed of honour, and how much honour
Picked from the chaff and ruin of the times
To be new varnished? (2.9.36–48)

While arrogant Arragon's speech includes some generic reflection about honor and merit, his courtship scene is rife with dramatic irony. On the one hand, English audiences "know" that this humorously repulsive egoist does not deserve *their* Portia. After all, hadn't Elizabeth's father, as recalled by John Foxe, demonstrated the necessity of rejecting England's entangling relationship with Aragon? On the other, they suspect that Spain's native "honour" and "command" have been "purchased" with wealth co-opted and coerced from the Americas. Arragon's superciliousness—his disdain for "the fool multitude" (2.9.25) and readiness "to assume desert" (2.9.50)—thus plays upon stock conceits of Spanish greed and hubris. While the Hispanophobic temper of Arragon's lines is mild in comparison with many of the representations that circulated during the 1590s, his "ambitious pride" would have seemed "natural" to audiences that had been immersed in such propaganda. Hadn't they experienced as much themselves during their ongoing national conflict?[40] This late in the decade the ethos expressed by Shakespeare's character, like that of his earlier comic figure Don Adriano de Armado in *Love's Labour's Lost*, would have given many in his audience about what they expected—from a Spaniard.[41]

All of this is to say that by constructing Portia as a character forced by birth and circumstance to receive the "foreign spirits" catalogued in act 2, *The Merchant of Venice* entertains—but only entertains—the possibility of the kind of foreign dynastic union Shakespeare's English sovereign had spent nearly forty years rejecting. In a manner that recalls the marital politics of the younger Gloriana as celebrated by poets as various as Gascoigne, Peele, Davies, and others, and recorded so authoritatively by Camden, an international cast of potential allies and traditional adversaries—represented most (im)potently by Morocco and Arragon—are alike dismissed in favor of the local favorite, Bassanio. The play thus inscribes an argument mirroring the "comic" historical vision that had already become the official story of the Elizabethan state as pronounced and promoted in emblems as public and various as court pageants, encomiastic verses, chronicle histories, and royal coinage.

"Civilitie, Kindnesse, and Courtesie"

Precisely why Shakespeare would put forth Bassanio as the worthiest investment among those who seek Portia's hand has always presented a problem; when we meet him he is debt-ridden, utterly dependent upon the kindness of friends (of his own kind), and untutored (or un-Tudored) in the gentle ways of Belmont. It may be that Portia's attraction to him is meant to signal nothing more than a lover's irrational desire: "The brain may devise laws for the blood," she says, "but a hot temper leaps over a cold decree" (1.2.15–17). Or perhaps the play reverses the kind of "miracle" we witnessed a moment ago in Sir John Davies's hymn, "To All the Princes of Europe," making a prince of a page.[42] But next to Bassanio, Portia finds her other suitors, each of whom has been dismissed for an inappropriate tick of national character, wanting. Although any of them would have represented a more appropriate match in terms of rank and social status—and though each had brought with him the prospect of a potentially powerful political union—in Portia's eyes, only penniless Bassanio brings to Belmont the kind of gentle (national) style that moves her.

Recalling that the English Renaissance held "a widespread fascination with the uses of stylized identity as a social tool," Frank Whigham has drawn our attention to some of the ways in which *The Merchant of Venice* "anatomizes this social rhetoric through parallel focuses of inclusion and exclusion."[43] In this world, where "material and aesthetic distinctions take on almost moral force," all of the suitors save one "are shown to be defective in style," and Portia's "mockery of them allows her to demonstrate her own impeccable credentials."[44] Thus "Bassanio's choice of the leaden casket" culminates in "the demonstration of stylistic class affinities" through which "Bassanio wins marital bliss, a splendid fortune, and solid class grounding."[45] Germane as these observations are, they tell only part of Bassanio's story. For *The Merchant of Venice* arrives at a moment when class association in England has become complicated by a new sense of *national* awareness. Not previously thought of as a seat of style—save perhaps during the era of international humanist florescence over which Katherine of Aragon presided—with the Virgin Queen as the focus of their courtly imaginings, the English sought during the course of her reign a reconstruction of their nation along more genteel lines. To a certain degree they were successful. As one French observer wrote, "In so much that England may by good right he accounted at this day the very Sanctuarie of all civilitie, kindnesse and courtesie."[46]

Edmund Spenser's *View of the State of Ireland* reveals some of the discursive processes by which the English undertook this national refashioning through an intense scrutiny of cultural difference. Spenser's dialogue locates the "barbarous rudenes" of the Irish in "those nations from whom that country was first peopled."[47] Since "the difference in manners and customs doth follow the difference of nations and people" (54), he argues that social degeneration may be observed most fully in Iberia, whose people are singled out as exemplifying the ill effects of an unfortunate mixing of ethnicities. It is a mark of Hibernian folly that the Irish, like their Celtic kindred the Scots, would "thinke to enoble themselves by wresting their auncientry from the Spaniard," Spenser writes,

> who is unable to derive himself from any in certaine. For the Spaniard that now is, is come from . . . as rude and savage nations . . . as there may be gathered by course of ages, and view of their owne history, (though they therein labour much to enoble themselves) scarce any drop of the old Spanish blood left in them. . . . And yet after all these Moores and Barbarians, breaking over out of Africa, did finally possesse all Spaine, or most part thereof, and did tread, under their heathenish feete, whatever they found there standing. The which, though after they were beaten out by Ferdinando of Arragon and Elizabeth his wife, yet they were not so cleansed, but that through the marriages which they had made, and mixture with the people of the land, during their long continuance there, they had left no pure drop of Spanish blood, no more than of Roman or Scythian. So that of all nations under heaven (I suppose) the Spaniard is the most mingled.[48]

Spenser's *View* also links Ireland to Africa. These African connections are shifting ones, however. In the earliest versions of Spenser's ethnography, Africa serves Ireland as a source of residual civility, exemplified by the fact of Irish literacy, which is recognized to predate that of its neighbors. When Eudoxius comments that the Irish are prone to "forge and falsifye everie thing as they liste" because they have been "alwaies without Lettres," Irenius corrects him. "Irelande hathe had the use of letters verie ancientlye, and longe before Englande," he responds, "from the Africans, whoe were always lettered and much resemblinge the Iryshe."[49] As Sujata Iyengar has usefully observed, by the time the *View* is redacted for its 1633 publication this positive association has disappeared. Now Irish lineage is shorn of its African roots, and Hibernians are taught letters by "the generous Gaules." While it is unclear just who these "Africans" are (Spenser offers the Irish Egyptian, Moorish, and Carthaginian antecedents), as Iyengar points out, we glimpse here a moment of apparent fluidity in which "skin color is, if not irrelevant, certainly far less important than their religious affiliation ('heathenishe'), their national origin (Moors, Africans, Carthaginians) and their language and culture" (92). But as Ann Rosalind Jones and Peter Stallybrass note, "One of the main aims of the English in the late sixteenth century was to disarticulate the Irish from the Spanish."[50] While they had been constructed initially as "very honorable people" in comparison to the wild Irish, the Spanish are reimagined as "of all nations under heaven . . . the most mingled, and most uncertaine" or, in an alternate copy, the "most bastardly."[51] Perhaps as a result of England's internalization of Black Legend perspectives between the years in which Spenser began his ethnological reflections and the *View*'s publication, "Africanness" recedes in the text while Hispanicity comes to the fore. As Barbara Fuchs has shown, the view of Spain that Irenius voices "foregrounds a diachronic view of Spain that serves to neutralize Irish recourse to Spanish allies while underscoring Irish otherness" and, insofar as "Spanish customs are collapsed into Moorish or African ones," transforms "Irish claims to Spanish origins into markers of racial, as well as cultural, otherness."[52] From a multiplicity of genealogical antecedents, then, a sort of primordial stew of Hibernian ethnicity, Spenser located the ethnos of Spain as a probable source of Irish recalcitrance and incivility.

Although in one breath Spenser voices an attenuated monogenism, the belief in a common human root—"I think there is no nation now in Christendome, nor much further, but is mingled, and compounded of others"—he warns in another that the mixing of peoples may be effected only under a government capable of providing "due order of discipline and good rule."[53] In this construction, which opposes Ireland's wrongly mingled "manners and customes" with "such sweet civility as England affords" as a land ruled by a "Sacred Maiestie" who is "by nature full of mercy and clemencie,"[54] we glimpse the logic of ethnos in which *The Merchant of Venice* is also grounded. "Native" behaviors, traditions, and values, while not necessarily a function of genetics—all nations have been mingled, after all—are esteemed as having failed to congeal in the manner most appropriate to "civilitie" as exemplified by the English nation. Thus the remedy for the Irish situation can only be to ensure that any future "intermingling" will be done in a context so disciplined as "to reduce things into order of English law" and lead the Irish toward a knowledge commensurate with "English inhabitants and customes."[55] Spenser's colonialist calculus thus mirrors the limits of intermingling that Shakespeare allows in his *Comical History*. Although contemporary theories of color might argue that royal "light sciental" could "blanch an Ethiop" (or an Irishman) into civility, this is not a power the queen of Belmont wishes to wield.[56] The potential ethnonational admixtures offered Portia are all rejected in favor of the suitor who comes closest to her own civil values, customs, and hue, even though he is far from an ideal match in terms of the international political and social connections characteristically valued in European dynasty building.

In Belmont's second problematic match, presumably because her "native" gentility is borne out by her "adventurous" use of Shylock's patrimony, Jessica demonstrates sufficient style to gain admission to the charmed community, simultaneously manifesting her class allegiance and choosing Venetian nationality over Jewish ethnicity.[57] What appears to be an immature or resentful squandering of inheritance from one angle—especially the ceremonious way in which her mother's ring is dispatched in Genoa—looks from another perspective like a performance of group loyalty and shared values. Especially given that, in Jewish culture, faith and blood are conceived as being transmitted through the mother, in selling off the symbol of this important bond Jessica embraces not merely the social mores and religion of her Christian husband, so famously expressed in the Pauline notion that she will be saved by him;[58] she also embraces his nationality—an identity based not on the blood or culture of her father but on a social choice that is (in the world of the play) eminently rational.

Structurally, Jessica's options are not unlike those available to English Catholics, who were required to subordinate, if not trade outright, their allegiance to a universal Madonna in favor of a more local English one. In point of fact, Jessica makes the kind of choice the Reformation had demanded of English subjects, whose place in the new society could only be guaranteed by the rejection of inherited transnational traditions supported by Mother Church in favor of developing national ones. Like Portia, she deems the local candidate most appropriate and most attractive; like Bassanio— who is led by right reason (and Portia's will) rather than by the presumption of monetary gain—she ventures all in order to perform loyalty and civility. And yet, rational choice and social style are not the sole determining factors. There remains the issue of Jessica's "kindness." For like Bassanio, who is "best deserving a fair lady" (1.2.99), and unlike Morocco, Arragon, and her father Shylock, Jessica too is "fair."

"A Kind of Hard Conscience"

While the figural mode we associate with the royal cult generates meaning throughout *The Merchant of Venice*, discussions of the play's allegorical register have tended to focus more on universal thematics than on the culturally specific representational practices embodied in Portia.[59] But its Christian universalist strains notwithstanding, *The Merchant of Venice* is much invested in particularism.[60] Its two most ardent advocates of "we're all the same under the skin" humanism, Shylock and Morocco, are also those from whom the bounties and kinship of Venice/Belmont are most ceremoniously withheld. From act 2 onward, the play begins to incorporate a discourse of color, the implications of which are both theological and racial. In his fit of "conscience," Launcelot worries: "To be ruled by my conscience I should stay with the Jew my master who, God bless the mark, is a kind of devil; and to run away from the Jew I should be ruled by the fiend who, saving your reverence, is the devil himself. Certainly the Jew is the very devil incarnation; and in my conscience, my conscience is but a kind of hard conscience to offer to counsel me to stay with the Jew. The fiend gives the more friendly counsel. I will run fiend. My heels are at your commandment. I will run" (2.2.16–25). Wracked with guilt and uncomfortably marked by his membership in the play's Jewish household, Launcelot must flee if he is to reclaim his identity from "the devil" with whose figurative "blackness" he risks becoming tainted should he fail to extricate himself. Even more problematically, Shylock's own daughter reemphasizes these issues as she flees home and the father who has presumably raised her. But to focus on the play's anagogical "unity" is to turn a deaf ear to the far more literal evocations of color that run throughout the work. For in addition to linking them to the powers of darkness, *The Merchant of Venice*, as James Shapiro has shown, rehearses an early modern tendency that "pointed to the Jews' dark or 'black' skin color as a marker of their racial difference."[61] It is a construction of difference we cannot ignore, for the distancing of its Christian characters from the "taint" of color becomes an important aim of the play.

The problem of Jessica's vaunted "fairness," as well as her receptivity to Christian conversion, complicates the play's color question. How can Jessica be "fair," as Lorenzo and Gratiano remark a number of times in act 2, scene 4—and thus a suitable mate for the "white" Christian Venetian Lorenzo—if her father Shylock is neither fair in his dealings with Antonio nor fair in his pigmentation? Mary Janell Metzger has substantially advanced our understanding of the terms of Jessica's integration into the world of the play, observing that Jessica "nullifies the claims of filial attachment by insisting that she is a different kind of Jew, one whose manners take precedence over blood and who thus can see the truth of Christianity."[62] Jessica's sanctification is therefore made possible by a "marriage [that] reconstitutes her as a body, for according to Christian ecclesiastical and legal authorities, a woman was incorporated into the body of her husband in marriage, becoming both one with and subject to him" (57). While the theological justification for Jessica's conversion is obviously consistent with both universalist and more culturally specific understandings of the play, as important to the meaning of *The Merchant of Venice* may be the national-ideological implications of her match, which reflect important developments in Elizabethan society (as well as Shakespeare's efforts to bend the material of this play toward the genre of comedy). For if, as Metzger argues, "Jessica's conversion from dark infidel to fair Christian" requires "the conversion of her body in distinctly racial and gendered terms" (57), we are left with the racialist implications of the play's denial of a like "salvation" to Launcelot's Moorish lover. Indeed, it is in the context of their discussion of Jessica's incorporation into Christian society that Lorenzo raises the problem of Launcelot's issue. Taking exception to Launcelot's comments about Jessica's conversion, Lorenzo turns the tables on him, claiming "I shall answer that better to the commonwealth than you can the getting up of the Negro's belly. The Moor is with child by you, Launcelot" (3.5.31–33). Private indiscretion here becomes a public matter: miscegenation affects the "commonwealth."[63]

While Shakespeare will emphasize the thematics of interracial marriage more thoroughly in his later Venetian play, *The Comical History* links both its Moroccan prince and Launcelot's Moor to Shylock's Jewish ethnicity even as Jessica reports that she has heard her father

> swear
> To Tubal and to Chus, his countrymen,
> That he would rather have Antonio's flesh
> Than twenty times the value of the sum
> That he did owe him. (3.2.283–87)

In recent years a number of scholars, Lynda Boose among them, have puzzled over how we should read "the odd racial geography within which Jessica denominates her father by referring to Shylock's 'countrymen' as 'Tubal and . . . Chus'—the latter being the name which Elizabethans widely recognized as the original black African" (38).[64] By yoking Shylock with Chus (Cush in the more common orthography), Shakespeare participates in the racialization of Jewish ethnicity that was a feature of several early modern discourses regarding the

Jews. As Shapiro observes, "The conventional critical view that what sets Shylock apart is his religion has deflected attention away from the more complex ways in which Shakespeare situates Jews within a larger, confused network of national and racial otherness. For Shakespeare's contemporaries, Jews were not identified by their religion alone but by national and racial affiliations as well. We ought to remember that this is a play in which the heroine laughingly dismisses her dark-skinned suitor, the Prince of Morocco, with the words, 'Let all of his complexion choose me so.' "[65]

That genealogies of faith and blood compete in the play becomes increasingly evident with each foreign spirit that enters Portia's world. But although the Prince of Morocco's universalist appeal evokes consanguinity, Shylock's primordialist invocations of "our sacred nation" and "my tribe" (1.3.46, 52), along with the many puns on "kind" and "kindness" that follow in the scene (1.3.137, 138, 139, 149, 174), emphasize the play's modulation from the key of "friendship," which Antonio and Bassanio remain insistent upon hearing in Shylock's discourse, to that of lineage, patrimony, and, to the degree that the sacred may be associated with a particular geographical space, also to land. Though in an ideal sense the New Dispensation should have erased the association of blood, faith, and territory from the salvific formula, as Christianity became institutionalized in specific nationalist contexts, the constellation of values linking nation and salvation often returned with a vengeance.[66]

If for Elizabethan England the nexus of Jewish "national and racial affiliations" was often Iberia, we ought also to remember that the Spains were equally a nexus for Elizabethan contacts with Africa and Africans. Recent studies have also shown that Shakespeare's characterization of the Prince of Morocco may have been informed by knowledge of actual Muslims encountered by the English in the ports of North Africa and the Levant, or perhaps even on the streets of London.[67] As Kim Hall observes, "England began its involvement in what was known as the Barbary and Guinea trades during Elizabeth's reign when merchants who dealt in Iberian trade began to see and act on the weaknesses of Portugal's hold on Africa" (17). The Moroccan trade in particular brought the English into contact with both Iberians and Africans "because it crossed the Spanish routes to the Indies, which meant that English traders would have had access to the slave trade in Spain."[68] Even during times of intense Anglo-Spanish hostility, a number of English traders—often in the face of protests from their own government—took great pains to keep the Iberian trade alive, for there they gained legitimate access to the resources, material, mineral, and human, that the combined fleets of Spain and Portugal made available even as they were able to profit mightily from the distribution of

English goods.[69] An adjunct of this experience was that Englishmen began to publish reports describing the diverse ethnic environment they encountered, adding new textual evidence to the store of knowledge about Spain's "mixed" heritage that England had acquired during centuries of prior Iberian involvement. Amplifying the perception that Spain and Africa were linked was the fact that English privateering fleets returning from Spanish waters were disembarking evidence of Iberia's African connections in England's home ports. In the tense religiopolitical climate of the later sixteenth century, this ethnic complexity began to register far more negatively than in earlier generations.

And as the series of royal letters and proclamations issued between 1596 and 1601 treating the importation of Africans into the realm confirms, the Elizabethans were not above considering the Spanish solution (that is, expulsion) to their "diversity" problems:

> Whereas the Queen's majesty, tendering the good and welfare of her own natural subjects, greatly distressed in these hard times of dearth, is highly discontented to understand the great number of Negroes and blackamoors which (as she is informed) are carried into this realm since the troubles between her highness and the King of Spain; who are fostered and powered here, to the great annoyance of her own liege people that which co[vet] the relief which these people consume, as also for that the most of them are infidels having no understanding of Christ or his Gospel: hath given a special commandment that the said kind of people shall be with all speed avoided and discharged out of this her majesty's realms.[70]

The black/white binary Elizabeth appears to invoke has received ample critical attention.[71] But the "Spanish connection" the document also reveals has not. The presence in the realm of these "Negroes and blackamoors"—"negars and blackamoores" in alternate transcriptions—had come as the result of continuing English privateering raids in Spanish America.[72] Certainly African slaves had been entering England since well before the 1590s. Captain John Lok's return from Guinea with "Five blacke Moores" during the reign of Mary and Philip provided a memorable example of such an importation.[73] But their number had grown sufficiently—"since the troubles between her highness and the King of Spain"—for them now to be seen as a disruptive, "infidel" presence rather than a profitable one. Complicating the issue was the fact that these displaced Africans, initially taken as prisoners of war, were, like the strangers frequenting London's Dutch and French churches, suspected of harboring Spanish loyalties.[74] Like the Prince of Morocco and Launcelot's

Moorish lover and child—who, unlike the "fair" Jessica, are denied a place in gentle (and gentile) Belmont—these descendants of Cush had become ethnic undesirables in the Elizabethan Commonwealth. Again we should note the irony that Protestant England's answer to this Hispano-African problem was to issue an edict of expulsion, much in the vein of the resolution Catholic Spain had forced upon its Jews and Moors in 1492, and would resort to again in 1609 in order to solve its *morisco* problem.[75]

Shakespeare's choice to exclude "blackamoors" from Portia's fiefdom thus suggests that important structural tensions had begun to exert themselves in England as the war with the Spanish continued. The calculus of ethnicity and nationality, gentility and fairness, conversion and expulsion that we find in *The Merchant of Venice* becomes even more complex when we observe that the playwright has construed the "race" of Shylock and Jessica not solely in relation to Cush, the biblical progenitor of black Africa, but within an additional web of significance as well. For when Shylock calls out the name of his "countryman," "Tubal, a wealthy Hebrew of my tribe" (1.3.52), Shakespeare gives his play's Jewish characters a yet more specific geographical origin.

"At Our Synagogue, Tubal"

In 1592, even as, amid the deluge of Hispanophobic polemic, Henslowe was putting Marlowe's *Jew of Malta* into rotation with *The Spanish Tragedy*, the great Spanish humanist Juan de Mariana (1535–1624) honored Philip II by presenting him with the massive *Historiae de rebus Hispaniae*. Published again in 1601, this time in vernacular translation, the narrative became the standard history of the Spanish Empire. It would be appended to at least two more times during the seventeenth century, until the whole—Englished by Captain John Stephens—was published with a title page appropriate to its length: *The General History of Spain. From the first peopling of it by Tubal, till the Death of King Ferdinand, who United the Crowns of Castile and Aragon. With a Continuation to the Death of King Philip III. Written in Spanish by the R.F.F. John de Mariana. To which are added Two Supplements, The First By F. Ferdinand Camargo y Salcido, the other by F. Basil Varen de Soto, bringing it down to the present Reign* (London, 1699).[76]

The extended titles of early modern texts tend to advertise not merely the content found within; they often signal the matter their producers held most significant. Thus the title given Mariana's history tells us much about the significance of Spain in English national consciousness. In spite of the 110 years that separate the publication of Stephens's translation from the defeat of the Armada and the beginning of Spain's decline into "decadence," Spanish history remains an important source of precedent. As late as 1699, the union of the Crowns of Castile and Aragon was still being seen as the empire's seminal accomplishment, the event from which the many global achievements of Ferdinand and Isabella's successors had sprung. More important in the present context is the fact that Mariana's history begins with this sentence: "*Tubal*, the son of *Japheth*, was the first Man that Peopled *Spain* after the Flood."[77]

Not that this Noachic reference was a revelation. On the contrary, as early as the seventh century, as Colin Kidd points out, Isadore of Seville had "told the story of the peopling of Europe by the stock of Japhet," and by "the late medieval period, the extension of this ethnology had contributed to the myths of origin which accompanied the rise of regnal solidarity in many kingdoms of Europe,"[78] a pattern confirmed by Marianna's history. While foregrounding connections between the peoples of Spain and their biblical forebears, the explicit link to a patriarch could also represent a source of Spanish pride, a symbolic precursor of the Spanish Hapsburgs' devotion and discernment; as Mariana emphasized, "Many grave Authors testify that he [Tubal] planted several Colonies in this part of the World, and governed Spain with Piety and Justice."[79] But while, as Kidd stresses, "the Mosaic paradigm emphasized affiliation and relationships with the Noachic family tree rather than notions of difference and otherness which we associate with modern nationalism,"[80] the Hispanophobic discourses being deployed in England suggest that this formulation of affiliation and relationship was gradually breaking down. Shakespeare suggests as much in *The Merchant of Venice*. For when we bring Mariana's *General History of Spain*—which announces "the first peopling" of Iberia "by Tubal"—into relationship with his play, we activate an interpretive matrix that has until recently remained dormant.

If by the time Shylock took the English stage the association of Noah's grandson with Iberia was such a widely held commonplace of history and culture, then Shakespeare could not have been much more explicit. For the presence of the "Spanish" patriarch's namesake is announced as early as act 1, scene 3, when Shylock reveals to Antonio that the guarantor of the "full three thousand ducats" he will be advanced is "Tubal, a wealthy Hebrew of my tribe" (1.3.51–52). And in act 3, scene 1, three lines after Shylock's famous "Hath not a Jew eyes?" speech, Shakespeare's text directs "*Enter Tubal*"—after which Solanio demonizes Shylock's compatriot as "another of the tribe," who "cannot be matched unless the devil himself turn Jew" (3.1.65–66). Soon Shylock appeals for news of Jessica: "How now, *Tubal*? What news from Genoa?

Hast thou found my daughter?" (3.1.67–68). And then, during the course of bemoaning, "The curse never fell upon our nation till now—I never felt it till now," Shylock repeats "good *Tubal*" (3.1.88), "Thou torturest me, *Tubal* (3.1.100), "Go, *Tubal*, fee me an officer" (3.1.104–5), before concluding the scene with "Go, *Tubal*, and meet me at our synagogue. Go, good *Tubal*; at our synagogue, *Tubal*" (3.1.107–8). In concert with the historiographic commonplaces regarding the ancient peopling of Spain, Shylock's repeated appeal to "Tubal" as member of both his "tribe" and their "synagogue" suggests that English audiences were being asked to perceive Spain as, if not their primordial place of "origin," the Jews' ancestral homeland. This is to say that Shakespeare's Shylock, like Marlowe's Barabbas, is a figure representative of the Sephardim—the Jews of Spain. Thus it may be that our own epoch's portrayals, which tend to give Shylock an Eastern European or Yiddish-sounding accent, are, from a sixteenth-century perspective, quite anachronistic: the more historical intonation would have been Spanish.

We have already seen that the issue of Spain's "questionable" origins was being addressed elsewhere in the precursor public sphere than on the stages of London. Much in the manner of Spenser—who, as we have also observed, denigrated Spain's ancestry even as he reflected on the unifying accomplishment of "Ferdinando of Arragon and Elizabeth his wife" (and figured Isabella of Castile as a type of his own queen)—the polemicist Edward Daunce claimed: "Touching therefore the significations of that countrie . . . [it] was not long after the division of tongues, first inhabited by the third sonne of Japhet named Jobel or Tubal, signifying worldly, or of the world, confusion and ignomie: which significations meet so jumpe regarding the state of that countrie, and the customes of that nation, as nothing could be devised apter."[81] Here *A Brief Discourse of the Spanish State* reverses the cultural significance of Spain's biblical patriarch. Rather than symbolizing the "Piety and Justice" Mariana had invoked, Daunce's "Tubal" comes to signify "confusion and ignomie," the conditions associated in Black Legend discourse with the Old Testament types of Philip II's Spain: Nimrod, Babel, and the confusion of tongues (the thematics that were so vital to Kyd's *Spanish Tragedy*). But Daunce takes his false derivation even further, asking his readers to observe that these "significations meet so jumpe"—that is, with such exact coincidence[82]—that they serve to explain an entire culture, whose "state" and "customes" are defined by their un-English "confusion and ignomie."[83]

And yet, by itself Spain's biblical lineage would seem to provide insufficient material for the kind of demonization Iberia undergoes in Daunce's Hispanophobic rhetoric. All of Europe's national cultures claimed common descent from the stock of Noah, after all. If, as a number of analysts have argued, monogenism indeed remained the prevailing explanation for the origins of nations,[84] one biblical grandparent should have been as good as another—unless that grandparent had inherited the curse of Ham. Daunce suggests as much when he reveals that the "customes of that [Spanish] nation" which most disturb him are those that have produced its "racial" impurity. Thus he "reasons" that "a compound is lesse perfit, & more daungerous for nature than a simple, if therefore Spaniards which descended only of Tubal, have in respect . . . what shall we think of the Spaniards of these days, which are confected of the pilferers of the wo[r]ld? truely that there is no vice in which they have not a surplussage above anie other nation of the earth. . . . The naturall Spaniard, being . . . mixed with the Gothes and Vandals, given to theevery and drunkenness: mingled with Mores cruell and full of treacherie: and consequently, tasting of everie one, [is] a spring of filthinesse."[85] Whereas, at some early moment of its national development Spain may have existed in a state more "simple," it is because the "naturall Spaniard"—that is, being both "native" and "illigitimate"[86]—has been compounded in the years since antiquity, mixed "with the Gothes and Vandals" and "mingled with Mores," that *A Discourse of the Spanish State* finds him unredeemable. Showing his hand in this manner, Daunce discloses that a major aim of his treatise—which has this much in common with Spenser's *View of the State of Ireland*—is to delegitimize Spanish authority and demonize Spanish custom by racializing "mingled" Iberia as "a spring of filthinesse."

In Daunce's formula, as in Spenser's, we see a shift, not merely from a universalist discourse of ethos to a particularizing rhetoric of ethnos, but also to an emerging Anglo-Saxonism, a precursor, perhaps, of the virulent nativist impulse that would energize the nationalist discourses of later epochs.[87] A further irony, of course, is that England's Spanish rivals had already elevated *limpieza de sangre*, purity of blood, to a national ideal. In spite of (or perhaps inspired by) Spain's official *pureza*, a number of Black Legend propagandists focus on Spain's ethnic "uncleanness."[88] It was a formula that racialized Spain by emphasizing the admixture (or miscegenation) at its roots. It is worth recalling how the most influential of all Black Legend promoters recognized the persuasive power of this racial rhetoric. "In Castile and Spayne," writes William I of Orange, whose namesake William III will be called on to ensure a Protestant succession at a future moment of national crisis, "I will no more wonder at that, which all the worlde beleeveth, to witte, that the greatest parte of the Spanyardes, and especially those, that coounte themselves Noble men, are of the blood of the Moores and Jews."[89] The various icons of ethnos inscribèd by writers as diverse as Edmund Spenser, Juan de Mariana, Edward Daunce, and William of Orange are recombined in Shakespeare's *Comical History of the Merchant of Venice, or Otherwise Called the Jew of Venice*, and, as we have seen, many of these icons implicate Spain.

"A Daniel Come to Judgment"

To the degree that it caricatures perceived Jewish cultural values in the figure of Shylock, *The Merchant of Venice* evidences the stereotyping sometimes given as the "reason" behind the historic antipathy of Christendom toward the Jews. But the play casts its stones from a number of trajectories—which is to say that Shylock, like so many other Renaissance figures, signifies multivocally. Though obviously embodying Jewish faith and Jewish ethnicity, he may also suggest the philosemitic or Judaizing tendencies of Shakespeare's own culture. As Michael Ferber and others have suggested, "Shylock is a kind of surrogate Puritan," and as such he puts us in mind of the English Hebraists of the period, who were "Christians of the Book, especially fond of the Old Testament," and "considered themselves, although with frequent anxiety, as the chosen people or the elect."[90]

But as we learn in the opening scene, Shylock is not the sole hub of the play's Protestant anxieties.[91] "Sadness" of the kind Antonio experiences, for example, could also be associated, as it was for Spenser, with the burden of Puritan sobriety.[92] Shakespeare emphasizes the discourses of reform even more obviously during Bassanio's courtship of the "aweary" Portia, where they are also linked with Elizabethan monarchical values. When Portia directs his trial of the leaden casket, she also schools Bassanio in religion. Commanding him to "confess and live," Portia invokes the epithalamic music that will also frame their return to Belmont in act 5, linking "those dulcet sounds in break of day / That creep in to the dreaming bridegroom's ear / And summon him to marriage" (3.2.51–53), with "the flourish when true subjects bow / To a new-crownèd monarch" (3.2.49–50). As he resolves to turn his back on the "gaudy gold" and "pale and common" silver, Bassanio frames his choice in language that verges on Puritan polemic:

> So may the outward shows be least themselves.
> The world is still deceived with ornament.
> In law, what plea so tainted and corrupt
> But, being seasoned with gracious voice,

Obscures the show of evil? In religion,
What damnèd error but some sober brow
Will bless it and approve it with a text,
Hiding the grossness with fair ornament. (3.2.73–80)

Surely this is another moment at which the play's Venetian setting betrays its English "origins," describing more the pressures Protestant reform was exerting in London than life in the Venetian Empire. But if Bassanio's "lesson" suggests he has been led toward a Protestant cast of mind, his confirmation becomes yet more evident during his participation in Portia's trial of the suit Shylock has brought against Antonio.

The scene that commences with entrance of Portia into the Duke's courtroom in act 4—when Portia utters the unforgettable rhetorical question, "Which is the merchant here and which the Jew?" (4.1.169)—and ends with her judgment against Shylock, provides what many consider the play's most compelling dramatic moments. We sometimes fail to notice, however, that when Portia arrives at the Duke's courtroom, the Christian mercy and Venetian law she brings are clothed in decades of Elizabethan religiopolitical ceremony. Further, the tension between Portia's injunction that "The quality of mercy is not strained" (4.1.179)—a sentiment that resonates strongly with any number of contemporary appeals to Elizabeth's merciful nature—and the stony inflexibility of Shylock's response, "I crave the law" (4.1.201), dramatizes the gulf in meaning associated with the difference between the Old Dispensation and the New, underscoring the religious tensions that have been building throughout each of the preceding scenes.

If the logic of *The Merchant of Venice* accepts the logic of the New Dispensation—and formal features such as the Launcelot–Old Gobbo allegory and Portia's "quality of mercy" intervention plainly argue that it does—this logic stands on the Christian assumption that the terms of God's covenant had changed since the "original" had been made with the Children of Israel. While Portia's invocation of mercy and Antonio's lamblike nonresistance may put us in mind of the Gospels, the Old Testament book of Daniel also provides an important textual backdrop for Shakespeare's hermeneutic confrontation.

In the climactic scene of a play foregrounding the historical relationship between Judaism and Christianity, especially as characterized by their different orientations toward scripture, Shakespeare could have evoked a number of female precedents in order to cast Portia as an embodiment of justice. Elizabeth was frequently compared to Judith or Deborah, and we have already noted her ceremonial association with the goddess Astraea.[93] But at this decisive moment, when Portia enters bearing a letter from the "learn'd *Bell*ario" (4.1), Shylock types the young "doctor of laws" as "A Daniel come to judgement, yea, a Daniel!" (4.1.218). Even before Shylock praises her, however, this interpretive matrix has been activated by the "Balthazar" identity Portia assumes. While contemporary exegetes could apply a range of figural significations to this Old Testament name, Shakespeare's choice resonates as strongly in *The Comical History* as did Kyd's in *The Spanish Tragedy*. Recall that Daniel's Babylonian appellation Balthazar, or *Bel*teshazar, signified "he that storeth riches" or "keeper of the treasure," even as it is Portia who keeps the rich treasure of *Bel*mont.[94] While these textual associations suggest relevant thematics, it is probable that the Elizabethans brought to the theater a far more prophetic intertext also associated with the book of Daniel. For, as Shapiro reminds us, "In scores of sermons and tracts produced in the late sixteenth century, Daniel called to mind first and foremost the Jewish prophet who foresaw the final judgment, an event precipitated by the conversion of the Jews" (133).[95] In a play that culminates with two Jewish conversions—Jessica's willing acceptance of her husband's faith and Shylock's forced one—the apocalyptic Daniel must also be apposite.[96]

As we saw in Chapter 3, the Augustinian theory of "the Four Monarchies"— a tradition raised on a prophetic reading of Daniel 2:24–49—was for the early moderns a master narrative tracing the biblically authorized "translation" of imperial power from East to West. This global religiopolitical chronology, as Mario Góngora recalls, "was based on the empires of the Assyrians, the Medes and Persians, the Greeks (under Alexander the Great) and of Rome (and the states which were the successors to Rome); the final empire, in eschatological terms, would be a Messianic Fifth Monarchy."[97] This march of history—at work on the Catholic side in Allen's *Admonition to the Nobility of England* no less than in the Protestant Daunce's *Brief Discourse of the Spanish State*[98]—depended upon the concept of *translatio imperii*.[99] For it was the fifth of these translations that was to authorize the empire that would preside over the Last Days while also overseeing the conversion of the Jews.[100] This figural framework must surely lend significance to *The Merchant of Venice*.[101] However uncomfortable we may be with the rationale of the punishment laid upon Shylock, which confiscates "one half of his goods" and leads him not "to the gallows" but "to the font" (4.1.376, 396), it is a logic that replicates contemporary inquisitional practices, both Catholic and Protestant, even as it is a conversion of two Jews that Portia, twice emphasized as the play's "second Daniel" (4.1.328, 335)—representative of both divinely inspired justice and imperial translation—so eloquently (and juridically) effects.

"Sweet Harmony"

There has been much recent debate as to whether the English had begun to see themselves as *the* chosen nation or simply *a* chosen nation.[102] In either case, England's sense of nationhood was substantially different from the kind of community imagined by Shylock. Though European understandings of national constitution as social contract had yet to reach Enlightenment articulation, the growing complexity of English society seems to have been moving the Elizabethans partly in that direction, even though it was also pushing them, at least in the short run, toward a monarchy that was increasingly absolute. Spenser was among those, as were Lewis Lewkenor and James I, who had begun to look toward Venice as a model that might help the English think through the complex problems that came with the necessity of incorporating others. Though Spenser would praise its "policie of right," his colonial experience led him to second Machiavelli's judgment that because the Venetians "limit their chiefe officers so strictly" and "thereby they have oftentimes lost such happy occasions, as they could never come unto againe" (160), their right policy ought to be backed up by royal prerogative of the kind Elizabeth might exercise in Ireland if only "the cumberous times" did not "hinder the regard thereof" (155). The notion that Venice's republican system could be perceived as "cumberous" resonates strongly in *The Merchant of Venice*, as does Spenser's sense that good governmental structures do not diminish the need for an absolute arbiter. Indeed, Venice's reputed reverence for the letter of its laws—even to the detriment of their spirit—helps to produce the play's most engaging conflict. For Antonio is redeemed not by Venice's law alone, nor is he saved by Venice's legally hamstrung Duke.[103] It is only when the Republic's vaunted laws are interpreted by *The Comical History*'s stand-in for Elizabeth Tudor, a virtual embodiment of Spenser's "mercy and clemency," that Antonio is spared.

Portia's double identity, like the dual-gendered dynamism of a number of Shakespeare's comic heroines, must surely mirror the shaping power of Elizabeth Tudor's "two bodies." As Carole Levin has shown, the queen could be conceived "as having two identities simultaneously, one male and the other female, both incorporating sovereignty."[104] The plot of *The Merchant of Venice* is clearly structured around such a duality. Elizabeth—whether courting local favorites such as Robert Dudley and Christopher Hatton or "foreign" contenders like Archduke Charles of Austria and the French Duke of Alençon—"took on what might be perceived as the male role, certainly the position of power, controlling courtship and intimacy."[105] Even so, the women who will be "bonded" and vindicated in the play's denouement, Portia, Nerissa, and Jessica, multiply our attention to the androgynous spirit of Elizabethan power by assuming male roles in order to move the plot toward its closing reconciliation. While each of these gender-bending ruses is significant in its way, it is Portia's action that commands the most attention (even as it is Portia who is most commanding in the play).

Declaiming that "the moon shines bright" (5.1.1), Lorenzo and Jessica announce Portia's return to Belmont, where she will preside over the play's conclusion. While this dreamy opening works to emphasize the radical difference of *The Merchant of Venice*'s green world in relation to the bustle of the Rialto or the intensity of its Senate chambers, the catalogue of famous lovers invoked with each repetition of "In such a night" (5.1.1, 6, 9, 12, 14, 17, 20) functions like a royal triumph welcoming Queen Portia home from victory. As Jessica and Lorenzo compare themselves to the some of the most storied couples of classical (and English) literature—Troilus and Cresida, Pyramus and Thisbe, Dido and Aeneas, Jason and Medea—they are bathed in a moonlight that also suggests the "imperial moon" iconography with which the Elizabethans had long memorialized their monarch.[106] As the lovers sit down to contemplate how the "Soft stillness and the night / Become the touches of sweet harmony" (5.1.55–56), Lorenzo orders the entering musicians to "wake Diana with a hymn" so that "With sweetest touches" they might "pierce" their "mistress' ear / And draw her home with music" (5.1.65–67). Shakespeare's allusiveness to the royal cult could hardly be more plain. And when Portia and Nerissa enter discussing how far "Shines a good deed in a naughty world" (5.1.90), the mistress of Belmont elaborates a theory of monarchical substitution that virtually describes the role she performs in the play:

A substitute shines as brightly as a king
Until a king be by, and then his state
Empties itself as doth an inland brook
Into the main of waters. (5.1.91–96)

Apprehending the lovemaking of Lorenzo and Jessica, Portia orders a temporary end to the play's music with a final allusion to one of the Elizabethans' cherished myths: "Peace, ho! The moon sleeps with Endymion, / And would not be awaked" (5.1.108–9). The queen of Belmont has returned to oversee the coupling—which may not continue until each pair of lovers has received her blessing—a scenario recalling not only the faerie world of the slightly earlier *Midsummer Night's Dream* (c. 1594–96), which features Shakespeare's most fully realized comic resolution, but also John Lyly's famous *Endimion: The Man in the Moone* (c. 1588) and the role Elizabeth played when presiding over England's aristocratic nuptials.[107]

Attractive though we may find the trio of couples who gather in Belmont to close the play, as significant to *The Comical History* are those who are left out of its moonlit reverie. The Tudored Bassanio, the delivered Antonio, the converted Jessica and her seemingly no longer conflicted manservant Launcelot are all blessed with the bonds of community, even if they do not all find true love. Of Shylock, now a *converso*, all that remains is his wealth, forcibly expropriated to the service of the state and his Christian son-in-law. The "fair" Jessica is saved by her husband and as such is allowed at least outward blessing, though we might reasonably wonder whether as an actual converted Jew she could ever experience full membership here. Launcelot's Moorish lover is shoved aside, as is their mixed-race offspring, with scarcely a trace of either to be found in this world of civility, privilege, and service. In *Merchant*'s concluding representation of Belmont's social body—gentile natives and genteel converts inside, bastardized progeny and racialized others outside—is mirrored the structure of a society that was beginning to emerge under Elizabeth's imperial aegis and in England's imperial historiography.

As Shakespeare portrays a militantly merciful Portia, who bonds herself maritally to a native son over and against all of the play's foreign spirits, he explores and neatly allegorizes—in a much more "gentle" manner, but to much the same ends, than Marlowe's *Jew of Malta* engages the same issues—the external pressures being exerted upon both Venice and England by their sometime ally, sometime enemy, imperial Spain. In this dynamic, we may have arrived at what is Hispanophilic in the play. Although Shakespeare's Belmont clearly figures Elizabethan England, the actual Belmont, the "Italian" Belmonte, was from the 1440s among the Neapolitan kingdoms of the Spanish monarchy.[108] So while Portia may in significant ways embody Elizabeth, her rejection of the play's ethnic outsiders also performs for England the essentialist logic of Inquisition Spain (even as it endorses a "purity" the historical Spaniards had, to their perceived detriment, failed to preserve).[109] Teasingly raising the possibility of creating a society in which others like Morocco, Arragon, and the Jew might be incorporated, Shakespeare's *Comical History* revokes this possibility in a way that prefigures the vision of ethnonational purity that has begun to emerge (as it had a century earlier in Spain) during the late Elizabethan and early Jacobean years. By 1605, rather than continuing to locate identity in the divisive primacy of religion, a nascent ethnonationalism, theorized by (the formerly Hispanized) Richard Verstegen, would appeal to the essentials of Anglo-

Saxon lineage, seeking the potential for national solidarity in common "racial" roots. Against those who "do call us a mixed nation,"[110] Verstegen insisted that—unlike the Spanish, whose heritage his Protestant countryman Spenser had identified as "the most mingled, and most uncertaine"—the English had "ever kept themselves unmixed with forrain people" and were "undoubtedly descended . . . of [the] German race."[111]

Shakespeare's first Venetian play thus turns upon an axis of ethnic admixture and national preservation, staging a critique not merely of the transnational dynasty building examined by Thomas Kyd but of racial mixing of the kind contemporary ethnographers located in the Spains. Further, as it contextualizes its argument within the commercial empire of Venice and in relation to a set of trials engaging the three "nations" associated with "mingled" Iberia—the Moorish, Roman Catholic, and Judaic—the play reselects, recombines, and recodifies a wealth of widely recognized cultural materials in order to recommend traditions of national solidarity, state religion, and ethnonational contraction much in line with those that were being promoted in the name of a unifying "Englishness." But the dissonant overtones we sense underlying the play's concluding harmonies betray a human remainder, a not-so-distant memory of prior cultural connection best emblematized, perhaps, in the "sweet music" (5.1.68) Jessica cannot abide. Though Shakespeare's drama may finally achieve a kind of concord, it does so at a cost at once generic and human. In spite of its concluding appeal to song, the denouement of *The Comical History* is haunted by the specter of those left out of its concluding "harmonies."[112] And like *The Jew of Malta*, *The Merchant of Venice* begs a question that both of the plays, in their late sixteenth-century context, loudly and emphatically raise: "Which is the Spaniard here? And which the Jew?"

CHAPTER SIX

Othello's Spanish Spirits

Or, Un-sainting James

Santiago of Spain,
Killed my Moors,
Scattered my company,
Broke my standard.
　　　—*Poem of Alfonso XI*, c. 1344

Wyat.　　　　　　　　　　　Who can
　　Disgest a Spaniard, that's a true Englishman?
Soldier. Would he might choake that disgests him.
　　　—*The Famous History of Sir Thomas Wyat. With the*
　　　　Coronation of Queen Mary, and the coming in of King
　　　　Philip, c. 1602

IT WAS SAID of Venice during the sixteenth century, "If you are curious to see men from every part of the earth, each dressed his own different way, go to St. Mark's square or the Rialto and you will find all manner of persons."[1] Even as Shakespeare was turning his dramatic eye toward the commercial republic, "when Antwerp and many other 'world markets' were suffering from political disruptions, when Jewish refugees drew to Venice trade from the Levant and Balkans, and when the boom of its textile industries reached new heights," cosmopolitan Venetian merchants were operating "in Sweden and, extensively, in Poland," and extending their sphere of traffic so far from the Mediterranean as to be "trading in gems and fabrics in Indian cities."[2]

In an address to Doge Andrea Gritti, the poet, playwright, and satirist Pietro Aretino, who had taken sanctuary in the city after being forced to flee Rome for having directed one too many witticisms at papal excess, evoked the city-state's international reputation in this way: "Venice opens her arms to all whom others shun. She lifts up all whom others abase. She welcomes those whom others persecute. She cheers the mourner in his grief and defends the despised and the destitute with charity and love. And so I bow to Venice with good reason. She is a living reproach to Rome."[3] Doubtless Aretino's encomium exaggerates, for, its legendary freedoms notwithstanding, Venice was no totally open society. Strictures were placed on the behavior of outsiders, who were often kept under surveillance within its territories. But as the diarist Girolamo Priuli confirmed, Venice's self-image and international prestige were very much linked to its storied liberality. The city of Saint Mark "was open to foreigners," wrote Priuli, "and all could come and go everywhere without any obstacle."[4] "Venice," as Garry Wills observes, even "allowed certain foreigners (*forestieri*) to become *cittadini*, giving them higher rank than native *popolani*."[5]

Recognitions such as these—about the international character of Venice and the breadth of that city-state's reach as a global center of trade and industry—failed until quite recently to register in discussions of Shakespeare's Venetian tragedy. By constructing Venice as a homogeneous society in relation to which "the Moor" represents a singular other, a stranger or an outsider,[6] traditional criticism declined to view *The Tragedy of Othello* in the cosmopolitan setting it granted Shakespeare's *Comical History of the Merchant of Venice*— where trade and profit "Consisteth of all nations."[7]

I argue in this final chapter that Shakespeare represents in *Othello* a culture so marked by external relationships and connections that it resembles a multiethnic metropolis far more than any insular whole.[8] When we extend Venice's vaunted openness to *Othello*, we see quite clearly that Shakespeare's second Venetian play raises the specter of Spain in order to mediate an uneasy local/global relationship through the "humorous" invocation of a "spirit" known throughout Europe since medieval times—a spirit not natively English, but one that entered England, as it did the rest of pre-Reformation Europe, during its long contact with the culture of Iberia.[9]

My appeal to the *longue durée* notwithstanding, I will resort at times to a narrative of actors and events. But I do so in order to bring into relief the selective nature of our cultural (and disciplinary) memory with regard to the play. As the poets, playwrights, and historians of the various nations of early modern Europe held a common store of exemplary tales to be invoked or reworked—much in the way they mobilized scriptural or classical precedents—as occasion demanded (their principal figures often named in order that they might metonymically represent their respective "races"), so the redeployment of these histories can help us observe the ways in which these emerging national cultures felt themselves positioned in relationship to each other, and how their narratives could be reconfigured in response to, or in order to explain, historical change.[10] When we listen for these early modern codes, we find that *The Moor of Venice* is animated, on the one hand, by a Protestant historical and theological revisionism authorized by the "English" sovereign James and, on the other, by the Black Legend of Spanish Cruelty, that highly ethnocentric discourse which sought, as we have seen time and again, to discover the "nature" of a "nation" by "lively decyphering" or "portraying" its motivating "humors" or "spirits"—spirits that had long infused the Mediterranean world.[11]

If we imagine Venice as Shakespeare and his contemporaries imagined the Republic—as a nexus of cultural mobility situated at the hub of an early modern global economy, where one could see, perhaps more clearly than from anywhere else on the European mainland, evidence that the Mediterranean was "the meeting place of many peoples, and the melting pot of many histories"—we find the play significantly transformed.[12] To construct a Shakespearean Venice as "open" as the Venice of Aretino and Priuli—open to men and women from every part of the earth, not merely to "Italians" and Mauritanians—is to raise from *Othello* Spanish spirits that we can no longer reasonably ignore.

"Fayre *Venice*, Flower of the Last Worlds Delight"

> The witness I purpose to produce, . . . who discoursing in the Senate of Venice, of the humours of this Spanish generation: beholde what good testimonie he gives of their integritie. The Spanish Nation (sayth he) is unfaithfull, ravenous, and insatiable above all other Nations. And where is (I pray you) that place of the world, where those infamous Harpyes have once set footing without defiling of it with . . . their abominable vices?
>
> —R.A., *A Comparison of the English and Spanish Nation* [13]

Even as our discipline has planted standards of cultural diversity, most readings of *Othello* have continued to lump together "Iago, Brabantio, Roderigo, and Cassio" as "Venetians."[14] A question not often posed is, "How do we know that all these four are *Venetians?*" Shakespeare's characters do each happen to be residing in Venice at the moment the play opens. But what can we say of their origins? As we have seen, Renaissance culture was obsessed with such genealogical concerns; so it should not come as a surprise that Shakespeare loaded his play with significant indices that point toward the European nations from which we may assume his characters have sprung. While we can say with some certainty that Brabantio, a man of means and a senator by rank, is Venetian (though his name, we will observe, suggests a different nationality), as are Desdemona and the Duke, along with Gratiano, Lodovico, and presumably Montano; beyond these six, national identities become a bit harder to discern. Cassio is a Florentine, if we can believe Iago. Emilia reports to Othello that "Cassio . . . hath killed a young Venetian called Roderigo" (5.2.111–12). But as Braudel reminded us, the global commercial center fielded a military force that could be composed of troops recruited from virtually any nation connected to the Mediterranean world, from Bavaria, say, or even Scotland.[15] A remark like Emilia's, then, in the context of an enterprise as collective as the storming of Cyprus for Western Christendom (though it is by no means clear that Roderigo is a military man) informs the general of not much beyond the fact that his former lieutenant has killed one of their own rather than a native Cypriot or a Turk. At an earlier moment in the play, when Iago speaks of "*our* country disposition," wishing to convince Othello that Desdemona "may fall to match [him] with *her* country forms" (3.3.201, 237, my italics), the ancient seems to do so in order to distinguish the difference between *ours*, meaning Othello's and his own, and *hers*, meaning Venice. Why the indirection? To which "country" might Iago be referring? By now it should be clear that Shakespeare is raising here the specter of Spain.

The most important event of *Othello*'s historical moment, 1604, the first full year of Stuart rule and the year in which the play was produced, is the peace the new Anglo-Scottish king makes with the Spanish Empire (Figure 10).[16] While influential noblemen in James's court (and later in the court of Charles) favor a close Spanish alliance, both Parliaments, but especially the House of Commons, remain hostile to England's traditional enemy. On the streets of London, news of the Spanish Peace is "greeted with an ominous silence."[17] Many still fear Spain's aggressive Catholicism. English Protestant clergymen "inveigh against the peace from the pulpit."[18] Memories of the Marian persecutions and the Armada are not easily displaced, nor have

Figure 10. Artist unknown, *The Somerset House Conference*, 1604, showing the negotiators of the Spanish Peace. Seated on the right are the English representatives, led by Robert Cecil, who sits in the foreground with pen, ink, and papers. On the left sits the Spanish embassy, led by Juan de Velasco, Duke of Frías and Constable of Castile, seated second from the open window, wearing the mantle of the Order of the Knights of Santiago. Image © National Portrait Gallery, London.

important overseas trading rivalries been resolved. "Neutral" Venice observes that "the English," caught up in a kind of nostalgia for the heroism of a not-so-distant past and "moved by hatred of Spain and their own interests, desire war, for the peace has stopped them from privateering, by which they grew rich."[19] At the center of this foreign policy tempest the Stuart regime, stressing the expanded possibilities of the new peacetime economy, holds up Venice as a mirror of political stability and commercial success.[20] While England's merchants and adventurers covet access to Venice's global marketplace, among the nation's statesmen are those who, praising the Republic's "policie of right," lionize Venice as a luminous example of the *status mixtus*—a place where "right of government" goes not by the rule of "nobility of lineage alone" but to "every other citizen whosoever . . . ennobled by virtue, or well deserving of the commonwealth."[21]

The Venice of *Othello*, what little we see of it, inscribes the idealized view in favor at James's court. In act 1 Shakespeare allows us to glimpse an oligarchical Republic in which citizens of different ranks—Senators, Officers, and Attendants—meet before a magisterial Duke to discuss matters of state. Othello himself, the "valiant Moor" who has so distinguished himself among the *cittadini* that he has been welcomed in their highest circles, is summoned to the parley. Knowing that "the fortitude" of Cyprus is best known to his general, the Duke reasons that while there is on the island "a substitute of most allowed sufficiency" (1.3.221–23), the Moor must straightaway be employed "against the general enemy Ottoman" (1.3.49). So things would have gone without a hitch had Brabantio not interrupted the council with his "particular grief" (1.3.55).[22] But *Othello's* opening scenes afford us far more than a glimpse of the celebrated Venetian government in action. They also serve to underscore the recognition among Shakespeare's contemporaries that the geography that favored Venetian commerce also rendered the city-state vulnerable to the changing seas of European politics.

In the late 1950s G. K. Hunter, restating what was probably even then a critical commonplace, wrote that "Italy became important to the English dramatist only when 'Italy' was revealed as an aspect of England."[23] This is no less true of *Othello* than of the other "Italian" plays of the period. What even the historically minded among us tend to forget, however, is that Sicily and much of the present-day Italian state were for several hundred years part of the Kingdom of Aragon, which, in concert with Castile, had carried the Iberian *reconquista* across the Strait of Gibraltar and was by the early sixteenth century securing a network of imperial outposts in North Africa. The accession of Charles V added Milan to the Spanish orbit, which accounts for the presence of Allesandro Robida, senator of Milan, at the Somerset House Conference (in Figure 10, he is seated on the Spanish side, third from center), along with Charles's German kingdoms and the Netherlands; in 1580, Charles's son Philip II had united the Spains by absorbing Portugal and its extensive colonial system. In order to maintain its vital trade relations with the Hapsburg dynasty's French adversaries, and yet preserve its favored-nation status with the expanding empire, Venice was often forced to juggle the priorities and interests of its various clients. While the Republic remained officially Roman Catholic in matters of religion, in matters of policy many sixteenth-century Venetians came to regard papal power as "Spanish power in disguise."[24] Thus the Lion City sometimes found its political interests sufficiently divergent from those of the Papal States, and that its foreign policies did not always coincide with those of its Italian neighbors.[25]

There was, for example, the matter of tolerance toward Protestants, which the Republic found politically and economically expedient. Indeed, by the 1590s "there were so many English in Venice that the Pope twice complained loudly about the 'heretics' congesting the city."[26] From late 1603—when James I establishes full diplomatic relations and dispatches Sir Henry Wotton to the Republic—one might even attend Church of England services there and witness "the true worship of God in the middest of Popery, superstition, and idolatry."[27] It is, then, a culturally diverse and ideologically contested environment that Shakespeare sketches in *Othello*, and while I am not trying to suggest that the play attempts to rehearse an actual historical situation, Shakespeare's play does reflect an awareness of the complexities of both the recent historical past in which it is set and the problems of the political present during which it was produced. It is precisely early modern Venice's historical and cultural complexity that Shakespeare exploits in powerfully significant ways. A brief look at Cinthio's *Hecatommithi* reveals how he sets about doing so.

Among the striking differences between Shakespeare's adaptation and Giraldi Cinthio's original is the fact that in the source tale the Moor and his wife are not separated as they are in act 2, scene 1, nor do they endure any storm; rather, Il Moro "embarked on board the galley with his wife and all his troops, and, setting sail, they pursued their voyage, and with a perfectly tranquil sea arrived safely at Cyprus."[28] Through the introduction of the scene in the Duke's war room, and the subsequent "battle," Shakespeare recasts the Cinthio story—much in the manner that Marlowe had typologically conflated the Hospitaller sieges of 1523 and 1565 in *The Jew of Malta*—from the period of the first Holy League of 1537–40, which won from "the Turk" Venice's "thirty-year peace" and significant economic concessions, into the period of the second Holy League alliance of the 1570s, which convened in response to Sultan Suleiman's demand that the Republic surrender the prosperous island. A number of critics over the years have noted how Shakespeare's scene suggests the 1572 naval engagement that saw Venice and its allies finally halt the advancing Ottomans at Lepanto, memorable to most students of literature only as the place where Cervantes received his "shining" wounds.[29] Since 1573, when Pope Pius V instituted a special feast of the Virgin, the Roman Catholic Church has kept October 7 as the Feast of the Rosary in commemoration of the providential victory.[30]

Less globally significant was the Lepanto commemoration of Shakespeare's new poet-king, whose long heroic poem on the subject had been published in Edinburgh in 1591 and was printed again in London in 1603, to commemorate the Stuart succession. *The Lepanto* of James I bears the following disclaimer:

"And for that I knowe, the special thing misliked in it, is, that I should seeme, far contrary to my degree and Religion, like a Mercenary poet, to penne a worke, ex processo, in praise of a forraine Papist bastard, I will by setting downe the nature and order resolve their ignorant error, & mak[e] the other sort inexcusable of their captiousnes." The sovereign assures his reading subjects that the poem is not meant to praise the "forraine Papist bastard"—the hero of Lepanto, Philip II's half-brother, Don John of Austria—he is merely attempting to render "true history." Further, he has been "hereof mooved" to write "by the stirring uppe of the league and cruell persecution of Protestants in all countries." What is more, King James's poem bears an "invocation of *the true God only,* and not *to all the He and She Saints* for whose *vaine honors* Don-Joan fought in all his warres" (my italics).[31] We cannot say with certainty that Shakespeare intended to honor his new king's lately republished "true history" by incorporating the event into the setting of his play.[32] However, the recording of several court performances during Shakespeare's lifetime—performances we will soon consider more fully—seems to suggest a certain fondness for the play on the part of James. And *Othello* does indeed stage attitudes quite in tune with those expressed in James's defensive preface.

If Shakespeare's improvisation upon Cinthio pays homage to the incoming monarch, it also appeals to the memory of the one recently departed. For act 2, scene 1, recalls not merely one battle but the two most important sea battles of the sixteenth century. Even as it evokes the Holy League's 1572 triumph at Lepanto, *Othello's* storm and bonfires also conjure England's own triumph, its 1588 "deliverance" from Philip's Armada. George Gower's famous portrait of Elizabeth (Figure 11), with its representation of divine agency in the right-hand panel, can stand here for the many commemorations of this early modern finest hour: that sign of "God's obvious design" which marked the covenant between the Almighty and Protestant England. The improvisational blending of the two victories in *Othello* suggests not merely a situational correspondence between but also a spiritual identification with the Venetian Republic and the divinely preserved, and therefore anointed, English monarchy. However, Shakespeare's evocation of the Lepanto event—which Cervantes, at the beginning of the second part of *Don Quixote,* will call "the greatest occasion which any age, past, present, or future, ever saw or can ever hope to see"[33]—is not as important as his invocation of the battle's symbolic or iconographic significance for Roman Catholic Europe. Though Protestant and Catholic versions concur on the importance of keeping the "circumsised Turband Turke" at bay, in accord with the prevailing line on saintly mediation, *Othello* disallows—as does the revisionist "true history" of Shakespeare's

Figure 11. George Gower's *Armada Portrait*, c. 1589, represents England's deliverance from Philip's fleet in November 1588. Agencies human and divine can be seen in diptych through its windows. The artist's placement of Elizabeth's right hand securely upon the globe was more political ploy than historical reality, for the Anglo-Spanish conflict was far from decided. By kind permission of His Grace the Duke of Bedford and the Trustees of the Bedford Estate, Woburn Abbey, Bedfordshire, England.

Protestant sovereign—Don John, Philip II, and the Communion of Saints any agency whatsoever in the divinely orchestrated victory.[34]

Returning to the *Hecatommithi*, we find Cinthio even less clear than Shakespeare when it comes to the "racial" identities of the Moor of Venice and his retinue. The general is simply *un Moro*. And of the *alfiero*, or standard bearer, we know only these things: Cinthio introduces him as one "amongst the soldiery"; he is neither "Iago" nor "ancient"; in the story's denouement he is said to have "returned to his own country."[35] Cinthio gives only "Disdemona" a name and mentions no character that resembles Iago's "foil," Roderigo.

Among Shakespeare's obvious improvisations, then, are his various namings. These may be not only his most significant improvisational choices; they also provide interpretive keys that open the play in telling ways. If we consider Shakespeare's use of Spanish names in accord with their public, symbolic meaning, *Othello*'s "racial riddle"—and the "Italy is England" matter of the play—may be discovered.[36] For there is but one thing rotten in the ideal Republic Shakespeare has drawn for us: as we have known from act 1, scene 1, line 1, and as Thomas Rymer long ago found it necessary to stress, characters named Iago and Roderigo can be seen "by Night in the Streets."[37]

"¡Sant Iago y cierra España!" [Saint James and close ranks Spain!]

> *Los moros llaman Mafómat   e los cristianos Santi Yagüe.*
> [The Moors call on Mohamet   and the Christians Saint James.][38]
>   —*Cantar de mio Cid*, c. 1140

> Ireni: *Orourk surely comes of Rodoricke which some say is a Spanishe name: and it maye well bee that his ancestor was a Spaniarde: and also that some spaniardes came over with the other Africans, to flye from those troblous times . . . as namely when the Moores invaded the king-dome of Granado and Portugall.*
>   —Edmund Spenser, *A vewe of the present state of Irelande* (1598)[39]

Discussions of *Othello*'s reception in the seventeenth century commonly begin with Rymer's condemnation of "our Poet" for making "so much ado, so much stress, so much passion and repetition about an Handkerchief."[40] We know that the first recorded performance of the play is that of Hollowmas Day, 1 November 1604, before King James at Whitehall, and that it was presented again during Shakespeare's lifetime in 1612–13 as part of the celebration marking the marriage of Princess Elizabeth and Frederick, the Elector Palatine, but the possibility of any occasional significance has been dismissed.[41]

There exists, however, a ballad that provides an early response to *Othello*, which has been curiously neglected by literary historians. Though no known printed version is extant, this ballad, a portion of which I offer here, seems to have been written by a contemporary, or near contemporary, of Shakespeare's. If we consider this text in relation to the situation of the play's initial performance as recorded by James's master of entertainments, and in concert with the cultural significance of the name Iago down the long centuries of pan-European cultural aspiration and exchange, we begin to hear startling resonances that have remained largely inaudible in the years since the play's initial reception:

The foule effects of jealousie,
Othelloe's deadly hate,
Iagoe's cruell treacherie,
And Desdemonae's fate,
In this same ballad you may reade,
If so you list to bye,
Which tells the blackest, bloodiest deede
Yet ever seen with eye.

. . . .

Now while upon the Isle they stayde,
The luckelesse lotte befell,
By a false Spaniard's wicked ayde,
Which I am now to tell.
He was the Antient to the Moore
For he so closely wrought,
He held him honest, trusty, sure,
Until he found him nought.
Iago was the monster's name.[42]

More than attesting to the popularity of the play, the anonymous "Tragedie of Othello the Moore" is unequivocal in attributing the tragedy's "blackest, bloodiest deede" to the agency of a "false Spaniard." To at least one early reader, Iago seems not to have posed much of a riddle. What led the balladeer to fix upon Iago's "Spanishness"? Surely it was a knowledge, however incomplete, of the cultural codes that pointed toward Iberia's central role in the development of Europe's Roman Catholic heritage. As Ophelia's pilgrim song confirms, it was a heritage still very much alive on either side of the Reformation divide at the dawn of the seventeenth century. Like Hamlet's victimized lover, our balladeer was caught up in at least some of the strands that composed, in Weber's famous phrase, the "web of significance" that hung about the name Iago.[43]

By the time Shakespeare introduced the archvillain through whom Western culture has continued to allegorize evil,[44] centuries of accumulated meaning have crystallized around his name. Had Shakespeare wanted to mobilize the cultural codes through which the early modern period represented an essential "Spanishness" by improvising upon "type"—in order that he might imply that two of his characters were of Spanish nationality—he could not have animated a more powerfully and symbolically appropriate sign than "Iago." The same is true of Iago's accomplice Roderigo. No two names are more indelibly written into the discourse of Spanish nationhood than these: Rodrigo, the

Christian name of "Ruy" Díaz de Bivar, El Cid Campeador—the epic hero of Iberian culture;[45] and Iago—which Shakespeare surely derived from Sant-Iago, the patron saint of Spain—who had intervened at the battle of Clavijo in 844, who had been invoked as Rodrigo El Campeador reconquered Valencia during the 1090s, and who was shortly to become known across the globe on "grounds Christen'd and heathen" as Saint James, the Moor-killer.

If we bring this cultural knowledge into textual relation with *Othello*, we can see that as culturally hyperbolized characters constructed for the English stage in the early years of the seventeenth century both Iago and Roderigo have "good" (but certainly not virtuous) reasons for behaving the way they do.[46] Iago can hate the Moor so completely and Roderigo can pursue Desdemona so blindly and persistently because they embody what the members of Shakespeare's audience—steeped, like our anonymous balladeer, in the discourse of *la leyenda negra*—recognized as "Spanish spirits." This, I submit, is the key to the agency riddle that has perplexed criticism at least since Samuel Taylor Coleridge and has remained the play's "great unsaid": "the motor" at the matrix of *Othello*, which overdetermines its significance and drives Iago's relentless pursuit of "the Moor," is a Spanish one—it is Santiago Matamoros.[47]

"Abenámar, Abenámar, moro de la morería"[Abenamar, Abenamar, Moor of the Moorish lands]

Neither have they beene less injurious to our marchants: they having arrested some, burnt others, and stayed the goods of many without retribution: upon this pretence, they had in their ships or chambers, the Psalmes of David, or some treatise of Scripture in the vulgar: the same being either the Erle of Surries sonets, or some other like matter: but neither were our countrie men so happie to bee afflicted for righteousnesse, or the Spaniards so just in censuring their lightnesse, which should have bin reformed at home: for if the reading a Sonet, or the bookes of Amadis du Gaul, which they have increased to a great volume be death, which of them are free from judgement? their chiefest Lectures consisting . . . in such light and vaine matter.
    —Edward Daunce, *A Briefe Discourse of the Spanish State* (1590)[48]

We have, with good reason, come to bristle at the racism apparent in Coleridge's *Table Talk* remark that "Othello must be conceived not as a negro, but as a high and chivalrous Moorish chief."[49] When we come across such statements as these, the distance we feel with regard to certain nineteenth-century discourses of race can feel sanctifying. Though events confirm that such essentializing habits of mind have continued to persist throughout modernity, however masked they once were by the master narrative of the East-West ideological struggle, we tend to notice proximity in the attitudes of others. But we should remain sensitive to difference with regard to the cultures of the past as well as those of the present. It is not clear that the sixteenth century racialized people along precisely the same lines that Coleridge did, or along the lines that individuals, subcultures and national cultures do today. While we do see emerging in early modernity a discourse of race resembling our own, monogenism—the belief in a common human root—seems then to have been the prevailing mode and "the general commitment to race as *lineage* was overriding."[50] But as Benjamin Braude has cautioned, "It should be acknowledged that belief in common Noachic descent gave no guarantee of human compassion, let alone mere indifferent acceptance."[51] And the language of the play makes it plain that Coleridge was wrong: Shakespeare did indeed conceive of his character as black.[52] Still, the matter of nobility and its links to lineage—Coleridge's "high and chivalrous"—is worth considering, as is the insight Coleridge half-realizes (half-realizes because he still sees Iago's malignity as motiveless) when he asserts that "Shakespeare learned the spirit of the character from the Spanish poetry, which was prevalent in England in his time."[53]

Disquieting though it could be to inquisitors Catholic and Protestant, texts—Spanish poems and novels no less than English biblical commentaries—have a way of traveling beyond the borders of the national cultures that produce them.[54] And as Coleridge observes, there *are* many Spanish ballads—indeed, one can talk of an entire genre of Spanish ballads—that sing the valor of "chivalrous Moorish chiefs" or "noble Moors," and England, like much of Europe during the period of Iberia's political and cultural ascendance, did express a Hispanophilic taste for Spanish literature.[55] During the late sixteenth century the figure of the noble Moor becomes a conventionalized type. Some of the poems that feature noble Moors, *romances nuevos* such as those written by world-class poets like Lope de Vega and Luis de Góngora, reinvent the old ballad of the frontier, or *romancero viejo*, investing its conventionally colloquial patterns with the Petrarchan formal elements that infuse so much of the verse of the age. This antiquarian appeal to Spain's Moorish past, a counterpart to the idealized world of the pastoral, reaches into the novel as well. The anonymous and often reprinted *Historia de Abindarráez y Xarifa* (*History of Abindarráez and Xarifa*) (c. 1564), for example, more commonly known as *El Abencerraje*, represents nostalgically a world in which Christians and Moors embraced shared values of chivalry, honor, and courtly love. But these texts also comment on the recurrent ethnic tensions that were reaching a flashpoint in Spain, which would lead to Philip III's expulsion of the *moriscos* during the first decade of the seventeenth century. In common with Miguel de Luna's *Verdadera Historia del rey Rodrigo* (1592) (*The True History of King Rodrigo*) and Pérez de Hita's *Las guerras civiles de Granada* (1595) (*The Civil Wars of Granada*), which incorporate features from epic romances such as Matteo Boiardo's *Orlando Inamoratto* and Ludovico Ariosto's *Orlando Furioso*—one of the heroes of which, it may be recalled, is the noble Moor Ruggiero (Italian for Roderick or Rodrigo)—these novels often bestow prestige on Spain's Islamic past by announcing derivation from Arabic pseudo-sources.[56] *Don Quixote* realizes this spirit: Cervantes claims that he is inventing no mere fiction; rather, he is translating a history set down by the learned Moor Cide Hamete Benengeli. Cervantes's gesture, which itself underscores romantically Iberia's multicultural heritage, resounds in Don Rodrigo "Ruy" Díaz's title as well. Like El Cid, Hamete Benengeli's title derives from the Arabic *sidi*—"leader" or "lord."[57]

But English writers too inherited this Spanish literary spirit, which had infused European culture from the first hours of the sixteenth century. Anthony Munday's Hispanophilic translations of the already widely disseminated *Palmerin* romances (1581–95) and *Amadis of Gaul* (1588) and the Bartholomew Yong translation of Jorge Montemayor's oft-imitated *Diana*, which, years prior to its 1598 publication in English, had inspired Philip Sidney's *Arcadia* (c. 1581), made available to a vernacular readership schooled in scripture these strangely transnational Iberian romances.[58]After Montemayor, Yong's *Diana* recalled the sad tale of an "Abenceraje" or "noble Moor" called Abyndaraez (a story humorously reinscribed by Cervantes in one of Don Quixote's earliest adventures),[59] "whose valiant deeds, and grave personages, as well in martiall adventures, as in peaceable and wise government of our commonwealth, were the mirrours of that kingdome"; Abyndaraez's rival, "whose singular virtues and approved manhood were so great, that as well in peace, as in war, he got the Sirname of the best knight of all those that lived in his time," is "Rodrigo of Narvaez."[60] This Rodrigo's actions along the Moorish frontier mark him as a latter-day Cid, and this typology, transmuted as *Othello*'s culturally hyperbolic Iberian presence, suggests that Spanish spirits are more pervasive in this play—and politically more charged—than Coleridge senses.

In response to the "vividly racialized rhetoric" of the barnyard epithets with which Roderigo and Iago open the play, several recent critics have written of the "monstrous" view of interracial sexuality that pervaded early modern culture.[61] Strange to say, Shakespeare's English epithets seem to play on the various significations of the Spanish masculine substantive, *el moro*. While in Spain the noun *moro* has signified above all, in "todas las épocas," a follower of Mohammed, or otherwise a gentile, pagan, or unbaptized individual, it also has referred since medieval times quite emphatically to black horses ("a los caballos negros"), to black cattle ("a las vacas negras"), to other black animals, and finally, to human beings ("y tambien a otros animales y eventualmente a las personas").[62] Along the Hispano-Muslim frontier, particularly in the Cid's homeland of Valencia, *moro* had so derogatorily come to signify "dog" that the church instituted the term *morisco* in an attempt to remove its beastly stigma and encourage "Christian charity" toward Moslem converts.[63] True, any number of negative metaphorical associations would have been available in English, including those that identified "blackness" with the "powers of darkness" or the "curse of Ham."[64] But could Shakespeare have had some sense of this more racially specific cultural knowledge—that in Iberia Moors, like Iberian Jews, or *marranos* (that is, "pigs"), were often denigrated in this way? As Iago dubs Othello "black ram" and "Barbary horse," and informs Brabantio he will soon have "coursers" and "gennets"—typically glossed as "Spanish horses"—for blood relatives, it begins to appear so.[65]

Setting Shakespeare's "grange" scene in its larger European context, we should recall that the Protestant north's anti-Spanish polemicists and pamphleteers, from virtually the moment that Bartolomé de Las Casas's nationally reflexive polemics become available, latch onto the accusations that the Dominican friar raises in the defense of the aboriginal Americans and essentialize the Spaniard by projecting upon Iberians a legendary taste for the bestial.[66] That model Hispanophobic text, translated as *A Pageant of Spanish Humours: Wherein are naturally described and lively portrayed the kinds and qualities of a Signior of Spaine* (London, 1599), which "blazon[s] the severall and sundry naturall humors of a Spanish Signior, as the limitation of time will permit" (A3), was particularly thorough in this regard.[67] Insofar its stereotypes draw upon the classical civility/barbarism binary, they constituted a movable ethnocentric frame that might be used to draw the "humours" from whichever "adversary" happened onto the national horizon.[68] It is not uncommon to hear the "wild Irish" or the "rude Scots" fashioned in similar terms, and sometimes they may even be described as "black."[69] But the sheer bulk of the printing we might assign to this emergent Hispanophobic genre—its "kindes and qualities" are repeated again and again in broadside, ballad, pamphlet, and treatise—indicates the wide dissemination of these stereotypes mobilized with a view to the slander of the Spanish race in particular.[70] Indeed, because it reduces "Signior" to his "essentials" by reinscribing via sixteen aphoristic me-morials virtually the whole range of early modern Hispanophobic common-places, we can position *A Pageant of Spanish Humours* so that it might stand synecdochically for the ethnocentric discourses that collectively make up *la leyenda negra*.[71] If we reimagine Roderigo and Iago, then, not as Venetians but as culturally hyperbolized Spanish "allies" in the service of a State whose "Cittizens . . . are deprived of the honors belonging to warres . . . and are con-tented to transferre them over to Straungers"[72]—*Othello*, from act 1, scene 1, rings with a new, Hispanophobic intensity.

Section 6 of the *Pageant* is particularly telling. After warning its read-ers of the dangers of the "Spanish Pockes" the pamphlet cautions, "Signior is stuffed with all manner of subtil devices to deceive women, which is his continuall studie. As the foxe often (not by force but by subtlety) catcheth a prize, to Sig[nior] where he can espye one of his lyking . . . he frieth in Love's scorching flames like a . . . Furnace"—not a little like Roderigo's yearning for Desdemona (or Othello's). Alongside such essentializing commonplaces, Brabantio's "The worser welcome!"—in response to the announcement "My name is Roderigo" (1.1.92)—takes on an entirely new tonality. On hearing the name Roderigo, Brabantio (like our balladeer or some other member of Shakespeare's early modern audience) perceives its indexicality:[73] the name is a sign of its bearer's nationality: "Roderigo" signifies "Spaniard." We can now note that Brabantio's name bears within its own telling cultural significance: "opened," its root is "Brabant"—as in that occupied kingdom of the Spanish Netherlands.[74] The worser welcome, indeed.

The recognition that "Spanishness" is so clearly typed in the various dis-courses that circulate early modern England invites a similar question about "Moorishness": is "the Moor" similarly blazoned? Not so irreversibly as we might imagine. While many in England, as throughout Christendom, remain in some sense shackled to the crusade mentality,[75] and although the English stage sports its share of negative representations, because Protestantism and Islam share the Deuteronomistic prohibition against images, one also encoun-ters new attitudes, "expressions . . . of the compatibility between Christian and Moslem beliefs, both of which included a God and his prophet and which abhorred idolatry."[76] The Reverend Richard Hakluyt, for one, delivered to his readership Edmund Hogan's report that the Moor Mully Abdelmelech of Bar-bary bore "a greater affection to our Nation then to others because of our reli-gion, which forbiddeth the worship of Idols."[77] And the fact that the English embassy represented its queen to "the Turk" as the "most mighty defender of the Christian faith against all kind of idolatries" suggests that these Protestants and Muslims saw at least the potential for a holy league of their own.[78] When Elizabeth authorized the Barbary patents, emphasizing the necessity and convenience of the region's "divers Marchandize . . . for the use and defense" of England and forbidding the importation and selling of these goods by "strangers of what nation or countrey soever," her wording, like Shakespeare's, was of political necessity ambiguous.[79] Abdelmelech was clearer. He was eager to sign over exclusive trading rights to the English because he wanted to "punish the Spanish whose ambassador and religion he dislikes."[80]

The treaty that ensues between England and the former infidel lasts well into the next century. Indeed, their mutual antipathy toward Spain inspires Moroccan emissaries in 1589 and 1595 to go so far as to suggest an allied Muslim and Protestant invasion of the Iberian homeland.[81] As recently as 1601, the state visit of Ambassador Abd el-Ouahed ben Messaoud ben Mohammed Anoun of Barbary had been commemorated by the official portrait sitting that has so often been reproduced in contexts such as this one.[82] We should be misled neither by inherited cultural stereotypes nor by literary-critical traditions; and we should not be too hasty to cast "the Moor of Venice" as necessarily other. There were "noble Moors" who had of late been as welcome in Elizabeth's court as Othello is in the Venetian Senate of Shakespeare's play.

The Chair of El Cid

Rubet Ensis Sanguine Arabum
[Red is the sword with the blood of the Moors]
    —Motto of the Knights of Santiago[83]

Against those . . . the captaine of the Spaniardes with a troupe of souldiers . . . had given them charge, that at a certaine appointed houre, they should all cast them upon those dauncers, and hee himself for his own part, casting himselfe into the thronge, the Indians mistrusting nothing, but onely intending their disport, he saith Saynctiago, let us amongst them, & upon them fire.
    —Bartolomé de Las Casas, *The Spanish Colonie* (1583)[84]

Samuel Johnson once complained,

A quibble is to Shakespeare, what luminous vapors are to the traveler; he follows it at all adventures, it is sure to lead him out of his way, and sure to engulf him in the mire. It has some malignant power over his mind, and its fascinations are irresistible. Whatever the dignity or profundity of his disquisition, whether he be enlarging knowledge or exalting affection, whether he be amusing attention with incidents, or enchanting it in suspense, let but a quibble spring up before him, and he leaves his work unfinished. A quibble, poor and barren as it is, gave him such delight, that he was content to purchase it, by the sacrifice of reason, propriety, and truth. A quibble was to him the fatal Cleopatra for which he lost the world and was content to lose it.[85]

After Johnson, Stephen Mullaney, writing of the ways in which prophecies and riddles came to constitute a "rhetoric of rebellion" for those unable to speak openly against the monarch's policies, has also called our attention to the preponderance of "uncomic puns" that pepper the language of English dramatic literature prior to the Restoration.[86] Shakespeare's linguistic improvisations do freely exploit the sorts of ambiguities Johnson and Mullaney identify. But his drama is also full of puns and riddles we either miss altogether or find "uncomic" because we fail to grasp the multiple referents he puts into play. I would not go so far as to say that *Othello* constitutes an act of rebellion (though much in the play does appear pitched toward resistance). And I find little in the play written in the prophetic mode (unless the tenor of the play as a whole foreshadows an end to the Pax Hispanica as inevitable as Othello's fall). But I do think that Shakespeare's wordplay provides us with signs that the play's "humors" draw not only upon the Hispanophobic inheritance of the Tudor era but also on a knowledge of things Spanish that England had imbibed during the long run of cultural interchange that preceded the Reformation. Placed at the moment of James I's Spanish Peace, *Othello* counters the new Stuart openness with Tudor discrimination: its riddles and puns tell the tale, for they hang "humorously" on the Black Legend rhetoric of the Elizabethan years. What is more, thus situated the play seems to sink, both into the mire of Hispanophobic sentiments that were an inheritance from the Armada period and generically, from "high" tragedy to "low" farce.

In act 1, scene 3, for example, Iago (in quite unheroic prose) tells the lovesick Roderigo, burning in the furnace of love: "Come, be a man! Drown thyself? Drown cats and blind puppies! I have profess'd me thy friend, and I confess me knit to thy deserving with cables of perdurable toughness. I could never better stead thee than now. Put money in thy purse; follow thou the wars; defeat thy favor with an usurp'd beard. I say, put money in thy purse. It cannot be long that Desdemona should continue her love to the Moor"

(1.3.335–43). Leaving aside the "de-serving" quibble which resounds so powerfully in *King Lear*, and which, albeit not so grandly, possesses the same sense of ironic foreshadowing here, let us bring into clearer focus what we might call Shakespeare's "Cid-riddle." That Iago would tell the epic hero's namesake to "be a man!" constitutes both an international insult and a powerfully suggestive inversion. But the line I would like to turn an ear to is that strange "follow thou the wars; defeat thy favor with an usurp'd beard." Typical editions gloss this line as Iago's suggestion that Roderigo should assume a disguise—a "false beard." Some suggest a quibble on Roderigo's immaturity—his inability even to grow facial hair. But when we consider Iago's prodding of Roderigo in relation to the Cid legend, the line becomes activated in telling ways.

The *Cantar de mio Cid,* no longer so well known in the Anglo world as in centuries past, begins *in medias res* with Rodrigo's banishment from Castile.[87] To make a long story short, El Cid's crime has been an offense of rank. On his way to collect from Mu'tamid, king of Seville, the tribute due King Alfonso VI (of Castile), Rodrigo engages the Moors of Granada who are allied with Count García Ordoñez. In a fit of triumphant bravado, the young hero plucks the beard of his "better." Offended at Rodrigo's presumption, the count claims that the young knight has embezzled the tribute with which he has been entrusted. The Cid's lord, King Alfonso, cannot let the young knight's offensive breach of honor go unpunished, so he banishes El Cid from the kingdom.[88] Rodrigo then begins an epic quest motivated by his effort to win back the "favor" of his king. While Alfonso remains distrustful, El Cid—ever loyal— sends the spoils of his many raids back to his lord. In response to the greatest of Rodrigo's victories, the conquest of Valencia, the Cid poet sings:

> There is great rejoicing   among all those Christians
> with My Cid Ruy Díaz,   who in good hour was born.
> His beard grows on him,   it grows longer upon him;
> these words My Cid   spoke it of his mouth:
> "For love of King Alfonso,   who sent me into exile."
> No scissors would touch   it nor one hair be cut,
> and let Moors and Christians   all tell of this.[89]

In the epic poem of Iberia, as elsewhere in medieval Europe (we might recall that Gloucester is similarly plucked in *King Lear*), the beard becomes a powerfully charged metonym signifying nobility. In the first incident, Rodrigo is worthy of blame—he has "usurped" the beard of his superior, García Ordoñez. In the second, however, the assumption of the beard of Valencia becomes a matter of praise. Growing with each victory El Cid dedicates to his lord, it becomes a sign of a new, dignified maturity.

If we bring the matter of Rodrigo's beard back to *Othello*, such a reading is surely consonant with Iago's "be a man!" One thinks of Hamlet's "Assume a virtue if you have it not" (3.4.151). And we cannot fail to note the undeniable association with monarchy that "usurp" would retain—we are, after all, speaking of a play performed at court and concerned with court matters.[90] But "usurp" also means simply "to claim unjustly" or "to seize or obtain possession of."[91] In such a context as this scene sets up, another sense of "beard" is consonant as well (I'm thinking of the "backdoor" view associated with Chaucer's Absolon in "The Miller's Tale"). Considering the perspective on sexuality which Iago has been encouraging up to this point, and that which the English propagandists obsessively ascribe to "the Spaniard,"[92] I don't think it overreading to attribute such wanton wordplay to Iago, whose pun activates yet another metonymic association as well. In English as in Spanish, "favor" may be associated with "sexual favors." In this context, Iago, by urging Roderigo to "defeat" his "favor," advises our young "hero" to conquer—to grab, as El Cid would Moorish territory in "the wars," that which he desires from Desdemona. Again we are reminded of the "debased sexuality" commonly associated with Iago—a "Spanish" sexual humor quite like that given off by *A Pageant of Spanish Humours*—and the fact that he already views Desdemona as a wanton: one who will simply "change for youth; when she is sated" (1.3.349–50).[93]

But all of this quibbling represents more than the sacrifice of propriety and the purchase of a moment's delight. Shakespeare's linguistic dallying turns high Romance to low by refashioning Don Rodrigo "the Challenger"—who is, in the *Cantar de mio Cid* and its several chronicle and many ballad variants, the upholder of Castilian honor and family values—as the inversion of the very ideals he had come to embody for Iberian culture. Further, these ideals, "purpose, courage and valor" (4.2.214), are the ones that Iago ironically attributes to Roderigo, who "challenges" Othello, not over matters spiritual—here Othello defends, loses, yet ultimately reclaims the high ground—but over matters oh-so-carnal. Roderigo's namesake, El Cid "Ruy" Diaz, is here not to be seen as the "original" of the Spanish spirit; rather, Shakespeare refashions Spanish virtues as the vices of a prior Rodrigo—precisely the move made by Robert Ashley, the "faithful translator" of *A Comparison of the English and Spanish Nation*, who, as we have seen, had "lively decyphered" the "nature" of both nations: "Being now entered into this discourse, it will not bee impertinent to speake of the originall of our Spaniardes at this day. For evé as waters which run out of sulphur springs, have always the taste of brimstone, so men alwaies imprinted in their manners, the vertuous or vitious qualitie of their ancestors. . . . About the year of Christ 717, Julian Count of Biscay being extreemly greeved, and exceeding desirous to be revenged the outrage done unto him by Rodericke king of the Gothes, who had defloured his daughter, called and drew unto him the Moores for his succor."[94] "Rodericke king of the Gothes"—the "originall" Roderigo—is figured as the blameworthy, "deflouring" progenitor; the Spanish nation is, by "virtue" of its "history," by *nature* a kingdom that flows from wellsprings so tainted with the "usurpations" of lust, rape, and revenge that it turns to "the Moores" in a desperate attempt to set things right.

Although English polemicists made much ado of Spain's Moorish antecedents, they were also well aware that Spain's Gothic past provided a related set of historical and genealogical precedents. Further, they knew how important Spain's Gothic roots were to its own efforts at national self-definition. For "early modern Spain attempted," as Barbara Fuchs explains, "to distinguish itself from Islam in no uncertain terms through the emphasis on a genealogically verifiable Gothic identity for true Spanish subjects . . . and the construction of a national myth that cast Spain as heir to imperial Rome and defender of the Church."[95] But the appeal to Gothic antecedents was fraught with instabilities. If the Goths could serve as a font of "pure" Germanic Christian origins, they were also those who had brought down, from within, the very Roman Empire Spain claimed to inherit. As Francesca J. Royster has suggested in reference to *Titus Andronicus*, if the play "invites its viewers to identify with the Romans," it "represents Goths as well as Moors as barbaric, uncivilized and racially other."[96] If the relationship of the Goths to Roman history was thus problematic, this was all the more the case with regard to the history of Spain. For if the storied Islamic invasion of the eighth century had come as a result of Visigothic sexual inconstancy, it had been the "original sin" of the Goths themselves that brought on seven hundred years of Moorish rule and the resultant potential for miscegenation that Spain's "purity of blood" ideologues sought to confront. As might be imagined, the Spanish chroniclers themselves were quite aware of the negative implications of a genealogy derived from "Rodericke king of the Gothes." Israel Burshatin has pointed out that "while the Cid harnesses the duality of the poet and soldier by his extraordinary deeds in both domains, King Rodrigo's failures in discernment and *mesura* (dignity, moderation, restraint) make him a flawed reader of symbols. In place of Cidian mastery over word and sword, stands Roderigo's intemperance. His thirst for knowledge and appetite for sex invite condemnation—and usher in the Arab conquest of Spain."[97] In other words, the appeal to a Gothic past did raise the specter of a primordial Christian purity. But this lineage also destabilized the very "whiteness" it sought to recover, opening the door to all manner of genealogical manipulation and falsification as Spaniards sought to establish lineal "cleanliness"—a notion that Black Legend polemicists were all too eager to exploit as laughable.[98]

With regard to Shakespeare's character, we need also to consider an additional web of significance that his application of the multivocal sign "Roderigo" would certainly have evoked in its early performance contexts. While pointing to Spain's Gothic past and its heroic *reconquista*, the presence of a Roderigo onstage must also have raised the specter of a Spanish *converso* present. After all, England's most renowned Roderigo was Roderigo Lopez, the Iberian doctor, merchant, and double agent who had been implicated in the infamous plot to kill Elizabeth Tudor. Shakespeare's Roderigo, unlike Rodrigo Díaz and his type Roderigo de Narvaez (but like Marlowe's Barabbas), appears to be no military man. Whether he is Christian or Jew, the text does not specify. We do know that the obsessed lover whom Iago has brought from Venice is adept at generating funds and thereby vulnerable to the repeated demands, "Put money in thy purse" (1.3.333, 335, 336–37, 339, 344), "make money" (1.3.354), and "provide thy money" (1.3.360). The trial of "Lopez the Jew," the wealthy and endlessly resourceful (if not avaricious) *converso* who "loved the queen as well as he loved Jesus Christ" cannot but have been called to the minds of many playgoers.

Shakespeare's condensation of the essential characteristics of all these Rodrigos collapses (much in the manner of Peele's conflation of the two Eleanors) all historical and genealogical difference in order to intensify Spanish type. Consumed with his lust for Desdemona, *Othello*'s unheroic Cid is completely incapable of reading signs himself (therefore completely vulnerable to Iago's manipulation of them); like Lopez the Jew, he has apparently endless strategies for putting money in his purse; and, like Rodrigo the Goth, he forsakes his patrimony in order to satisfy his carnal desire: "I'll sell all my land" (1.3.380). And if we place these Roderigos in textual relation with another of the commonplaces reinscribed by *A Pageant of Spanish Humours*, we can hear yet more clearly how Shakespeare's culturally hyperbolized character "decypers" the "nature" of "the Spaniard": "In a place of garrison, where nothing is to be don[e] but bragging and domineering, there turn a Signior loose, he wil play his part, he esteemes his skil, far to surpasse all others, but no sooner doth he heare the thundering rumor of *Los Ennemigos*, or see them plant their Tents and Standards with any advantage, he is in a moment wholly metamorphosed, his heart shrinkes like a piece of wet leather by the fire; all his lyon like courage vanisheth like smoake, for that from a Lyon he becomes a hare; yet he wil seeme to cloake it, but never so wel, but you shall see him making of vowes to *Signior Iago*."[99] Driven to become "the Challenger" by an ignoble passion, "wholly metamorphosed"— Roderigo calls on his "Signior Iago" to help him achieve his wholly unholy design: the "usurpation" of Desdemona. By way of this demonization the "essence" of the Spanish spirit, and the hero of Spain's national epic—once a figure to be emulated by all Christendom, now a cowering "hare"—is discovered. And Iago, himself a demonized inversion, rather than bringing spiritual aid and guidance to this "Cid's" cause, indulges Roderigo's lower aspirations—just as he does Othello's—encouraging him to "burn."

It is in act 5, however, that *Othello*'s Hispanophobic subtext comes more clearly into focus; here, several cherished Spanish cultural icons appear on stage in order that they may be played upon. These enter the play by way of several puns, which, depending on where one stands in relation to their spirit, may or may not be regarded as "uncomic." The scene is "a street" once again, where Cassio and Roderigo have tangled. Iago turns his blade on Roderigo, who cries, "O damned Iago! O inhuman dog!" (5.1.64). With his dying breath Roderigo blasphemes his mediator's name, cursing the spirit of Spain in terms used to denigrate *el moro*—"O inhuman dog!" As Bianca enters, calling for her "dear Cassio" (5.1.78), Iago feigns concern for the Florentine, asking, "Cassio, may you suspect / Who they should be that have thus mangled you?" (5.1.79–80). When Cassio answers, "No," Iago, recognizing he has yet to be implicated in the ambush, self-consciously (and a bit melodramatically) improvises the role of the concerned bystander: "Lend me a garter. So. O for a chair / To bear him easily hence" (5.1.83–84). Now let us tune a Johnsonian ear to *Othello*'s intercultural wordplay:

> *Iago.* Gentlemen all, I do suspect this trash
>   To be a party in this injury.—
>   Patience awhile good Cassio.—Come, come.
>   Lend me a light. Know we this face or no?
>   Alas, my friend and my dear countryman
>   Roderigo? No.—Yes, sure.—Yes, 'tis Roderigo!
> *Gratiano.* What, of Venice?
> *Iago.* Even he, sir. Did you know him?
> *Gratiano.*   Know him? Ay.
> *Iago.* Signior Gratiano? I cry your gentle pardon.
>   These bloody accidents must excuse my manners
>   That so neglected you.

> *Gratiano.*   I am glad to see you.
> Iago. How do you, Cassio?—O, a chair, a chair!
> *Gratiano.* Roderigo.
> *Iago.* He, he, 'tis he!
>   [*Enter attendants with a chair*]
>   O, that's well said, the chair!
>   Some good man bear him carefully from hence. (5.1.82–101)

Replaying the scene, Iago—having stabbed Roderigo from behind and thus provoking his blasphemous curses, having acknowledged the fallen Roderigo as "my friend and my dear countryman" and then lamenting "these bloody accidents," and having begged Gratiano's "gentle pardon" in order to remain in control of the scene while maintaining the appearance of proper deference—expresses his concern for Cassio: "How do you, Cassio?—O, a chair, a chair!" Gratiano, presumably addressing the other body on stage, answers, "Roderigo?" Iago, somewhat unaccountably, responds, "He, he, 'tis he! [*Enter attendants with a chair*] O that's well said, the chair!" Why this response at the mention of "Roderigo"? What has been "well said"? (Modern editions uniformly gloss "well said" as "well done.") The quibble is both verbal and visual: Iago is directing our gaze from "the chair" to "Roderigo" and from Roderigo ("he") back to "the chair." The riddle is intercultural:

> I would tell you of him   who in good hour girded on the sword:
> By the stone ledge of El Poyo   he set up his camp;
> as long as there are Moors   and Christian people
> it will be called: The Chair of My Cid.[100]

The "stone ledge of El Poyo" is a natural formation that dominates the landscape of the border region between Valencia and Aragon from which El Cid Campeador, Don Rodrigo Díaz, carried out his raids during his exile. There is a famous convent marking the site—El convento del Cid.[101] The prophecy of the Cid-poet presently came to pass. Don Rodrigo's hideout, knowledge of which was disseminated by the various retellings of the Cid legend—but perhaps most materially by *La crónica del famoso cavallero Cid Ruy Díez Campeador*, which went through fourteen printed editions between 1498 and 1589[102]—gained renown as "the Chair" of El Cid—a geological reminder or "natural sign" of Cid Campeador's prowess and piety. "Let a quibble spring up before him and he leaves his work unfinished," indeed. When Iago says "well said"—he means "well said": here is your "chair," Roderigo; just as Dr.

Johnson warns he will, Shakespeare becomes stuck in the mire, holding up this "sublime" tragedy to stoop for the "wretched golden apple" of a quibble.[103] Shakespeare's "ethnic joke" rests on a pun that reduces Spain's national hero—a cultural touchstone who had "girded on the sword" with the purest of motives—from moral exemplum to dallying wanton: Iago's fallen "countryman," the gulled Roderigo, king of the Goths, assumes the Chair of El Cid.

"Sword of Spain"

> Even as vipers do eate out, and tear into pieces the bellies of their breeders, that themselves may get out: So, not the Jewes onely, but the Papists also, do mangle and tear in pieces the law of God, and do rent, and corrupt the words and doctrine of the holy prophets of God.
> —Anthonie Fletcher, Certain very proper, and profitable Similies (1595)[104]

As *Othello* rolls to its inevitable end, Shakespeare's intercultural wordplay takes a turn more serious. Before Roderigo, "seeming dead," awakes to inform us, "Iago hurt him, / Iago set him on" (5.2.337–38)—before the discovery of the three letters in Roderigo's possession (at lines 315, 317, and 322); before Iago ends his own role by guilefully answering Othello, "Demand me nothing. What you know, you know. / From this time forth I never will speak word" (5.2.309–10)—the Moor reveals his "sword of Spain, the ice-brooks temper" (5.2.260). Entering the bridal chamber to discern "the matter," Gratiano warns Othello not to "attempt it." Upon which note Othello, reassuring Gratiano, "Be not afraid though you do see me weaponed" (5.2.266), resumes his praise of the blade we sense he is soon to turn on himself.[105] "Here is my journey's end," Othello recognizes, "here is my butt," addressing both his "fate" and the hilt of his "good sword" (5.2.267). Even as Othello incants his coming descent into hellfire, Lodovico's officers enter with their prisoner, Iago, in tow. To Lodovico's demand, "Where is the Viper? Bring the villain forth," Othello riddles a reply: "I look down towards his feet—but that's a fable. / If thou be'st a devil, I cannot kill thee" (5.2.285–86). Turning the sword fated for himself upon Iago, Othello makes a last, desperate run at "the Viper," who parries, "I bleed, sir, but not killed" (5.2.288). As the noble Moor draws Iago's blood with his sword of Spain, Shakespeare draws out a humor yet more essential from the Spanish spirit. For when Iago responds, "I bleed, sir, but not killed," he does indeed riddle Othello an answer. In the teasing logic of the passage, "If I cannot kill you, you are a devil. You cannot kill me; therefore, I must be." This riddle of the "cloven-footed viper" finds an answer in *A Pageant of Spanish Humors* as well: "In fine, a *Signior* is a Saint, [he] want[s] but workes (lurks under the greenest grasse, the most venemous serpeant). As *Signior* [appears] an Angell in the Church, to the contrary . . . he is a Divel or Furie."[106] Through Iago, the "demi-devil," Shakespeare rehearses for his seventeenth-century English audience the "more than Turkish cruelty" lurking behind the seductive "workes" of the "Church militant"—a spirit which, though it presents itself as holy, "hath," as the *Pageant* warns, "at sundry times through . . . cruelty, without mercy, tyrannized and supressed whole Countries & Kingdomes."[107] It is this "crusading spirit" that Othello cannot kill with his sword of Spain, and it is this spirit that Shakespeare's villain "humorously" embodies: Iago is a demonic reduction of the "official" Spanish self-image represented most profoundly by the cult of Saint James and *la orden de la cavalleria del señor Santiago de la espada*—the Order of the Knights of the Sword of Saint James.[108]

As Roderigo, the simpering womanizer, represents in Shakespeare's play "the contrary" of Spain's epic hero, so "honest Iago," who appears to Othello and to the play's other characters the embodiment of duty and faithfulness, demonizes the spirit of Spanish Catholicism—*la Santa Fé*—as faithless "workes." But more important, just as Iago, whose "cause is hearted," and Roderigo, whose heart "hath no less reason" (1.3.366–67)—twin inversions of the official Spanish ethos—are, both in the anti-Hispanic propaganda tracts and in Shakespeare's play, culturally inseparable, so are their identities both dependent upon Othello's. As is suggested by that strange riddle-like passage from act 1, which produces, in Stephen Greenblatt's powerful phrase, a kind of "vertigo," the three characters are, in theological, genealogical, as well as dramaturgical senses, consubstantial:[109] "It is as sure as you are Roderigo, / Were I the Moor I would not be Iago" (1.1.56–57), says the "false Spaniard," and indeed, this muddying rhetorical conflation shadows forth the fact that all three—Roderigo, I[ago], and the Moor—are culturally inseparable, each from the other.[110] In other words, Iago and Roderigo need Othello's "blackness," his Moorishness, because this Moorishness defines them both.

We are now in a position to see that in the manner of the revised *Spanish Tragedy*, Marlowe's *Jew of Malta*, and Shakespeare's own *Merchant of Venice*, *Othello*'s incorporation of early modern England's Hispanophobic commonplaces stages an English view of the obsession that defined early modern Spain's sense of itself, *limpieza de sangre*, or "purity of blood"—which should also give us pause to consider Shakespeare's choice of the term "ancient" rather than Cinthio's *alfiero*, "lieutenant" or "standard bearer," to indicate Iago's rank. As representatives of the ancient spirit of Hispano-Catholicism, which considers neither baptism nor deeds sufficient to remove the stigma of a Moorish lineage, "Old Christian" Iago and "New Christian" Roderigo can claim superiority over Othello—a *morisco* who has risen above them in status by virtue of his celebrated abilities—only by virtue of blood.[111] Iago's fixation on the Moor, then, may be as much cultural pathology as personality disorder: the "ancient" has reason not to want it "thought abroad" that "twixt his sheets" Othello has done his "office" (1.3.387–88), for such a discovery could ruin him. And when Othello—a converted Moor, a *morisco*—turns his blade upon the "circumciséd dog" in renunciation of both his humanity and his baptism, he does so in recognition of the fact that in a Europe policed by the Inquisition the one depended on the other. For nothing provided "unimpeachable proof" of Islamic heritage like circumcision.[112]

We repeat the Protestant propagandists' essentializing error, however, if we do not recognize that Spain itself had not been uncritical of the double-edged spirit of its national character. It was precisely this orientation toward the crusading past that Las Casas, among others, sought to expose as apostasy. Having witnessed that among his contemporaries were those who had cast the story of Spain's New World exploits in terms of the ballads and chivalric romances that glorified the *reconquista* of the Old, saying masses in honor of El Cid and calling on Sant-Iago as they waged holy war upon the Amerindian "Moors," Las Casas wrote: "All that I have seen and your reverences have heard, will seem perhaps like the fables and lying tales of Amadis of Gaul, for all that has been done in these Indies is by natural, divine and human law, null, inane and invalid, and as if it had been done by the Devil."[113]

The Promotion of Lazarillo de Tormes

> *Lazaro deserves no blame,*
> *but praise to gaine,*
> *That plainely pens the Spaniards prankes,*
> *and how they live in Spaine.*
> *He sets them out to shew*
> *for all the world to see,*
> *That Spaine when all is done, is Spaine,*
> *and what those gallants be.*
>   —David Rouland, *The Plesant Historie of Lazarillo de Tormes*
>   (1586)[114]

The process through which cultural icons of Spanish origin could acquire Hispanophobic significance when adapted to new discursive contexts is nowhere more evident than in what is perhaps the most hyperbolic and literarily jarring of all the Black Legend constructions printed in London during the 1590s. We have already heard "Gentleman" Edward Daunce weigh in on the question of Spain's racial heritage: "The *Mores* in eight monthes conquered *Spaine* . . . and . . . the *Spaniards* were eight hundred years before they recovered that losse: during which time, we must not thinke that the *Negroes* sent for women out of *Aphrick*."[115] But his argument from ethnos becomes yet more estranging when it offers as further supporting evidence what is surely one of the oddest conflations of fact and fiction in the history of Anglo-Spanish relations. Wishing to "display some Spanish colours" for his "most mightie Princesse" Elizabeth, and also to convince a "noble and vertuous" readership that Iberia is ripe for English invasion, Daunce appeals to one of the most famous figures in Spanish literature as though to a living authority. In *A Breife Discourse of the Spanish State* we find that, in order to perform ethnologically, Lazarillo de Tormes has stepped from the pages of the widely printed picaresque novel and into the genre of Hispanophobic polemic.

As *La vida de Lazarillo de Tormes* (1554) is not widely known among English-speaking audiences, it might be helpful to consider the "origins" of both the novel and the famous protagonist whose name it bears.[116] While Lazarillo possesses a kind of native intelligence—watching the *pícaro* navigate Spain's complicated social hierarchy by living on his wits, readers have tended to find him immanently likable—about all he can claim in the way of patrimony is a dubious ancestry: his low-born miller "father" had gone off to fight the Moors never to return, after which his mother, in the words of English translator David Rouland, "had occasion to make often resort unto the stables, where in continuance of time, a black Morren . . . becaime to be familiarly acquainted with her."[117] Indeed, of his lineage all he can say is, "I was borne within the river called Tormes, whereof I toke my surname" (Av).

The ethnopoetic work the novel is made to perform in England becomes quite obvious when, incredibly, Daunce offers the travels and travails of this fictional protagonist as factual evidence of both Spain's mixed racial heritage and its advancing decadence. "But what heare I?" asks Daunce, "Spain not onely abounding with fruitful fields and rich mines, but with such men as have been parentes of all good customes[?] It sufficeth. But let this be tried by Lazarillo di Tormes, he being lesse partiall . . . who finde[s] nothing in their hostelries but a mat to lye upon, and a candle to bring them to bed" (32). *Lazarillo de Tormes* is co-opted as a kind of intelligence report revealing

Spain's internal depletion and its overreliance upon external sources of wealth, even as it is used to ridicule Spanish values. With the invocation of this seminal character of the picaresque genre, Daunce simultaneously appeals to, and undermines, that key ideological component of Spain's official self-image, its valorization of *limpieza de sangre*, purity of blood—for Lazarillo's heritage is nothing if not mixed.

In much the same way that the writings of Las Casas were put to work in order to discover essential elements of the Spanish national character, the archetypal picaresque novel—a nationally self-reflexive examination of inequities and hypocrisies within Spanish culture—had been recast by the English as Hispanophobic propaganda. Even as Las Casas's defenses of the Indians were mobilized to serve the darker purposes of Spain's international rivals, so was this product of Spain's Erasmian humanist underground read against the grain in order to discover an essential Hispanicity. It was a strategy the proponents of the Black Legend found both effective and irresistible. By appropriating Spanish cultural icons to their own propagandistic uses—Hispanophilically dressing their arguments in "Spanish colours"—Protestant polemicists were able to lend their Hispanophobic rhetoric an air of authenticity.

English playwrights were able to do the same. Thomas Dekker's *Blurt, Master Constable*, a play we find circulating in print by 1602, also foregrounds the nationality of a principal character through an obvious intertextual association with Daunce's acquaintance, Lazarillo.[118] In Dekker's play we find that the *pícaro* has again moved across genres—from Spanish novel, to Black Legend polemic, to English stage comedy. And rather than employing Spain itself as his backdrop, Dekker, like Shakespeare, sets his play in Venice in order to stage a confrontation between his Venetian protagonist, an assortment of Venetian nobles, and a variety of outsiders, including the Spanish "Captain Lazarillo de Tormes."

Much in the mold of *The Merchant of Venice* and *Othello, Blurt, Master Constable* represents the convergence of multiple national cultures in the Republic's famous marketplace. By opposing the French Fontinell and the Spaniard Lazarillo Dekker neatly allegorizes a key geopolitical tension associated with Venice's unique position at the economic crossroads of East and West, including the historical rivalry between Spain and France for control of the Italian Peninsula. Their conflict becomes particularly relevent when we see Fontinell vying with Lazarillo for the favors of the Venetian "Curtizan," Madona Imperia (whose name and sexual appetites bear striking resemblances both to Kyd's Bel-Imperia, the vexed heroine of *The Spanish Tragedy*, and to Marlowe's Bellamira, the courtesan of *The Jew of Malta*). More important in the present context are some of the ways in which Dekker's deployment of the name Lazarillo both mediates and intervenes in the Anglo-Spanish crisis that raged on inconclusively during the final moments of Tudor rule. For clearly, *Blurt, Master Constable* runs through the litany of Hispanophobic typologies that by 1600 had come to constitute the commonplaces of the Black Legend.

At Captain Lazarillo's entrance we learn that he is overcome with certain humors: "Boy," he tells his servant, "I am melancholy because I burne / . . . I pine away with desire of the flesh" (1.2.1–3). Such a line might at first appear to be a somewhat melodramatic marker of a more generic kind of villainy. While it certainly marks the villain, this index of Spain's national character is, as we have seen, precisely that found time and again in Protestant propaganda. Indeed, in the manner of the pamphlets printed by Wolfe and Field, Lazarillo himself attributes this taste for "lac'd mutton" to his own national origin: "So it pleaseth the destinies that I should thirst to drinke out of a most sweete Italian vessel, *being a Spaniard*" (1.2.17–19, my italics). In the object of this desire, "the moyst handed Madona Imperia," we find a character not as chaste as Shakespeare's high-toned Venetian ladies (though we might recall that, once possessed by the green-eyed monster, Othello perceives in Desdemona a like "moistness").[119] The allegorical possibilities implied by her name suggest that her voluptuousness is as much a sign of Venetian economic plenty (here we might think of Shakespeare's Portia) as sexual appeal. And like Kyd's Bel-imperia, this imperial lady wants to be taken.

Most of Dekker's farcical action turns on Captain Lazarillo's romp through Venice in pursuit of Madona Imperia, who will have none of him—although she is, as are all of the play's characters, deeply interested in his Spanish gold. Lazarillo's lust for Madona Imperia, in turn, causes him a number of brushes with Constable Blurt, a city officer who answers directly to the Venetian Duke. While it is doubtful that Dekker's crude comedy will ever find its way into our dramatic canon, his play speaks volumes about the way the Black Legend had come to shape the repertory of England's stage villains. It may also tell us something about the way these stage villains contributed reciprocally to the development of the Black Legend.

Engineering a bed trick to tempt the play's hot-blooded Spaniard, Madona Imperia resolves to gull the love-struck Lazarillo by arranging a midnight rendezvous: "Heere is a key," she says, and "that is your chamber . . . about twelve a clocke you shall take my beauty prisoner" (3.3.189–92). But there is a hitch: "I will come by my virginitie," she blushes, "but I must tel[l] you one thing, that all my chambers are many nightes haunted with what sprites none can see: but sometimes we heare Birdes singing; sometimes Musicke playing;

sometimes voices laughing; but stirre not you, nor be frightened at any thing" (3.3.195–200). Brashly, Lazarillo replies, "By Hercules, if any spirits rise, I will / Conjure them in their owne Circles with *Toledo*" (3.3.201–2), at which moment the captain brandishes a blade reminiscent of Othello's "sword of Spain." Instead of finding the comely Madona Imperia laying in wait, Lazarillo encounters the set of trap doors that will complete her ruse.

As the gulling commences, we find the "amazed" Lazarillo pacing with his Toledo blade in hand. Hearing the musical strains for which Madona Imperia has primed him, the captain boldly invokes the apostle James, patron saint of Spain: "Saint Jaques and the seven deadly sinnes (that is, the seven wise masters of the world) pardon me, for this night I will kill the devill" (4.2.1–3). Hearing laughter within, Lazarillo threatens: "Thou Prince of Black-amoores, thou shalt have small cause to laugh, if I run thee through" (4.2.5–6). But as Lazarillo bursts into the room he finds that he recognizes the tune: "The Spanish Pavin," he says. "I thought the devill could not understand Spanish: but since thou art my countriman, thou tawnie Satan, I will daunce after thy pipe" (4.2.30–32). The Moorish sprite dances the Spanish captain around the room until, tiring of the merriment, Lazarillo begs off so that he might "fall to sleep, / And dreame" (4.2.35–36) of his beloved Madona Imperia.

The purpose of Dekker's rather bizarrely orchestrated ritual has been mainly to set up the ensuing bed trick. So as Lazarillo dreams longingly for his Venetian lover, her trapdoors open to receive him. We can now smell out the humors of Madona Imperia's cozening. Dekker has employed the French form of James in order to pull off a gag at once visual, aural, and presumably olfactory. For this is precisely where Lazarillo falls—into "the Jaques" (or "jakes"). The Jaques/jakes pun is a common one, most famously employed by Shakespeare in the name of his melancholy courtier in *As You Like It* (1600). But here, from the mouth of a Spaniard, the "humorous" wordplay is all the more potent, for who should appear at the invocation of Saint James but Satan as a "Black-amoore," Satan singing in Spanish, a "tawnie" Satan, whom Lazarillo recognizes as his "countriman."

While recalling for English audiences the intense identification of the Spanish with their patron saint, Dekker also creates in *Blurt, Master Constable* precisely what we see in Peele, Greene, the period's Black Legend pamphlets, and *Othello*: a powerful moment of identification between the Spaniard and the "Moorish spirit" of Spain. Dekker's cross-cultural act demonizes the two most important icons of Spanish Catholicism (for the other desacralized figure in the play is surely the courtesan, *Madona* Imperia) in such a way as to render the Spanish and their Moorish adversaries as both spiritually and physically of the same essence. The ethnopoetic constructions of Peele and Greene pale in comparison to Dekker's, calculated at once to produce laughter at the expense of the Spanish and to fly in the face of their professed racial purity.

Before we exit the ethnopoetical stench of Dekker's Spanish comedy, we should also note the attention to which another of the play's Sant-Iago tropes calls to itself. In an attempt to avoid the embarrassment of incarceration, Captain Lazarillo offers Master Constable "golde enough to discharge all, from the Indies" (4.3.115–16). When Blurt will not be bought, Lazarillo reminds him, "I am kin to Don Dego the Spanish Adelanto" (4.3.132). Blurt's response evokes both more topical humor and another commonplace of Hispanopobia:

> If you be kin to Don Dego (that was smelt out in
> Paules) you packe; your Lantedoes . . .
> cannot serve your turne: I charge you, let me commit
> you to the tuition. (4.3.33–36)

Dekker nods here to a Spaniard of legend who, during the period of Philip II's courtship of Elizabeth Tudor (c. 1560), was purported to have "fouled" Saint Paul's Cathedral by defecating in its rood-loft. It was never determined that the episode actually took place. Nonetheless, the "perpetrator" appeared first in numerous pamphlets and subsequently in this play and another written by Dekker and John Webster, *The Famous History of Sir Thomas Wyatt* (c. 1602). Indeed, the Wyatt play poses the riddle even more precisely than does Constable Blurt: "There came but one Dondego in England, and hee made all / Paules stinke agen, what shall a whole army of Dondegoes doe / My sweete countriman?" (4.2.56–58).[120] Of course, "Dondego" (*Don* Dego) is yet one more corruption of "James"—that is, Diego—encountered here en route to becoming the formerly common Hispanophobic term of abuse. Dekker's English captain parses the name for us in the play—punning "villain" or "vile" and "Iago"—"a Dondego is a desperate Viliago, a very Castilian, God / Blesse us" (4.2.54–55).[121] Typologically, the Spaniard "smelt out in Paules," Don Dego, prefigures those "dagoes" or "vile-Iagos" who would be readmitted to England if ever another Spanish match were made—or more proleptically, if James I's Spanish Peace were to become a reality. We begin to get a sense of how deeply the epithet cuts when we recognize the degree to which this final Rabelaisian inversion farcically turns the official Spanish worldview upside down. In Dekker's refashioning of Santiago, a high theological symbol, the patron saint of Hispano-Catholicism and reputed inventor of the Romish mass, reenters the English national imaginary as the scatologically low Don Dego.[122]

The Devil's Faith

> *Don Quixote rode up to the diners and, after first saluting them courte-*
> *ously, asked them what lay under their linen covers. To which one of*
> *them replied: "Sir, beneath these sheets are some images, sculptures in*
> *relief. . . ."*
>
> *"If you would be so kind," said Don Quixote," I should like to see*
> *them, for images carried with such care must certainly be good ones."*
>
> *"Yes, that they are," said the other, "considering their price, for*
> *there's not one of them that didn't cost more than fifty ducats. . . ."*
>
> *Then, getting up, he left his dinner and went to take the cover off*
> *the first image, which proved to be St. George mounted on horseback*
> *with his lance thrust through the mouth of a serpent. . . .*
>
> *Don Quixote laughed and begged them to take off another of the*
> *cloths, beneath which was revealed the image of the patron of Spain on*
> *horseback with bloody sword, trampling down Moors and treading on*
> *their heads. And when he saw him Don Quixote said: "This is a knight*
> *indeed, and of Christ's squadrons. He is called Saint James the Moor-*
> *killer, one of the most valiant saints and knights the world ever possessed*
> *or Heaven possesses now."*
> —Miguel de Cervantes, *Don Quixote de la Mancha*, book 2[123]

> *Seeing then, the worshipping of Images is the worshipping of divels.*
> —John Dod and Robert Cleaver, *A Plaine and familiar*
>   *exposition of the Ten commandements* (1606)[124]

Though Shakespeare is perhaps the most "artful," he is, then, by no means the only "un-sainter" of James: *Othello* both draws on and participates in a world of discourse that includes the writings of Erasmus and Luther, the earliest critics of the cult of Saint James to be read widely among the advocates of church reform, as well as those of Spanish Erasmians like Cervantes who would have preferred openness to inquisition, and "Puritans" of the north and south who found the bipolar discord of the old order more comfortable than the openness of the new.[125] In the disquiet of this Reformation conjuncture Shakespeare's play moralizes a spectacle of spiritual errancy that, via the Iberian arch-Catholic who prefers Roman ritual to saving faith, engages one of early modern culture's deepest spiritual anxieties.

For as the exchange between Elizabeth and Mully Abdelemech emphasized, it was neither national nor ethnic origin that necessarily othered the

Spaniard, though given the right rhetorical purpose either might be invoked; rather, Spanish Catholicism had become detestable to both Moslem and Protestant because it so actively encouraged the "worship of Idols," Saint James the Moor-killer among them (Figure 12). As John Vernon had observed early in Elizabeth's reign, "The Spaniardes and Gallycians, have yet at this houre their holy Saint James, whom they do rather call upon, then uppon the eternall everlysting god, in their moste perillous affayres."[126] Shakespeare would have been catechized and confirmed in a post-Marian church whose clergy had attempted to erase the temptation of saintly mediation by replacing each parish's "images" with Deuteronomistic tables intended to represent the "pure milk" of the biblical text. Spain's national obsession with purity of blood had met its ideological reverse in an English Protestant obsession with purity of faith that subsumed the devotion to "dead saints" within a general theological argument which affirmed Roman Catholic doctrine to be, in John Foxe's phrase, "that false doctrine whereof St. James speaketh."[127] This theological crux—the problem of justification by "Works" (which Spain, as temporal advocate of the church militant, sought to uphold) versus justification by "Faith" (whereby, through a collective interpretation of *solo fides,* outlaw England transformed itself into the "nation of the elect")—in response to which differing interpretations of the Gospel of James were mobilized, came to split Protestant from Catholic so thoroughly that both would consider it worth going to war over.[128] Militantly Protestant texts such as *A Discoverie of the Jesuitical Opinion of Justification* revealed the "original" of Catholic belief: "Papists . . . doe by a double sophistrie beguile themselves and others. That is to wit, in this word faith, & in the word Justification, for faith in that place of St. James, is taken for such a faith as the Devill hath, as Pharoa[h] . . . and such others, that for a time believed, and such a one as Judas and Simon Magnus had, and like unto the Jesuits, call faith, and I think, worse than the Devil's faith."[129] Let us consider the darkness that this "Devil's faith" in James—emphasized, as we have seen, even in tracts as mundane as *A Pageant of Spanish Humors*—casts upon Othello's fall.

The tragedy in *Othello,* viewed from a Protestant perspective, is brought on by the characters' embrace of a false, "idolatrous" religion, Roman Catholicism. In Othello's case, his conversion—his "official" transformation from *moro* to *morisco*—has so contaminated him with the "pollution" of "idolatrie" that he has been "wholly metamorphosed" from proto-Protestant Muslim to "one addicted and bent to the service of idols."[130] As we know, it is through the pollution of images, not "proofs of Holy Writ" (3.3.324), that Iago ensnares the valiant Moor's soul.[131] We even have it from Othello's mouth: "It is not words

Figure 12. *Santiago Matamoros*, fifteenth century, artist unknown. This polychrome image of the militant "twin brother" of Christ was fashioned for the world-famous pilgrimage site in Compostela, Galicia. Note Saint James's "cockle hat" and the facial resemblance to his peace-making "sibling." Photo courtesy of Les Archives Jean Dieuzaide, Toulouse.

that shake me thus" (4.1.41–42). A catechized and confirmed *luterano* could not have failed to appreciate the irony—or the allegory.[132] For if Iago, as the spirit of the Spanish "Old Christian," embodies "justification by works," the allegorical implications of the play, which from even a moderately Reformed point of view are "theologically correct," are thrown suddenly into relief. For though *Othello*'s characters are caught up in the events associated with one of the church militant's great "works"—the triumph of the Holy Catholic League in the War of Cyprus—"faith," other than the faith each character places in Iago, or the faith Desdemona places in her erring husband, is conspicuously absent from the play. This absence is crucial, and it enables us to see why the play might have been considered an appropriate occasional piece for James's 1613 wedding of state.

Among the ways in which idolatry, something of a master sin in early modernity, could often be defined was "setting the heart inordinately upon any creature, by fearing, loving, trusting in it, more then in God and above him."[133] An audience catechized in the Reformed tradition of the late sixteenth century would have seen that Othello is a man to double business bound.[134] On the one side, the idolatrous "loving" relationship Othello enters into with his new wife comes between him and the duty to both church and state that his religion and rank demand; on the other, Othello's idolatrous "trusting" relationship with Iago the demon of Works has eroded his faith—"Christian" that he claims to be, Othello never calls on the heavenly mediator. To the degree that Desdemona draws Othello from this higher responsibility, she is indeed, in the anti-idolatry parlance of the day, a "cunning whore." It is, therefore, this "spiritual whoredome"—idolatry—that is in a strong sense "the cause" of the tragedy.[135] "It is the cause, it is the cause" for the profoundly simple reason that as the hero of this tragedy places the love of his wife before his God and his office, she becomes his "demon." As she allows Othello so to "idolize" her, Desdemona repeats Eve's primal error: she unwittingly comes between her husband and his God and thereby becomes an agent of his tragic fall—a fall from which only divine election can save him. Of course, like the fall of every sinner, Othello's descent "to hell" is mediated by "the Viper," represented in this particular circumstance by Iago.

Recognizing how insistently the English reformers characterized idolatry as "infectious pollution," and their belief that "faith in that place of St. James is taken for such a faith as the Devill hath," we can listen once again to the oaths Iago swears in act 2, scene 3: "Diablo" (3.2. 161)—his curse is Spanish, not the Italian *diavolo*—and "Divinity of hell!" (3.2.350), oaths that resonate chillingly with Iago's inversion, early in act 1, of Exodus 3:14—"I am *not* what I am" (1.1.65, my italics). Thus there is ample precedent in the Protestant theology of the day to justify Stanley Cavell's more recent intuition that the names of Ot*hell*o and Des*demon*a may be "opened"—indeed, as a Reformation hermeneutic might have opened them—so that "hell and demon come staring out."[136] Shakespeare's Protestant sovereign could not but have been pleased by the obvious religiopolitical message the play must have delivered at his daughter's marriage: for no kind of "idolatrous" relationship should one "traduce the state"—a Reformation variation on the theme, so common to all tragedy, of the dangers inherent in life at the top, where public and private so easily conflate.[137]

But we are jumping ahead nine years to the marriage of the Winter Queen and the elector Frederick. In its 1604 court context *Othello*, no less than the other great tragedies of the early Stuart years, captures the immediate concerns of the newly unified island realm. As it allegorizes Spanish devotion to works and stages the disastrous consequences for those who become seduced by such idolatrous "pagan" practices, the play also records the anxieties of a culture that had become caught up in the Elizabethan propaganda blitz (or information explosion) of the 1580s and 1590s. To the degree that *Othello* hearkens back to the glorious days that saw the providential scuttling of Philip's Armada, the play re-sounds the sentiments found in one of the most notorious pieces of patriotic propaganda to come off an English press—a tract in which the militantly Protestant and English nationalist strains of the Black Legend wore the authorization of the queen's own "pure image"—*A Fig for the Spaniard, or Spanish Spirits* (see Figure 5):

> Lastly, [the Spaniard] so loveth, imbraceth, and nourisheth the Gospel, that he maketh his Jesuites, and Shavelings forget all Gospel, and mangleth, and massacreeth all true professors of the Gospell. That he is milde by nature, and seeketh no mans bloud, First aske . . . the millions of Moores, and poore Portingales, aske thousands of Neopolitanes, and Dutchmen, aske Frenchmen, and Italians, yea and the English that have been tortured, and tormented to death by him . . . notwithstanding he possesseth at this day more large territories, and greater store of wealth, then any of his progenitors, or any other prince Christian ever did . . . we may couragiously say, God the Lord of hostes (who is, and hath alwaies been our defender) is our right, and cheerfully vaunt, *a Fig for the Spaniard*.[138]

Like his countrymen who had come of age during the second half of the sixteenth century, Shakespeare would have found the sudden peace with Spain both threatening and destabilizing. By demonizing Spain's national hero and patron saint after the manner of the Protestant propagandists, and dramatizing their "polluting influence" upon the Moor, a very English playwright both resurrects and improvises on his nation's anti-Hispanic heritage, and, at the moment during which a new era of intercultural relations has begun to emerge, bids "a Spanish fig" in respect of his king's new foreign policy. The uncanny number of resonances between England's Black Legend publications and *Othello* indicates the wide dissemination of these cultural typologies. It also suggests that the Protestant anti-Spanish propaganda network was exceedingly successful in its production of this cultural knowledge, guiding "public opinion" in the direction of Hispanophobia. Indeed, *Othello* draws upon so many "socially established structures of meaning," to call once more on Clifford Geertz's formulation, that it is *as if* Shakespeare had this material at hand when sat down to write *The Moor of Venice*.

It is tempting to speculate from our historical vantage point about how *Othello* was received—we might wonder whether James recognized something of himself in the drama's setting and the Protestant attitudes it animates, or whether the members of the Spanish embassy felt their honor stung as they watched the English players so demonize their cultural icons—that day upon which the King's Men performed Shakespeare's play at court: 1 November 1604, "Hollowmas," All Saints' Day—or *el Día de los Santos*. In any case, both the Britons and the Iberians present that November would probably have recognized that the name Iago pointed at once to the storied Moor-killer as well as to Juan Baptista de Tassis, who, seated alongside Juan Fernandez de Velasco y Tobar, the Constable of Castile in the Somerset House portrait, had ceremoniously worn the mantle of the Order of Santiago for the occasion and may even have attended the performance of the play (see Figure 10).[139] They might have noticed too that it pointed to Shakespeare's Scottish sovereign, who had himself, just fifteen months earlier, un-sainted James the Greater by nationalizing that most Spanish of saint's days, which also marked the anniversary of the coronation of the previous "English" king, Philip of Spain: Saint James's Day, 25 July—*el Día de Santiago*. Speculation aside, however, what we can now *observe*—even from our historical remove—are the ways in which the various spirits that hover around the name Iago in early modernity *all* point toward Spain. Indeed, by tracking the strands of cultural significance that attach the play's Spanish names we may have discovered the root of that line of criticism which has sensed the farcical structure of the play. Like its jokes, quibbles, and sleights of hand, *Othello*'s action is so overdetermined by the ethnocentric attitudes, popular commonplaces, politicotheological disputes, and other kinds of cultural knowledge that cluster around the figure of Santiago Matamoros, that the play can, depending upon one's angle of vision, appear less high tragedy than "bloody farce."[140]

*   *   *

To situate *Othello* thus—as a play which registers the anxieties of a culture that finds itself suddenly faced with change, as the product of a society that traffics in propaganda as well as art and which draws upon both to mediate its involvement with other nations—is to read Shakespeare both as a writer of the historical conjuncture we know as the European Reformation and of our own ethnically (and ethically) uneasy moment. Caught up in this unsettling dialectic between the local concerns of early seventeenth century England and the historical wide angle suggested by a more global sense of relationship and connection, Shakespeare himself seems less saintly, more darkly political than we imagined, certainly more *English*, yet strangely familiar; while his dramatic vision still ranges the Globe, it appears more clearly that of his Protestant countrymen in "humor" and "spirit." Until now we have, as through a tremendous, collective exercise of Anglocentric will—our Renaissance, Reformation, and disciplinary inheritance—repressed the multiethnic cast of *Othello*. But Spanish spirits will again inhabit this play, as surely as there is a city across the border from Brownsville, Texas—in a nation once colonized as New Spain—named Matamoros.

Afterword

A Natural Enemy

Mar. Good Master Spaniard doe not kill us,
  Take any thing we have, but save our lives.
1 Spa. How the young brattes cling about our swords.
2 Spa. Zwounds, dash out their braines. . . .
Wif. O my sweet children.
2 Spa. Out you Brabant bitch, thinke you whining
  To preserve your whelpes?
Wif. O spare the infants, and the aged blinde,
  These have not might, nor power to do you hurt.
1 Spa. Cut all their throates. . . .
  Stabs the Children.
Wif. Ah bloudie Spaniard, that hast slaine my children.
1 Spa. Bitch, art thou rayling? take thou this. *Stabs her.*
2 Spa. And this. *Stabs him.*
  Get you together with your damned brats.
Har. O cruel Spaniard, that dost spare no age nor sexe.
  —Anonymous, *A Larum for London*, 1602

LIKE SO MUCH of Shakespeare's dramatic achievement, *Othello: The Moor of Venice* transcends the historical context in which it was born. *Othello*'s poetry, its characterizations, even its farcical structure, rise above the ethnopoetics in which Shakespeare indulged his early Jacobean audience. We do not need to know that the mud being slung as the play opens has something to do with the typical (or typological) animus "the Spaniard" harbored toward "the Moor," nor must we recall the moment of James I's Spanish Peace and the many relationships and connections that continued to link England with Spain, even during the most heated moments of their storied international conflict. It is enough to know that the drama's hero/victim is black, while those who conspire to undo him are not. We empathize with the vulnerability of difference: such universals are what bring most of us to literature, at least initially. *Othello* lives, Black Legend or no.

But the Black Legend also lives. Though we have willfully declined to notice, Shakespeare played a part in its Hispanophobic generation. Indeed, *Othello* may have been shaped by (even as it helped to shape) an entire genre of Hispanophobic plays. Although recent scholarship suggests that we may be reacquiring a taste for Dekker's *Lust's Dominion*,[1] in which Marlowe may have had a hand, we no longer read his *Noble Spanish Soldier: or, A Contract Broken, Justly Revenged* or *Match Mee in London*, or Middleton and Rowley's *Spanish Gipsy*, *All's Lost By Lust*, and *The Spanish Curate*, or Beaumont and Fletcher's *The Chances* and *The Island Princesse*, or Heywood's *Challenge for Beauty*, dramas that failed to transcend their temporal (and national) origins. A quick scan of their dramatis personae, however, reveals among these plays five "Moors," two "Roderigos," two "Don Johns," a "Lazarillo," a "Ruy Dias," and even one "Iago." To the these we can add any number of lost or forgotten plays, such as *The Spanish Moor's Tragedy*, which Dekker, Day, and Haughton seem to have been working on for the Lord Admiral's Company in February 1600, or the anonymous *Spanish Fig*, "for which Henslowe made a partial payment on 6 January 1601/2,"[2] works that almost certainly would have resonated with *The Moor of Venice* in much the manner that Dekker's *Blurt, Master Constable* does. The unknown balladeer who read Spanish treachery in Shakespeare's *Othello* was privy to no special knowledge: Hispanicity had become so overcoded that, among early modern English audiences, recognition of the era's Hispanophobic nods and winks would have been assured. Thanks to the Elizabethans, the meaning of "the Spaniard" had become fixed.

By first decade of the seventeenth century, Hispanophilic attractions— such as those Marlowe writes into his early history play *Edward II*, which constructs "King Edward, England's Sovereign" as "Son to the lovely Eleanor of Spain" (3.1.10–11)—were becoming difficult to voice, even for English Catholics. Not all of the era's Hispanophobic drama cribbed as overtly from Las Casas as *A Larum for London* (1602), an anonymous play once assigned to Shakespeare,[3] which fleshed out Gascoigne's *Siege of Antwerp* (1576) in order to discover that "the Spaniard waites to take your lives, / That he may spoyle your towne, your wealth, your wives" (lines 463–64), with episodes drawn directly from *The Spanish Colonie*. The more ethnopoetically typical mode of representation may be witnessed in the obsessive De Flores of *The Changeling*, or the utterly degenerate Aragonese brothers of Webster's *Duchess of Malfi*, which, like *Othello*, locate their evils in the untoward excesses and obsessions of Spanish blood. And when James I's prolonged negotiations for a Spanish match for his son Charles revived the old Protestant fears of absorption by Spain's Catholic monarchy, a spate of new Hispanopobic plays (along with a revival of the old ones) hit the playhouses. Of these, the White versus Black endgame of Middleton's *Game at Chess* (1624) was perhaps the most "artful." Voicing militant anti-Hispanism in spite of the official prohibition, Middleton precipitated an international incident that resulted in the temporary closing of the Globe, as well as an arrest warrant reminiscent of those once issued for Marlowe and Kyd.

As England's internal religiopolitics pushed the nation toward the Civil War, obsession with the "Spanish threat" subsided for a time. But with the Interregnum, the English Republic sought to bring Protestant light to the Indies over which England's "natural enemy" had for so long cast Romish darkness. Even as the Western Design fixated on Spain's New World Empire in precisely the way Richard Hakluyt had recommended, the English began to fix again on Spanish otherness. At the opening of Parliament in 1656, Oliver Cromwell gave the Anglo-American world what may be the most essentializing expression of anti-Hispanism ever uttered. "Why, truly, your great enemy is the Spaniard," the Lord Protector said. "He is. He is a natural enemy, he is naturally so, throughout . . . through that enmity that is in him against all that is of God in you, or which may be in you, contrary to that his blindness and darkness, led on by superstition and the implicitness of his faith in submitting to the See of Rome, acts him unto."[4] In support of his expansionist aims the Black Legend typologies of the Elizabethans were revived, and Hispanophobia was retooled to suit England's "new model" foreign policy.[5] Perhaps most tellingly, a new edition of Las Casas's *Brief Account of the Devastation of the Indies*, dedicated to the Lord Protector himself, was brought out as *The Tears of the Indians* (1656), translated this time by Milton's nephew, John Phillips, a budding Hispanophile who would turn to less political endeavors after the Restoration, Englishing *Don Quixote*.[6] Even as dramas (including "Marloe's" *Lust's Dominion*) that had once set "the Spaniard" on London's public stages were printed for public consumption or given in private performance, new productions like Sir William Davenant's 1658 "operas" *The History of Sir Francis Drake* and *The Cruelty of the Spaniards in Peru* reveled in England's Black Legend heritage.

Returning to England with his exiled court, Charles II brought in a number of controversial Francophile fashions, among them a taste for the mimetic potential of women in the drama. The French had yet to become the "sweet enemy" the English would often face following the radical reorientation of their foreign policy under William and Mary.[7] Recognizing that Hispanophobia had grown so deeply connected with his nation's self-image, Charles II, unlike his grandfather James I, would not presume to dampen England's anti-Spanish energies. After the Restoration, William Davenant's contributions to the Black Legend were printed together in his *Play-house To Be Lett* (1663) and then included among the poet laureate's collected *Works* (1673).[8] One of John Dryden's most successful efforts, *The Indian Emperour: Or, The Conquest of Mexico by the Spaniards* (1667), would similarly bring Spanish cruelties to the stage. With performances spanning the years 1665 to 1737, Dryden's play achieved a longevity eclipsing even that of *The Spanish Tragedy*.[9]

The spirit of Hispanophobia was translated to North America by our earliest colonial writers. Captain John Smith, for example, could count on an immediate nod of recognition among his readers when, recalling his role in helping to maintain England's tenuous foothold in the New World, he wrote (representing himself in third person), "The Spaniard never more greedily desired gold than he victual, nor his soldiers more to abandon the country than he to keep it."[10] More famously, and certainly more influentially, Plymouth governor William Bradford recorded that the New Englanders' sojourn in the Low Countries had only been possible because of "the twelve years of truce" resulting from Philip III's Pax Hispanica, after which time "there was nothing but beating of drums and preparing for war."[11] The pilgrims had decided to sail west, Bradford recalled, because "the Spaniard might prove as cruel as the Savages of America, and the famine and pestilence as sore here as there" (28). Whereas the adventurer Smith mixed Hispanophobia with Hispanophilia by viewing the heroism of the "worthy Ferdinando Cortus" as exemplary in spite of "the Spaniard's" legendary greed,[12] the Reformed Protestant Bradford evidenced no such ambivalence in his reference to Spanish cruelty.

From these formative moments, Anglo-America has harbored an abiding suspicion of all things Hispanic. The essentializing spirit thrived after Independence (which, ironically, Spain had helped the colonies to gain).[13] Unmoored from the historical conjuncture that first launched its ethnopoetic categories, this discursive formation drifted down the centuries, anchoring itself at moments of cultural stress, wherever and whenever the Anglo and the Hispanic worlds rubbed uncomfortably together. Throughout the nineteenth century the Hispanophobic discourses of early modernity would be summoned in order to prop up the Manifest Destiny ideologies that aspired to "all Mexico," Cuba, and the Philippines, or to influence subsequent foreign (and immigration) policy.[14] As the United States began flexing its imperial muscle in a region that would become its imperial "workshop,"[15] the "mixed race" and "mongrel" typologies that had Hispanized Spain mapped all too easily onto the nations of Latin America, whose vices sounded suspiciously like those that had circulated in *A Pageant of Spanish Humours*.[16]

As late as 1990, the U.S. National Park Service would issue a pamphlet urging public awareness of how the negative stereotypes of the Black Legend "have impeded . . . the struggle [of Hispanics] for acceptance in American society, especially in education, housing and the workplace."[17] In that slightly calmer era, immigration and demographic redistribution toward the Sun Belt was thought to merit critical, government-sponsored reflection upon how "Hispanics in Texas, New Mexico, Arizona and California were frequently in the courts defending their citizenship rights, which, throughout the nineteenth century . . . were constantly being questioned by Anglo-Americans."[18]

"Why We Fight"

> The only difference between Philip II and Osama bin Laden is that the former enjoyed—if he may be said to have enjoyed anything—official power and formal authority, while Osama bin Laden had to construct his power and convince men of his authority. But their souls are bitter twins.
>
> —Lieutenant Colonel Ralph Peters, U.S. Army (retired), "Why We Fight" (2002)[19]

> The FBI has knowledge of individuals from countries with known Al Qaeda connections who have entered the United States leaving false Hispanic identities, pretending to be illegal immigrants and entering the country and disappearing.
>
> —Rep. John Culberson, Fox News (2005)[20]

In the intense political climate that would arrive with the September 11, 2001, attacks on the United States, Hispanophobia would undergo another strange translation. With a Machiavellian executive branch,[21] a complicit corporate media,[22] and a press "grown too close to the sources of power" exploiting the fears of a grieving and benighted public,[23] it is perhaps not surprising that Shakespeare too would be called to serve in the "War on Terror." It was difficult to imagine an American officer corps (let alone its poorly educated volunteers and ill-equipped National Guard units) being moved to "link the great past to the great present" in the way the "greatest generation" had been inspired to do by Laurence Olivier's 1944 film adaptation of *Henry V*, which had warranted a *Time* cover story in 1946.[24] And yet, taking its cue from a publishing effort of the last "good war," in 2002 the U.S. State Department authorized an official edition of that most eloquent expression of Elizabethan martial values in order to inspire coalition forces "once more into the breach"—a prospect made all the more difficult by an armed insurgency that offered coalition forces few opportunities to engage in traditional combat heroics.[25]

Shakespearean patriotism was not the only Elizabethan artifact drummed into service. In one of the strangest rhetorical gestures of the new millennium, administration apologists also deployed sixteenth-century anti-Hispanism. Though it might sound absurd in the extreme that sixteenth-century typologies would surface in the context of what one media giant branded "America's New War,"[26] an essay published in the September 2002 issue of *American Heritage* both commemorated and clarified the nature of the previous year's attacks on "the Homeland" by simultaneously resuscitating the Hispanophobic commonplaces of the Elizabethan age and appealing to the archetypical patriotism of World War II. Evoking filmmaker Frank Capra's classic propaganda series of 1943, the venerable public history magazine offered "Why We Fight" by Lieutenant Colonel Ralph Peters, which sought to explain the psychology of the adversary by proclaiming, "It has become clear that ours is a very old enemy."[27] Juxtaposing images of the camouflaged and bearded Osama bin Laden with a sixteenth-century polychrome of Philip II in gilded ceremonial armor, Peters observed not merely that "their bitter souls are twins" (40) but also that these exemplary evildoers were together "the enduring foes of liberty, of conscience and warm faith" and "a reflection of the enemy who lurks within us all, of Cain" (41).

Cleary, the colonel's rather imprecise application of biblical and historical typology revealed far more about the limits of the neoconservative historical imagination than it did about either of its subjects. But what Peters, who, following his 1998 retirement from the U.S. Army Intelligence Unit, had been a regular contributor to the *Armed Forces Journal*, *USA Today*, and the *New York Post*, as well as military analyst for media outlets such as MSNBC, Fox News, and National Public Radio (and, under the pseudonym "Owen Parry," a prolific writer of military pulp fiction),[28] may also have revealed about "why we fight" is perhaps more troubling than the strained logic of the essay itself. For Peters's reduction of Philip II and bin Laden to an identical "type" evidenced as little understanding of the sixteenth century's Wars of Religion as it did of the cultural currents that were rocking Islamic culture in the twenty-first.

That the actions of a legitimate European monarch, whatever his personal religious obsessions, should be yoked with the leader of a fundamentalist paramilitary fringe group and a network of nationless conspirators was absurd in the extreme. But Peters made this argument not merely in order to prove the errancy of both Roman Catholic and Islamic extremism, which he implicitly opposed to the "warm faith" of today's "Christian" right (41). At the same time, he indulged in the anti-intellectualism so characteristic of today's right-wing politics by taking the opportunity to defame the writers of "the Annales school," whom he dismissed alongside all "fashionable . . . academic historians" as "those profound enemies of history." Among the sins of their scholarship was the attempt "to discount the 'black legend' of Spanish misbehavior." While taking "the vivid Protestant writers" who had chronicled Spain's injustices at their word, and wallpapering his essay with images representing the 1573 siege of Harlem, Peters predicted that, "were Osama bin Laden to realize the power for which he longs, his reign would be no less savage" (42) than Philip II's pacification of the Netherlands.

Such distortions beg for comment here because, while disfiguring Spanish history and culture more egregiously than the sentiments of perhaps any other writer since William of Orange, they misread altogether our critical reassessment of the Black Legend. None of us, I think, wishes to whitewash the atrocities that were carried out under the Spanish flag during the period of Hapsburg rule, which were certainly many and certainly "vivid." But these "Spanish" acts did not stand outside their time. In attempting to look behind the rhetoric of *la leyenda negra* in order to sort out the various cultural relationships—colonial, imperial, and dynastic, northern European, Mediterranean, African, and American—in which Hispanophobia was born, many of us have found that, relative to the imperial and colonial practices common to the era, Spain's actions seem to have been no "blacker" than those of other nations (to bear this out we need proceed no further than England's Henrician tyrannies, its Marian persecutions, France's Saint Bartholomew's Day Massacre, or the Elizabethans' public drawing and quartering of Jesuit missionaries). If the analysis of Black Legend discourse yields any lessons, certainly one of them concerns the poverty of typology. For with the sweeping application of timeless truths and master narratives, historical and cultural understanding (along with earnest dialogue) are often among the first casualties. That a writer whose understanding of history reduces complex causalities and cultural divisions to a search for "the enduring human archetype" (42) should be called on for his expertise in military intelligence does not bode well for a future of intercultural communication and transaction.

And insofar as it exemplifies a pattern of assertion and acquiescence that was increasingly evident after the U.S. election of 2000, "Why We Fight" may be relevant for yet another reason. Appearing in an imprint of Forbes Incorporated, whose links to conservative business and political interests are patent, the essay was as devoid of any actual historical substance as it was of critical analysis. Rather, it existed solely to promote an ideology, to *guide* a public toward the passive acceptance that the members of its current leadership, with their "truer" conception of faith and its relation to historical process, had embarked on the right course of action. Set within the theater of the "War on Terror"—with its embedded reporting, scripted town meetings, "swift-boat" character assassinations, and "no-spin zones"—the essay was of a piece with its own historical type, the "vivid" accounts Peters valued as objective historical sources. The only American "heritage" put on display here was a centuries-old proclivity for Hispanophobia.

As two 2006 *New York Times* op-ed pieces pointed out, Hispanophobic attitudes also sit at only a slight remove from recently proposed U.S. immigration legislation.[29] In an effort to lend authority to a war that most now felt had been built on dubious assumptions, and in connection with increasing public hostility to undocumented immigration patterns, paramilitary groups such as the Minutemen were being encouraged to patrol the American Southwest, even as the U.S. president had called upon the U.S. National Guard to help defend what a popular CNN commentator insisted are our "broken borders."[30] While Black Legend representations of Hispanics continued to circulate internationally via the film media,[31] fear-mongers went so far as to proclaim that Islamist agents of terror were being taught Spanish in order to "pass" as Mexicans and thereby gain entry into the United States.[32] Such assertions continued to fuel the color prejudice being felt alike by Americans of Hispanic and Middle Eastern descent, even as they raised the old specters of xenophobia, anti-Catholicism, and nativism.[33]

One of the great paradoxes of our historical moment is that, even as national boundaries are characterized by fluidity unknown since before the Reformation, religiopolitical identities have grown as polarized as they often were during the Wars of Religion which that epoch spawned. The trend makes it all the more urgent that we lay down the burden of comedy. To do so is to recognize that in every corner of our increasingly interconnected globe lurk similarly essentializing polarities. As the fading twentieth century taught us so many times, and as the nightmarish events that opened the twenty-first confirmed, when the eschatological pretensions of religious "election" come together with particularist claims to political legitimacy, all of humanity has cause for worry—the more so when these discourses appeal to the virtues (or vices) of blood and the nativist promise of land. Let all such discourses be discovered, wherever (and whenever) they live.

NOTES

All Shakespeare quotations are from *The Norton Shakespeare*, ed. Stephen Greenblatt et al. Chaucer passages are from *The Riverside Chaucer*, ed. Larry D. Benson.

INTRODUCTION

1. Eriksen, *Ethnicity and Nationalism*, distinguishes processes of "complementarisation," which recognize difference as "an asset" in order to produce a "shared field" for "We-You" relationships, from the process of "dichotomisation," which "essentially expresses an Us-Them kind of relationship," 26–28.

2. On England's return to the region, see Braudel, *Mediterranean*, 1:611–28.

3. From Robert Dodsley [pseud. Nathan ben Saddi], *Chronicle of the Kings of England* (London, 1821), 95–102. See also Dodsley, *Trifles* (London, 1745), and for context Solomon, *Rise of Robert Dodsley*, 82–87.

4. My conceptualization "ethnopoetics" differs from the term employed by anthropologists such as Dell Hymes, Richard Tedlock, Joel Sherzer, and others. As defined by Sammons and Sherzer, *Translating Native American*, "an approach to verbal art . . . is *ethnopoetic* [when] textual representations and translations are based on native canons of performance and aesthetic appreciation," xii. Their usage describes verbal art (literally, the "poetry" of specific language groups); mine refers to the making or marking of ethnicity.

5. *Elizabeth: The Golden Years* © 2007, Universal Pictures Working Title Films. Two Oscar-winning films *Elizabeth* (1998) and *Shakespeare in Love* (1998) brought in a new era of fascination with the Tudors. More recently we have seen the BBC miniseries *Henry VIII* (2003), the BBC/Masterpiece Theater production of *Elizabeth I: The Virgin Queen* (2005), the award-winning HBO Films Channel Four miniseries *Elizabeth I* (2006), and a BBC/Showtime series, *The Tudors* (2007–10).

6. After Armitage, *Ideological Origins*, I adapt "Greater Britain" from J. R. Seely's 1881 attempt to describe the "encompass[ing] of the colonies of white settlement in North America, the Caribbean, the Cape Colony, and Australasia, all bound together into an 'ethnological unity' by the common ties of 'race,' religion, and 'interest,'" to underscore its ethnocentric anachronicity, 16–21. Seely, *Expansion of England*, argued that "the simple

obvious fact of the extension of the English name into other countries of the globe, [is] the foundation of Greater Britain," 12.

7. On the "inventedness" of national traditions, see Hobsbawm and Ranger, *Invention of Tradition*, 1–14. Literary traditions are as invented as those of any other national institution. See, for example, Dobson, *Shakespeare and the Making*.

8. Camden, *History of Elizabeth*, 10–11.

9. White, *Metahistory*, 9; Frye, *Anatomy*, 163.

10. I follow the fourfold schematic of historical emplotment articulated in White, *Metahistory*, which utilizes "the fourfold conception of the tropes, conventional since the Renaissance, for distinguishing among different stylistic conventions within a single tradition of discourse." As White recognizes, "sixteenth-century rhetoricians, following Peter Ramus, classified the figures of speech in terms of the four tropes (or modes) of Metaphor, Metonymy, Synecdoche, and Irony, but without stressing their mutual exclusiveness, and thereby providing a more subtle differentiation of literary styles than that offered by modern linguisticians," 32. The scheme was widely disseminated through early modern rhetorical and biblical-exegetical handbooks such as Wilson, *Christian Dictionarie*, the first comprehensive Bible concordance in English.

11. Montrose, "The Elizabethan Subject," discovers the mystery of Elizabethan imperial ideology in the refusal "to enact the female paradigm," so that "Elizabeth perpetuates her maidenhood in a cult of virginity; transfers her wifely duties from the household to the state; and invests her maternity in her political rather than her wifely body," 310.

12. White, *Metahistory*, 25.

13. Ibid., 9. As Frye, *Anatomy*, observed, "New Comedy," with which Shakespearean comedy shares many structural affinities, "normally presents an erotic intrigue between a young man and a young woman which is blocked by some kind of opposition, usually paternal, and resolved by a twist in the plot which is the comic form of Aristotle's 'discovery.' . . . At the beginning of the play the forces thwarting the hero are in control of the play's society, but after a discovery in which the hero becomes wealthy or the heroine respectable, a new society crystallizes around the hero and his bride . . . making the struggle of the repressive and the desirable societies a struggle between two levels of existence, the former like our own world or worse, the latter enchanted and idyllic," 44.

14. Hannaford, *Race*, finds the "classical" distinction between civility and barbarity as "most essential" in the Renaissance, 182. We will have to wait, he assures us, until after the more "scientific" investigations of Descartes, Hobbes, and Locke to "begin to see increasing use of the terms 'race,' 'espèces' and 'ethnic groups' to describe the ordering of the many different varieties [of humankind]," 188.

15. Daunce, *Brief Discourse* (London, 1590), 31. Bartlett, "Language and Ethnicity in Medieval Europe," observes that "while the language of race—gens, natio, 'blood,' 'stock,' etc.—is biological, its medieval reality was almost entirely cultural. . . . The most notorious twentieth-century variants either, like colour racism in the United States, seize on clear biological markers, or, like Nazi anti-Semitism, insist on invisible biological differences in the absence of such markers," 127.

16. Hall, *Things of Darkness*, 7.

17. Burton, *Traffic and Turning*, 196.

18. Shapiro, *Shakespeare and the Jews*, 14.

19. Matar, *Britain and Barbary*, 13; *Turks, Moors and Englishmen*, 3–35.

20. As Loades, *Reign of Mary Tudor*, notes, "Even the lurid reports put about in Devon that the Spaniards would land there and 'woold ravyshe ther wyves and daughters and robbe and spoile the commons' failed to produce the desired reaction" of provoking "a general and spontaneous movement of the kind which had put Mary on the throne," 78–79.

21. This discussion also applies to related words such as "hispanicize," "hispaniolate," "hispaniolize," "spanify," "spaniolate," "spaniolize." See the applicable *OED* entries.

22. "Fictive ethnicity" is Étienne Balibar's phrase. "No nation," writes Balibar, "possesses an ethnic base naturally, but as social formations are nationalized, the populations included within them, divided up among them, or dominated by them are ethnicized—that is, represented in the past or future as if they formed a natural community, possessing itself an identity of origins, culture and interests which transcends individuals and social conditions. . . . It is fictive ethnicity which makes it possible for the expression of pre-existing unity to be seen in the service of the nation, and as a consequence, to idealize politics." See Balibar and Wallerstein, *Race, Nation, Class*, 96–97. Of course, the same sort of processes enable the ethnicization of others. As Eriksen, *Ethnicity and Nationalism*, writes, "Like other ethnic identities, national identities are constituted in relation to others; the very idea of the nation presupposes that there are other nations, or at least other peoples, who are not members of the nation," 111.

23. Shapiro, *Shakespeare and the Jews*, 3.

24. Little, *Shakespeare Jungle Fever*, 2.

25. Loomba, *Shakespeare, Race*, 39; Sweet, "Iberian Roots," 143–66.

26. After Williams, *Marxism and Literature*, which attempted to inject "feeling" into "structure" in order to emphasize the processual nature of social relations and institutions, 128–35.

27. 43 Elizabeth I, 804.5: Licensing Casper van Senden to Deport Negroes (ca. January 1601), in Hughes and Larkin, *Tudor Royal Proclamations*, 3:221; See also Loomba, *Shakespeare, Race*, 52.

28. Iyengar, *Shades of Difference*, 1.

29. Hall, *Things of Darkness*, 6–7.

30. Hannaford, *Race*, 188.

31. According to Hendricks and Parker, *Women, "Race," and Writing*, "At the beginnings of this era, *raza* in Spanish, *raça* in Portuguese or 'race' in French or English variously designated notions of lineage or genealogy, as in the case of a noble (or biblical) 'race and stock,' even before its application in Spain to Moors and Jews or its eventual extension to paradigms of physical and phenotypical difference that would become the basis of later discourses of racism and racial difference," 2.

32. Habib, *Shakespeare and Race*, 2. For a useful summary, see Loomba, *Shakespeare, Race*, 22–44.

33. Hall, "New Ethnicities," 168.

34. *OED*, sense 2.a. Williams, *Keywords*, observes that "ethnic has been in English

since mC14. It is from fw *ethnikos*, Gk—heathen (there are possible but unproved connections between ethnic and *heathen*, fw *haethan*, oE). It was widely used in the senses of heathen, pagan or Gentile, until C19, when this sense was generally superseded by the sense of a RACIAL characteristic," 119. I employ *ethnos* in order to distinguish these early modern discourses from more modern ones of "race," though in certain rhetorical situations the distance between them may not have been as great as we have believed. In any case, I refer to this marking as "ethnic" rather than "racial" in order to suggest historical difference. Further, like "race," the word "ethnos" seems to have been moving in the direction of otherness earlier than philological authorities recognize.

35. Perceval [John Minsheu], *Dictionarie in Spanish and English* (London, 1599), 133, 295.

36. Montanus, *Discovery and playne Declaration*.

37. Foxe, *Acts and Monuments* (London, 1837–41) 4:7, 451. It was the institution's interference in the affairs of self-identified "kingdoms and nations" that Foxe found most disturbing, not the Inquisition's focus on cultural outsiders.

38. My usage corresponds roughly to Smith, *Myths and Memories*, who distinguishes between "ethnic categories" and "ethnic communities." While the former denote "populations distinguished by outsiders as possessing the attributes of a common name or emblem, a shared cultural element (usually language or religion), and a link with a particular territory," whereas "ethnic communities . . . are human populations distinguished by both members and outsiders" as "a named human population with myths of a common ancestry, shared historical memories and one or more common elements of culture, including an association with a homeland, and some degree of solidarity, at least among elites," 12–13. Following Connor, "A Nation Is a Nation," I adopt the further qualification that an "ethnic group may be readily discerned by an anthropologist or other outside observer," but "until the members are themselves aware of the group's uniqueness, it is merely an ethnic group and not a nation. While an ethnic group may, therefore, be other-defined, the nation must be self-defined," 45–46.

39. Kinney and Swain, *Tudor England*, 693; Gurr, "The Shakespearean Stage," 1031.

40. Beeman, "Anthropology of Theater," 386.

41. An important exception is Lamana, "Of Books, Popes, and *Huacas*," 117–49.

42. For Bakhtin, "Problem of Speech Genres," "Language is realized in the form of individual concrete utterances (oral and written) by participants in the various areas of human activity. These utterances reflect the specific conditions and goals of each area not only through their content (thematic) and linguistic style, that is, the selection of the lexical, phraseological and grammatical resources of the language, but above all through their compositional structure. All three of these aspects—thematic content, style, and compositional structure—are inseparably linked to the whole of the utterance and are equally determined by the specific nature of the particular sphere of communication. Each utterance is individual, of course, but each sphere in which language is used develops its own relatively stable types of these utterances. These we may call speech genres. . . . Each sphere of activity contains an entire repertoire of speech genres that differentiate and grow as the particular sphere develops and becomes more complex. Special emphasis should be placed on the extreme heterogeneity of speech genres (oral and written)," 60.

Bakhtin's critique of Saussurean linguistics is also apropos: "The single utterance, with all its individuality and creativity, can in no way be regarded as a completely free combination of forms of language, as is supposed, for example, by Saussure (and by many other linguists after him), who opposed the utterance (la parole), as a purely individual act, to the system of language as a phenomenon that is purely social and mandatory for the individuum. . . . When we select a particular type of sentence, we do so not for the sentence itself, but out of consideration for what we wish to express with this one given sentence. . . . The idea of the form of the whole utterance, that is, of a particular speech genre, guides us in the process of our speaking. . . . The chosen genre predetermines for us their type and their compositional links," 81. Or, as per Volosinov, *Marxism and the Philosophy,* "Social psychology exists primarily in a wide variety of forms of the 'utterance,' of little speech genres of internal and external kinds—things left completely unstudied to the present day. . . . All these forms of speech interchange operate in extremely close connection with the conditions of the social situation in which they occur and exhibit an extraordinary sensitivity to all fluctuations in the social atmosphere," 20.

43. Floyd-Wilson, *English Ethnicity and Race,* parses the period's appropriations of classical geohumoralism; Kidd, *British Identities Before Nationalism,* focuses on the biblicism and Gothicism underwriting English constructions of nationality.

44. After Eco, *Theory of Semiotics*: "Overcoded entities float among the codes, on the threshold between convention and innovation. It is by a slow and prudent process that a society admits them to the ranks of rules upon which it bases its own raison 'd'être.'" And "frequently a society does not recognize overcoded rules that in fact allow the social exchange of signs," 134.

45. After Greenblatt, "Remnants of the Sacred," 342.

46. Juderías, *La leyenda negra* (Barcelona, 1929). Among the more useful studies are Powell, *Tree of Hate*; Maltby, *Black Legend in England*; García Cárcel, *La leyenda negra.*

47. Weber, *Spanish Frontier,* 336.

48. H. W., *Pageant of Spanish Humours* (London, 1599), A3.

49. See Braudel, *Mediterranean,* 833. On the Treaty of Vervins, see Baumgartner, *France,* 231–32.

50. Jonson, *The Alchemist,* 245.

51. Braudel, *Structures,* 317–18.

52. Fuchs, *Mimesis and Empire,* 2–4.

53. See Greer, Mignolo, and Quilligan, *Rereading the Black Legend,* passim.

54. See Hegel, *Introduction to the Philosophy of History.* 1840 (Indianapolis, 1988), 52, 67; De Grazia, "Teleology, Delay, and the 'Old Mole.'"

55. Burckhardt, *Civilization of the Renaissance,* 4, 101.

56. Taine, *Histoire de la littérature anglaise* (Paris, 1863), identified two strains within the literature of England: its "Christian Renaissance" authors evidence "the hatred of the ecclesiastical hierarchy, which is the Reformation," while its "Pagan Renaissance" writers offer a "the return to the senses and to the natural life," 139. Emblematic are Tillyard, *Elizabethan World Picture,* who wrote of the era "as a period between two outbreaks of Protestantism: a period in which religious enthusiasm was sufficiently dormant to allow the

new humanism to shape our literature" (3), and Rouse, *Elizabethan Renaissance*, although he did say in closing that "foreigners coming to the island on a voyage of discovery found the English of that age much more as we conceive of Continentals," 353.

57. Williams, *Marxism and Literature*, suggests that in "'epochal' analysis, a cultural process is seized as a cultural system, with determinate dominant features," whereas "it is necessary at every point to recognize the complex interrelations between movements and tendencies both within and beyond a specific and effective dominance," 121. "The residual, by definition, has been effectively formed in the past, but is still active in the cultural process, not only and often not at all as an element of the past, but as an effective element of the present," 122, while "emergent," concerns the "new meanings and values, new practices, new relationships and kinds of relationship" that "are continually being created," 123. I intend the "deeper" sense of "tradition": "a deliberately selective and connecting process which offers a historical and cultural ratification of a contemporary order . . . tied to many practical continuities—families, places, institutions, a language—which are indeed directly experienced . . . [the] struggle for and against [which] . . . is understandably a major part of all contemporary cultural activity"; and I employ "formations" as "those effective movements and tendencies, in intellectual and artistic life, which have significant and sometimes decisive influence on the active development of a culture, and which have a variable and often oblique relation to formal institutions," 116–17.

58. Within the Shakespeare canon alone there exists a substantial subset of plays that suggest connections to the very Hispanic world the Elizabethans incontrovertibly othered. Setting aside moments in which his characters rather unaccountably utter Castilian "palabras" (*Taming of the Shrew, Much Ado About Nothing*), invoke "Diablo" (*Othello*), bid each other "Spanish Figs" (*2 Henry IV, Henry V*), wield Spanish swords (*Romeo and Juliet, All's Well That End's Well, Othello*), express envy of Spain's Indies or anxieties about the Spanish Netherlands (*Comedy of Errors*), plays like *Love's Labour's Lost, Much Ado About Nothing, The Winter's Tale*, and *The Tempest* are by implication as much Spanish plays as Kyd's famous tragedy. For Navarre, Sicily, Naples, Milan, and Algiers are in Shakespeare's day either among the Kingdoms of the Spanish Monarchy or within the Spanish orbit.

59. On New Historicism's orientation toward time, see Ingham, "Contrapuntal Histories," 74–75.

60. Greene, *Unrequited Conquests*, 26.

61. After Rosaldo, *Culture and Truth*, 20.

62. Braudel, *Mediterranean*, 16. Wallerstein, *Modern World System,* 38–63, provides a view of Iberia's place within the global network. See Jardine, *Worldly Goods*, on commercial interconnectedness.

63. Fuchs, "Imperium Studies," 72.

64. Most suggestive are Greene, *Unrequited Conquests*, and Fuchs, *Mimesis and Empire*. On the "ambivalence and contradiction" of Anglo-Hispanic relations, see Griffin, "The Specter of Spain in John Smith's Colonial Writing"; Hart, *Representing the New World*, 5 and passim; Scanlan, *Colonial Writing*, 38–67. For an anthropological perspective on the perception of otherness in a nation's "imaginary," see Hamilton, "Fear and Desire."

65. Fuchs, "Imperium Studies," adds a useful elaboration: "In order to address this

history of expansion, imperium studies brings some of the central preoccupations of post-colonial theory to the early modern metropole. The differenda of power within a society; the 'othering,' racialization, and exploitation of marginalized peoples; the resistance of those peoples to centralized power; the discursive strategies that serve to control and transform territory; the cultural significance of borders and contact zones—all these inquiries potentially reveal as much about European nations-in-the-making as they do about colonized territories. For the metropole is not a uniform locus of political power, even if it might occasionally appear thus from the colonies. Instead, it too is marked by conquests, migrations, cultural transformations, and enduring tensions between center and peripheries. Imperium studies is an effort to write the story of those tensions and the cultural dynamics that characterize them," 74.

66. See, for example, the work of Bartels, Vitkus, Burton, Matar, and Raman.

67. See Gunn, "Globalizing Literary Studies," 16; Jay, "Beyond Discipline?" 32–47.

68. Ginzburg, *No Island Is an Island.*

69. Greenblatt, "Racial Memory," 59.

70. Geertz, *Interpretation of Cultures,* 12.

71. After Comaroff and Comaroff, *Ethnography and the Historical Imagination*: "The historicity of all social fields, political communities and cultural milieus . . . resides in a complex equation, the elements of which are (1) the internal dynamics of local worlds, their dialectics of the short run and (2) the articulation, over the long term, between those local worlds and the structures and agencies—at once regional and global—that come to make up their total environments," 98.

72. Clifford, "On Ethnographic Allegory," 110.

73. Geertz, *Interpretation of Cultures,* 453.

CHAPTER 1. FROM ETHOS TO ETHNOS

Note to epigraph: Middleton, *Game at Chess,* induction: 41–43.

1. Froude, *History of England* (London, 1862–70), 12:530.

2. See also Fernández-Armesto, *Spanish Armada*; Gallagher and Cruikshank, *God's Obvious Design.*

3. Because *A Game at Chess* stands outside my main purview, and because there is substantial recent commentary on its relation to the Spanish match, I have chosen not to discuss the play at length. See Taylor, "Cultural Politics of Maybe"; Howard-Hill, ed., *Middleton's "Vulgar Pasquin,"* 10–17; Dutton, "Receiving Offense"; Patterson, *Censorship and Interpretation,* 81–87.

4. Helgerson, *Forms of Nationhood*; McEachern, *Poetics of English Nationhood.*

5. Smith, *Myths and Memories,* 98.

6. Rosaldo, *Culture and Truth,* 20.

7. On links between European nationalism, nineteenth-century philology, "and the historiography of the romantic epoch," see Smith, *Myths and Memories,* 29–30, 71–73.

8. Connor, "A Nation Is a Nation," 45; Smith, *Myths and Memories,* 57, passim.

9. Williams, *French Fetish*. In an illuminating and otherwise inclusive anthology, *Empire and Others*, ed. Daunton and Halpern, the Spanish appear as only a marginal presence.

10. On Henry V and nationalism, see Holderness, "What Ish My Nation?"

11. Comaroff and Comaroff, *Ethnography and the Historical Imagination*, 50–51.

12. Habermas, *Structural Transformation*, whose model "may be conceived above all as the sphere of private people who come together as a public" and claim "the public sphere regulated from above against the public authorities themselves, to engage them in a debate over the general rules governing relations in the basically privatized but publicly relevant sphere of commodity exchange and social labor," 27.

13. Mattingly, *Catherine of Aragon*, 6, 15. Katherine of Aragon was known variously as "Catalina," "Catherine," "Katharine," which Foxe preferred, and "Kateryne."

14. In "Speke Parrot," his famous court satire, Skelton writes of "Kateryne incomporabyll, owur royall quene . . . / That pereles pomegarnat, Cryst save hyr noble grace!" *Complete English Poems*, 231.

15. Eriksen, *Ethnicity and Nationalism*, 26–28.

16. This is more than a bit ironic, considering that the "national" culture into which she is born is moving by increments toward the dead-end of ethnopolitics by elevating *limpieza de sangre* even as influential factions within her adoptive nation will soon court delusions of purity of faith.

17. Hall, *Union of the Two Noble Illustre Famelies* (London, 1809), 519–20 (hereafter, *Hall's Chronicle*).

18. Ibid., 520. "Sydney" is William Sidney (1482–1554), grandfather of the famous courtier-soldier-poet, Sir Philip. For the mixed success of English involvement in Granada and North Africa during this period, see Hillgarth, *Mirror of Spain*, 15–16.

19. On the shifting borders of the region, and the relationship of "successive English governments" with Aragon, Castile, and Portugal, see Russell, *English Intervention*, xxiii–iv, passim.

20. On the social processes of pilgrimage, "which seem to have contributed to the maintenance of some kind of international community in Christendom," and a fifteenth-century account of the "Arrival at Compostela," see Turner, *Dramas, Fields, and Metaphors*, 179–82. See also Arsuaga, "Shrine as Mediator."

21. Livermore, *New History of Portugal*, 120–22.

22. Mattingly, *Catherine of Aragon*, 236.

23. Ibid., 256. See also Griffin, "From Ethos to Ethnos," on Foxe's construction.

24. Arguments claiming Katherine's prior marital knowledge depended upon an anecdote that asserted that the fifteen-year-old Arthur Tudor had "confessed the act done, by certain words spoken," Foxe, *Acts and Monuments*, 5:51. It was not, however, generally believed that the marriage had in fact been consummated.

25. Bernstein, *Foregone Conclusions*, argues "Back-shadowing is a kind of retroactive foreshadowing in which the shared knowledge of the outcome of a series of events by narrator and listener is used to judge the participants in those events as though they too should have known what was to come," 16.

26. Haller, *Elect Nation*, 13.

27. Foxe, *Acts and Monuments*, 5:44.

28. On the high esteem in which Katherine was held by the English people, and their acts of resistance to Henry's divorce, see Montrose, *Subject of Elizabeth*, 11–15. On Foxe's rhetorical strategies and handling of sources, see King, *Foxe's* Book of Martyrs, 21–22.

29. Firth, *Apocalyptic Tradition*, 69ff. On the Elizabethan regime's shifting positions, see Kouri, "True Faith or National Interest?" 411ff.

30. I mean to suggest the root sense of "ethos," that is, "character" or "custom"; but I also want to imply the moral dimension suggested by cognates such as "ethics" and "ethical."

31. Fabian: *Time and the Other*, 30–31.

32. Duffy, *Stripping of the Altars*, 524. Collinson, *Birthpangs*, seconds Scarisbrick, *Reformation and the English*: "On the whole, English men and women did not want the Reformation and were slow to accept it when it came," but notes the "readiness with which these 'most' people abandoned religious habits which seem to have been meaningful and dear to them simply at the behest of the government," 40. Or as Haigh says in *English Reformations*, "There was no sign of Catholic collapse, no suggestion that Mary's Church might be in terminal decline," 235.

33. Elder, *Copie of a letter* (London, 1555), quoted in Armitage, *Ideological Origins*, 38.

34. Martyr, *Decades* (London, 1555), 43–200.

35. See Prescott, *History of Philip II*, 1:126.

36. Loades, *Reign of Mary Tudor*, 158.

37. Loades, ibid., notes that "the behaviour of the Spaniards was not exemplary, in spite of Philip's efforts and the emperor's copious advice"; among the problems was "a rooted conviction in Spain that the English were all heretics and savages, a preconception which seems to have informed many of the earliest comments made by Philip's followers," 160.

38. In addition to noting the Saint James's Day marriage and Bishop Gardiner's sermon on Saint James and his "works," among the incidents from England's "Spanish period" on which Foxe casts an ironic eye are Philip's arrival with a "naked sword" and the "Spaniards" playing "at knaves" in the cloister of Saint Paul's. In each case, Foxe deploys antithesis in order to suggest that the Spaniards have not the virtues they claim to represent, but embody instead their "Antichristian" opposite. See *Acts and Monuments*, 5:554–83.

39. Helgerson, *Forms of Nationhood*, 249–68; *Acts and Monuments*, "Pertaining to the Last Three Hundred Years from the Loosing Out of Satan," 4:3–556. Helgerson partially vindicates Haller's *Elect Nation* thesis, which has fallen into disfavor among scholars who believe that the idea of national election did not take hold before the 1640s. It does seem clear, however, that a similar sense of election pervades Foxe's book. If the "God is English" rhetoric of the Civil War is not present, the "England as Israel" topos amounts to much the same thing. As Parry, "Elect Church or Elect Nation?" suggests, when we consider the "international political context . . . which conditioned the way in which [English readers] 'received' Foxe's history," we can recognize the "troubling ease with which they persuaded themselves that his ideas contained a manifesto for Elizabethan England's priority in successfully ending [the international] struggle," 168. Like Helgerson, Parry argues that Foxe's

"binding of Satan to the reign of Constantine" helped to create "a tradition of reading the *A & M* as a manifesto for England's ruler to lead the Protestant cause, a reading which continued to be echoed into the seventeenth century, though less finally and xenophobically than Haller allows," 170–71. Armitage, *Ideological Origins*, distances himself from Haller, writing that Foxe "clearly placed the history of the English Church within a universal scheme of salvation and reprobation, the small, persecuted elect leaven within the lump of unregenerate mass of humanity being as unequally distributed within his own nation as anywhere else," 79. I would argue that Foxe's book goes to great lengths to suggest that the leavening is larger in England than in any other nation. Wooden, *John Foxe*, takes a reasonable middle position: Foxe is simultaneously internationalist and nationalistic, 34–36.

40. Fabian, *Time and the Other*, 26.

41. Holinshed, *Chronicles* (London, 1807–8), notes that Philip had prayed at his shrine at Compostela, where "the English Ambassadors met him. . . . And after he had in the presence of a great number of noble men and gentlemen there ratified the contract, and swoorne to observe the covenant, he departed towards Corone, where within a few daies after he imbarked, and accompanied with the number of an hundred and fiftie saile, directed his course toward England," 4.57.

42. One of these works is the "error" of the mass itself, wrongly attributed by Foxe to Saint James, "once bishop at Jerusalem," *Acts and Monuments*, 6:369. For a discussion of "Justification by Faith Alone, and its Consequences," see Davies, *Worship and Theology*, 17–25.

43. "Works" extended to a broad range of Roman Catholic practices, including the granting of indulgences and dispensations, the adoration of images, the consecration of the host, the lighting of candles, and the saying of the mass itself. The notion of "hot-gospelling" biblical literalism I derive from Collinson, *Elizabethan Puritan Movement*, an orientation toward what Tyndale described as "the whole course of scripture," 27. Collinson, *Religion of Protestants,* emphasizes the "Chillingworth dictum": "The Bible, the Bible only I say, is the religion of Protestants," which Collinson finds "profoundly true of the Elizabethan and Jacobean Church," viii–ix.

44. Bozeman, "Federal Theology," notes that English reformers may have adapted the notion of the "national covenant" from Heinrich Bullinger, who by 1534 had published "the first major Reformed treatise structured by the covenant idea," 398–99.

45. On the pageantry of Katherine's arrival, see Anglo, *Spectacle, Pageantry*, 56–97.

46. Hakluyt, *Discourse of Western Planting*, 1584 (London, 1993), 1:166–70, 11:1437–41.

47. We have tended to think of this emulation as primarily colonial. On the unification of the Spanish Crowns as a model for national consolidation, see Morrill, "The British Problem," 11; Armitage, *Ideological Origins*, 22–23.

48. Cecil, William. "An Antidote Against Jesuitism," cited in Edwards, "Divisions Among the English Catholics," 25.

49. The Star Chamber edict of 1586 goes a long way toward achieving this goal. As Greg observed, "By concentrating the craft of printing books, and to a considerable extent their distribution, in the hands of a single society in London . . . the government rendered the task of surveillance and control of the nation's reading comparatively easy. . . . The mo-

nopoly it ensured to the members of the [Stationers] Company was valuable and gratifying, and no other interests existed of sufficient weight to form an effective opposition or even raise a vocal protest." Quoted in Bennett, *English Books and Readers*, 58–59.

50. Parmellee, *Good Newes from Fraunce*, 32–33; Woodfield, *Surreptitious Printing*, 6–7. See also Brennan, *Patriotism, Power and Print*, especially 94–107.

51. See Coldiron, "Public Sphere/Contact Zone," 209.

52. Ibid., 207, 211; Loewenstein and Stephens, "Charting Habermas's 'Literary' or 'Precursor,'" 201–5.

53. Maravall, *Culture of the Baroque*, 19–53, 57–148. Building on Maravall's model, Cascardi, *Ideologies of History*, describes this "crisis-structure" in relation to a problematic of "subject-formation," 112–14.

54. See also Maravall, "From the Renaissance to the Baroque," 3–40, for his notions of structure and periodization. On Maravall's Burckhardtian tendencies, see Gilbert, "Ideology and Image," 172–74; on his debt to Wölfflin, see Lollini, "Maravall's Culture of the Baroque," 187–94.

55. Beverley, "On the Spanish Literary Baroque," 221–22.

56. Mignolo, "What Does the Black Legend Have to Do with Race?" 312–24.

57. On the *la leyenda aurea*, or "gilded legend," see Gibson, *Black Legend*, 6–7; alternatively, pro-Spanish discourses may be figured as *la leyenda rosa*, the "red legend" of Hapsburg apologists. See García Cárcel, *La leyenda negra*, 113.

58. Schmidt, *Innocence Abroad*, 17–23.

59. Martyr, *Decades*, 50; Hart, *Representing the New World*, 62.

60. On Fernández's *Virgin of the Navigators* (or "Seafarers"), and the problematic identification of its figures, see Phillips, "Visualizing Imperium."

61. Schmidt, *Innocence Abroad*, 71; Pagden, *Lords of All*, 74–75.

62. The Latin phrase is from Tacitus. See Pagden, *Lords of All*, 13. For the White Legend as Hispanophobia's ideological opposite, see Gibson, *Black Legend*, 5–27.

63. On William of Orange, Dutch, and German uses of Las Casas, see Schmidt, *Innocence Abroad*, 87–99, 115–22; Keen, *Aztec Image*, 162–66.

64. William of Orange, *Apologie* (Delft, 1580), O2 (probably written by Pierre Loyseleur).

65. For the Dutch context of the Black Legend, see Schmidt, *Innocence Abroad*, 17–23. See also Hilgarth, *Mirror of Spain*, 309–27; Hadfield, *Literature, Travel*, 85–104.

66. Schmidt, *Innocence Abroad*, 25–30.

67. On Benzoni and Challeux, see Elliott, *Old World and the New*, 95–96; Gibson, *Black Legend*, 78–89, Schmidt, *Innocence Abroad*, 43–46; Hart, *Representing the New World*, 70–82; Hillgarth, *Mirror of Spain*, 333.

68. Las Casas, *Devastation of the Indies*, trans. Herma Briffault, 125.

69. On Las Casas's "predilection for numbers," see Schmidt, *Innocence Abroad*, 117–21.

70. Scanlan, *Colonial Writing*, 1.

71. Scanlan writes, "In their insistent focus on the cruelty of the Spanish toward the native populations, the prefaces [to Las Casas's *Brevíssima relación* and Hakluyt's *Discourse*

of Western Planting] forge the crucial link between the behavior of colonizing nations and their identities," 9. As Scanlan accurately observes, "What these early translations show is that Spanish colonization—or, more precisely, the Spanish treatment of the native populations in the colonial setting—could be made to signify something about the Spanish nation," 19.

72. For the relationship between Foxe and Day, see King, *Foxe's* Book of Martyrs, passim.

73. Las Casas, trans. M. M. S., *Spanish Colonie* (London, 1583), A4r, and passim.

74. Greenfeld, *Nationalism*, 29–87. While I question Greenfeld's failure to consider that both Portugal and Castile might have seen themselves as "firstborn," and her failure to note Spain's role in the constitution of national consciousness, her observations about the depth of England's sense of national election seem fundamentally sound. See also Helgerson, *Forms of Nationhood*, especially 181–87 and 254–68.

75. A text as potentially inflammatory as Gascoigne, *Spoyle of Antwerpe* (London, 1577), (sometimes attributed to Bernard Gardet), which described the harsh treatment of English subjects present during the siege, also commended the efficiency of the Spanish troops, whose "victorye was obtyened with losse of but fyve undreth Spanierds, or sixe at the most," diminished the significance of the Spanish violence by observing that the "outrages and cruelties done to our nation, proceeded but from the cōmon Souldiers" and not by "a man of any charge or reputacion," Ai.

CHAPTER 2. A LONG AND LIVELY ANTITHESIS

Note to epigraphs: Quoted in King, *Foxe's* Book of Martyrs, 70; Ashley, *Comparison of the English and Spanish* (London, 1589), A3v–r, D3v, E1v.

1. Foxe, *Acts and Monuments*, 3:719–20.

2. King, *Foxe's* Book of Martyrs, 80–92; King, *English Reformation Literature*, 425–43. England's Black Legend texts have been partially catalogued by Parmellee, *Good Newes from Fraunce*; Powell, *Tree of Hate*; and Maltby, *Black Legend in England*.

3. Peele, *Life and Works*, ed. Tyler; see also Chambers, *Elizabethan Stage*, 3:460.

4. For Edward's Jewish policy, see Prestwich, *Edward I*, 343–46.

5. Holinshed, *Chronicles*, 2:492.

6. Camden, *Britannia*, 1:390–91, quoted in Parsons, *Eleanor of Castile*, 223.

7. For Eleanor as an agent of positive cultural exchange, see Walker, "Leonor of England," 69–76.

8. Anon., *Coppie of the Anti-Spaniard*, 27–35.

9. Fuchs, "Spanish Race," 90–91.

10. This is yet another improvisation, for the office of the Prince of Wales was not created until ten years after Eleanor's death. See Prestwich, *Edward I*, 226–27.

11. Anon., "The Lamentable fall of Queene Elenor for her pride and wickednesse, by Gods judgement, sunke into the ground at Charing crosse, and rose up againe at Queene hive." To the tune of, Gentle and curteous (London: William Blackwall [c. 1600]), one sheet.

12. Anon., "[Queen Eleanor's confession] shewing how King Henry, with the Earl Martial, in fryars habits, came to her instead of two fyars from France, which she sent for." To a pleasant new tune (London, 1690), one sheet.

13. See, for example, G. B., *A Fig for the Spaniard* (London, 1591, 1592).

14. William of Orange, *Apologie* (Delft, 1580), or the catalogue of abuses in Anon., *Briefe discourse of the cruel dealings* (London, 1599), 11–13.

15. Chambers, *Elizabethan Stage*, 3:460–61.

16. Aston, *Queen's Two Bodies*, 101–4.

17. Dreher, *Chronicle of King Edward*, argues that the play echoes several details noted by the medieval chronicler Matthew Paris, who had written that the Spaniard's dwellings, "hung with palls of silk and tapestry . . . it being in accordance with the custom of their country," were signs of "excessive pride," which "excited the laughter and derision of the people," and that "Serious and prudent persons . . . were deeply grieved on a careful consideration of the pleasure manifested by the king at the presence of any foreigners," xiv–xv.

18. See Shapiro, *Shakespeare and the Jews*, 46–49.

19. Rishanger, *Chronica et Annales,* quoted in Prestwich, *Three Edwards*, 24.

20. Douglas, *Purity and Danger*, 122.

21. For Robert Wilson's Puritan connections, see Greene, *Life and Complete Works*, 238–40.

22. See Burton, *Traffic and Turning*, 219–21; Vitkus, *Turning Turk*, 173–77.

23. Early Protestant dramas like John Bale's *King Johan* (c. 1536) and Foxe's *Christus Triumphans* (c. 1556) depend heavily on this mode. On the vitality of Protestant allegory and the tendency toward "generic hybridization and mutation," see King, *Spenser's Poetry*, 5, 75–79.

24. Hough, in *Preface to the Faerie Queene*, writes, "In naïve allegory theme is completely dominant, image merely a rhetorical convenience with no life of its own. . . . Where theme is so completely dominant, image tends to become incoherent, insipid, or characterless; and we are on the verge of passing out of literature altogether, into moral suasion, political propaganda, or what not," 106.

25. R. W., *The Three Lords and Three Ladies of London* (London, 1590), 43ff.

26. On Richard Field, see Woodfield, *Surreptitious Printing*, 34–45.

27. Cates, *Summarie and True Discourse* (London, 1589), 244–46.

28. Greene, *Plays and Poems*, 1.75.

29. On *Alphonsus, King of Arragon*, see Burton, *Traffic and Turning*, 33; on Alfonso "the Battler," see Barton, *Short History of Spain*, 51–57, 85.

30. Greene, *Spanish Masquerado* (London, 1589), title page.

31. Ibid., C4v.

32. Daunce, *Brief Discourse*, 31.

33. Hall, *Things of Darkness*, 7.

34. Handelman, *Models and Mirrors*, 22–31; Kertzer, *Ritual, Politics, and Power*, 9–14.

35. Eriksen, *Ethnicity and Nationalism*, 111; Connor, "A Nation Is a Nation," 36–46.

CHAPTER 3. THOMAS KYD'S TRAGEDY OF "THE SPAINS"

Note to epigraphs: Spenser, "A letter of the Authors," in *Faerie Queene*, ed. Hamilton, 737–38; in Allen, *Admonition* (Antwerp, 1588), XLV–XLIX.

1. Anonymous, *Explanation of the True* (Leyden, 1585).

2. Braudel, *Mediterranean*, 1184.

3. See Bartels, *Speaking of the Moor*, 21–44; Burton, *Traffic and Turning*, 20–21; Matar, *Britain and Barbary*, 13–20; Olsen, *Calabrian Charlatan*, 6–11.

4. Quoted in Parker, *Grand Strategy*, 166.

5. More than fifty years ago William Empson taught us that "the question" Kyd explores in *The Spanish Tragedy* was "a major one of current politics." Yet this seminal text has remained strangely resistant to critical efforts that import history, whether by anecdote or allusion. Perhaps because the political currents of the day were so complex and so volatile, we have lacked Empson's confidence with respect to precisely which question could help us unfold the play. So generally we have tended to think about *The Spanish Tragedy* in light of the historical dynamics of the short run, by fixing it either to the Armada crisis or to the birth of English revenge tragedy. See Empson, "The Spanish Tragedy," 16–29.

6. See Siemon, "Sporting Kyd," and Ardolino, *Apocalypse and Armada*. Díaz-Fernández, "Thomas Kyd: A Bibliography," indicates the steady interest in *The Spanish Tragedy*.

7. Wolf, *Europe and the People*, 387.

8. Collinson, *Elizabethan Puritan Movement*, 27; Collinson, *Religion of Protestants*, viii–ix.

9. Geertz, *Interpretation of Cultures*, 5.

10. Parker, *Grand Strategy*, 96.

11. I am not referring to any "hidden meaning." Rather, after Geertz, *Interpretation of Cultures*: "Culture is public because meaning is," 12.

12. Neale, *Elizabeth I*, 272.

13. As with the historical viceroyalties of Sicily, New Spain, and Peru, the Portugal that Kyd represents is governed by a viceroy subordinate to the Crown of Castile.

14. Hill, "Senecan and Virgilian Perspectives," 163–64.

15. Hill notes, "The tragedy is providential in that it is a *Spanish* tragedy that implies an English comedy," 158–59. But unlike contemporary productions that emphasize Hispanophobia by evoking cultural stereotypes, *The Spanish Tragedy* favors elevated Senecan rhetoric. We might, then, shift the emphasis of Hill's formula by saying that "the tragedy is *providential*" in its dramatization of the coming *translatio imperii*. Justice, "Spain, Tragedy," and Mulryne, "Nationality and Language," suggest that audiences would have been predisposed toward Spanish villainy, which accounted for the play's enduring popularity.

16. Hill, "Senecan and Virgilian Perspectives," 161. While we differ on several details, I find fundamentally sound Hill's conclusion that *The Spanish Tragedy* "reveals a poet closer in his meaningful playfulness to Spenser than to the crowd-pleasing hack critics have so often mistaken him" (165).

17. The line occurs at 1.1.10. See Empson, "The Spanish Tragedy," 68.

18. The sexual readiness Empson recognizes may account for unconvincing attempts

to link the fictional Bel-imperia with the historical Elizabeth. For example, Ardolino, *Apocalypse and Armada*, argues that because "Bel-imperia turns against Balthazar by helping Hieronimo to cause the fall of Babylon/Spain-Portugal . . . she becomes the analogue of Queen Elizabeth, the image of 'beautiful power,' " 113.

19. Spenser, "Letter of the Authors," in *Faerie Queene*. For Kyd, Spenser, and the Merchant Taylors' School, see Freeman, *Thomas Kyd*, 6–10.

20. *Faerie Queene*, book I, canto 2, stanzas 13–45. As does Duessa, Bel-imperia seems related to characters like Marlowe's Bellamira (*Jew of Malta*) and Dekker's Madona–Imperia (*Blurt, Master Constable*), figures who possess outer beauty that, like the Whore of Babylon's, belies an unchaste spirit.

21. See Hill, "Senecan and Virgilian Perspectives,"161; and Ardolino, *Apocalypse and Armada,* 151–52.

22. The text is explicit at 1.2.52—"Now while Bellona rageth here and there. . . ." The dangerous lure of Bel-imperia is evident in her dialogues with Horatio; their love scenes (2.2.28–40 and 2.4.28–49) are also charged with the language of battle.

23. Johnson, "*The Spanish Tragedy,* or Babylon Revisited"; Broude, "Time, Truth, and Right"; and Ardolino, *Apocalypse and Armada*, 1–80.

24. Nashe's objection, from the preface to Greene's *Menaphon*, is quoted from Freeman, *Thomas Kyd*, 39.

25. After Victor Turner, Eriksen, *Ethnicity and Nationalism*, stresses that it is the "ambiguity or 'multivocality' of symbols" that "makes it possible to manipulate them politically," 73, 101.

26. Even a sound can be construed as seductive in the iconoclastic discourse of the Protestant reformers. As Spenser's commentator, E. K., instructs, glossing *The Shepeardes Calender*: "By such trifles are noted, the reliques and ragges of popish superstition, which put no small religion in Belles . . . Idoles . . . and such lyke trumperies." See *Spenser's Minor Poems*, ed. de Sélincourt, 59. Foxe, *Acts and Monuments*, also ridicules the Catholic's desire "to be rung for" in "A Christian Man After the Pope's Making, Defined," 1:86. Knappen, *Tudor Puritanism* notes, "Church bells were rung to call people to services but not at other times—a Protestant rule of the sort frequently found in Episcopal injunctions of the period. The use of the hand bell, formerly carried before corpses, and bidding prayers for the dead were also banned," 254.

27. Isaiah 45 and 46. Wilson, *Christian Dictionarie,* instructs: "[Bel a contract of Behel, which commeth of Bahall] A Lord, it was not onely the particular Idoll of the Babylonians, but a generall name to the Idols in the East, agreeing to all the Idols of the Gentiles, as some write, Jer. 19.5, I Kin. 18.25." Bel-imperia's name also evokes the Apocryphal Bel and the Dragon, and by extension virtually the whole typological chain of Babel/Babylon from Genesis through Revelation. The *Oxford Dictionary of the Christian Church* defines "Bel" as "another form of 'Baal' . . . the tutelary god of Babylon, the empire which held the Jews captive," 151.

28. Here I second Scanlan, *Colonial Writing*: "Protestants in general, and the English Puritans in specific, were constantly allegorizing everything. They lived in a world, in which every person, object, and event was filled with signifying potential," 12. That we

have neglected this biblical/allegorical presence in "Bel-imperia" may be a measure of the effectiveness of Kyd's allegorizing strategy. As Fletcher, *Allegory*, writes, "The whole point of allegory is that it does not need to be read exegetically; it often has a literal level that makes good enough sense by itself. But *somehow* . . . this literal surface suggests a peculiar doubleness of intention, and while it can, as it were, get along without interpretation, it becomes much richer and more interesting if given interpretation," 7. In *The Spanish Tragedy* this *somehow* is that the play immediately announces its allegorical mode by staging the appearance of Don Andrea's Ghost, who, in the presence of the allegorical figure of Revenge, suggests the play's "doubleness" by invoking the character that is at once his lover and the figure around which the drama turns, "hight sweet Bel-imperia by name" (1.1.10–11).

29. Quilligan, *Language of Allegory*, 22.

30. Quilligan theorizes that the "pretext" is the source that always stands outside any allegorical narrative and becomes the key to its interpretability (though not necessarily to its interpretation), ibid., 23.

31. After de Baeque, "Allegorical Image of France," 114. We might say that in Bel-imperia, the idol of Empire, *The Spanish Tragedy* quite literally embodies *allegoria*, which Puttenham, *Arte of English Poesie* (1589), calls variously the "false" and the "faire semblant" (both of which seem apt to describe Bel-imperia). "Of this figure," he writes, "therefore which for his duplicitie we . . . will speake first as of the chief ringleader and captaine of all other figures, either in the Poeticall or oratorie science," 197. Puttenham then adds, "And ye shall know that we may dissemble, I meane speake otherwise then we thinke, in earnest as well as in *sport*, under covert and darke termes, and in learned and apparent speeches," 305 (my italics).

32. Fletcher, *Prophetic Moment*, 106. Quilligan, *Language of Allegory*, argues that allegory begins at the level of *sound*: "We may easily sense the essential affinity of allegory to the pivotal phenomenon of the pun, which provides the basis for the narrative structure characteristic of the genre." After Quilligan, we might sat that the play unfolds as an investigation "into the literal truth inherent in individual words [Bel, bella, bellum], considered in the context of their whole histories as words," 33.

33. Both Bel-imperia's father and brother recognize her lack of chastity. See 3.10.54–55, 3.14.11.12. Here we might compare Redcrosse's attraction to Duessa.

34. Camões, *Lusiads*, trans. Atkinson, 129. First published in 1572, Camões's ten cantos are replete with appeals to "national pride" and allusions to the Hapsburg Empire that is about to absorb Portugal. To commemorate simultaneously the poet's death and the inevitable union, two editions of Camões' epic were published in Spain in 1580—the earliest date suggested for Kyd's play.

35. Jan. 7, 1584. Richard Hakluyt, preacher, to the same [Fr. Walsingham]. *Calendar of State Papers, Domestic,* CLXVII:28.

36. Whetstone, *English Myrror* (London, 1596), 84.

37. Cervantes, *Numancia*, 1:512. On the Roman siege of the Celtiberian city of Numancia and Spanish national identity, see Schmidt, "Development of *Hispanitas.*"

38. King, "Cervantes' *Numancia* and Imperial Spain," 215. On generic and thematic ambivalence in Cervantes's play, see Simerka, "That the rulers should sleep."

39. See Siemon, "Sporting Kyd," for a discussion "the mysteries of hierarchy and class solidarity" implied by the Lorenzo/Balthazar subplot, 556–58.

40. The play may support Lynch's thesis that, their long history of dynastic infighting notwithstanding, the former competitors had come to appreciate what might be gained by combining resources. See *Spain*, 432.

41. The "errant" Israel provides preachers with the more common typology. See Collinson, *Birthpangs*, especially 17–27.

42. See Johnson, "*The Spanish Tragedy,* or Babylon Revisited,"36; Ardolino, *Apocalypse and Armada,* 113.

43. Daniel 1:7, Geneva gloss.

44. Daniel 4:6, gloss *e*. See also the "Briefe Table of the interpretation of the proper names which are chiefly found in the Old Testament" which appends the Geneva translation. "Beel [*sic*], Baal, Bealim," signifying "lord, lords," is given as "the name of the idol of the Sidonians, or a generall name to all idoles, because they were as the lords and owners of all that worshipped them"; "Belshatsar," "Baltasar," "Belteshazar," "Beleshatsar," or "Beleshazzar" signify "without treasure, or searcher of treasure." "Babel," "confusion," and "Babylon" are given as synonyms.

45. Ardolino, *Apocalypse and Armada,* 4.

46. Eire, *War Against the Idols,* writes, "Idolatry is a fighting word," suggesting that the term can be understood to refer not simply to "the worship of a physical object, but rather [to] any form of devotion that is judged to be incorrect," 5. See also Aston, *England's Iconoclasts,* 343–479; Collinson, *Iconoclasm to Iconophobia,* 22–25.

47. Allen, *Admonition,* VI.

48. John Hawkins to Walsingham, February 1587: "God will defend us, for we defend the chief cause, our religion, God's own cause; for if we would leave our profession and turn to serve *Baal* (as God forbid, and rather to die a thousand deaths, we might have peace, but not with God." Quoted in Fernandez-Armesto, "Armada Myths," 23 (my italics).

49. Tanner, *Last Descendant,* observes, "In the Monarchy of Spain which he had dedicated to Philip at the end of the sixteenth century, Tomasso Campanella proclaimed that Philip had realized that plan that God had prognosticated through his prophets: Spain had become the Last World Monarchy. These words expressed a long-held conviction at the Hapsburg court, one that was visually expressed in a treatise dedicated to Philip, where the prophet Daniel reveals his dream of the Four Monarchies directly to Philip," 145. See also Elliott, *Spain and Its World,* 8–10.

50. Foxe writes, "We affirm and say, that our church was, when this church of theirs was not yet hatched out of the shell . . . that is, in the time of the apostles, in the primitive age . . . when as yet no universal pope was received publicly . . . nor this doctrine of abuse and sacraments yet heard of. In witness whereof we have the old acts and histories of ancient time to give testimony with us, wherein we have sufficient matter to shew that . . . this our present reformed church, are not the beginning of our own but the renewing of the old ancient church of Christ," *Acts and Monuments,* 1:8.

51. Via a rhetoric of inversion (we should recall that *inversio* and *allegoria* are virtual synonyms), Kyd "corrects" the Roman Catholic mobilization of Daniel's Imperial prophe-

cies by subjecting them to a thoroughly Protestant figuration. See McGinn, *Anti-Christ*, 200–230.

52. Church of England, "Homelie, or Sermon," 103–13.

53. Knewstub, *Lectures Upon the Twentieth* (London, 1577), 34. See Aston, *England's Iconoclasts*, for a review of this theological orientation, 342–79. From 1560 onward, the Geneva Bible glosses the condemnation of idolatry in Hosea, chapters 1–3, under the headings "Spiritual Whoredome" and "Spiritual Marriage."

54. Helgerson, *Forms of Nationhood*, 1–2.

55. Geertz, *Interpretation of Cultures*, 119.

56. Ibid., 118.

57. Quoted in Fernández-Armesto, *Spanish Armada*, 39–40.

58. From Tacitus, the phrase is often used by Allen and the Catholic theorists of universal monarchy. See Pagden, *Lords of All*, 13.

59. Eire, *Madrid to Purgatory*, 172.

60. Gardiner, *Explications* (1551), 150. Quoted in the *OED*. Protestant divines rail against propitatory practices. John Bradford, for example, preaches (hand-in-hand with his anti-Hispanism) that the Catholic view is "perverted and used to a contrary ende, as of sacrifycing propitiatorely for the syns of the quicke and of the dead"; see, for example, *Two notable Sermons* (1579 [1561]), Bi, Biv.

61. Diehl, *Staging Reform*, 112.

62. Justice, "Spain, Tragedy," suggests that it is "the *world* of *The Spanish Tragedy*" that Kyd wants to examine in the play, 276 (my emphasis). Without denying that Hieronimo elicits our sympathies, Justice argues that, "as Hieronimo takes upon himself the divine prerogatives of vengeance, he makes his divinity in Spain's image, the image of the society which 'colde not atteine unto the Law of righteousness . . . / Because they soght it not by faith, but as it were by workes of the law' (Rom. 9:31–32)," 285.

63. Ardolino, *Apocalypse and Armada*, ix.

64. Foxe, *Acts and Monuments*, 1:84.

65. Allen, *Defense and Declaration* (Antwerp, 1565), 242. The Protestant preacher Samuel Cottesford, *Treatise against traitors* (London, 1591), identifies as "hispanated" those English Catholic priests, like Allen, who have chosen to study at Catholic universities abroad and thereby commit a treasonous, un-English act.

66. *Hamlet* (1.5.1–90).

67. Foxe, *Acts and Monuments*, 1:84. It is widely thought that Nashe played a role in the production of the anti-Martinist tracts.

68. Church of England, "Homile or Sermon concerning the Nativity."

69. Vernon, *Huntynge of Purgatorie* (1561), 101–3.

70. Foxe, *Acts and Monuments*, 1:84–85.

71. Vernon, *Huntynge of Purgatorie*, 100–103.

72. Ibid.

73. Ibid., 106–7. On the presence of "both a 'Virgilian' and a Christian eschatology" in the writings of Saint Jerome, see Scourfield, *Consoling Heliodorus*, 98–100.

74. Edwards, "Thrusting Elysium into Hell," 117–32.

75. Allen, *Admonition*, XLIX.

76. Daniel 2:44.

77. Pagden, *Lords of All*, 42–43; Schmidt and Skinner, eds,, *Cambridge History*, 750–52.

78. In the Hapsburg view, a succession of events—the completion of Iberian *reconquista*, the discovery of America, the conquests of the Aztecs and Incas, victories over "the Turk" at Tunis and Lepanto, the pacification of the Philippines and the unification of the Spains—provided the unambiguous, visible signs of this translation. Their interpretation becomes sufficiently well known that in the mid-seventeenth century it could be revived in order to foment anti-Spanish feelings in service of the Western Design: "The Spaniards," wrote one Protestant polemicist, "hold this as a Delphic oracle and most infallible prophesy that the last *Monarchy shall be fixed in Spain.*" Quoted in Pagden, *Lords of All*, 43. See also Fuchs, "Imperium Studies," 72–77.

79. Pagden, *Lords of All*, defines extended Empire as "the pattern of political relationships which held together groups of peoples in 'an extended system the terms of whose association were not permanently established,' " 13.

80. Allen, *Admonition*, XII.

81. Hill argues, "The illogic of the Spanish King's explanation is patent, although it goes unremarked amid the carousing. England has compelled one Portuguese King 'To bear the yoke of the English monarchy' and 'captured,' on another occasion, a second 'King of Portingale'; the English have also taken a King of Spain prisoner; *therefore* (!) the Portuguese should be less discomforted by their loss to the Spaniards, while the Spanish should not boast too much," 160 (italics his).

82. An English contingent is known to have participated, but without the aid of Robert of Gloucester, King Stephen's bastard brother, who does not seem to have been present. See Bevington's gloss of the scene, and Livermore, *New History of Portugal*, 54–61.

83. The siege was not of itself a "conquest" but one event among the many that contributed to the ongoing project of the Iberian *reconquista*.

84. John Foxe, *Acts and Monuments*, includes a lengthy examination of the spread of the Islamic Antichrist, 6:88–122.

85. Edmund of Langley *did*, "When Richard wore the diadem" (1.4.151–53), come to Lisbon. He *did not*, however, fight *against* the Portuguese, he fought *with* them. In other words, he never "razèd Lisbon walls," nor did he take "the King of Portingale in fight" (154–55). See Russell, *English Intervention*, 302–44. Langley was, however, "For . . . other suchlike service," against the troublesome Scots, "after created Duke of York" (156–57). See *DNB* entry.

86. Well-known accounts include such histories as Bourchier's translation of Froissart, and the chronicles of Hall and Holinshed. Gaunt's expedition and subsequent marriage were also celebrated in Spain: the "English" monarchs Katherine of Aragon and Philip of Hapsburg traced their lineage through the Duke of Lancaster.

87. Freeman, *Thomas Kyd,* notes the similarity between this episode from Hieronimo's act 1 masque and the Ocland text, 55–56. Sharrock's verse translation of Christopher Ocland's Latin "epic" *Anglorum Proelia* (London, 1558) was published as *The Valiant Actes*

and victorious Battailes of the English Nation (London, 1585), by Waldegrave, a printer with an undeniably Protestant pedigree. See McKerrow, ed., *Dictionary of Printers,* 277–79.

88. Ocland, *Valiant Actes,* sig. D3.

89. The ascension of Elizabeth does not relieve these difficulties, for, as Cardinal Allen points out, she too could be demonstrated a product of "bastardie" according to the prevailing logic of succession—which had allowed Philip, through an appeal to his mother's ancestry, to displace the "illegitimate" Don Antonio's claim to Portugal. Allen, *Admonition,* XI and XLIX.

90. In lines that may allude to *The Spanish Tragedy,* Shakespeare refers to the expedition in *3 Henry VI* ("great John of Gaunt, / Which did subdue the greater part of Spain" [3.3.81–82]), which also seems to have been the subject of a lost play commissioned by Henslowe, *The Conquest of Spayne by John a Gant.* See *Henslowe's Diary,* 167–68, 294.

91. According to Froissart, Edmund Langley, Duke of York, and his brother, John of Gaunt, returned from the Spains linked by marriage to the House of Castile. See *Chronicle of Froissart,* 2:372ff. and 4:332, 404. The Portuguese ambassador is therefore right to counsel his viceroy that "English warriors likewise conquered Spain" because they did enforce a suit, that of Gaunt's wife Constance to the throne of Castile (against the usurpation of the bastard Henry of Trastamara), much like Philip's claim to Portugal. For a summary, see Livermore, *New History of Portugal,* 100–110.

92. Pagden, *Lords of All,* 37–52. In the Ciceronian tradition, Allen draws this distinction with regard to English activities in the Low Countries. See *Copie of a Letter* (Antwerp, 1587), 8–9.

93. "Bellibone" appears in the "Aprill" eclogue of the earlier *Shepheardes Calender* (1579) and Belphoebe in *The Faerie Queene.* These names may also play against "Bel-imperia."

94. On these Elizabethan personae, see Yates, *Astraea,* 29–87.

95. After Montrose, "The Elizabethan Subject," 310. This is precisely the political strategy (or subject position) that *The Spanish Tragedy*'s Bel-imperia is denied.

96. Like the eclogues of *The Shepheardes Calender,* the epic romance of *The Faerie Queene* and any number of reinscriptions by Raleigh, Sidney, Lyly, Drayton, and others, *The Spanish Tragedy* works, in Montrose's phrase, "to suggest that the ruler and the ruled are mutually defining, reciprocally constituted." See "The Elizabethan Subject," 320.

97. Ardolino, *Apocalypse and Armada,* writes, "*The Spanish Tragedy* is a mystery of divine vengeance exacted against Spain in which Hieronimo, the Danielic figure, the judge, bearer of the sacred name (*hieros nym*), anglophile representative of God's will at the court of Babylon/Spain, author, actor, and revenger, causes the 'fall of Babylon' in his revenge playlet, ostensibly intended to celebrate the marital and dynastic union of Spain and Portugal," 12.

98. This Latin corruption inspires many a lengthy treatise, the most widely known being the prefatory matter of the *Acts and Monuments.*

99. After Geertz, *Interpretation of Cultures:* "Not only is the semantic structure of the figure a good deal more complex than it appears on the surface, but an analysis of that structure forces one into tracing a multiplicity of referential connections between it and social reality, so that the final picture is one of a configuration of dissimilar meanings out of

whose interworking both the expressive power and the rhetorical force of the final symbol derive. This interworking is itself a social process, an occurrence not 'in the head' but in that public world where 'people talk together, name things, make assertions, and to a degree understand each other,' " 213.

100. Diehl, *Staging Reform*, 126.

101. Diehl quotes Foxe, *Acts and Monuments*, 5:303.

102. Significantly, since the reign of the patriarch Rudolf I the ritual of the Eucharist had been an important icon of the Hapsburg Empire. Tanner, *Last Descendant*, recalls that by "vowing on the Eucharist in battles against the Turks and the Protestants," and by establishing by imperial edict "that in processions celebrating . . . military triumphs, the Eucharist would be displayed in a monstrance carried by the archbishop," the Hapsburgs made the public ritual of the Eucharist a powerful ideological tool, "for under Philip's sovereignty the mass was said in all four parts of the world for the first time," 215.

103. Wisdom 14:13 and 15, in Kohlenberger, ed., *Parallel Apocrypha*, 306–8. My discussion is indebted to Diehl, *Staging Reform*, 137ff.

104. See Allen, *Defense and Declaration*, whose appeal to "St. Hieronyme" is ridiculed by Fulke, in *Confutation of the popish Churches* (London, 1577), 318–21, which reprints the whole of Allen's *Defense* and answers the Catholic position point by point over some 460 pages.

105. *Geneva Bible* (London, 1599), Gggv.

106. Acts 2:1 (gloss 1) and 5.

107. Ibid., 2:21 (gloss 4).

108. It is appropriately ironic it is that the fall of Babylon/Spain should come at the hands of a character posing as "the Turk." Shepherd, *Marlowe*, 144, and Mulryne, "Nationality and Language," are among those who note this Turkish connection, 75–81.

109. Johnson, "*The Spanish Tragedy*, or Babylon Revisited," 27; Justice, "Spain, Tragedy," 285–86; Mulryne, "Nationality and Language," 85–86; and Ardolino, *Apocalypse and Armada*, 39, have drawn attention to these resonances with the Pentecost of Acts 2.

110. After Hill, Mulryne, "Nationality and Language," has emphasized the play's *translatio imperii*, 70; Justice, "Spain, Tragedy," arrives at a similar conclusion independently, 285–86.

111. Ardolino, "Hieronimo as St. Jerome in *The Spanish Tragedy*," 435–37.

112. Justice, "Spain, Tragedy," notes, "The persistence of Babel manifests the persistent corruption of self-will that eventually corrupts communication itself. . . . In his search for justice he [Hieronimo] more nearly recapitulates the sin of Nimrod than any of [the play's other characters]," 285–86.

113. Though his civil jurisdiction as Knight Marshall may have extended throughout "the verge," as Johnson, "*The Spanish Tragedy,* or Babylon Revisited," argued, in neither England nor Spain would it have extended to those above him in rank, 30.

114. Wheatcroft, *The Hapsburgs*, 145–46.

115. See *Catholic Encyclopedia*, 7:345; *New Catholic Encyclopedia*, 6:1099–1100. Ardolino notes resonances between the Hieronymites, El Escorial, San Lorenzo, and *The Spanish Tragedy*.

116. Geertz, *Interpretation of Cultures*, 453.

117. See the editions by Boas, lxxxix; Edwards, lxi; Cairncross, xxii–iii; Mulryne, xxxi.

118. At least not by the play's major editors, Boas, Edwards, Cairncross, Mulryne, and Bevington.

119. On *The Spanish Tragedy*'s revisions, see Griffin, "Nationalism, the Black Legend."

120. See Mayer, "'The Papist and His Poet,'" 116–29; Hogge, *God's Secret Agents*, passim.

CHAPTER 4. MARLOWE AMONG THE MACHEVILLS

Note to epigraphs: G.B., *A Fig for the Spaniard*, B3—on this pamphlet's government sponsorship, see Kamen, *Spanish Inquisition*, 310; citations of "A Libell, fixte upon the French Church Wall, in London. Anno 1593," are from Freeman, "Marlowe, Kyd, and the Dutch Church Libel," 45; Florio, *World of Wordes*, 219. Florio, *Queen Anne's New World of Words* (London, 1611), amplifies: "One descended of Jews or infidels, and whose parents were never christened, but for to save their goods they will say they are Christians. Also as Marana," 300.

1. This remained the drama's full title as late as 1633. See Chambers, *Elizabethan Stage*, 3:424–25.

2. Eliot, *Elizabethan Essays*, 28.

3. Freeman, "Marlowe, Kyd," 45.

4. Pettegree, *Foreign Protestant Communities*, 293–94.

5. According to Archer, *Pursuit of Stability*, by hearing popular grievances the courts gave the appearance of ruling "for the benefit of all citizens," 259.

6. Pettegree, *Foreign Protestant Communities*, 293; Archer, *Pursuit of Stability*, 5.

7. Although contemporary accounts refer to the "Dutch" libel, the surviving transcription reads "fixte upon a *French* Church wall." See Freeman, "Marlowe, Kyd," and *Jew of Malta*, ed. Siemon, 115–18.

8. Freeman, "Marlowe, Kyd," notes Stowe's observation, "the French Church, St. Anthony's, stood hard by the Dutch, on Broad Street at the junction of Three Needle (or Threeneedle) Street, Ward of Broadstreet," 51.

9. Pettegree, *Foreign Protestant Communities*, 274–75. The inconsistency may suggest that these émigrés were discriminated against indiscriminately, alike considered an "un-English" presence. If it was in fact a "French" church, most members of the congregation would have been Huguenots, among whom French-speaking Netherlanders and Walloons would have been worshipping, if "Dutch," most would have been "German." In either case, the church may have been attracting a significant number of English congregants.

10. Munday, *Sir Thomas More*: Passages attributed to Shakespeare, Addition II.D.15–17; II.D. For historical context, see Honigmann, "Play of *Sir Thomas More*"; Long, "Occasion of *The Book of Sir Thomas More*," 45–56. On censorship and textual problems, see McMillin, *Elizabethan Theatre*.

11. Braudel, *Structures of Everyday Life*, notes "that [the] long blood-letting of France that began in 1540 with the first systematic persecutions [of the Protestants] and only ended in 1752–3, with the last great emigration movement following the bloody repressions of Languedoc," 54.

12. Pettegree, *Foreign Protestant Communities*, 293. Pettegree also observes, "Whether or not one is justified in talking of a 'crisis of the 1590s' with general European manifestations, certainly the coincidence of endemic plague, poor harvests, high taxation, and political insecurity as a result of the war with Spain put abnormal strains on the fabric of society, and inevitably the problems were most acute in the capital. As in previous periods of high domestic tension, the strangers were an easy scapegoat for society's ills. A rising tide of protest against alien competition in trade and handicrafts issued in a new proposal, backed by the city of London, to prevent strangers selling by retail, and a bill to this effect was debated at some length in the parliament of 1593," 291.

13. Hakluyt, *Discourse of Western Planting*, 218.

14. Hunt, *Puritan Moment*, 60.

15. On the English colleges in Spain, see Loomie, *Spanish Elizabethans*.

16. Lewkenor, *Discourse of the Usage*, B, A3.

17. Haigh, *English Reformations*, 254–64.

18. On Stanley and York, see Mattingly, *Armada*, 49. On the Spanish succession, see Hurstfield, "Succession Struggle," 376–79.

19. See Riggs, *World of Christopher Marlowe*, 319–21.

20. Chambers, *Elizabethan Stage*, dates the play c. 1589, after the death of the duc de Guise, 13 December 1588. Henslowe records seventeen performances by Strange's men between 26 February 1592 and 1 February 1593. Sussex's, the Queen's, the Admiral's, and the Chamberlain's men all seem to have performed the play between 4 February 1594 and 23 June 1596, which attests to its continuing Elizabethan popularity, as does a further revival in 1601, 3: 424–25.

21. See Loewenstein, "For a History," 395–96; Hoppe, "John Wolfe, Printer and Pubisher," 263–67.

22. Estimates suggest that Wolfe was responsible for upwards of 25 percent of the "nearly one hundred and thirty translations of French pamphlets and books concerning the religious wars" printed in English between 1500 and 1601. See Parmellee, *Good Newes from Fraunce*, 27–51; Woodfield, *Surreptitious Printing in England*, 24–33.

23. Quoted in Donaldson, *Machiavelli and Mystery of State*, 99, who suggests that Wolfe may have earned the epithets from his "amoral ambitiousness," 102. See also Meyer, *Machiavelli and the Elizabethan Drama*, 49.

24. Donaldson, *Machiavelli and Mystery*, 102; Loewenstein, "For a History," 404.

25. Verstegen, *Declaration of the True Causes*, 52, 74.

26. Ibid., 76–77 (italics in original). The epithet may play upon Wolfe's association with the "Fishmonger's" guild.

27. Huffman, *Elizabethan Impressions*, 53. Verstegen's linking of Wolfe with Cecil, and his assessment of the latter's role in the propaganda wars, seems to have been accurate. Shortly after the Armada crisis, Wolfe had been contracted to print the surreptitious letter,

the *Essempio d'una lettera mandata d'Inghilterra a don Bernardino di Mendoza,* an original copy of which exists in Cecil's own hand. Pleased with the effects of the ruse, Lord Burghley continued to enlist the services of Wolfe and his associate Richard Field in order to issue false letters, translations of propagandistic foreign tracts, and newly commissioned diatribes, which ceased appearing with his death in 1598.

28. See Gentillet, maxim 17, in *Discourse upon the Meanes.* See also Boyer, *Villain as Hero,* 241–45.

29. See Parmellee, *Good Newes from Fraunce,* passim.

30. Kocher, "Contemporary Pamphlet Backgrounds," 151–73; Tilley, "Some Pamphlets," 451–70. Similarly, Shepherd, *Marlowe and the Politics,* has observed the way Faustus "speaks a discourse of English Protestantism" in *Doctor Faustus,* incorporating material that was "a stock part of Protestant propaganda," 137.

31. Praz, *Machiavelli and the Elizabethans,* observed that "Machiavelli had become a sort of rallying-point for whatever was most loathsome in statecraft, and indeed human nature at large," 6; see also Boyer, *Villain as Hero,* 34.

32. Quoted in Minshull, "Marlowe's 'Sound Machevill,'" 44; Praz, *Machiavelli and the Elizabethans,* noted, "The French origin of the Elizabethan Machiavellian is made evident by his very covetousness," 3–4.

33. Gentillet, *Discourse upon the Meanes,* maxims 21, 23 and 25.

34. On Barabbas's Turkish turn, see Vitkus, *Turning Turk,* 183–86; Burton, *Traffic and Turning,* 203.

35. *A Relation, or Rather a True Account,* quoted in Knapp, *Empire Nowhere,* 30–31.

36. Pettegree, *Foreign Protestant,* 276.

37. Cecil, *A Politike Discourse,* 10.

38. While stressing "remarkable congruence between theories of nationalism and anthropological theory of ethnicity," Eriksen, *Ethnicity and Nationalism,* observes that "ethnic identities tend to attain their greatest importance in situations of flux, change, resource competition and threats against boundaries," 100.

39. Church of England, *Liturgies and Forms of Prayer,* 519.

40. Ibid., 524.

41. On the relation of the *Antichristi typus* to the play, see Hunter, "Theology of Marlowe's *The Jew of Malta.*"

42. "58 miles south of Sicily, 220 miles north of Libya and 180 miles east of Tunisia," "Malta road" provided both a gateway to North Africa and a way station between Europe the Levant. Of strategic importance since ancient times, as the Holy Land came under siege during the Ottoman expansions of the fourteenth, fifteenth, and sixteenth centuries, the Hospitallers of Jerusalem were displaced first to Tripoli, next to Acre, then to Rhodes, which they lost to "the Turk" in 1522, and finally, in 1530, to their famous stronghold at Malta. See Sire, *Knights of Malta,* 268ff.

43. Pole continued, "If I wanted to examine the exact words that are spoken of the reign of Antichrist," he wrote, "I should not find even one word that he [Henry VIII] does not embody so closely that a painter could never present a more exact image of anyone." Quoted in Donaldson, *Machiavelli and Mystery,* 13.

44. Bartels, "Malta, the Jew," 5.

45. Brennan, "Two Newsletter Accounts," 157–60.

46. Anonymous, *Certayn and tru good nues*.title page. For a contemporary Spanish perspective, see Corregio, *The Siege of Malta, 1565.*

47. Anonymous, *Certayn and tru good nues*, A2r.

48. Braudel, *Mediterranean*, 1014.

49. See ibid. for the rumor of the Turkish invasions and reprisals feared as a result of the Maltese victory, 1021.

50. Spivak, *Shakespeare and the Allegory*, 346.

51. Anonymous, *Begynnynge and foundacyon*, (London, 1524).

52. See ibid., Bi.

53. Hakluyt, *Principal Navigations*, 5:1–60.

54. See Freeman, "Marlowe, Kyd," 45.

55. Archer, *Pursuit of Stability*, estimates closer to five thousand, 132; Pettegree, *Foreign Protestant Communities*, suggests three thousand, or 3.5 percent, 293.

56. For the disagreement on numbers, Kamen, "Mediterranean and the Expulsion," 30–55.

57. Katz, *Jews in the History*, 1–2.

58. On the Portuguese Inquisition, see Kamen, *Spanish Inquisition,* 287–90; Shapiro, *Shakespeare and the Jews*, 68; Roth, *Spanish Inquisition*, 135–38.

59. As Kamen, "Mediterranean and the Expulsion," has shown, *marranos* and *conversos* continued to leave for many years after the edict of expulsion, either because they wished to join "with their brethren" abroad or, "while wishing to remain Christian, preferred to escape the injustices of the Inquisition and find security in another Christian country." Kamen suggests that "historians have, consciously or not, identified *converso* emigration as 'Jewish' and have thus further confused a problem that could do with more clarity," 49–50.

60. On the Lopez case, see Campos, "Jews, Spaniards, and Portingales," 599–616.

61. See Katz, *Jews in the History*, 49–106, for a discussion of the Lopez case.

62. Ibid., 59–61.

63. Ibid., 73; Marcham, *Lopez the Jew*, 10.

64. Marcham, *Lopez the Jew*, 2.

65. See Dutch Church Libel, lines 42, 22.

66. According to the statement of Philip Gawdy of Clifford's Inn. See Katz, *Jews in the History*, 89.

67. *Calendar of State Papers, Domestic*, 1594, March 9, 455.

68. See stage direction at 1.1.1. After Geertz, *Interpretation of Cultures*: "What in a place like Morocco," or in this case, early modern London," most prevents those of us who grew up winking other winks . . . from grasping what people are up to is not ignorance as to how cognition works . . . as a lack of familiarity with the imaginative universe in which their acts are signs," 13.

69. Greenblatt, "Marlowe and Renaissance Self-Fashioning," suggests that Barabbas functions as "the embodiment of a category," 53.

70. G.B., *Fig for the Spaniard*, B3 (my italics).

71. *Calendar of State Papers, Domestic*, 1594, February 28, 446.

72. See *DNB*, 132.

73. Freeman, "Marlowe, Kyd," 50. See also *DNB*, 133. After Lopez's first petition for a monopoly on these herbs was denied, Walsingham himself seems to have intervened in his behalf. See *Calendar of State Papers, Domestic*, 1589, July 12, 609.

74. For a summary, see Rodríguez-Salgado, "Anglo Spanish War," 1–44.

75. Andrews, ed., *English Privateering Voyages*, 86, 154. See also Griffin, "Nationalism, the Black Legend," on Terceira references in the revised *Spanish Tragedy*.

76. Peele, *Farewell* (London, 1589).

77. On the English adventure in Lisbon, see Campos, "Jews, Spaniards, and Portingales," 599–616. For the Portuguese perspective, see Olsen, *Calabrian Charlatan*, 87–93. On Portugal's "Babylonian Captivity" under Spain, see Nowell, *History of Portugal*, 135–49.

78. Woodfield, *Surreptitious Printing*, 26.

79. Marcham, *Lopez the Jew*, 3.

80. Persons [pseud. Doleman], *Conference* (1594).

81. Freeman, "Marlowe, Kyd," 50.

82. On the Spanish Infanta as Elizabeth's successor, see Hurstfield, "Succession Struggle," 373–79.

83. See Katz, *Jews in the History*, 94, 106; and the List of prisoners in the Tower, 14 April 1594, in *Calendar of State Papers, Domestic*, 1594, 484.

84. See Braudel, *Mediterranean*, 814–23.

85. Netanyahu, *Origins of the Inquisition*, points out that although some maintained that "the Jew, upon conversion, left not only his faith, but also his people," Jewish law "insisted that the convert from Judaism, though he renounced his faith, remained a member of his people, thereby retaining also some of the rights which that status conferred on him," 993.

86. Quoted in Lynch, *Spain*, 4.

87. Elliott, *Imperial Spain*, 128.

88. Quoted in Lynch, *Spain*, 4.

89. On Spanish language use within the Ottoman Empire, see Lewis, *Jews of Islam*, 134–35.

90. Via Dyce, modern editors such as Fraser and Rabkin, *Drama of the English Renaissance*, 1:273, render line 39 as *Bueno para todos mi ganado no era*. Siemon in his edition of *The Jew of Malta*, offers *ganada*, which he derives from the 1633 Quarto, 36, note 39. Marlowe probably meant *ganancia* (gain, increase, earnings, profit) rather than *ganado*, which is associated with "livestock"—unless, of course, his Spanish is sophisticated enough to intend the metaphor. Such a usage would suggest the sort of bestiality attributed to Spain and the Jews in Black Legend discourse, which, in turn, would be consistent with the language Shakespeare associates with Iago.

91. Wallerstein, *Modern World System*, 86–90.

92. On the antagonism between Jewish merchants and the "evil monks" of Malta, see Braudel, *Mediterranean*, 822.

93. Hakluyt, *Principal Navigations*, 10:7.

94. Ibid., 10:64–74. On England's withdrawal from the Guinea–Caribbean trade, see Andrews, *Trade, Plunder and Settlement*, 111, 127–28; Thomas, *Slave Trade*, 154–58.

95. Hakluyt, *Principal Navigations*, 10:8. On England's resumption of slaving, see Thomas, *Slave Trade*, 175–78. On English attitudes toward slavery, see Guasco, "Settling with Slavery," 236–53.

96. Wallerstein, *Modern World System*, 86–129.

97. See Orange, *Apology*, O2; Cecil, *Politike Discourse*, D2; Ashley, *Comparison of the English and Spanish Nation*, D2; L.T.A., trans., *Masque of the League*, B3; Anonymous, *Coppie of the Anti-Spaniard*, D2.

98. The othering effect of this sort of ethnopoetic conflation, a willful disinclination to distinguish accurately between non-Christian cultures, may be observed in Montanus's influential *Discovery and playne Declaration*. Locating the roots of the institution in Spanish history, Montanus wrote: "After the warres were ended wherein *Ferdinando* and *Isabella* of famous memory expelled the Turkes out of the territorie and Citie of *Granata*, and other places in *Spaine*. . . . The occasion whereof as wel by the *Mores*, that being conquered, had libertie to remain in *Spaine*, and to enjoy all their goods with condicion that they shold receive the christā faith: as by the Iewes that were in number as many as the other, who were permitted to cōtinue stil under the same condition" (B.iii.). As signs of Islamic otherness, "Turkes" and "Mores" function as virtual synonyms. As Montanus asks his readership to consider the demographic consequences, arguing that "it is easie for any man to perceive, that wil consider with us but thus much, that of so many thousands of people either Turkes or Iews, or true chrisitans or heretickes (as they terme them) and revolters from the romish faith, as have come within the Inquisitors jurisdiction from the very first beginnings of the Inquisition, till this day," he simultaneously links and declines to distinguish between the national, ethnic and genealogical identities of "Turkes" and "Jews," adding yet two more distinct culture groups to the ethnic mix, Biiiv.

99. Roth, "Jews of Malta," noted that "the problem of the crypto-Jew, which formed the pretext for the banishment from Spain, was virtually unknown in Sicily and its dependencies," including Malta, 207.

100. Roth adds that while it was "not impossible that one or two Jews remained in Malta even after the edict of expulsion" (ibid., 207), still, "[e]very inducement was accordingly offered to throughout the kingdom for the Jews to become converted to Christianity, in which case they would of course be permitted to remain without interference," 212.

101. Ciappara, *Society and the Inquisition*, 198–201.

102. For a comparison between Ferdinand's Machiavellianism, which "sought to appear ethical and religious; for he accurately assessed the crucial part played by ethics and religion in human affairs," and Cesare Borgia's "openly defying morality," see Netanyahu, *Origins of the Inquisition*, 1031–34.

103. According to Roth, "Jews of Malta," the actual cost "to purchase the privilege of Baptism" would have been "the surrender of 45 per cent of their property," 212.

104. Cassar, *Society, Culture and Identity*, xxx.

105. Defoe, "True-born Englishman."

106. See Bartels, *Spectacles of Strangeness*, 91.

107. Cassar, *Society, Culture and Identity*, xxxi.

108. Critics have long grappled with the Machiavellian ethos that permeates the drama. Along with Meyer, Boyer, and Praz, see Babb, "Policy"; Bawcutt, " 'Policy,' Machiavellianism," 195–209.

109. Minshull, "Marlowe's 'Sound Machevill,' " argues, "Although presented in a deliberately outrageous and provocative way, this image is compatible with what Machiavelli actually wrote," 38.

110. Machiavelli, *Prince*, 77. Machiavelli's *Arte of Warre* (1562, 1574, 1588), in Peter Whitehorne's translation, was the only of his works to have been published in English during Marlowe's lifetime.

111. Machiavelli, *Prince,* 119.

112. Ibid., 119–20.

113. On the knights' fealty to the Crown of Sicily, see Sire, *Knights of Malta*, 60–61.

114. See Minshull, "Marlowe's 'Sound Machevill,' " 41.

115. Pope Paul III conferred the Priory of Venice on his grandson Ranuccio Farnese in 1535. See Sire, *Knights of Malta*, 168.

116. On Parma's brilliance, see Hanson, *Confident Hope*, 143–58. Marlowe would evoke Farnese in *Dr. Faustus*, where his "Dutch" protagonist longs to "levy soldiers . . . / And chase the Prince of Parma from our land, / And raigne sole king of all the provinces" (1.1.94–96).

117. Huralt, *Discourse upon the present*, 40.

118. Mattingly, *Armada*, 43.

119. Indeed, "Fernese" is typologically appropriate for several reasons. In addition to his victories in the Low Countries, Parma's first brush with fame had come as a member of Don John's officer corps at the battle of Lepanto in 1571, and thus the young Alessandro became associated with the vanquishing of "the Turk." Further, it was his grandfather, Charles V, who bequeathed the island of Malta to the knights after their defeat at Rhodes, ushering in the order's "Spanish period."

120. Rodríguez-Salgado, "The Anglo Spanish War," 12–20; Persons [pseud. Doleman], *Conference*, 173–84.

121. Boutcher, " 'Who taught thee Rhetoricke,' " 14–15.

122. Heywood, "Defence of drama" (c. 1608), 494–95 (my italics).

CHAPTER 5. SHAKESPEARE'S COMICAL HISTORY

Note to epigraphs: *Taming of the Shrew*, induction 2: 124–35; Dekker, *Pleasant Comedie of Old Fortunatus*, prologue: 1–6.

1. White, *Metahistory*, observes that in comedy "hope is held out for the temporary triumph of man over his world by the prospect of occasional reconciliations of the forces at play in the social and natural worlds. Such reconciliations are symbolized in the festive occasions which the Comic writer traditionally uses to terminate his dramatic accounts of change and transformation," 9.

2. Ibid.

3. Admittedly, *Merchant* should fit the pattern: Shakespeare participated in the realization of the very archetype White's analysis discovers.

4. Stressing the play's Englishness are Rackin, "Impact," 73–76; Gillies, *Shakespeare and the Geography*, 66; Ferber, "Ideology," 448.

5. Barber, *Shakespeare's Festive Comedy*, 166. As Boose, "Comic Contract," has observed, "The comic contract is always fulfilled through a formulaic closure of marriage that at times seems so blatantly imposed on top of a recalcitrant narrative as to approach becoming a device that parodies the demands of the patriarchal formula it so determinedly reproduces," 242.

6. Smith, *Nationalism*, 20.

7. On the "flexibility" of Elizabethan iconography, see Yates, *Astraea*, especially 86–87.

8. As Ferber, "Ideology," puts it, "Wherever they are set, all of Shakespeare's plays are 'about' England," 448.

9. Williams, *Marxism and Literature*, 128–35.

10. See Shapiro, *Shakespeare and the Jews*; Katz, *Jews in the History*; Roth, *History of the Marranos*; Gerber, *Jews of Spain*; Ginio, ed., *Jews, Christians and Muslims*; and Lewis, *Jews of Islam*.

11. See Wallerstein, "Construction of Peoplehood," 71–85.

12. From Spenser's sonnet, "The antique Babel, Empresse of the East," which prefaced Lewkenor, *Commonwealth and Government of Venice* (London, 1599), a translation of Contarini, *De magistratibus et republica Venetorum* (1543). See Spenser, *Shorter Poems*, 776.

13. See Floyd-Wilson, *English Ethnicity and Race*, on "geo-humoral" ethnology, especially 23–86.

14. Examining the unstable quality of English identity in relation to the increasing importation of and reliance on foreign commodities are Burton, *Traffic and Turning*, 15–16; Vitkus, *Turning Turk*, 37; and Rackin, "Impact," passim.

15. Geertz, *Interpretation of Cultures*, 10.

16. Shapiro, "Which is *The Merchant* here, and which *The Jew*?" observes, "Shakespeare's echoes of Marlowe pervade not only the world of Venice but that of Belmont as well," 272–73. See also Rosen, "Rhetoric of Exclusion," 74–75.

17. In this courteous spirit Portia offers a politic reply that is quite out of tune with the conversation she and Nerissa have shared in private: "the lott'ry of my destiny / Bars me the right of voluntary choosing. / But if my father had not scanted me, / And hedged me by his wit to yield myself / His wife who wins me by that means I told you, / Yourself, renownèd Prince, then stood as fair / As any comer I have looked on yet / For my affection" (2.1.15–22).

18. See Little, *Shakespeare Jungle Fever*, 63, 71; Ungerer, "Portia and the Prince," 112.

19. For a discussion of how "Shakespeare has contributed to the obsession with color," see Palmer, "Merchants and Miscegenation," 55–58.

20. On possible sources for the "casket-plot," see Shakespeare, ed. Furness, *New Variorum* 7:314–19.

21. Whigham, "Ideology and Class," 103–4.

22. Although Norman, "Morocco's Reference to Spain," 363–64, offers this interesting surmise, it does not follow necessarily that this construction constitutes a reference to Spain.

23. On the Anglo-Moroccan alliance, see Ungerer, "Portia and the Prince," 89, and Matar, *Turks, Moors, and Englishmen*, 9, and *Britain and Barbary*, 12–37.

24. Smith, *Myths and Memories*, 16.

25. Challis, *Tudor Coinage*, passim.

26. On "Numismatic Miscegenation," see Ungerer, "Portia and the Prince," 105–6.

27. Dubrow, *Echoes of Desire*, 189.

28. Freer, "John Donne and Elizabethan Economic Theory," 498.

29. Ungerer, "Portia and the Prince," speculates that "Shakespeare may have recognized an opportunity to attract and regale Londoners with the Prince of Morocco's pilgrimage to Belmont (a displacement of an English country seat and estate) as an allegory of the political and cultural rapprochement between Saadian Morocco and Elizabethan England," 103.

30. On Portia's xenophobia, see Adelman, "Her Father's Blood," 6; and Rackin, "Impact," 81.

31. Peele, "Decensus Astraeae," lines 40–41, in *Life and Works*, 2:214–19.

32. See "Speech to a Joint Delegation of Lords and Commons, November 5, 1566," and Cecil's "Report to the Full House of Commons, November 6, 1566, on Elizabeth's Speech of November 5," in Marcus et al., *Elizabeth I*, 93–100.

33. Gascoigne's Kenelworth Entertainment resonates strongly with the "Comical History." See "briefe rehearsall, or rather a true Copie" (1576), in *Complete Works* 2:95–97, 99, 102–3. See also Montrose, *Purpose of Playing*, 154–55; King, "Queen Elizabeth I," 45–46; Yates, *Astraea*, 59.

34. Davies, *Complete Poems* 1:136.

35. See Lewkenor, *Commonwealth and Government*, sig. A4, although his translation appeared two years later than we commonly date *Merchant*. Whittled, "Sir Lewis Lewkenor," 123–33, speculates that Shakespeare may have used Lewkenor's manuscript, or perhaps spoken to him while writing the play. In this instance Lewkenor claims to be repeating proverbial knowledge. The connection between Lewkenor, *Othello, Volpone*, and later Venetian plays has been well established by Mcpherson, "Lewkenor's Venice," 459–66, and *Shakespeare, Jonson, and the Myth of Venice*, passim.

36. Marcus, *Unediting the Renaissance*, 57 (my italics).

37. Hough, *Preface to the Faerie Queene*, 106ff.

38. For Burton, *Traffic and Turning*, "Portia's Belmont represents the unsettling new world of early modern trafficking . . . a place where Christian and Muslim venturers meet in contention, and where Portia is rendered one more commodity," 207.

39. Raman, *Framing India*, 222–29; Elliott, *Spain and Its World*, 19–24.

40. For example, G.B., *Fig for the Spaniard*, B.

41. Shapiro, *Shakespeare and the Jews*, writes, "Portia's other unsuccessful suitor, the Prince of Arragon, offers another example of the disjunctive imposition of a Marlovian

figure in the play" and "the unsuitable (and Marlovian) voices of Morocco and Arragon are exposed and dismissed," 274. I would argue that it is as much the ethnicized bodies uttering these speeches that render them "unsuitable" as it is their "voices."

42. Davies, *Complete Poems* 1:136.

43. For Whigham, "Ideology and Class," the play's marriage plot thus "takes place in a context where insecurity is held at bay by reassuring assertions of class solidity and value," 93–94. This is quite in tune with Camden, *History of Princess Elizabeth*, who in his rendering of "The Third Year, 1560," notes Elizabeth's entertaining of Archduke Charles of Austria mediated by the Count of Elphenstien, James Earl of Arran, and Eric King of Sweden, whose suit had been presented by his brother, John Duke of Finland, as well as her courting by the unsuitable Sir William Pickering Knight and Henry Earl of Arundell, who are eclipsed by Robert Dudley, "a man of flourishing age and comely Features of body and limbs," 12, 51–53.

44. Whigham, "Ideology and Class," 94.

45. Ibid., 95–97. Thus Portia, who shows herself to be a "more discriminating member of a more differentiated society," enables the "displacement of typical Elizabethan ethnocentrism to Italy, where one of the victims is an Englishman, [which] emphasizes the exclusive motive itself," 99.

46. Ashley, *Comparison of the English and Spanish*, C2.

47. Here Spenser's *View* chastens the Old English who have degenerated on Irish soil. Eudoxus wonders, "Is it possible that an Englishman, brought up in such sweet civility as England affords, should find such likeing in that barbarous rudenes, that he should forget his owne nature, and forgoe his owne nation! how may this bee, or what (I pray you) may be the cause thereof?" (54).

48. Ibid., 50. As Kidd, *British Identities Before Nationalism,* has noted, contemporaries such as George Saltern, *Of the antient lawes of Great Britaine* (1605), could also argue that "the various nations of Britain were all derived from 'branches of the same stock, namely the Cimbri of Gomer, and likewise the Saxons and Danes of Ashkenaz, and the Scots, if Iberi, of Tubal, and all of Japhet," 62. See also, Rackin, "Impact," 83.

49. See Spenser, *Variorum*, 10:85n; Iyengar, *Shades of Difference*, 91.

50. Jones and Stallybrass, "Dismantling Irena," 157–71, 159–60.

51. Spenser, *View,* 50; Spenser, *Variorum*, 10:91.

52. Fuchs, "Spenser and the Irish Moriscos," 52.

53. Spenser, *View*, 51, 144.

54. Ibid., 102.

55. Ibid., 143. As editors Hadfield and Maley note of Spenser's *View*, "Irenius/Spenser's political analysis is vitiated by an apparent contradiction. On one hand, the attempt appears to be to convince the reader that Ireland is not beyond reform and that the land can be salvaged from its current abject situation. On the other, the argument seems to cast the Irish as irremediably 'other,' implacably opposed to such English efforts by dint of their being Irish and wanting to remain that way," xxi.

56. Jonson, *Irish Masque*, quoted in Iyengar, *Shades of Difference*, 92–93.

57. As Whigham, "Ideology and Class," observes, "Jessica proves her truth by false-

hood to her father, and she is finally a more faithless Jew" than he is; but "she is true . . . to the canons of truth of the class she has joined, both in her acquisition of her financial inheritance and in her celebration with Lorenzo in Genoa, where they display their credentials by lavish spending and revelry, trading Leah's ring for a monkey," 113. Observing here that "true love, exploitation, and the demonstration of identity . . . coalesce" in Jessica's actions (113), Whigham builds upon Stone, *Crisis of the Aristocracy*, which is worth quoting here: "Money was the means of acquiring and retaining status, but it was not the essence of it: the acid test was the mode of life, a concept that involved many factors. Living on a private income was one, but most important was spending liberally, dressing elegantly, and entertaining lavishly. Another was having sufficient education to display a reasonable knowledge of public affairs, and to be able to perform gracefully on the dance-floor, and on horseback, in the tennis court and the fencing school," 50.

58. Steinsaltz, *Essential Talmud*, 136.

59. Lewalski, "Biblical Allusion and Allegory," suggests that "comprehension of the play's allegorical meanings leads to a recognition of its fundamental unity, discrediting the common critical view that it is a hotchpotch which developed contrary of Shakespeare's intention," 328.

60. Rackin, "Impact," notes a resemblance of the ethos represented in the play and the way Samuel Purchas "optimistically imagines that the influence of global trade will resolve the differences between the English and their foreign others into a world united in universal obedience to the Christian God of the English," a "benevolent universalism that looks very much like a rationale for English imperialism," 77.

61. Shapiro, *Shakespeare and the Jews*, 7.

62. Metzger, " 'Now by My Hood,' " 56.

63. See Rackin, "Impact," for another view of Launcelot's miscegenation, 84.

64. See Shapiro, *Shakespeare and the Jews*, 172; Metzger, "Now by My Hood" 55.

65. Shapiro, *Shakespeare and the Jews*, 173. Burton, *Traffic and Turning*, observes appropriately, that for reasons of profit and policy, "in the changing world of Mediterranean trafficking, Portia may have her preferences, but like it or not the Muslim must be treated 'as fair / As any comer' (2.1.10–21)," 208.

66. O'Brien, *God Land*, 24–26.

67. See Ungerer, "Portia and the Prince," 89–126; Vitkus, *Turning Turk*, 25–27; Matar, *Turks, Moors, and Englishmen*, 20–21, 33–34.

68. On England's involvement in the slave trade, see Ungerer, "Portia and the Prince," 90; Rackin, "Impact," 79, and Chapter 3 above.

69. As Loomie, "Sir William Semple," points out, "In 1591 alone, ninety-eight English merchants freighted ships for southern Adalucia," 177.

70. "43 Elizabeth I, 804.5: Licensing Casper van Senden to Deport Negroes" (c. January 1601), in Hughes and Larkin, eds., *Tudor Royal Proclamations*, 3:221.

71. See Hall, "Guess Who's Coming?" 87–111; Newman, *Fashioning Femininity*, 81; Boose, "Getting of a Lawful Race," 53.

72. Bartels, "Too Many Blackamoors," has recently drawn attention to this issue.

73. "The second voyage to Guinea set out by Sir George Barbe, Sir John Yorke, Thomas

Lok, Anthony Hickman and Edward Castelin, in the yere 1554. The Captaine whereof was M. John Lok," in Hakluyt, *Principal Navigations*, 6:176. For Hawkins's taking of "500 Negroes" for "traffique to the West Indies" in 1568, see "The travailes of Job Hortop, which Sir John Hawkins set on land within the Bay of Mexico," *Principal Navigations*, 9:447. On Hawkins's 1562–68 ventures into the transatlantic slave trade with "unprecedented royal support," see Appleby, "War, Politics, and Colonization," 59–60.

74. Bartels, "Too Many Blackamoors," 315.

75. In *Don Quixote*, Cervantes comments in various ways on this cultural loss. See especially Sancho's encounter with his former neighbor, Ricote the *morisco*, part II, chapter LIV, "Concerning matters relevant to this history and not to any other."

76. Kagan, "Clio and the Crown," 73–99.

77. As Castro, *Spaniards*, writes, "As early as the thirteenth century, Rodrigo Jiménez de Rada believed that Iberians and Spaniards descended from Tubal, fifth son of Japheth," adding, "I myself was taught in school to repeat that 'Tubal, son of Japheth and grandson of Noah, was the first settler of Spain,' " 23, 20. See also Kagan, "Clio and the Crown," 77; Genesis 10:2.

78. See Kidd, *British Identities Before Nationalism*, 30. Braude, "Sons of Noah," notes that such uses of biblical genealogy "reflect the ethnic and geographical assumptions of each age," 108.

79. So focused have we been on identifying Jewish individuals Shakespeare may have known that we have not often asked, with reference to a play that is very much about "kindness," what *kind* of Jewish identity did Shakespeare mean to evoke in his play? See Edelman, "Which Is the Jew?"

80. Shapiro, *Shakespeare and the Jews*, 13, 18. See Florio, *World of Wordes*, 216; *Queen Anne's New World*, 300.

81. Daunce, *Brief Discourse*, 3, 27. *OED*: "Ignomie," variant short form of ignominy: 1. Dishonor, disgrace, shame; infamy; the condition of being in disgrace, etc. 2. Ignominious or base quality or conduct; that which entails dishonour or disgrace, disgraceful or dishonorable conduct, quality or action.

82. *OED*: "jump," adv. "with exact coincidence or agreement; exactly, precisely." Obs. Usage current from 1539–1656.

83. Daunce's argument takes on an even darker tone when "confusion" is read against the Leviticus 18:23 prohibition: "Thou shalt not . . . lie with any beast to be defiled therewith, neither shall any woman stand before a beast, to lie down thereto: for it is an abomination," which the Geneva Bible glosses "or confusion," and the King James translation gives primacy.

84. Goldberg, *Racist Culture*, 63; Hannaford, *Race*, 147–84.

85. Daunce, *Brief Discourse*, 35–36.

86. *OED*: "naturall," Obs. 17.a. Of a country or language: being that of a person's birth; native. 17. b. Of a person: native to a country; native born. Obs. 17.d. That is native of the specified place. Obs. But also 15.a. Of a person: related genetically but not legally to his or her father; born outside of marriage, illegitimate.

87. On the relationship between sixteenth- and early seventeenth-century Anglo-

Saxonism and the nineteenth-century ideology, see Horsman, *Race and Manifest Destiny*, 7–16. On Cecil, Camden, Verstegen, and emerging Anglo-Saxonism, see MacDougall, *Racial Myth*, 31–49.

88. Adelman, "Her Father's Blood," 4–30.

89. Orange, *Apologie*, O2.

90. Ferber, "Ideology," 444. See also Fisch, "Shakespeare and the Puritan Dynamic," 81–92; Millward, *Shakespeare's Religious Background*, 158–61; Siegel, "Shylock and the Puritan Usurers."

91. Danson, *Harmonies*, has suggested a relationship between the play and the paradoxes of law as expressed in Hooker's *Lawes of Ecclesiastical Polity*, 94.

92. Trevor, "Sadness in *The Faerie Queene*."

93. While Kyd may have incorporated this coding by echoing Bel-imperia against Belphoebe, the most immediately striking resonance between the several personae adopted by Portia and the poetics of English nationhood may be Elizabeth's own early identification with the biblical Daniel. Levin, *Heart and Stomach*, notes that "ironically, in *The Merchant of Venice* Shylock also compares Portia to Daniel when he thinks she is the lawyer Balthazar, though of course this 'Daniel come to judgement' does not in the end help Shylock," 132.

94. See my discussion of Kyd's wordplay in Chapter 3, above.

95. Shapiro, *Shakespeare and the Jews*, observes that editors of *The Merchant of Venice* as "uniformly note that the characters are alluding to the apocryphal story of Susannah and the elders, where Daniel is described as a 'young child' who convicts the lying elders out of their own mouths. The explanations go no further, perhaps because the similarities between the young Portia and Daniel end there" (133).

96. Ibid.

97. Góngora, *Colonial History of Latin America*, 220.

98. The precedence of the model was apparent to Daunce, *Brief Discourse*, who observed, "It is certain the Spaine is of great antiquity, bearing that name under the first Monarchie," though he argued that in the case of this particular nation "her age [is] no ornament (as it hath bene in the names of the other foure Monarchies, and some of other nations)," 2. Thus the Danielic narrative could also serve as a straw man against which Spain's imperial rivals, many of whom harbored their own eschatological pretensions, would take aim—a rhetorical strategy deployed by the English from the Elizabethan period through the era of the Commonwealth's Western Design and well into the eighteenth century. Edward Gibbon would write, "Among the nations who have adopted the Mosaic history of the world, the ark of Noah has been of the same use, as was formerly to the Greeks and Romans the siege of Troy. On a narrow basis of acknowledged truth, an immense but rude superstructure of fable has been erected; and the wild Irishman, as well as the wild Tartar, could point out the individual son of Japhet from whose loins his ancestors were lineally descended. The last century abounded with antiquarians of profound learning and easy fait, who, by the dim light of legends and traditions, of conjectures and etymologism conducted the great-grandchildren of Noah from the tower of Babel to the extremities of the globe." Quoted in Kidd, *British Identities Before Nationalism*, 9–10.

99. Pagden, *Lords of All*, 42–43; Scmidt and Skinner, eds., *Cambridge History*, 747–52.

100. In Anglo-American history, we are most familiar with the example of the "Fifth Monarchy Men" whose apocalyptic energies contributed to the English Civil War. The more universal view had been voiced during the Armada crisis by Allen, *Admonition*, vi, XLV–XLIX.

101. Hadfield, "Late Elizabethan Protestantism," 311–20.

102. Venice's republican system provided a model against which European nations measured their own political needs. See Fink, *Classical Republicans*, especially 28–45.

103. Shakespeare's contemporary Laurence Aldersley noted the Duke's powerlessness, as "but a servant, for himself he can doe litle . . . if any man having a suite, come to him, and make his complaint, and deliver his supplication, it is not in him to help him, but he will tell him, You must come this day, or that day, and then I will refer your suite to the Seigniorie." See "The first voyage or journey, made by Master Laurence Aldersley, Marchant of London . . . in the yeere 1581," Hakluyt, *Principal Navigations*, 5:205.

104. Levin, *Heart and Stomach*, 121. Marcus, "Shakespeare's Comic Heroines," adds, "There are remarkable correlations between the sexual multivalence of Shakespeare's heroines and an important strain in the political rhetoric of Queen Elizabeth I," 137.

105. Addressing the play's sexual energies, Levin, *Heart and Stomach*, writes that a "boy actor playing a female disguised as a male could be either a powerful professional young man, like Portia as Balthazar in *The Merchant of Venice*, or a sexually attractive but powerless boy, like Jessica in her male disguise as she elopes with Lorenzo in the same play," 126.

106. Yates, *Astraea*, 76–80.

107. After Montrose, *The Purpose of Playing*, I see "the play's connection to the monarch and to the culture of the court" was "dialectical rather than causal" and "structural rather than incidental." Thus, "whether or not the play was first (or ever) performed for an aristocratic wedding, the pervasive cultural presence of the Queen was a condition of the play's imaginative possibility. And, in the sense that the royal presence was itself presented within the play, the play appropriated and extended the imaginative possibilities of the Queen," 159–61.

108. Barton, *Short History of Spain*, 85–86, 96–97.

109. Neill, *Putting History to the Question*, suggests the Inquisition connection, pointing out that "one reason why Shylock remains such a deeply troubling figure at the end of *The Merchant* is the unspoken possibility that his forcible conversion (like that of the Jews in sixteenth-century Spain), will only institutionalize the very uncertainly it is designed to efface," 272. See also Vitkus, *Turning Turk*, 191.

110. Verstegan, *Restitution* (London, 1605), 187. See also Hamilton, "Richard Verstegen and Catholic Resistance," 90.

111. See Verstegan, *Restitution,* 1, 43, and Kidd's discussion of the same in *British Identities Before Nationalism*, 77, 86–87. MacDougall, *Racial Myth*, 45–49, observes that Camden was beginning to draw conclusions similar to Verstegen's. See also Clancy, *Papist Pamphleteers*, 113.

112. Bartels, "Too Many Blackamoors," has noted that we see "a more guarded and insular nationalism" surfacing between 1596 and 1601 in royal letters and attendant proclamations, and that "with it comes a more insistent racism," 317. See also Hall, "Guess Who's Coming?" on "the exclusionary values of Belmont," 98.

CHAPTER 6. *OTHELLO*'S SPANISH SPIRITS

Note to epigraphs: Anonymous, "Poem of Alfonso Onceno," fourteenth century—for its Iberian cultural significance, see Castro, *Spaniards*, 411–13; Dekker, *Famous History of Sir Thomas Wyat. With the Coronation of Queen Mary, and the coming in of King Philip*. See Bowers ed., *Dramatic Works*, vol. 1., 4.1.20–21.

1. Braudel, *Perspective*, 30.

2. See Lane, *Venice*, 331.

3. Quoted in Wills, *Venice*, 181.

4. Aretino, quoted in Wills, *Venice*, 181.

5. Priuli, quoted in Wills, *Venice*, 181.

6. Gillies, *Shakespeare and the Geography*, critiques this traditional model, drawing our attention to Venice's "disturbing porosity," 137. The construction of Othello as outsider is advanced primarily by Iago, Roderigo, and Brabantio; I don't think we can attribute it to the play's more "Italian" characters: the Duke, his officers, Cassio, and Desdemona. Fiedler, *The Stranger in Shakespeare*, is the classic discussion of this perspective.

7. *Merchant of Venice*, 3.3.30–31.

8. The diversity of Venice was hardly Braudel's discovery. As Priuli wrote, "In Venice nearly everyone, apart form the nobles and a few *cittadini*, is a foreigner," *I diari*, 4:101, quoted in Martin, *Venice's Hidden Enemies*, 163. While such observations are present in any of the histories of the Venice, I privilege Braudel, whose particular contribution was to downplay national borders in favor of geographical (un)boundedness. The view from Lane's *Venice* is, by way of contrast, often that of native "Doges," "Noble Gentlemen," and "Resident Merchants." For Lane's influence, see Braudel's foreword to *Venice and History*, v–xiii. On Braudel's tendency to diminish "politics" and "the state," see Hill, "Braudel and the State," 125–42.

9. After Clifford, "Traveling Cultures," "the representational challenge" concerns "the portrayal and understanding of local/global historical encounters, co-productions, dominations and resistances . . . hybrid, cosmopolitan experiences as well as native ones," 101.

10. "History" in the Renaissance is often "heroic," the more so when rendered in such a "high" genre as tragedy. Sahlins, *Islands of History*, on the "structure" of nineteenth-century Fijian history resonates strongly with much Renaissance historiography: "This really is a history of kings and battles, but only because it is a cultural order that, multiplying the action of the king by the system of society, gives him a disproportionate effect," 41.

11. Three important Black Legend tracts employ this terminology in order to advertise their common ethnographic project. See the title pages of R. A., *Comparison*, G. B., *Fig for the Spaniard*, and H. W., trans. *Pageant of Spanish Humours*.

12. Braudel, *Mediterranean*, 31.

13. R.A., *Comparison*, 21. The heading is from Spenser's sonnet "The antique Babel, Empresse of the East."

14. See Newman, *Fashioning Femininity*, 85.

15. See Lane, *Venice*, 415; Braudel, *Perspective*, 37.

16. Trevor-Roper, "Spain and Europe," 269.

17. Maltby, *Black Legend in England*, 100.

18. Ambassador Giustinian, "to the Doge and Senate," in *Calendar of State Papers, Venetian*, 11:6. See also Wright, "Propaganda Against James I's 'Appeasement,'" 149–72.

19. "Report on England presented to the Government of Venice in the year 1607, by the Illustrious Gentleman Nicolo Molin, Ambassador there," *Calendar of State Papers, Venetian*, 11: 501.

20. See Kernan, *King's Playwright*, for James's high esteem for the Venetian oligarchy, 93. On the importance of Venice for European political culture, see Bouwsma, *Usable Past*, 266–91.

21. Lewkenor, *Commonwealth and Government of Venice*, 15ff. Lewkenor was James's master of ceremonies. See also Mcpherson, "Lewkenor's Venice."

22. On the tensions between "family honor," the changing value of "love," and "the honor of the Venetian government," see Ruggiero, *Boundaries of Eros*, 15–44.

23. Quoted in Cohen, *Drama of a Nation*, 200.

24. Lane, *Venice*, 394.

25. On conflicts between Venice, Spain, and the Papal States, see Bouwsma, *Usable Past*, 247–65.

26. Lewkenor, *Commonwealth and Government*, 15ff. On Venice's foreign Protestant communities, see Martin, *Venice's Hidden Enemies*, 226–33; Lane, *Venice*, 393–96. On Venetian relations with Protestant Europe during and after the Papal Interdict of 1606–7, see Bouwsma, *Venice and the Defense*, especially 506–8.

27. *Coryat's Crudities*, vol. 1, quoted in Levith, *Shakespeare's Italian Settings and Plays*, 14.

28. *Hecatommithi*, in *Othello*, ed. Kernan, 173.

29. Elliott, *Shakespeare's Invention of* Othello, 78; Winstanley, *"Othello" as the Tragedy of Italy* (1924), was more emphatic. On Cervantes's Lepanto experience, see the prologue to book 2of *Don Quixote*, 467.

30. On the Holy League and the significance of Lepanto, see Braudel, *Mediterranean*, 1027–42; Bouwsma, *Venice and the Defense*, 190–93; Lane, *Venice*, 369–74.

31. *"Lepanto* of James VI, King of Scotland" (1591), in *His Majesties Poetical Exercises* my italics.

32. See Mcpherson, *Shakespeare, Jonson, and the Myth of Venice*, 75–81, and Kernan, *King's Playwright*, 60–61, on the play and James's poem.

33. *Don Quixote*, book 2, 467.

34. *Lepanto* of James VI, line 6.

35. *Othello*, ed. Kernan, 171–84.

36. After Geertz, *Interpretation of Cultures*, "Culture is public because meaning is," 12. Noting the connection between Iago and Santiago are Murphy, "A Note on Iago's Name"; Macey, "Naming of the Protagonists"; Everett, "'Spanish' Othello"; Parker, "Fantasies of 'Race' and 'Gender,'" 90; and Newman, *Fashioning Femininity*, 164 n. 31.

37. The phrase is from Rymer, *Short View of Tragedy* (1693), 96.

38. Anonymous, *Cantar de mio Cid*, canto 36:88. My section heading is the famous Spanish battle cry.

39. Spenser, *Variorum,* 10, Copy P: 92.

40. Rymer, *Short View of Tragedy,* 139. On the Restoration's construction of Shakespeare as "our Poet," see Dobson, *Shakespeare and the Making,* 17–133.

41. *Othello,* ed. Sanders, 1. Edmund Tilney, Master of Revels, recorded the 1604 performance thus: "By the Kings Maiesties plaiers. Hallamas Day being the first of Novembar. A play in the Banketing house at Whithall called The Moor of Venis. Shaxberd." Indeed, the performance of the play at such seemingly divergent occasions has led Goldberg, *James I and the Politics of Literature,* to suggest that there is no correspondence between occasion and text whatsoever, that it is not "even topically suitable," 231.

42. Shakespeare, ed. Furness, *New Variorum*: "In the list of ballads, as given by Collier (New Particulars, & c., 1836, p. 45), there appeared the following Tragedy of *Othello* the Moor, 'Anonymous, but following Shakespeare's Tragedy very closely. Not printed. . . . There can be no doubt,' Collier goes on to say, 'that this Ballad was written subsequently to Shakespeare's Tragedy; it was founded upon the play in consequence of its popularity, and not the play upon it. . . . It varies slightly from the play, and makes Iago a Spaniard, as indeed his name indicates. The change was, perhaps, made in accordance with the prejudice of the time when it was written, possibly about 1625, after the breaking off of the Spanish Match,'" 4:398. I would argue that the ballad did not "vary" from the play at all. Rather, the balladeer reads the codes of "Hispanicity" in a sensible and obvious manner.

43. There is, perhaps, no more important name in Iberian history than Santiago, alternatively spelled San Tiago or Sant-Iago, excepting, of course, the sacred names of Jesus Christ and the Virgin Mary. According to Roman Catholic tradition, Saint James the Greater, brother to Saint John the Evangelist and first of the Twelve to be martyred for the Faith, brought Christianity to Iberia. See Benedictine Monks, *Book of Saints,* 157. For more comprehensive views, see Castro, *Santiago de España*; Kendrick, *Saint James in Spain*; Myers et al., *Santiago*; Melczer, *Pilgrim's Guide.*

44. Walt Disney Pictures' animated feature *Aladdin* (1992) is one of the more recent dramatic works to mobilize the typology—the evil sorcerer Jafar's duplicitous parrot-sidekick is named Iago.

45. Referring to Shakespeare's character, I use the Englished "Roderigo"; when referring to the Spanish historical figures, I prefer the Spanish, "Rodrigo." The name is so (arch)typically Spanish that it could, of course, have evoked any number of more contemporary "Spaniards." Another suggestive possibility would be Rodrigo Borgia [de Lanzol y Borja] (Alexander VI), the "Spanish pope."

46. I borrow "cultural hyperbole" from Newman, *Fashioning Femininity,* who writes that Iago, "the representative of 'the white male sexual norm'" who implicates us "by virtue of his manipulative power and his superior knowledge and control over the action, which we share . . . is a cultural hyperbole . . . he does not oppose cultural norms so much as hyperbolize them," 85.

47. After Riffaterre, *Semiotics of Poetry,* I adapt the "hypogram," or "the generator of textual derivation," and isolate two elements: the *matrix,* or "Santiago," and the *model,* "killing Moors." Together these *overdetermine,* or "create the special meaning" of, the play, 19–22.

48. Daunce, *Brief Discourse*, 24–25. Section heading is from Trend, ed., *Oxford Book of Spanish Verse*, 60.

49. From *Table Talk*—22 December 1822. See *Coleridge's Literary Criticism*, 244.

50. Goldberg, *Racist Culture*, 63 (emphasis his); Hannaford, *Race*, 147–84.

51. Braude, "Sons of Noah," 104.

52. Gillies, *Shakespeare and the Geography*, notes that *Othello*'s Moor is drawn more sharply than the other Moors seen on the Elizabethan stage; he speculates that "the gap between Coleridge's 'veritable negro' and Shakespeare's moor is partly explained by the institutionalization of plantation slavery in the New World in the course of the seventeenth century," 32–33.

53. *Coleridge's Literary Criticism*, 244.

54. On the international book trade and efforts to control dissemination, see Jardine, *Worldly Goods*, 135–80; Febvre and Martin, *Coming of the Book*, 216–44.

55. Perhaps the most well known of the genre, from Trend, ed., *Oxford Book of Spanish Verse*, 33. Entwhistle, *European Balladry* (1939), observed that "the Castilian 'romances' are unsurpassed in Europe for their number, vigour, influence, dramatic intensity, and veracity," 152. Tyler, *Early Guitar*, notes that other *romances*, like *Passeavase el Rey Moro*, circulated in popular songbooks written for the *vihuela*, 28.

56. Carasco-Urgoiti, *Moorish Novel*, 48–52, 97–101.

57. *Don Quixote* was known in England long before its 1612 translation by Shelton. See Knowles, ed., *Don Quixote in England*.

58. Romance protagonists travel the length and breadth of the Mediterranean world: from Constantinople to London (Palmerin), from Gaul to Scotland (Amadis), and from Greece to California (Amadis's son, Esplandían). On the impact of the Spanish novel on English literary culture, see Randall, *Golden Tapestry*, especially 39–94; O'Connor, *Amadis de Gaule and Its Influence*, 131–225. On the complicated textual history of *El Abenceraje*, see Carrasco-Urgoiti, *Moorish Novel*, 53–72. For a recent discussion of Sidney's *Old Arcadia* in an imperial context, see Lockey, *Law and Empire*, 47–79.

59. See *Don Quixote*, book 1, chapters 5 and 6. An expurgated *Diana* is one of the romances preserved in the "inquisition" of Don Quixote's library.

60. Montemayor, trans. Yong, *Diana of George Montemayor* (London, 1598), 161–62, 166.

61. See, for example, Parker, "Fantasies of 'Race,'" Newman, *Fashioning Femininity*, and Neill, "Unproper Beds," 187ff., who also answer Coleridge.

62. *Diccionario Crítico Etimológico Castellano e Hispánico*, 5:151. See Harvey, *Muslims in Spain*, 2–10, for a historically sensitive survey of *moro* and its derivatives.

63. For the Moor as "dog," and the institutionalization of the term "morisco," see Hess, *Forgotten Frontier*, 151.

64. See Vaughan and Vaughan, "Before *Othello*," 27.

65. In Venice a verbal assault such as Iago's and Roderigo's might well have constituted a crime against the state. See Ruggiero, *Violence in Early Modern Venice*, 125–37.

66. See Maltby, *Black Legend in England*, 12–28.

67. H. W., trans. *A Pageant of Spanish Humours* (London, 1599), A3.

68. Adversary," with its "Satanic" Hebrew etymological inheritance, may be more appropriate than "other" to describe the demonizing rhetorical practices of Reformation Europe.

69. Iyengar, *Shades of Difference*, 81–93.

70. See Parmelee, *Good Newes from Fraunce*, on the political context in which these texts were "published to enlighten the English public as to the nefarious activities of the Spanish," 33.

71. The *Pageant's* sixteen "naturall kindes of a Signior of Spaine" are precisely those stereotypes that comprise *la leyenda negra.* See Gibson, Maltby, Powell, Weber, Juderías, Fernández Retamar, and Sánchez.

72. Quoted in Mcpherson, *Shakespeare, Jonson, and the Myth*, 73.

73. See Peirce, *Peirce, On Signs*, for his famous example of "indexicality" or "second-ness," 239–40.

74. Burelbach, "Name-play and Internationalism," writes, "Shakespeare often does not connect his characters' names with his settings. . . . All of the names in Othello sound Italian but actually have non-Italian roots." Brabantio is "reflective of the divided history of Brabant, a duchy in the Low Countries," 144–47. My "opening" of "Brabantio" was suggested first by Alan F. Nagel and then by my encounter with Wilson, *Christian Dictionarie* (London, 1612), which emphasizes "opening the signification of the chiefe wordes of the Old and New Testament," title page.

75. The figure of "the Turk" as mediated by Foxe surely held a certain sway in the Protestant view of the Islamic adversary. But although he claims that "the Turk is the more open and manifest enemy of the church" than the papist, the rhetorical purpose of Foxe's interpolation is that the reader might judge "the acts of them both." See *Acts and Monuments*, 4:122. It was left for Protestants to discern the more than Turkish cruelty of the papist, most especially the archpapist Spaniard.

76. Bartels, "Making More of the Moor," 439.

77. Hakluyt, *Principal Navigations,* 6:289. See also Burton, *Traffic and Turning*, 246–48.

78. Hakluyt, *Principal Navigations,* 5:226.

79. Ibid., 5:420–26.

80. Ibid., 5:287.

81. Matar, *Britain and Barbary*, 13.

82. Harris, "Portrait of a Moor," 89–97; Griffin, "Un-sainting James," 72–73.

83. Quoted from Starkie, *Road to Santiago*, 41.

84. Las Casas, *Spanish Colonie*, sig. D4.

85. Johnson, "Preface" to Shakespeare (1765). See *Johnson on Shakespeare*, 22–23.

86. Mullaney, *Place of the Stage*, 119–20.

87. The early pages of the poem have been lost. The incident is written in *La Crónica de Veinte Reyes*, versified and published throughout the sixteenth century. See Powell, *Epic and Chronicle.* El Cid began to appear fairly often on the stage during the seventeenth century, most significantly in Lope de Vega's *Las Hazañas del Cid, y su muerte, con la tomada de Valencia* (1603) (could Shakespeare have known this play?), Guillén de Castro y Bellvís,

Las Mocedades del Cid (1618), and its more famous offspring, Corneille's *Le Cid* (1636). A principal character in Cornielle's slightly less well known *L'Illusion* (1635) is "Matamore."

88. An important thematic strain of *Othello* is also that of "honor." There is a sense in which Shakespeare's play stages a northern view of this more broadly Mediterranean cultural value: Brabantio's honor is stung by Desdemona's elopement, Roderigo's by her choice of Othello, Iago by Othello's choice of Cassio, Cassio's by his demotion, Desdemona's by Othello's mistrust, and so forth. See Wilson, "A Hispanist Looks at *Othello*," 201–19. Baroja, "Religion, World Views," notes the importance of the military saints, Santiago and San Jordi (Saint George), in this complex, 91–102. On the wider social complex, see Peristiany, ed., *Honor and Shame*, especially 19–137.

89. *Cantar de mio Cid*, canto II:76.

90. *OED*, senses I and II.

91. Also ibid.

92. Among many other observations, Daileader, "Back Door Sex," notes that we often see "Italians (and Spaniards, Egyptians, Ethiopians, and Hebrews) scapegoated for more general masculinist, Anglophile anxieties (sometimes released through humor) about sex," 326.

93. Following Dr. Johnson, Hollander, "Dallying Nicely with Words," has recognized that Shakespeare's punning tends to "eroticize" them, 123–24.

94. R.A., *Comparison*, 19.

95. Fuchs, *Passing for Spain*, 10.

96. Royster, "White-limed Walls," 436.

97. See Burshatin, "Moor in the Text," on the fifteenth-century *Crónica Saracina*, 123.

98. On the instability of whiteness, see Royster, "White-limed Walls." On the problems associated with proving *limpieza*, see Kamen, *Spanish Inquisition*, 241–42; Lynch, *Spain*, 37.

99. H.W., *Pageant*, "kind" 8: "A Signior is a Hare in a besieged place," sig. B2.

100. *Cantar de mio Cid*, canto 1:50.

101. The "Poyo" is located in the province of Teruel. *Diccionario Enciclopédico Espasa* 10:313; Menéndez Pidal, *Cid and His Spain*, 235–37.

102. Viña Liste, ed., *Mio Cid Campeador*, xlviii–ix, 377–80.

103. *Johnson on Shakespeare*, 22–23.

104. Fletcher, *Certain very proper, and profitable Similies* (London, 1595), 17.

105. The superiority of Spanish blades was an early modern commonplace. See my Introduction's discussion of Jonson, *Alchemist* (4.4.14–15).

106. H.W., *Pageant*, sig. A2–A3.

107. Ibid., sig. B3.

108. According to Lomax, *La Orden de Santiago*, "The ideals [the Order of Santiago] presented to the people of the peninsula were based upon the spirit of the crusade: religion, war, Church, nation-state, nobility and purity of blood—themes wholly Santiagan—would come together in a single concept, which marks distinctively the Hispanic mentality of the Golden Age," 217 (my translation). See also Kendrick, *Saint James in Spain*, 13–24.

109. Greenblatt, *Renaissance Self-Fashioning*, 235 and 298–99.

110. Burke identifies Iago as a "demon of Rhetoric" in *Rhetoric of Motives* (1950), 36. In *Grammar of Motives* (1945), Burke had identified Iago as "consubstantial with Othello in that he represents the principles of jealousy implicit in Othello's delight in Desdemona as a private spiritual possession." Had Burke placed a little more weight on the "scenic" component of his pentad, that is, on "Shakespeare qua Englishman" circa 1604, rather than "Shakespeare qua poet," he might have figured Roderigo into his analysis, 414–15.

111. Lynch, *Spain*, writes, "Of all [the Inquisition's] activities, however, one of the most characteristic and perhaps the most pernicious was related to the question of *limpieza de sangre*, or purity of blood," 37. There is probably no better example (unless we want to turn to our own century) of institutionalized "miscegenation" paranoia than the Spanish Inquisition. Lynch also recalls that while converts were officially members of the faith, they "were objects of suspicion and prejudice which took the form of a spirit of exclusiveness among Old Christians," and "anyone who desired a tranquil career in church or state applied to the Inquisition for certificates attesting their purity of blood," which "encouraged perjury, bribery, and collusion, and offered . . . an occasion for the gratification of spite," 36–37—and which describes the antics of Roderigo and Iago quite "faithfully."

112. Vincent, "Moriscos and Circumcision," 78–92.

113. Las Casas, *Short Account*, ed. Griffin, 50. See also Pagden, *European Encounters*, 79. For the infusion of this "novel" spirit into the New World, see Leonard, *Books of the Brave* (1949).

114. Anonymous, *Plesant Historie of Lazarillo de Tormes* (London, 1586), sig. Ai. The commendatory verse is by George Turberville.

115. Daunce, *Brief Discourse*, 31.

116. Published simultaneously in Burgos, Alcalá, and Antwerp in 1554, the year in which England and Spain renewed their traditional alliance with the marriage of Mary and Philip, the much-imitated *novela picaresca* was the product of a nationally self-reflective Erasmian faction that took recourse to fiction in order to expose inequities within Spanish society. See Schevill, "Erasmus and the Fate of a Liberalistic Movement," 103–14. Because of its satirical anticlericalism, *Lazarillo* was the source of considerable controversy in Counter-Reformation Spain. Placed on the Index in 1559, the novel continued to circulate widely. Eventually, Philip II ordered its expurgation, which resulted in the edition of 1573. By 1576, *Lazarillo* had been published in David Rowland's popular English translation, which was reprinted at least five more times during the sixteenth and seventeenth centuries. Other translations also circulated.

117. Anonymous, *Plesant Historie of Lazarillo*, sig. Av.

118. Quotations are from *Blurt, Master Constable* (1602). The play has sometimes been attributed to Middleton.

119. *Othello*, 3.4.36.

120. Salomon, "Don Diego," discovers that Don Diego also appears in plays by Marston, *The Malcontent* (1604), Heywood, *Fair Maid of the West, Part 1* (1609–10), Beaumont and Fletcher, *Maid in the Mill* (c. 1623), and Shirley, *Humorous Courtier* (c. 1631).

121. According to the *OED*, "Viliago" is a variant of "villiaco," "a vile or contemptible person; a villain, scoundrel."

122. Scatological inversion was a rhetorical strategy long favored by Reformation ideologues. McGinn, *Anti-Christ*, points out that Roman icons and "trumpery" were shown as emanating from the devil's ass in publications as serious as Martin Luther's collected works, and "the association of farting and shitting . . . was part of a conscious program of insult by inversion of values," 206–7. Bakhtin, *Rabelais and His World*, notes "a number of extremely free parodies of the names of saints" that were invented "for laughter's sake," 191–92.

123. See Cervantes, *Don Quixote*, book 2, 838–39.

124. Dod and Cleaver, *Plaine and familiar exposition* (London, 1606), 69.

125. See Stone, *Cult of Santiago*, 346–60, for a discussion of Luther's role in "The Passing of Santiago." Erasmus, *A pylgremage, for pure devocyō*, the 1536 English edition of *Peregrinatio religionis ergo* (Basel, 1526), was prefaced with an iconoclastic polemic that railed against "the desperate synne of ydolatrye" in all of its forms, singling out the "brotherhoodes and sisterhoodes" as especially "pernycyouse" because they "counterfayte" the passion of Christ at "Saynt James in Compostella" and "set forthe uncertayne relyques as certayne" and "prostytute to set theym forthe for fylthye lukre," 7–8.

126. Vernon, *Stronge Battery against the Idolatrous invocation* (London, 1562), Aiii.

127. Foxe, *Acts and Monuments*, 10:559.

128. The Council of Trent clearly came down on the side of "Works": "For which reason it is most truly said that *faith without works is dead* (James 2:17–20) and of no profit, and *in Christ Jesus neither circumcision availeth anything or uncircumcision, but faith that worketh by charity* (Galatians 5:6, 6:15). See Olin, ed., *Reformation Debate*, 120. As Justice, "Spain, Tragedy," has shown, "justification" provided a provocative problem for English tragedians, who fall back upon "the vocabulary of intra- and inter-ecclesiastical polemics" that circulated in late sixteenth-century England "emphasizing salvation by faith alone" rather than "the Roman emphasis on works," 273. On the distinctively Iberian conflation of James the Lesser (author of the canonical New Testament epistle) with James the Greater as Santiago, the "twin-brother" of Christ, see Castro, *Spaniards*, 380–470.

129. White, *Discoverie of the Jesuitical Opinion* (London, 1582), 37–38. Saint Ralph Sherwin—an English Jesuit arrested with Campion and executed in 1581—was canonized in 1970 as one of the Forty Martyrs of England and Wales. See Benedictine Monks, *Book of Saints*, 474.

130. Wilson, *Christian Dictionarie*.

131. On *Othello*'s "idolatrous" relationship, the possibility that Desdemona's handkerchief might have been perceived as an "idol," and the play's relation to iconophobia, see Diehl, *Staging Reform*, 166–71.

132. Iago seems to embody "inversio," the figure of "dissimulation" or the "false semblant"—that is, allegory: to speak "otherwise then we think." See Puttenham, *Arte of English Poesie* (1589), 196–97.

133. Wilson, *Christian Dictionarie*, sense IV.

134. On use of the Decalogue to instruct English children, see Aston, *England's Iconoclasts*, 342–479.

135. "Spiritual Whoredome" is another common figure for idolatry in sixteenth-century Protestant discourse. See, for example, Knewstub, *Lectures upon the twentieth* (Lon-

don, 1577), or the Geneva Bible's headings for Hosea, chapters 1–3, "Spirituall whoredome" and "Spirituall marriage."

136. Cavell, *Claim of Reason*, 495.

137. Orlin, *Private Matters and Public Culture*, has located the spirit of Santiago in *Othello* as well. In her reading, it is the Santiago of the zodiacal sign of Sagittarius (which governed the month of November in Agrippa's occult philosophy) that overdetermines the play's action, 193–228.

138. G. B., *Fig for the Spaniard*. This passage underscores the politically divided condition of the Italian Peninsula. While the obviously rude gesture, "giving the fig" or *dar la higa*, can be found throughout the Mediterranean world, it seems to come to England by way of Spain. Pistol gives "the Figge of Spaine" in *Henry V* (3.4.62), but *Othello*'s figs are delivered between "Spaniards." To Roderigo's moment of self-doubt, "I confess it is my shame to be so fond, but it is not my virtue to amend it," Iago responds, "Virtue? A fig!" (1.3.312–14); and a bit later on, when Roderigo praises Desdemona's "blessed condition," Iago responds with the yet more coarse, "Blessed fig's-end! The wine she drinks is made of grapes" (2.1.251–52).

139. On anti-Spanish sentiment and the Spanish mission to the court of James I, see Allen, *Philip III*, 127–41.

140. Rymer, *Short View of Tragedy*, 146, seems to be the first to have responded in print to the farcical structure of the play. Voltaire, "On Tragedy," 87, and Shaw, "Dressing Room Secret," 245, also read the play as farce.

AFTERWORD

Note to epigraph: Anonymous, *Larum for London* (1602), 1143–85.

1. See Bartels, *Speaking of the Moor*, 118–37; Iyengar, *Shades of Difference*, 136–38; Matar, *Britain and Barbary*, 25–26; Burton, *Traffic and Turning*, 121–25; Vitkus, *Turning Turk*, 102–3; Floyd-Wilson, *English Ethnicity*, 43–44.

2. Chambers, *Elizabethan Stage*, 3:300, 427.

3. Chambers, *Elizabethan Stage*, notes that the play has been assigned variously or in combination, to Shakespeare, Marston, Lodge, and Marlowe, 4:1.

4. Oliver Cromwell, quoted in Gibson, *The Black Legend*, 56–57.

5. Korr, *Cromwell and the New Model*, 138–47.

6. Paulson, *Don Quixote in England*, 32–34.

7. Tombs, *That Sweet Enemy*, 16.

8. Davenant, *Works* (London, 1673).

9. Dryden, *Works*, 9:294–310.

10. Smith, *Generall Historie*, 2:145.

11. Bradford, *Of Plymouth Plantation*, 28.

12. Smith, *General Historie*, 2:315.

13. A classic example of the undervaluing of the Hispanic contribution to U.S. history is the lack of recognition given to Bernardo de Gálvez, virtually absent from popular

history, though he fought a second front along the Mississippi River and Gulf Coast during the American Revolution. See Weber, *Spanish Frontier*, 267–70.

14. Sullivan, "Annexation" (1845), is the archetypal expression of these widely held sentiments. Horsman, *Race and Manifest Destiny*, especially 229–48, provides an excellent discussion of the nineteenth-century contexts. See also Powell, *Tree of Hate*, 113–58.

15. Grandin, *Empire's Workshop*, 11–51; Johnson, *Sorrows of Empire*, 39–47.

16. Weber, *Spanish Frontier*, 337.

17. Sánchez, *Spanish Black Legend*, ii.

18. Ibid., i.

19. Peters, "Why We Fight."

20. Fox News, November 21, 2005. John Culberson, 7th District, Houston, Tex.

21. Suskind, "Why Are These Men Laughing?" in which former domestic policy analyst John DiIulio reported, "It's the reign of the Mayberry Machiavels."

22. Barstow, "Behind TV Analysts."

23. Bennett, Lawrence, and Livingston, *When the Press Fails*, 1.

24. Agee, review of *Henry V*.

25. Legacy Project, "For the First Time in Fifty-Five Years."

26. CNN, *Larry King Live*, September 14, 2001.

27. Peters, "Why We Fight," 40.

28. Wikipedia, s.v. "Peters, Ralph." On the discovery that the CIA may be covertly editing this "free encyclopedia," see Fildes, "Wikipedia 'Shows CIA Page Edits.'"

29. Horowitz, "Immigration—and the Curse of the Black Legend"; Downes, "The Terrible, Horrible."

30. CNN, *Lou Dobbs: Tonight*, a regular feature. On Dobbs's fueling of resurgent American nativism, see Southern Poverty Law Center, "Broken Record"; see also Southern Poverty Law Center, "The Nativists."

31. Amayo, "Why Spaniards Make Good Bad Guys."

32. Downes, "The Terrible, Horrible."

33. Baumgarten, "Is FAIR Unfair?" 2–4.

BIBLIOGRAPHY

Catalogue numbers drawn from *Early English Books, 1475–1660* (Ann Arbor, Mich.: University Microfilms International, 1937 [?]–1997), selected from A. W. Pollard and G. R. Redgrave, *A Short Title Catalogue of Books Printed in England, Scotland, and Ireland, and of English Books Printed Abroad, 1475–1660* (London: Bibliographical Society, 1948, revised 1975), receive the abbreviation STC.

A., L. T., trans., *The Masque of the League and the Spanyard Discovered*. Tours and London, 1592. STC 7.

Adelman, Janet. "Her Father's Blood: Race, Conversion, and Nation in *The Merchant of Venice*." *Representations* 81 (Winter 2003): 4–30.

Agee, James. Review of *Henry V. Time*, April 8, 1946, 56–60.

Alexander, Catherine M. S., and Stanley Wells, eds. *Shakespeare and Race*. Cambridge: Cambridge University Press, 2000.

Allen, Paul C. *Philip III and the Pax Hispanica, 1598–1621*. New Haven: Yale University Press, 2000.

Allen, William. *An Admonition to the Nobility and People of England and Ireland*. Antwerp, 1588. STC 368.

———. *The Copie of a Letter written by M. Doctor Allen: Concerning the yeelding up of the citie of Daventrie, unto his Catholike Majestie*. Antwerp, 1587. STC 370.

———. *A Defense and Declaration of the Catholicke Churches Doctrine, touching Purgatory, and prayers for the soules departed*. Antwerp, 1565. STC 371.

Amago, Samuel. "Why Spaniards Make Good Bad Guys: Sergi López and the Persistence of the Black Legend in Contemporary European Cinema." *Film Criticism* 30, no. 1 (Fall 2005): 41–63.

Andrews, Kenneth R. *Trade, Plunder and Settlement: Maritime Enterprise and the Genesis of the British Empire, 1480–1630*. Cambridge: Cambridge University Press, 1984.

Andrews, Kenneth R., ed. *English Privateering Voyages to the West Indies, 1588–1595*. Cambridge: Cambridge University Press, 1959.

Anglo, Sydney. *Spectacle, Pageantry and Early Tudor Policy*. Oxford: Oxford University Press, 1969.

Anonymous. *The begynnynge and foundacyon of the holy hospitall & of the ordre of the knyghtes hospytallers of saynt Johan baptyst of Jerusalem.* London, 1524. STC 15050.

———. *A briefe discourse of the cruel dealings of the Spaniards.* London, 1599. STC 23008.

———. *Certayn and tru good nues, frō the syege of the Isle of Malta.* Gaunt, 1565. STC 17213.5.

———. *The Coppie of the Anti-Spaniard.* London, 1590. STC 684.

———. *La crónica del famoso cavallero Cid Ruy Díez Campeador.* 1562. In Viña Liste, ed., *Mio Cid Campeador.*

———. *The Explanation of the True and Lawfull Right and Tytle, of the Moste Excellente Prince Anthonie the first of that name, King of Portugal, concerning his warres, againste Phillip King of Castile.* Leyden, 1585. STC 689.

———. "The Lamentable fall of Queene Elenor for her pride and wickednesse, by Gods judgement, sunke into the ground at Charing crosse, and rose up againe at Queene hive." To the tune of, Gentle and curteous. One sheet. London: William Blackwall [c. 1600]. STC 7565.4.

———. *A Larum for London.* 1602. Oxford: Malone Society, 1913.

———. "A Libell, fixte upon the French Church Wall, in London. Anno 1593." Ed. Arthur Freeman. In Freeman, "Marlowe, Kyd, and the Dutch Church Libel," 45.

———. *The Plesant Historie of Lazarillo de Tormes a Spaniarde, wherein is conteined his marveilous deeds and life.* Trans. David Rouland. London, 1586. STC 15336.

———. "Poem of Alfonso XI." In *The Forgotten Frontier: A History of the Sixteenth Century Ibero-African Frontier.* Chicago: University of Chicago Press, 1978.

———. *Poema del Cid.* Texto de Menéndez Pidal. Trans. W. S. Merwin. New York: Meridian, 1975.

———. "Queen Eleanor's confession." One sheet. London, 1690. Early English Tract Supplement, A2:4 [88].

Appelbaum, Robert, and John Wood Sweet, eds. *Envisioning an English Empire: Jamestown and the Making of the North Atlantic World.* Philadelphia: University of Pennsylvania Press, 2005.

Appleby, John C. "War, Politics, and Colonization." In *The Origins of Empire,* ed. Nicholas Canny, 55–78. Oxford: Oxford University Press, 1998.

Archer, Ian W. *The Pursuit of Stability: Social Relations in Elizabethan London.* Cambridge: Cambridge University Press, 1991.

Ardolino, Frank R. *Apocalypse and Armada in Kyd's Spanish Tragedy.* Kirksville, Mo.: Truman State University Press, 1995.

———. "Hieronimo as St. Jerome in *The Spanish Tragedy.*" *Études Anglaises* 36 (1983): 435–47.

Armitage, David. *The Ideological Origins of the British Empire.* Cambridge: Cambridge University Press, 2000.

Arsuaga, Ana Echiverría. "The Shrine as Mediator: England, Castile, and the Pilgrimage to Compostela." In Bullón-Fernández, ed., *England and Iberia,* 47–65.

[A]shley, [R]obert, trans. *A Comparison of the English and Spanish Nation.* London, 1589. STC 842.

Aston, Margaret. *England's Iconoclasts*. Vol. 1. Oxford: Oxford University Press, 1988.

———. *The Queen's Two Bodies: Drama and the Elizabethan Succession*. London: Royal Historical Society, 1977.

B., G. *A Fig for the Spaniard, or Spanish Spirits. Wherein are lively portraihed the damnable deeds, misserable murders, and monstrous massacres of the cursed Spaniard*. London, 1591, 1592. STC 1026, 1027.

Babb, Howard S. "Policy in Marlowe's *The Jew of Malta*." *English Literary History* 24 (1957): 85–94.

Baecque, Antoine de. "The Allegorical Image of France, 1750–1800: A Political Crisis of Representation." *Representations* 47 (Summer 1994): 111–43.

Bakhtin, M. M. "The Problem of Speech Genres." In *The Problem of Speech Genres and Other Late Essays,* ed. Caryl Emerson and Michael Holquist, 60–102. Austin: University of Texas Press, 1986.

———. *Rabelais and His World*. Trans. Helene Iswolsky. Bloomington: Indiana University Press, 1984.

Balibar, É., and I. Wallerstein, eds. *Race, Nation, Class: Ambiguous Identities*. Trans. Chris Turner. London: Verso, 1991.

Barber, C. L. *Shakespeare's Festive Comedy: A Study of Dramatic Form and its Relation to Social Custom*. Princeton: Princeton University Press, 1959.

Baroja, Julio Caro. "Religion, World Views, Social Classes, and Honor During the Sixteenth and Seventeenth Centuries in Spain." Trans. Victoria Hughes. In *Honor and Grace in Anthropology*, ed. J. G. Peristiany and J. Pitt-Rivers, 91–102. Cambridge: Cambridge University Press, 1992.

Barstow, David. "Behind TV Analysts, Pentagon's Hidden Hand." *New York Times*, April 20, 2008. Available at http://www.nytimes.com/2008/04/20/washington/20generals. html (accessed April 22, 2008).

Bartels, Emily C. "Making More of the Moor: Aaron, Othello, and Renaissance Refashionings of Race." *Shakespeare Quarterly* 41 (Winter 1990): 433–54.

———. "Malta, the Jew, and the Fictions of Difference: Colonialist Discourse in Marlowe's *The Jew of Malta*," *English Literary Renaissance* 20, no.1 (Winter 1990): 1–16.

———. *Speaking of the Moor: From* Alcazar *to* Othello. Philadelphia: University of Pennsylvania Press, 2008.

———. *Spectacles of Strangeness: Imperialism, Alienation and Marlowe*. Philadelphia: University of Pennsylvania Press, 1993.

———. "Too Many Blackamoors: Deportation, Discrimination, and Elizabeth I." *Studies in English Literature* 46 (Spring 2006): 305–22.

Bartlett, Robert. "Language and Ethnicity in Medieval Europe." In *Ethnicity*, ed. John Hutchinson and Anthony D. Smith, 127–34. Oxford: Oxford University Press, 1996.

Barton, Simon. *A Short History of Spain*. New York: Palgrave Macmillan, 2004.

Baumgarten, Gerald. "Is FAIR Unfair? The Federation for American Immigration Reform." New York: Anti-Defamation League, 2000. Available at www.adl.org (accessed June 20, 2006).

Baumgartner, Frederic J. *France in the Sixteenth Century*. New York: St. Martin's Press, 1995.

Bawcutt, N. W. "'Policy,' Machiavellianism, and the Earlier Tudor Drama." *English Literary Renaissance* 1 (1971): 195–209.

Beeman, William O. "The Anthropology of Theater and Spectacle." *Annual Review of Anthropology* 22 (1993): 369–93.

Benedictine Monks of St. Augustine's Abbey. *The Book of Saints: A Dictionary of Servants of God*. 6th ed. Wilton, Conn.: Morehouse, 1993.

Bennett, H. S. *English Books and Readers, 1558 to 1603: Being a Study of the Book Trade in the Reign of Elizabeth I*. Cambridge: Cambridge University Press, 1965.

Bennett, W. Lance, Regina G. Lawrence, and Steven Livingston. *When the Press Fails: Political Power and the News Media from Iraq to Katrina*. Chicago: University of Chicago Press, 2007.

Bernstein, Michael André. *Foregone Conclusions: Against Apocalyptic History*. Berkeley: University of California Press, 1994.

Beverley, John R. "On the Spanish Literary Baroque." In Cruz and Parry, eds., *Culture and Control*, 216–30.

Boose, Lynda E. "The Getting of a Lawful Race: Racial Discourse in Early Modern England and the Unrepresentable Black Woman." In Hendricks and Parker, eds., *Women, "Race," and Writing*, 35–54.

———. "The Comic Contract and Portia's Golden Ring." *Shakespeare Studies* 20 (1988): 241–67.

Boutcher, Warren. "'Who taught thee Rhetoricke to deceive a maid?': Christopher Marlowe's *Hero and Leander*, Juan Boscán's *Leandro*, and Renaissance Vernacular Humanism." *Comparative Literature* 52, no. 1 (Winter 2000): 11–52.

Bouwsma, William J. *A Usable Past: Essays in European Cultural History*. Berkeley: University of California Press, 1990.

———. *Venice and the Defense of Republican Liberty*. Berkeley: University of California Press, 1968.

Boyer, C. V. *The Villain as Hero in Elizabethan Tragedy*. New York: E. P. Dutton, 1914.

Bozeman, T. D. "Federal Theology and the 'National Covenant': An Elizabethan Presbyterian Case Study." *Church History* 61 (1992): 394–407.

Bradford, John. *The copye of a letter sent out by J. Bradford to the erles of Arundel & Darby. Or An admonition to al Englishmen*. London, 1556. STC 3504.

———. *Two notable Sermons . . . the one of repentance, the other of the Lord's Supper*. London, 1579 [1561]. STC 3499.5.

Bradford, William. *Of Plymouth Plantation, 1620–1647*. New York: Modern Library, 1981.

Braude, Benjamin. "The Sons of Noah and the Construction of Ethnic and Geographical Identities in the Medieval and Early Modern Periods." *William and Mary Quarterly*, 3rd series, 54, no. 1 (January 1997): 103–42.

Braudel, Fernand. *The Mediterranean and the Mediterranean World in the Age of Philip II*. 2 vols. Trans. Siân Reynolds. New York: Harper and Row, 1973 [1949].

———. *The Perspective of the World*. Trans. Siân Reynolds. Berkeley: University of California Press, 1992.

———. *The Structures of Everyday Life*. Trans. Siân Reynolds. Berkeley: University of California Press, 1992.

Brennan, Gillian E. *Patriotism, Power and Print: National Consciousness in Tudor England*. Pittsburgh: Duquesne University Press, 2003.

Brennan, Michael G. "Christopher Marlowe's *The Jew of Malta* and Two Newsletter Accounts of the Siege of Malta." *Notes and Queries* (June 1993): 157–60.

Broude, Ronald. "Time, Truth, and Right in *The Spanish Tragedy*." *Studies in Philology* 68 (1971): 130–45.

Bullón-Fernández, María, ed. *England and Iberia in the Middle Ages: Cultural, Literary, and Political Exchanges, 12th*[th]*-15th Century*. New York: Palgrave Macmillan, 2007.

Burckhardt, Jacob. *The Civilization of the Renaissance in Italy*. 1860. Trans. S. G. C. Middlemore. New York: Random House, 1954.

Burelbach, Fredrick M. "Name-play and Internationalism in Shakespearean Tragedy." *Literary Onomastics Studies* 12 (1985): 144–47.

Burke, Kenneth. *A Grammar of Motives*. Berkeley: University of California Press, 1945 [1969].

———. *A Rhetoric of Motives*. Berkeley: University of California Press, 1950 [1969].

Burshatin, Israel. "The Moor in the Text." In *"Race," Writing, and Difference*, ed. Henry Louis Gates, Jr., 117–37. Chicago: University of Chicago Press, 1986.

Burton, Jonathan. *Traffic and Turning: Islam and English Drama, 1579–1626*. Newark: University of Delaware Press, 2005.

Calendar of State Papers, Domestic Series, of the reigns of Edward VI, Mary, Elizabeth [and James I]. 1547–[1625]. 12 vols. London: Longman, 1856–72.

Calendar of State Papers, Foreign Series, of the reign of Elizabeth: Preserved in the State Paper Department of Her Majesty's Public Record Office. 23 vols. London: Longman, Green, Longman, Roberts, and Green, 1863–1950.

Calendar of State Papers [Venetian], and manuscripts relating to English affairs, existing in the Archives and collections of Venice, and in other libraries of Northern Italy. 38 vols. London: Longman, HMSO, 1864–1947.

Camden, William. *The History of the Most Renowned and Victorious Princess Elizabeth, Late Queen of England*. Ed. Wallace MacCaffrey. Chicago: University of Chicago Press, 1970.

Camões, Luis Vaz de. *The Lusiads*. Trans. William C. Atkinson. London: Penguin Books, 1952.

Campos, Edmund Valentine. "Jews, Spaniards, and Portingales: Ambiguous Identities of Portuguese Marranos in Elizabethan England." *English Literary History* 69 (2002): 599–616.

Carasco-Urgoiti, María Soledad. *The Moorish Novel*. Boston: G. K. Hall, 1976.

Cascardi, Anthony J. *Ideologies of History in the Spanish Golden Age*. University Park: Penn State University Press, 1997.

Cassar, Carmel. *Society, Culture and Identity in Early Modern Malta*. Msida [Malta]: Mireva, 2000.

Castro, Américo. *Santiago de España*. Buenos Aires: Emecé Editorial, 1958.

———. *The Spaniards*. Berkeley: University of California Press, 1971.

Cates, Thomas. *A Summarie and True Discourse of Sir Frances Drakes West Indian Voyage. Wherein were taken, the Townes of Saint Iago, Sancto Domingo, Cartagena & Saint Augustine*. London: Richard Field, 1589. In *Sir Francis Drake's West Indian Voyage, 1585–86*, ed. Mary Frear Keeler, 210–77. London: Hakluyt Society, 1981.

Catholic Encyclopedia: An International Work of Reference on the Constitution, Doctrine, and History of the Catholic Church. Ed. Charles G. Heberman et al. New York: Encyclopedia Press, 1910.

Cavell, Stanley. *The Claim of Reason: Wittgenstein, Skepticism, Morality and Tragedy*. Oxford: Oxford University Press, 1979.

Cecil, William [pseud. F. M., trans.]. *A Politike Discourse, most excellent for this time present: Composed by a French Gentleman, against those of the League, which went about to perswade the King to breake the Allyance with England, and to confirme it with Spaine*. London: John Wolfe, 1589. STC 13101.

Cervantes, Miguel de. *The Adventures of Don Quixote*. Trans. J. M. Cohen. London: Penguin Books, 1950.

———. *El cerco de Numancia*. Ed. Robert Maranst. Salamanca: Biblioteca Anaya, 1970.

Challis, C. E. *The Tudor Coinage*. Manchester: Manchester University Press, 1978.

Chambers, E. K. *The Elizabethan Stage*. 4 vols. Oxford: Clarendon Press, 1923.

Chaucer, Geoffrey. *The Riverside Chaucer*. Ed. Larry D. Benson. Boston: Houghton Mifflin, 1987.

Church of England. "An Homilie or Sermon concerning the Nativity and birth of our Saviour Jesus Christ." In *Seconde Tome of Homilies* (1563). London, 1587. STC 13673.

———. "An Homelie, or Sermon, of Good Woorkes Annexed unto Faithe." In *Certaine Sermons and Homilies* (1547), ed. Ronald B. Bond, 101–19. Toronto: University of Toronto Press, 1987.

———. *Liturgies and Forms of Prayer Set Forth in the Reign of Queen Elizabeth*. Ed. William Keatinge Clay. Cambridge: Cambridge University Press, 1847.

Ciappara, Frans. *Society and the Inquisition in Early Modern Malta*. San Gwann [Malta]: PEG, 2001.

Cinthio, Giraldi. *Hecatommithi. Othello*. Ed. Alvin Kernan. New York: Signet Books, 1963 [1986].

Clancy, Thomas H. *Papist Pamphleteers: The Allen-Persons Party and the Political Thought of the Counter-Reformation in England, 1572–1615*. Chicago: Loyola University Press, 1964.

Clifford, James. "On Ethnographic Allegory." In *Writing Culture: The Poetics and Politics of Ethnography*, ed. James Clifford and George E. Marcus, 98–121. Berkeley: University of California Press, 1986.

———. "On Ethnographic Authority." *Representations* 1 (1983): 118–46.

———. "Traveling Cultures." In *Cultural Studies*, ed. Lawrence Grossberg et al., 96–111. New York: Routledge, 1992.

CNN. *Larry King Live*. September 14, 2001. Available at http://edition.cnn.com/transcripts/0109/14/lkl.00.html (accessed December 1, 2007).

CNN. *Lou Dobbs: Tonight.* Available at http://www.cnn.com/CNN/Programs/lou.dobbs. tonight/ (accessed December 1, 2007).

Cohen, Walter. *Drama of a Nation: Public Theater in Renaissance England and Spain.* Ithaca, N.Y.: Cornell University Press, 1985.

Coldiron, A. E. B. "Public Sphere/Contact Zone: Habermas, Early Print, and Verse Translation." *Criticism* 46, no. 2 (Spring 2004): 207–22.

Coleridge, Samuel Taylor. *Coleridge's Literary Criticism.* Ed. J. W. Mackail. London: Oxford University Press, 1948.

Collinson, Patrick. *The Birthpangs of Protestant England.* New York: Oxford University Press, 1988.

———. *The Elizabethan Puritan Movement.* Oxford: Oxford University Press, 1990 [1967].

———. *From Iconoclasm to Iconophobia.* Reading: University of Reading Press, 1985.

———. *The Religion of Protestants: The Church in English Society 1559–1625.* Oxford: Oxford University Press, 1982.

Comaroff, John, and Jean Comaroff. *Ethnography and the Historical Imagination.* Boulder: Westview Press, 1992.

Connor, Walker. "A Nation Is a Nation, Is a State, Is an Ethnic Group, Is a . . ." In *Nationalism*, ed. John Hutchinson and Anthony D. Smith, 36–46. Oxford: Oxford University Press, 1994.

Contarini, Gasparo. *The Commonwealth and Government of Venice.* [*De magistratibus et republica Venetorum.* 1543]. Trans. Lewis Lewkenor. London, 1599. STC 5642.

Corregio, Francesco Balbi di. *The Siege of Malta, 1565. A true account of all that took place in the Island of Malta in the year 1565, from the time before the arrival of the fleet of Soliman the Magnificent, until the landing of the last relief force of the Catholic King, our Lord Don Philip, second of the name. Barcelona, 1568.* Alcalá, 1567. Trans. Henry Alexander Balbi. Copenhagen: Bagsvaerd, 1961.

Cottesford, Samuel. *A treatise against traitors. Meete for all faithfull subiects in these dayes. Taken out of the 40. chapter of Ieremye.* London, 1591. STC 5840.

Cruz, Anne J., and Mary Elizabeth Parry, eds. *Culture and Control in Counter-Reformation Spain.* Minneapolis: University of Minnesota Press, 1992.

Daileader, Celia R. "Back Door Sex: Renaissance Gynosodomy, Aretino, and the Exotic." *English Literary History* 69 (2002): 303–34.

Danson, Lawrence. *The Harmonies of* The Merchant of Venice. New Haven: Yale University Press, 1978.

Daunce, Edward. *A Brief Discourse of the Spanish State.* London, 1590. STC 6291.

Daunton, Martin, and Rick Halpern, eds. *Empire and Others: British Encounters with Indigenous Peoples, 1600–1850.* Philadelphia: University of Pennsylvania Press, 1999.

Davenant, William. *The Works of William Davenant.* 1673. New York: B. Blom, 1968.

Davies, Horton. *Worship and Theology in England: From Cranmer to Baxter and Fox, 1534–1690.* Grand Rapids, Mich.: William B. Eerdmans, 1975.

Davies, Sir John. *Complete Poems.* Ed. A. B. Grosart. London: Chatto and Windus, 1876.

Defoe, Daniel. "The True-born Englishman." In *Oxford Book of Satirical Verse*, ed. Geoffrey Grigson, 96–109. Oxford: Oxford University Press, 1980.

de Grazia, Margreta. "Teleology, Delay, and the 'Old Mole.'" *Shakespeare Quarterly* 50, no. 3 (Fall 1999): 21–67.

Dekker, Thomas. *Blurt, Master Constable*. 1602. Ed. Thomas Leland Burger. Salzburg: Institut für Anglistik und Amerikanistik, 1979.

———. *Dramatic Works of Thomas Dekker*. 4 vols. Ed. Fredson Bowers. Cambridge: Cambridge University Press, 1962.

Díaz-Fernández, José Ramón. "Thomas Kyd: A Bibliography, 1966–1992." *Bulletin of Bibliography* 52, no. 1 (1993): 1–13.

Diccionario Crítico Etimológico Castellano e Hispánico. Madrid: Editorial Gredos, 1981.

Diccionario Enciclopédico Espasa. Vol. 10. Madrid: Espas–Calpe, 1978.

Dictionary of National Biography. Ed. Sir Leslie Stephens and Sir Sidney Lee. London: Oxford University Press, 1882.

Diehl, Huston. *Staging Reform, Reforming the Stage: Protestantism and Popular Theater in Early Modern England*. Ithaca, N.Y.: Cornell University Press, 1997.

Dobson, Michael. *Shakespeare and the Making of the National Poet: Shakespeare, Adaptation, and Authorship, 1660–1769*. Oxford: Clarendon Press, 1992.

Dod, John, and Robert Cleaver. *A Plaine and familiar exposition of the Ten commandements with a methodical short catechisme*. Third edition. London, 1606. STC 6969.

Dodsley, Robert [pseud. Nathan ben Saddi]. *The Chronicle of the Kings of England from William the Norman to the Death of George III, written in the manner of the Jewish Historians*. London: Fairburn, 1821.

———. *A Select Collection of Old Plays*. 1744. Ed. Carew Hazlitt. 15 vols. London, 1874.

———. *Trifles*. London, 1745.

Donaldson, Peter S. *Machiavelli and Mystery of State*. Cambridge: Cambridge University Press, 1988.

Douglas, Mary. *Purity and Danger: An Analysis of the Concepts of Pollution and Taboo*. London: Routledge, 1966 [1991].

Downes, Lawrence. "The Terrible, Horrible, Urgent National Disaster That Immigration Isn't." *New York Times*, June 20, 2006.

Dreher, G. K., ed. *The Chronicle of King Edward the First*. Second edition. Midland, Tex: Iron Horse Free Press, 1999.

Dryden, John. *The Works of John Dryden*. Vol. 9. Ed. H. T. Swedenberg, Jr. Berkeley: University of California Press, 1966.

Dubrow, Heather. *Echoes of Desire: English Petrarchism and Its Counterdiscourses*. Ithaca, N.Y.: Cornell University Press, 1995.

Duffy, Eamon. *The Stripping of the Altars: Traditional Religion in England, 1400–1580*. New Haven: Yale University Press, 1992.

Dutton, Richard. "Receiving Offense: *A Game at Chess* Again." In *Literature and Censorship in Renaissance England*, ed. Andrew Hadfield, 50–74. New York: Palgrave, 2001.

Dutton, Richard, Alison Findlay, and Richard Wilson, eds. *Theatre and Religion: Lancastrian Shakespeare*. Manchester: Manchester University Press, 2003.

Eco, Umberto. *A Theory of Semiotics*. Bloomington: Indiana University Press, 1976.

Edelman, Charles. "Which Is the Jew That Shakespeare Knew? Shylock on the Elizabethan Stage." *Shakespeare Survey* 52 (1999): 99–106.

Eden, Richard, trans. *The First Three English Books on America*. 1555. Ed. Edward Arber. Birmingham, 1885.

Edwards, Francis, S.J. "The Divisions Among the English Catholics: 1580–1610." *Elizabethan Review* 3 (Autumn 1995): 25–34.

Edwards, Philip. "Thrusting Elysium into Hell: The Originality of *The Spanish Tragedy*." *Elizabethan Theatre* 11, ed A. L. Magnusson and C. E. McGee (1990): 117–32.

Eire, Carlos M. N. *From Madrid to Purgatory: The Art and Craft of Dying in Sixteenth-Century Spain*. Cambridge: Cambridge University Press, 1995.

———. *War Against the Idols*. Cambridge: Cambridge University Press, 1986.

Elder, John. *The Copie of a letter sent into Scotland, of the arivall and landynge, and moste noble marriage of the moste Illustre Prynce Philippe, Prynce of Spaine, to the most excellente Princes Marye Quene of Englande*. London, 1555. STC 7552.

Eliot, T. S. *Elizabethan Essays*. New York: Haskell House, 1964.

Elizabeth I of England. *Collected Works*. Ed. Leah S. Marcus, Janell Mueller, and Mary Beth Rose. Chicago: University of Chicago Press, 2000.

Elizabeth: The Golden Years (film). Los Angeles: Universal Pictures, 2007.

Elliott, J. H. *Imperial Spain: 1469–1716*. London: Penguin Books, 1963 [1990].

———. *The Old World and the New, 1492–1650*. Cambridge: Cambridge University Press, 1970.

———. *Spain and Its World: 1500–1700*. New Haven: Yale University Press, 1989.

Elliott, Martin. *Shakespeare's Invention of Othello*. London: Macmillan, 1988.

Empson, William. "The Spanish Tragedy." *Nimbus* 3 (Summer 1956): 16–29.

Entwhistle, William J. *European Balladry*. Oxford: Oxford University Press, 1939.

Erasmus, Desiderius. *A pylgremage, for pure devocyō*. In *Tudor Translations of the Colloquies of Erasmus*. 1536–94. Ed. Dickie A. Spurgeon, 1–97. New York: Scholars Facsimiles and Imprints, 1972.

Eriksen, Thomas Hylland. *Ethnicity and Nationalism: Anthropological Perspectives*. London: Pluto Press, 1993.

Everett, Barbara. "'Spanish' Othello: The Making of Shakespeare's Moor." *Shakespeare Survey* 35 (1982): 101–12.

Fabian, Johannes. *Time and the Other: How Anthropology Makes Its Object*. New York: Columbia University Press, 1983.

Febvre, Lucien, and Henri-Jean Martin. *The Coming of the Book: The Impact of Printing, 1450–1800*. London: Verso, 1958 [1990].

Ferber, Michael. "The Ideology of *The Merchant of Venice*," *English Literary Renaissance* 20, no. 3 (Fall 1990): 431–64.

Fernández-Armesto, Felipe. "Armada Myths: The Formative Phase." In *God's Obvious Design*, ed. P. Gallagher and D. W. Cruikshank, 19–39. London: Tamesis Books, 1990.

———. *The Spanish Armada: The Experience of War in 1588*. Oxford: Oxford University Press, 1988.

Fernández-Retamar, Roberto. *Caliban and Other Essays*. Minneapolis: University of Minnesota Press, 1989.

Fiedler, Leslie. *The Stranger in Shakespeare*. New York: Stein and Day, 1973.

Fildes, Jonathan. "Wikipedia 'Shows CIA Page Edits.'" 15 August 2007, at http://news.bbc.co.uk/go/em/fr/-/1/hi/technology/6947532.stm (accessed September 17, 2007).

Fink, Zera S. *The Classical Republicans: An Essay in the Recovery of a Pattern of Thought in Seventeenth Century England*. Evanston: Northwestern University Press, 1945.

Firth, Katherine R. *The Apocalyptic Tradition in Reformation Britain, 1530–1645*. Oxford: Oxford University Press, 1979.

Fisch, Harold. "Shakespeare and the Puritan Dynamic." *Shakespeare Survey* 27 (1974): 81–92.

Fletcher, Angus. *Allegory: The Theory of a Symbolic Mode*. Ithaca, N.Y.: Cornell University Press, 1964.

———. *The Prophetic Moment: An Essay on Spenser*. Chicago: University of Chicago Press, 1971.

Fletcher, Anthonie. *Certain very proper, and profitable Similies*. London, 1595. STC 11503.

Florio, John. *Queen Anne's New World of Words*. 1611. Facsimile edition. Menston: Scolar Press, 1988.

———. *A World of Wordes, or most copious, and exact Dictionarie in Italian and English*. London, 1598. STC 11098.

Floyd-Wilson, Mary. *English Ethnicity and Race in Early Modern Drama*. Cambridge: Cambridge University Press, 2003.

Fox News. Monday, November 21, 2005. John Culberson, 7th District, Houston, Tex. Available at http://www.foxnews.com/story/0,2933,176216,00.html (accessed June 20, 2006).

Foxe, John. *The Acts and Monuments of John Foxe*. 8 vols. Ed. Stephen Reed Cattley. London: R. B. Seeley and W. Burnside, 1837–41.

Fraser, Russell A., and Norman Rabkin eds. *Drama of the English Renaissance*. Vol. 1: *The Tudor Period*. New York: Macmillan, 1976.

Freeman, Arthur. "Marlowe, Kyd, and the Dutch Church Libel." *English Literary Renaissance* 3, no. 1 (Winter 1973): 44–52.

———. *Thomas Kyd: Facts and Problems*. Oxford: Oxford University Press, 1967.

Freer, Coburn. "John Donne and Elizabethan Economic Theory." *Criticism* 38, no. 4 (Fall 1996): 497–520.

Froissart, Jean. *The Chronicle of Froissart Translated out of French by Sir John Bourchier Lord Berners, annis 1523–25*. 6 vols. London: D. Nutt, 1901–3.

Froude, J[ames]. A[nthony]. *History of England from the Fall of Wolsey to the Defeat of the Spanish Armada*. 12 vols. London, 1862–70 [New York, 1969].

Frye, Northrop. *Anatomy of Criticism*. Princeton: Princeton University Press, 1957.

Fuchs, Barbara. "Imperium Studies: Theorizing Early Modern Expansion." In Ingham and Warren, eds., *Postcolonial Moves*, 71–90.

———. *Mimesis and Empire: The New World, Islam, and European Identities*. Cambridge: Cambridge University Press, 2001.

———. *Passing for Spain: Cervantes and the Fictions of Identity*. Urbana: University of Illinois Press, 2003.

———. "The Spanish Race." In Greer, Mignolo, and Quilligan, eds., *Rereading the Black Legend*, 88–98.

———. "Spenser and the Irish Moriscos." *Studies in English Literature* 42, no. 1 (Winter 2002): 43–62.

Fulke, William. *A Confutation of the popish Churches doctrine touching Purgatory & prayer for the dead*. London, 1577. STC 11458.

Gallagher, P., and D. W. Cruikshank, eds. *God's Obvious Design*. London: Tamesis Books, 1990.

García Cárcel, Ricardo. *La leyenda negra: Historia y opinion*. Madrid: Alianza Editorial, 1992.

Gascoigne, George. "A briefe rehearsall, or rather a true Copie of as much as was presented before her majesti[e] at Kenelworth, during her last aboade there." 1576. In *The Complete Works of George Gascoigne.*, vol. 2, ed. John W. Cunliffe, Cambridge: Cambridge University Press, 1910.

———. [ascribed to Bernard Guardet]. *The Spoyle of Antwerpe. Faithfully reported, by a true Englishman, who was present at the same. Novem. 1576*. London: Richard Jones, 1577. STC 11644.

Geertz, Clifford. *The Interpretation of Cultures*. New York: Basic Books, 1973.

Geneva Bible. London, 1599. Facsimile edition. Pleasant Hope, Mo.: L. L. Brown, 1993.

Gentillet, Innocent. *A Discourse upon the Meanes of Wel Governing and Maintaining in God Peace, A Kingdom, or Other Principalitie . . . Against Nicholas Machiavel the Florentine*. London, 1602. STC 11743.

Gerber, Jane S. *The Jews of Spain: A History of the Sephardic Experience*. New York: Free Press, 1992.

Gibson, Charles. *The Black Legend: Anti-Spanish Attitudes in the Old World and the New*. New York: Basic Books, 1971.

Gilbert, Donald. "Ideology and Image in Maravall's Baroque." *Yearbook of Comparative and General Literature* 45–46 (1997–98): 172–74.

Gillies, John. *Shakespeare and the Geography of Difference*. Cambridge: Cambridge University Press, 1993.

Ginio, Alisa Meyuhas, ed. *Jews, Christians and Muslims in the Mediterranean World After 1492*. London: Cass, 1992.

Ginzburg, Carlo. *No Island Is an Island: Four Glances at English Literature in a World Perspective*. New York: Columbia University Press, 2000.

Goldberg, David Theo. *Racist Culture*. Oxford: Oxford University Press, 1993.

Goldberg, Jonathan. *James I and the Politics of Literature*. Baltimore: Johns Hopkins University Press, 1983.

Góngora, Mario. *Studies in the Colonial History of Spanish America*. Trans. Richard Southern. Cambridge: Cambridge University Press, 1975.

Grandin, Greg. *Empire's Workshop: Latin America, the United States, and the Rise of the New Imperialism*. New York: Henry Holt, 2007.

Greenblatt, Stephen. "Marlowe and Renaissance Self-Fashioning." In *Two Renaissance Mythmakers*, ed. Alvin Kernan, 41–69. Baltimore: Johns Hopkins University Press, 1977.

———. "Racial Memory and Literary History." *Publications of the Modern Language Association of America* 116, no. 1 (January 2001): 48–63.

———. "Remnants of the Sacred in Early Modern England." In *Subject and Object in Renaissance Culture*, ed. Margreta de Grazia, Maureen Quilligan, and Peter Stallybrass, 337–48. Cambridge: Cambridge University Press, 1996.

———. *Renaissance Self-Fashioning: From More to Shakespeare*. Chicago: University of Chicago Press, 1980.

Greene, Robert. *The Life and Complete Works in Prose and Verse of Robert Greene*. 15 vols. Ed. Alexander B. Grossart. London: Huth Library, 1881–86; reprt. New York: Russell and Russell, 1964.

———. *The Plays and Poems of Robert Greene*. 2 vols. Ed. J. Churton Collins. Oxford: Clarendon Press, 1905.

———. *The Spanish Masquerado*. London, 1589. STC 12309.

Greene, Roland. *Unrequited Conquests: Love and Empire in the Colonial Americas*. Chicago: University of Chicago Press, 1999.

Greenfeld, Liah. *Nationalism: Five Roads to Modernity*. Cambridge, Mass.: Harvard University Press, 1992.

Greer, Margaret R., Walter D. Mignolo, and Maureen Quilligan, eds. *Rereading the Black Legend: The Discourses of Religious and Racial Difference in the Renaissance Empires*. Chicago: University of Chicago Press, 2007.

Griffin, Eric. "Ethos, Empire, and the Valiant Acts of Thomas Kyd's Tragedy of 'The Spains.'" *English Literary Renaissance* 31, no. 2 (Spring 2001): 192–229.

———. "From Ethos to Ethnos: Hispanizing 'the Spaniard' in the Old World and the New." *CR: The New Centennial Review* 2, no. 1 (Spring 2002): 69–116.

———. "The Specter of Spain in John Smith's Colonial Writing." In Appelbaum and Sweet, eds., *Envisioning an English Empire*, 111–34.

———. "Nationalism, the Black Legend, and the Revised *Spanish Tragedy*." *English Literary Renaissance* 39, no. 2 (Spring 2009): 336–70.

———. "Un-sainting James: *Othello* and the 'Spanish Spirits' of Shakespeare's Globe." *Representations* 62 (Spring 1998): 58–99.

Guasco, Michael J. "Settling with Slavery: Human Bondage in the Early Anglo-Atlantic World." In Appelbaum and Sweet, eds., *Envisioning an English Empire*, 236–53.

Gunn, Giles. "Introduction: Globalizing Literary Studies." *Publications of the Modern Language Association of America* 116, no. 1 (January 2001): 16–31.

Gurr, Andrew. "The Shakespearean Stage." In *The Norton Shakespeare*, ed. Stephen Greenblatt et al. New York: W. W. Norton, 1997.

Habermas, Jürgen. *The Structural Transformation of the Public Sphere: An Inquiry into a Category of Bourgeois Society*. Trans. Thomas Burger. Cambridge, Mass.: Harvard University Press, 1991.

Habib, Imtiaz. *Shakespeare and Race*. Lanham, Md.: University Press of America, 2000.

Hadfield, Andrew. "Late Elizabethan Protestantism, Colonialism, and Fear of the Apocalypse." *Reformation* 3 (1998): 311–20.

———. *Literature, Travel, and Colonial Writing in the English Renaissance, 1545–1625*. Oxford: Oxford University Press, 1998.

Haigh, Christopher. *English Reformations: Religion, Politics, and Society Under the Tutors*. Oxford: Oxford University Press, 1993.

Hakluyt, Richard. *Discourse of Western Planting*. 1584. Ed. David B. Quinn and Allison M. Quinn. Hakluyt Society Extra Series 45. London: Hakluyt Society, 1993.

———. Letter to [Fr. Walsingham]. January 7, 1584. In *Calendar of State Papers, Domestic Series*. Vol. 167. London, 1865.

———. *The Original Writings and Correspondence of the Two Richard Hakluyts*. Ed. E. G. R. Taylor. London: Hakluyt Society, 1935.

———. *The Principal Navigations, Voyages, Traffiques, and Discoveries of the English Nation*. 12 vols. Glasgow: James MacLehose and Sons, 1903–5 [Augustus M. Kelley, 1969].

Hall, Edward. *The Union of the Two Noble Illustre Famelies of Lancaster & York, Beeing Long In Continual Discension for the Croune of this Noble Realm . . . Beginnyng at the Tyme of Kyng Henry the Fowerth, the First Auctor of this Division, and so succesively proceadyng to the Reigne of the High and Prudent Prince Kyng Henry the Eight, the Undubitate Flower and Very Heire of Bothe the Said Linages*. London: J. Johnson et al., 1809.

Hall, Kim F. "Guess Who's Coming to Dinner?" *Renaissance Drama* 23 (1982): 87–111.

———. *Things of Darkness: Economies of Race and Gender in Early Modern England*. Ithaca, N.Y.: Cornell University Press. 1995.

Hall, Stuart. "New Ethnicities." In *Black British Cultural Studies: A Reader*, ed. Houston A. Baker, Jr., Manthia Diawara, and Ruth H. Lindeborg, 163–72. Chicago: University of Chicago Press, 1996.

Haller, William. *The Elect Nation: The Meaning and Relevance of Foxe's Book of Martyrs*. New York: Harper and Row, 1963.

Hamilton, Annette. "Fear and Desire: Aborigines, Asians and the National Imaginary." *Australian Cultural History* 9 (1990): 14–35.

Hamilton, Donna B. "Richard Verstegen and Catholic Resistance: The Coding of Antiquarianism and Love." In Dutton, Findlay, and Wilson, eds., *Theatre and Religion*, 87–104.

Handelman, Don. *Models and Mirrors: Towards an Anthropology of Public Events*. Cambridge: Cambridge University Press, 1990.

Hannaford, Ivan. *Race: The History of an Idea in the West*. Baltimore: Johns Hopkins University Press, 1996.

Hanson, Neil. *The Confident Hope of a Miracle: The True History of the Spanish Armada*. New York: Alfred A. Knopf, 2005.

Harris, Bernard. "A Portrait of a Moor." *Shakespeare Survey* 11 (1958): 89–97.

Hart, Jonathan. *Representing the New World: The English and French Uses of the Example of Spain*. New York: Palgrave, 2000.

Harvey, L. P. *Muslims in Spain, 1500 to 1614*. Chicago: University of Chicago Press, 2005.

Hegel, G. W. F. *Introduction to the Philosophy of History*. 1840. Trans. Leo Rauch. Indianapolis: Hackett, 1988.

Helgerson, Richard. *Forms of Nationhood: The Elizabethan Writing of England*. Chicago: University of Chicago Press, 1992.

Hendricks, Margo, and Patricia Parker, eds. *Women, "Race," and Writing in the Early Modern Period*. London: Routledge, 1995.

Henslowe, Philip. *Henslowe's Diary*. Ed. R. A. Foakes and R. T. Rickert. Cambridge: Cambridge University Press, 1961.

Hess, Andrew. *The Forgotten Frontier: A History of the Sixteenth Century Ibero-African Frontier*. Chicago: University of Chicago Press, 1978.

Heywood, Thomas. "A defence of drama." C. 1608. In *English Renaissance Literary Criticism*, ed. Brian Vickers. Oxford: Clarendon Press, 1999.

Hill, Christopher. "Braudel and the State." *The Collected Essays of Christopher Hill*. Vol. 3. Brighton: Harvester Press, 1986.

Hill, Eugene. "Senecan and Virgilian Perspectives in *The Spanish Tragedy*." *English Literary Renaissance* 15 (1985): 143–65.

Hillgarth, J. N. *The Mirror of Spain, 1500–1700: The Formation of a Myth*. Ann Arbor: University of Michigan Press, 2000.

Hobsbawm, Eric, and Terrance Ranger. *The Invention of Tradition*. Cambridge: Cambridge University Press, 1983.

Hogge, Alice. *God's Secret Agents: Queen Elizabeth's Forbidden Priests and the Hatching of the Gunpowder Plot*. New York: HarperCollins, 2005.

Holderness, Graham. "'What Ish My Nation?': Shakespeare and National Identities." In *Materialist Shakespeare*, ed. Ivo Camps, 218–38. London: Verso, 1995.

Holinshed, Raphael. *Chronicles of England, Scotland and Ireland*. 6 vols. London: J. Johnson, 1807–8.

Hollander, John. "Dallying Nicely with Words." In *The Linguistics of Writing*, ed. Nigel Fabb et al., 123–34. Manchester: Manchester University Press, 1987.

Honigmann, E. A. J. "The Play of *Sir Thomas More* and Some Contemporary Events." *Shakespeare Survey* 42 (1990): 77–84.

Hoppe, H. R. "John Wolfe, Printer and Publisher." *The Library*, series 4, no. 14 (1933): 241–74.

Horowitz, Tony. "Immigration—and the Curse of the Black Legend." *New York Times*, July 9, 2006.

Horsman, Reginald. *Race and Manifest Destiny: The Origins of American Racial Anglo-Saxonism*. Cambridge, Mass.: Harvard University Press, 1981.

Hough, Graham. *A Preface to the Faerie Queene*. London: Gerald Duckworth, 1963.

Howard-Hill, T. H. ed., *Middleton's "Vulgar Pasquin": Essays on* A Game at Chess. Newark: University of Delaware Press, 1995.

Huffman, Clifford Chalmers. *Elizabethan Impressions: John Wolfe and His Press*. New York: AMQ Press, 1988.

Hughes, Paul F., and James F. Larkin, eds. *Tudor Royal Proclamations*. Vol. 3. New Haven: Yale University Press, 1969.

Hunt, William. *The Puritan Moment*. Cambridge, Mass.: Harvard University Press, 1983.

Hunter, G. K. "Elizabethans and Foreigners." In Alexander and Wells, eds., *Shakespeare and Race*, 37–63.

———. "The Theology of Marlowe's *The Jew of Malta*." In *Christopher Marlowe's* The Jew of Malta: *Text and Major Criticism*. New York: Odyssey Press, 1970.

Huralt, Michel. *A discourse upon the present estate of France*. Trans. E. Aggas. London: John Wolfe, 1588. STC 14004.

Hurstfield, Joel. "The Succession Struggle in Late Elizabethan England." In *Elizabethan Government and Society*, ed. S. T. Bindoff et al., 369–96. London: Athlone Press, 1961.

Ingham, Patricia Clare. "Contrapuntal Histories." In Ingham and Warren, eds., *Postcolonial Moves*, 47–70.

Ingham, Patricia Clare, and Michelle R. Warren, eds. *Postcolonial Moves: Medieval Through Modern*. New York: Palgrave, 2003.

Iyengar, Sujata. *Shades of Difference: Mythologies of Skin Color in Early Modern England*. Philadelphia: University of Pennsylvania Press, 2005.

James VI [and I]. King of Scotland [and England]. *His Majesties Poetical Exercises at Vacant Houres*. Edinburgh, 1591 [1818].

Jardine, Lisa. *Worldly Goods: A New History of the Renaissance*. New York: Doubleday, 1996.

Jay, Paul. "Beyond Discipline? Globalization and the Future of English." *Publications of the Modern Language Association of America* 116 (2001): 32–47.

Johnson, Chalmers. *The Sorrows of Empire: Militarism, Secrecy, and the End of the Republic*. New York: Henry Holt, 2004.

Johnson, Samuel. *Selections from Johnson on Shakespeare*. Ed. B. H. Bronson and J. M. O'Meara. New Haven: Yale University Press, 1986.

Johnson, S. F. "*The Spanish Tragedy*, or Babylon Revisited." In *Essays on Shakespeare and Elizabethan Drama*, ed. Richard Hosley. Columbia: University of Missouri Press, 1962.

Jones, Ann Rosalind, and Peter Stallybrass, "Dismantling Irena: The Sexualizing of Ireland in Early Modern England." In *Nationalisms and Sexualities*, ed. Andrew Parker et al., 157–71. New York: Routledge, 1992.

Jonson, Ben. *The Alchemist*. In *Ben Jonson's Plays and Masques*, ed. Robert M. Adams. New York: W. W. Norton, 1979.

Juderías, Julian. *La leyenda negra: Estudios acerca del concepto de España en el extranjero*. 1914. Barcelona: Casa Editorial Araluce, 1929.

Justice, Stephen. "Spain, Tragedy, and *The Spanish Tragedy*." *Studies in English Literature* 25 (1985): 271–88.

Kagan, Richard L. "Clio and the Crown: Writing History in Hapsburg Spain." In *Spain, Europe and the Atlantic World*, ed. Richard L. Kagan and Geoffrey Parker, 73–99. Cambridge: Cambridge University Press, 1995.

Kamen, Henry. "The Mediterranean and the Expulsion of Spanish Jews in 1492." *Past and Present* 119 (1988): 30–55.

————. *The Spanish Inquisition: A Historical Revision.* London: Weidenfeld and Nicolson, 1997.

Katz, David. *The Jews in the History of England, 1485–1850.* Oxford: Oxford University Press, 1994.

Keen, Benjamin. *The Aztec Image in Western Thought.* New Brunswick, N.J.: Rutgers University Press, 1990 [1971].

Kendrick, T. D. *Saint James in Spain.* London: Methuen, 1960.

Kernan, Alvin. *Shakespeare, the King's Playwright: Theater in the Stuart Court, 1603–1613.* New Haven: Yale University Press, 1995.

Kertzer, David I. *Ritual, Politics, and Power.* New Haven: Yale University Press, 1988.

Kidd, Collin. *British Identities Before Nationalism: Ethnicity and Nationhood in the Atlantic World, 1600–1800.* Cambridge: Cambridge University Press, 1999.

King, John N. *English Reformation Literature: The Tudor Origins of the Protestant Tradition.* Princeton: Princeton University Press, 1982.

————. *Foxe's* Book of Martyrs *and Early Modern Print Culture.* Cambridge: Cambridge University Press, 2006.

————. "Queen Elizabeth I: Representations of the Virgin Queen," *Renaissance Quarterly* 43, no. 1 (Spring 1990): 30–74.

————. *Spenser's Poetry and the Reformation Tradition.* Princeton: Princeton University Press, 1990.

King, Willard F. "Cervantes' *Numancia* and Imperial Spain." *Modern Language Notes* 94 (1979): 200–221.

Kinney, Arthur F., and David W. Swain, eds. *Tudor England: An Encyclopedia.* New York: Garland, 2001.

Knapp, Jeffrey. *An Empire Nowhere: England, America, and Literature from Utopia to the Tempest.* Berkeley: University of California Press, 1992.

Knappen, M. M. *Tudor Puritanism.* Chicago: University of Chicago Press, 1939.

Knewstub, John. *Lectures upon the twentieth chapter of Exodus, and certiane other places of Scripture.* London, 1577. STC 15042.

Knowles, Edwin B., ed. *Don Quixote in England.* New York: New York University Press, 1941.

Kocher, Paul H. "Contemporary Pamphlet Backgrounds for Marlowe's *The Massacre at Paris.*" *Modern Language Quarterly* 8 (1947): 151–73.

Kohlenberger, John R., III, ed. *The Parallel Apocrypha.* Oxford: Oxford University Press, 1997.

Korr, Charles P. *Cromwell and the New Model Foreign Policy.* Berkeley: University of California Press, 1975.

Kouri, E. I. "For True Faith or National Interest? Queen Elizabeth I and the Protestant Powers." In *Politics and Society in Reformation Europe,* ed. E. I. Kouri and Tom Scott, 411–36. London: Macmillan, 1987.

Kyd, Thomas. [*The Spanish Comedy,* or] *The First Part of Hieronimo* and *The Spanish Tragedy* [or *Hieronimo Is Mad Again*]. Ed Andrew S. Cairncross. Lincoln: University of Nebraska Press, 1967.

———. *The Spanish Tragedy*. Ed. David Bevington. Manchester: University of Manchester Press, 1996.

———. *The Spanish Tragedy*. Ed. Philip Edwards. Manchester: University of Manchester Press, 1977 [1959].

———. *The Spanish Tragedy*. Ed. J. R. Mulryne. London: Benn, 1970.

———. *The Works of Thomas Kyd*. Ed. F. S. Boas. Oxford: Clarendon Press, 1901.

Lamana, Gonzalo. "Of Books, Popes, and *Huacas*; Or, The Dilemmas of Being Christian." In Greer, Mignolo, and Quilligan, eds., *Rereading the Black Legend*, 117–49.

Lane, Frederic. *Venice: A Maritime Republic*. Baltimore: Johns Hopkins University Press, 1973.

———. *Venice and History: The Collected Papers of Frederic C. Lane*. Baltimore: Johns Hopkins University Press, 1966.

Las Casas, Bartolomé de. *The Devastation of the Indies: A Brief Account*. Trans. Herma Briffault. Baltimore: Johns Hopkins University Press, 1992.

———. *A Short Account of the Destruction of the Indies*. Ed. Nigel Griffin. London: Penguin Books, 1992.

———. *The Spanish Colonie, or the Brief Chronicle of the Acts and gestes of the Spaniardes in the West Indies*. Trans. M. M. S. London: William Brome, 1583. STC 4739.

Legacy Project. "For the First Time in 55 Years." At http://www.warletters.com.book/asedition.html (accessed March 3, 2004).

Leonard, Irving. *Books of the Brave*. Berkeley: University of California Press, 1949 [1992].

Levin, Carole. *The Heart and Stomach of a King: Elizabeth I and the Politics of Sex and Power*. Philadelphia: University of Pennsylvania Press, 1994.

Levith, Murray J. *Shakespeare's Italian Settings and Plays*. New York: St. Martin's Press, 1989.

Lewalski, Barbara K. "Biblical Allusion and Allegory in *The Merchant of Venice*." *Shakespeare Quarterly* 13, no. 3 (Summer 1962): 327–43.

Lewis, Bernard. *The Jews of Islam*. Princeton: Princeton University Press, 1983.

Lewkenor, Lewis. *A Discourse of the Usage of the English Fugitives by the Spaniard*. London, 1595. STC 15562.

Little, Arthur, Jr. *Shakespeare Jungle Fever: National-Imperial Re-Visions of Race, Rape, and Sacrifice*. Stanford, Calif.: Stanford University Press, 2000.

Livermore, H. V. *A New History of Portugal*. Cambridge: Cambridge University Press, 1976.

Loades, David. *The Reign of Mary Tudor: Politics, Government, and Religion in England, 1553–1558*. Second edition. New York: Longman, 1991.

Lockey, Brian C. *Law and Empire in English Renaissance Literature*. Cambridge: Cambridge University Press, 2006.

Loewenstein, Joseph. "For a History of Literary Property: John Wolfe's Reformation." *English Literary Renaissance* 18, no. 3 (Autumn 1988): 398–412.

Loewenstein, Joseph, and Paul Stephens. "Introduction: Charting Habermas's 'Literary' or 'Precursor' Public Sphere." *Criticism* 46, no. 2 (Spring 2004): 201–5.

Lollini, Massimo. "Maravall's Culture of the Baroque: Between Wölfflin, Gramsci and Benjamin." *Yearbook of Comparative and General Literature* 45–46 (1997–98); 187–94.

Lomax, D. W. *La Orden de Santiago*. Madrid: Consejo Superior de Investigaciones Científicas, 1965.

Long, William B. "The Occasion of The Book of Sir Thomas More." In *Shakespeare and Sir Thomas More: Essays on the Play and Its Shakespearean interest*, ed. T. Howard-Hill, 45–56. Cambridge: Cambridge University Press, 1989,

Loomba, Ania. *Shakespeare, Race and Colonialism*. Oxford: Oxford University Press, 2002.

Loomie, Albert J. "Sir William Semple and Bristol's Andalucian Trade, 1597–1598." *Transactions of the Bristol and Gloucestershire Archaeological Society* 82 (1963): 177–87.

———. *The Spanish Elizabethans*. New York: Fordham University Press, 1963.

Lynch, John. *Spain 1516–1598: From Nation-State to World Empire*. Oxford: Blackwell, 1991.

MacDonald, Joyce Green, ed. *Race, Ethnicity, and Power in the Renaissance*. Cranbury, N.J.: Associated University Press, 1997.

MacDougall, Hugh A. *Racial Myth in English History: Trojans, Teutons, and Anglo-Saxons*. Hanover, N.H.: University Press of New England, 1982.

Macey, Samuel L. "The Naming of the Protagonists in Shakespeare's *Othello*." *Notes and Queries*, n.s., 25 (1978): 143–45.

Machiavelli, Niccolò. *The Prince*. Trans. George Bull. London: Penguin Books, 1961.

Maltby, William S. *The Black Legend in England*. Durham, N.C.: Duke University Press, 1971.

Maravall, José Antonio. *Culture of the Baroque: Analysis of a Historical Structure*. Trans. Terry Cochrane. Minneapolis: University of Minnesota Press, 1986.

———. "From the Renaissance to the Baroque: The Diphasic Schema of a Social Crisis." Trans. Terry Cochran. In *Literature Among the Discourses: The Spanish Golden Age*, ed. Wlad Godsich and Nicholas Spadaccini, 3–40. Minneapolis: University of Minnesota Press, 1986.

Marcham, Frank, ed. *The Prototype of Shylock, Lopez the Jew, executed 1594: An Opinion by Gabriel Harvey*. Harrow Weald: Middlesex, 1927.

Marcus, Leah S. "Shakespeare's Comic Heroines: Elizabeth I and the Political Uses of Androgyny." In *Medieval and Renaissance Women: Literary and Historical Perspective*, ed. Mary Beth Rose. Syracuse, N.Y.: Syracuse University Press, 1986.

———. *Unediting the Renaissance: Shakespeare, Marlowe, Milton*. London: Routledge, 1996.

Marcus, Leah S., Janell Mueller, and Mary Beth Rose, eds. *Elizabeth I: Collected Works*. Chicago: University of Chicago Press, 2000.

Mariana, Juan de. *The General History of Spain. From the first peopling of it by Tubal, till the Death of King Ferdinand, who United the Crowns of castile and Aragon. With a Continuation to the Death of King Philip III. Written in Spanish by the R.F.F. John de Mariana*. Trans. Captain John Stephens. London: Richard Sare, 1699.

Marlowe, Christopher. *The Complete Works*. 4 vols. Ed. Fredson Bowers. Cambridge: Cambridge University Press, 1973.

———. *The Jew of Malta*. Ed. James R. Siemon. New York: W. W. Norton, 1994 [2002].

Martin, John. *Venice's Hidden Enemies: Italian Heretics in a Renaissance City*. Berkeley: University of California Press, 1993.

Martyr, Peter. *The Decades of the newe world or west India*. In Eden, trans., *First Three English Books*.

Matar, Nabil. *Britain and Barbary, 1589–1689*. Gainesville: University Press of Florida, 2005.

———. *Turks, Moors, and Englishmen in the Age of Discovery*. New York: Columbia University Press, 1999.

Mattingly, Garrett. *The Armada*. Boston: Houghton Mifflin, 1959.

———. *Catherine of Aragon*. Boston: Little, Brown, 1941 [1990].

Mayer, Jean-Christophe, "'The Papist and His Poet': Shakespeare's Lancastrian Kings and Robert Parsons *Conference about the Next Succession*." In Dutton, Findlay, and Wilson, eds., *Theatre and Religion*, 116–29.

McEachern, Claire. *The Poetics of English Nationhood, 1590–1612*. Cambridge: Cambridge University Press, 1996.

McGinn, Bernard. *Anti-Christ: Two Thousand Years of the Human Fascination with Evil*. San Francisco: HarperCollins, 1994.

McKerrow, R. B., ed. *A Dictionary of Printers and Booksellers in England Scotland and Ireland, and of Foreign Printers of English Books, 1557–1640*. Oxford: Oxford University Press, 1968.

McMillin, Scott. *The Elizabethan Theatre and* The Book of Sir Thomas More. Ithaca, N.Y.: Cornell University Press, 1987.

Mcpherson, David. "Lewkenor's Venice and Its Sources," *Renaissance Quarterly* 41, no. 3 (Autumn 1988): 459–66.

———. *Shakespeare, Jonson, and the Myth of Venice*. Newark: University of Delaware Press, 1990.

Melczer, William, trans. *The Pilgrim's Guide to Santiago de Compostela*. New York: Italica Press, 1993.

Menéndez Pidal, Ramón. *The Cid and His Spain*. 1934. Trans. Harold Sutherland. London: F. Cass, 1971.

Metzger, Mary Janell. "'Now by My Hood, a Gentle and No Jew': Jessica, *The Merchant of Venice*, and the Discourse of Early Modern English Identity." *Publications of the Modern Language Society of America* 113, no. 1 (1998): 52–63.

Meyer, Edward. *Machiavelli and the Elizabethan Drama*. Weimar: E. Felber, 1897.

Middleton, Thomas. *A Game at Chess*. Ed. T. H. Howard-Hill. Manchester: Manchester University Press, 1993.

Mignolo, Walter D. "What Does the Black Legend Have to Do with Race?" In Greer, Mignolo, and Quilligan, eds., *Rereading the Black Legend*, 312–24.

Millward, Peter. *Shakespeare's Religious Background*. Bloomington: Indiana University Press, 1973.

Minshull, Catherine. "Marlowe's 'Sound Machevill.'" *Renaissance Drama* 13 (1982): 35–53.

Montanus, Gonsalvius. *A Discovery and playne Declaration of the sundry subtill practices of the Holy Inquisition of Spayne*. London, 1568. STC 11996.

Montemayor, Jorge. *The Diana of George Montemayor*. 1598. Trans. Bartholomew Yong. Oxford: Oxford University Press, 1968.

Montrose, Louis A. "The Elizabethan Subject and the Spenserian Text." *Literary Theory/Renaissance Texts.* Baltimore: Johns Hopkins University Press, 1986.

———. *The Purpose of Playing: Shakespeare and the Cultural Politics of the Elizabethan Theater.* Chicago: University of Chicago Press, 1996.

———. *The Subject of Elizabeth: Authority, Gender, and Representation.* Chicago: University of Chicago Press, 2006.

Morrill, John. "The British Problem, c. 1534–1707." In *The British Problem, c. 1534–1707: State Formation in the Atlantic Archipelago,* ed. Brendan Bradshaw and John Morrill, 1–38. New York: St. Martin's Press, 1996.

Mullaney, Stephen. *The Place of the Stage: License, Play, and Power in Renaissance England.* Chicago: University of Chicago Press, 1988.

Mulryne, J. R. "Nationality and Language in Thomas Kyd's *Spanish Tragedy.*" In *Langues et Nations au Temps de la Renaissance,* ed. M. T. Jones-Davies, 67–91. Paris: Université de Paris-Sorbonne, 1991.

Munday, Anthony. *Sir Thomas More.* In *The Norton Shakespeare.* Ed. Stephen Greenblatt et al. New York: W. W. Norton, 1997.

Murphy, G. N. "A Note on Iago's Name." In *Literature and Society,* ed. Bernice Slote. Lincoln: University of Nebraska Press, 1964.

Myers, Joan, Marc Simmons and Donna Pierce. *Santiago: Saint of Two Worlds.* Albuquerque: University of New Mexico Press, 1992.

Neale, J. E. *Elizabeth I and Her Parliaments, 1584–1603.* New York: St. Martin's Press, 1957.

Neill, Michael. *Putting History to the Question: Power, Politics, and Society in English Renaissance Drama.* New York: Columbia University Press, 2000.

———. "Unproper Beds: Race, Adultery, and the Hideous in *Othello.*" In *Critical Essays on Shakespeare's Othello,* ed. Anthony Gerard Barthelemey, 187–215. New York: G. K. Hall, 1994.

Netanyahu, B. *The Origins of the Inquisition in Fifteenth-Century Spain.* New York: Random House, 1995.

New Catholic Encyclopedia. 16 vols. New York: McGraw Hill, 1967.

Newman, Karen. *Fashioning Femininity and English Renaissance Drama.* Chicago: University of Chicago Press, 1991.

Norman, Nathan. "Morocco's Reference to Spain." *Shakespeare Quarterly* 13 (1962): 363–64.

Nowell, Charles E. *A History of Portugal.* New York: D. Van Nostrand, 1952.

O'Brien, Conor Cruise. *God Land: Reflections on Religion and Nationalism.* Cambridge, Mass.: Harvard University Press, 1999.

Ocland, Christopher. *The Valiant Actes and victorious Battailes of the English Nation: from the yeare of our Lord, one thousand three hundred twentie and seven . . . to the yeere 1558.* London, 1585. STC 18777.

O'Connor, John J. Amadis de Gaule *and Its Influence on Elizabethan Literature.* New Brunswick, N.J.: Rutgers University Press, 1970.

Olin, John C., ed. *The Council of Trent on Justification, A Reformation Debate: John Calvin, Jacopo Sadoleto.* Grand Rapids: Baker Book House, 1966.

Olsen, H. Eric R. *The Calabrian Charlatan, 1598–1603: Messianic Nationalism in Early Modern Europe*. London: Palgrave Macmillan, 2003.

Orlin, Lena Cowen. *Private Matters and Public Culture in Post-Reformation England*. Ithaca, N.Y.: Cornell University Press, 1994.

Oxford Dictionary of the Christian Church. Second edition. Oxford: Oxford University Press, 1974.

Oxford English Dictionary. Second edition. Prepared by J. A. Simpson and E. S. C. Weiner. Oxford: Clarendon Press, 1989.

Pagden, Anthony. *European Encounters in the New World*. New Haven: Yale University Press, 1993.

———. *Lords of All the World: Ideologies of Empire in Spain, Britain and France, c. 1500–c. 1800*. New Haven: Yale University Press, 1995.

Palmer, Daryl W. "Merchants and Miscegenation: *The Three Ladies of London*, *The Jew of Malta*, and *The Merchant of Venice*." In MacDonald, ed., *Race, Ethnicity, and Power*, 36–66.

Parker, Geoffrey. *The Grand Strategy of Philip II*. New Haven: Yale University Press, 1998.

Parker, Patricia. "Fantasies of 'Race' and 'Gender': *Othello* and Bringing to Light." In Hendricks and Parker, eds., *Women, "Race," and Writing*, 84–100.

Parliamentary History of England: 1066–1803. Vol. 3. 1808. Ed. William Cobbett and John Wright. New York: Johnson Reprint, 1966.

Parmellee, Lisa Ferraro. *Good Newes from Fraunce: French Anti-League Propaganda in Late Elizabethan England*. Rochester: University of Rochester Press, 1996.

Parry, Glyn. "Elect Church or Elect Nation? The Reception of the *Acts and Monuments*." In *John Foxe: An Historcal Perspective*, ed. David Loades, 167–81. Brookfield, Vt.: Ashgate, 1999.

Parsons, John Carmi. *Eleanor of Castile: Queen and Society in Thirteenth-Century England*. New York: St. Martin's Press, 1995.

Patterson, Annabel. *Censorship and Interpretation: The Conditions of Writing and Reading in Early Modern England*. Madison: University of Wisconsin Press, 1984.

Paulson, Ronald. *Don Quixote in England: The Aesthetics of Laughter*. Baltimore: Johns Hopkins University Press, 1998.

Peele, George. *Battell of Alcazar, Fought in Barbarie, betweene Sebastian king of Portugall, and Addelmelec king of Marocco. With the death of Captaine Stukeley*. 1594. Facsimile edition. Oxford: Malone Society, 1907 [1963].

———. *A Farewell. Entitled to the famous and fortunate Generalls of our English forces: Sir John Norris & Syr Frauncis Drake Knights, and all theyr brave and resolute followers*. London, 1589. STC 19537.

———. *The Life and Works of George Peele*. 3 vols. Ed. Charles Prouty Tyler. New Haven: Yale University Press, 1952–70.

Peirce, C. S. *Peirce, On Signs*. Ed. James Hoopes. Chapel Hill: University of North Carolina Press, 1991.

Perceval, Richard [pseud. John Minsheu]. *A dictionarie in Spanish and English. . . . Now enlarged with many thousand words. . . . All done by John Minsheu professor of languages in London.* London, 1599. STC 19620.

Peristiany, J. G., ed. *Honor and Shame: The Values of Mediterranean Society.* Chicago: University of Chicago Press, 1966.

Persons, Robert [pseud. R. Doleman], *A Conference about the next Succession to the Crowne of Ingland.* 1594. Ed. D. M. Rodgers. Ilkley: Scholar Press, 1972.

Peters, Ralph. "Why We Fight." *American Heritage,* August–September 2002: 40–44.

Pettegree, Andrew. *Foreign Protestant Communities in Sixteenth-Century London.* Oxford: Clarendon Press, 1986.

Phillips, Carla Rahn. "Visualizing Imperium: *The Virgin of the Seafarers* and Spain's Self-Image in the Early Sixteenth Century." *Renaissance Quarterly* 58, no. 3 (Fall 2005): 815–56.

Powell, Brian. *Epic and Chronicle: The "Poema de mio Cid" and the "Crónica de veinte reyes."* London: Modern Humanities Research Association, 1983.

Powell, Philip Wayne. *Tree of Hate: Propaganda Affecting United States Relations with the Hispanic World.* New York: Basic Books, 1971.

Praz, Mario. *Machiavelli and the Elizabethans.* London: H. Milford, 1928 [Folcraft Library, 1973].

Prescott, William H. *The History of the Reign of Philip II.* 2 vols. Boston: Phillips, Samson, 1856.

Prestwich, Michael. *Edward I.* Berkeley: University of California Press, 1988.

———. *The Three Edwards: War and State in England, 1272–1377.* New York: St. Martin's Press, 1980.

Puttenham, George. *The Arte of English Poesie.* 1589. Facsimile Edition. Kent, Ohio: Kent State University Press, 1988.

Quilligan, Maureen. *The Language of Allegory.* Ithaca, N.Y.: Cornell University Press, 1979.

Rackin, Phyllis. "The Impact of Global Trade in *The Merchant of Venice.*" *Shakespeare Jahrbuch* 138 (2002): 73–88.

Raman, Shankar. *Framing India: The Colonial Imaginary in Early Modern Culture.* Stanford, Calif.: Stanford University Press, 2001.

Randall, Dale B. J. *The Golden Tapestry: A Survey of Non-chivalric Spanish Fiction in English Translation, 1543–1657.* Durham, N.C.: Duke University Press, 1963.

Riffaterre, Michael. *Semiotics of Poetry.* Bloomington: Indiana University Press, 1978.

Riggs, David. *The World of Christopher Marlowe.* New York: Henry Holt, 2004.

Rodríguez-Salgado, M. J. "The Anglo Spanish War: The Final Episode in 'The Wars of the Roses'?" In *England, Spain, and the Gran Armada, 1585–1604: Essays from the Anglo-Spanish Conferences, London and Madrid, 1988,* ed. M. J. Rodríguez-Salgado and Simon Adams, 1–44. Savage, Md.: Barnes and Noble, 1990.

Rosaldo, Renato. *Culture and Truth: The Remaking of Social Analysis.* Second edition. Boston: Beacon Press, 1993.

Rosen, Alan. "The Rhetoric of Exclusion: Jew, Moor, and the Boundaries of Discourse in *The Merchant of Venice.*" In MacDonald, ed., *Race, Ethnicity, and Power,* 67–79.

Roth, Cecil. *A History of the Marranos*. Fourth edition. New York: Herman Press, 1974.

————. "The Jews of Malta." *Transactions of the Jewish Historical Society of England* 12 (1931): 187–251.

————. *The Spanish Inquisition*. New York: W. W. Norton, 1964 [1996].

Rouse, A. L. *The Elizabethan Renaissance*. 3 vols. New York: Charles Scribner's Sons, 1972 [Chicago: Ivan R. Dee, 2000].

Royster, Francesca T. "White-limed Walls: Whiteness and Gothic Extremism in Shakespeare's *Titus Andronicus*." *Shakespeare Quarterly* 51, no. 4 (Winter, 2000): 432–55.

Ruggiero, Guido. *The Boundaries of Eros: Sex, Crime and Sexuality in Renaissance Venice*. Oxford: Oxford University Press, 1995.

————. *Violence in Early Modern Venice*. New Brunswick, N.J.: Rutgers University Press, 1980.

Russell, P. E. *The English Intervention in Spain and Portugal in the Time of Edward III and Richard II*. Oxford: Clarendon Press, 1955.

Rymer, Thomas. *A Short View of Tragedy*. 1693. Facsimile edition. London, 1970.

Sahlins, Marshall. *Islands of History*. Chicago: University of Chicago Press, 1985.

Salomon, Brownell. "Don Diego: Infamous Spaniard of English Renaissance Drama." *Journal of Popular Culture* 1 (1968): 433–38.

Sammons, Kay, and Joel Sherzer, eds. *Translating Native American Verbal Art: Ethnopoetics and the Ethnography of Speaking*. Washington, D.C.: Smithsonian Institution Press, 2000.

Sánchez, Joseph P. *The Spanish Black Legend: Origins of Anti-Hispanic Stereotypes*. Albuquerque: Spanish Colonial Research Center, 1990.

Scanlan, Thomas. *Colonial Writing in the New World, 1583–1671: Allegories of Desire*. Cambridge: Cambridge University Press, 1999.

Scarisbrick, J. J. *The Reformation and the English People*. Oxford: Basil Blackwell, 1984.

Schevill, Rudolf. "Erasmus and the Fate of a Liberalistic Movement Prior to the Counter Reformation." *Hispanic Review* 5, no. 2 (1937): 103–14.

Schmidt, Benjamin. *Innocence Abroad: The Dutch Imagination and the New World, 1570–1670*. Cambridge: Cambridge University Press, 2001.

Schmidt, Rachel. "The Development of *Hispanitas* in Spanish Sixteenth-Century Versions of the Fall of Numancia." *Renaissance and Reformation* 19, no. 2 (1995): 27–45.

Schmitt, Charles B., and Quentin Skinner, eds. *The Cambridge History of Renaissance Philosophy*. Cambridge: Cambridge University Press, 1988.

Scourfield, J. H. D. *Consoling Heliodorus: A Commentary on Jerome, Letter 60*. Oxford: Oxford University Press, 1993.

Seeley, J .R. *The Expansion of England*. 1881–82. Ed. John Gross. Chicago: University of Chicago Press, 1971.

Shakespeare, William. *The New Cambridge Shakespeare Othello*. Ed. Norman Sanders. Cambridge: Cambridge University Press, 1984.

————. *A New Variorum of Shakespeare*, vols. 6–7. Ed. H. H. Furness. Philadelphia: J. B. Lippincott, 1886–88.

————. *The Norton Shakespeare*. Ed. Stephen Greenblatt et al. New York: W. W. Norton, 1997.

Shapiro, James. *Shakespeare and the Jews.* New York: Columbia University Press, 1996.

———. "'*Which Is* The Merchant *here, and which* The Jew?': Shakespeare and the Economics of Influence." *Shakespeare Studies* 20 (1988): 269–79.

Shaw, George Bernard. "A Dressing Room Secret." In *Shaw on Shakespeare.* Ed. Edwin Wilson. New York: E. P. Dutton, 1961.

Shepherd, Simon. *Marlowe and the Politics of Elizabethan Theatre.* Brighton: Harvester Press, 1986.

Siegel, Paul N. "Shylock and the Puritan Usurers." *Studies in Shakespeare* (1953): 129–38.

Siemon, James R. "Sporting Kyd." *English Literary Renaissance* 24, no. 3 (Autumn 1994): 553–82.

Simerka, Barbara A. "'That the rulers should sleep without bad dreams': Anti-Epic Discourse in *La Numancia* and *Arauco domado.*" *Cervantes* 18, no. 1 (1998): 46–70.

Sire, H. J. A. *The Knights of Malta.* New Haven: Yale University Press, 1994.

Skelton, John. *The Complete English Poems.* Ed. John Scattergood. London: Penguin Books, 1983.

Smith, Anthony. *Myths and Memories of the Nation.* Oxford: Oxford University Press, 1999.

———. *Nationalism: Theory, Ideology, History.* Cambridge: Polity Press, 2001.

Smith, John. *The Generall Historie of Virginia, New England and the Summer Isles. The Complete Works of Captain John Smith (1580–1631).* 3 vols. Ed. Philip L. Barbour. Chapel Hill: University of North Carolina Press, 1986.

Solomon, Harry M. *The Rise of Robert Dodsley: Creating the New Age of Print.* Carbondale: Southern Illinois University Press, 1996.

Southern Poverty Law Center. Intelligence Report: "Broken Record." At http://www. splcenter.org/intel/intelreport/article.jsp?aid=589 (accessed December 1, 2007).

———. Intelligence Report: "The Nativists." At http://www.splcenter.org/intel/intelre port/article.jsp?aid=576 (accessed December 1, 2007).

Spenser, Edmund. *The Faerie Queene.* Ed. A. C. Hamilton. London: Longman, 1977.

———. *The Shepeardes Calender.* In *Spenser's Minor Poems,* ed. Ernest de Sélincourt, 1–121. Oxford: Oxford University Press, 1910 [1966].

———. *A View of the State of Ireland.* Ed. Andrew Hadfield and Willy Maley Oxford: Blackwell, 1997.

———. *The Works of Edmund Spenser: A Variorum Edition.* Vol. 10. Ed. Edwin Greenlaw et al. Baltimore: Johns Hopkins University Press, 1949.

———. *The Yale Edition of the Shorter Poems of Edmund Spenser.* Ed. William A. Oram et al. New Haven: Yale University Press, 1989.

Spivak, Bernard. *Shakespeare and the Allegory of Evil: The History of a Metaphor in Relation to His Major Villains.* New York: Columbia University Press, 1958.

Starkie, Walter. *The Road to Santiago.* New York: E. P. Dutton, 1957.

Steinsaltz, Adin. *The Essential Talmud.* Trans. Chaya Galai. London: Weidenfeld and Nicolson, 1977.

Stone, J. S. *The Cult of Santiago.* New York: Longmans, 1927.

Stone, Lawrence. *The Crisis of the Aristocracy, 1558–1641.* Oxford: Clarendon Press, 1965.

Sullivan, John L. "Annexation." *United States Magazine and Democratic Review*. 1845. In *Annals of America*, 7:288–92. Chicago: Encyclopedia Britannica, 1976.

Suskind, Ron. "Why Are These Men Laughing?" *Esquire* (January 2003). Available at http://www.esquire.com/features/esq0103-jan_rove_rev_2#story (accessed March 3, 2004).

Sweet, James H. "The Iberian Roots of American Racist Thought." *William and Mary Quarterly* 54, no. 1 (1997): 143–66.

Taine, Hippolyte. *Histoire de la littérature anglaise*. 3 vols. 1863. Trans. H. Van Laun. New York, 1871.

Tanner, Marie. *The Last Descendant of Aeneas: The Hapsburgs and the Mythic Image of the Emperor*. New Haven: Yale University Press, 1993.

Taylor, Gary. "The Cultural Politics of Maybe." In Dutton, Findlay, and Wilson, eds., *Theatre and Religion*, 242–58.

Thomas, Hugh. *The Slave Trade: The Story of the Atlantic Slave Trade, 1440–1870*. New York: Simon and Schuster, 1997.

Tilley, Arthur. "Some Pamphlets of the French Wars of Religion." *English Historical Review* 14, no. 55 (July 1899): 451–70.

Tillyard, E. M. W. *The Elizabethan World Picture*. New York, 1943.

Tombs, Robert, and Isabelle Tombs. *That Sweet Enemy: The French and the British from the Sun King to the Present*. New York: Alfred A. Knopf, 2007.

Trend, J. B., ed. *The Oxford Book of Spanish Verse: XIIIth Century–XXth Century*. 1940. Oxford: Clarendon Press, 1969.

Trevor, Douglas. "Sadness in *The Faerie Queene*." In *Reading the Early Modern Passions: Essays in the Cultural History of Emotion*, ed. Gail Kern Paster, Katherine Rowe, and Mary Floyd-Wilson, 240–52. Philadelphia: University of Pennsylvania Press, 2004.

Trevor-Roper, Hugh R. "Spain and Europe 1598–1621." In *The New Cambridge Modern History*, vol. 4, ed. J. P. Cooper, 260–82. Cambridge: Cambridge University Press, 1970.

Turner, Victor. *Dramas, Fields, and Metaphors: Symbolic Action in Human Society*. Ithaca, N.Y.: Cornell University Press, 1974.

Tyler, James. *The Early Guitar: A History and Handbook*. London: Oxford University Press, 1980.

Ungerer, Gustav. "Portia and the Prince of Morocco." *Shakespeare Studies* 31 (2003): 89–126.

Vaughan, Alden T., and Virginia Mason Vaughan. "Before *Othello*: Elizabethan Representations of Sub-Saharan Africans." *William and Mary Quarterly*, third series, 54, no. 1 (January 1997): 19–44.

Vernon [Veron], John [Jean Senonoys]. *The Huntynge of Purgatorie to death*. London, 1561. STC 24683.

———. *A Stronge Battery against the Idolatrous invocation of dead Saintes, and against the having or setting Up of Images in the house of prayer, or any other place where there is any paril of Idolatrye*. London, 1562. STC 24686.

Verstegen, Richard. *A Declaration of the True Causes of the Great Troubles Presupposed to be Intended Against the Realm of England*. Antwerp: [J. Tragnesius,] 1592. STC 10005.

————. *A Restitution of Decayed Intelligence.* 1605. Facsimile edition. Ed. D. M. Rogers. Ilkley, U.K.: Scolar Press, 1976.

Viña Liste, José María, ed. *Mio Cid Campeador.* Madrid: Biblioteca Castro, 2006.

Vincent, Bernard. "The Moriscos and Circumcision." In Cruz and Parry, eds., *Culture and Control*, 78–92. Minneapolis: University of Minnesota Press, 1992.

Vitkus, Daniel. *Turning Turk: English Theater and the Multicultural Mediterranean, 1570–1630.* New York: Palgrave Macmillan, 2003.

Volosinov, V. N. *Marxism and the Philosophy of Language.* Trans. Ladislav Matejka and I. R. Titunik. Cambridge, Mass.: Harvard University Press, 1973 [1929].

Voltaire. "On Tragedy." In *Letters Concerning the English Nation.* Ed. Nicholas Cronk. Oxford: Oxford University Press, 1994.

W., H., trans. *A Pageant of Spanish Humours: Wherein are decsribed and lively portrayed, the kinds and qualities of a Signior of Spaine.* London, 1592. STC 22620.

Walker, Rose. "Leonor of England and Eleanor of Castile: Anglo-Iberian Marriage and Cultural Exchange in the Twelfth and Thirteenth Centuries." In Bullón-Fernández, ed., *England and Iberia*, 67–87.

Wallerstein, Immanuel. "The Construction of Peoplehood: Racism, Nationalism, Ethnicity." In Balibar and Wallerstein, eds., *Race, Nation, Class*, 71–85.

————. *The Modern World System: Capitalist Agriculture and the Origins of the World Economy in the Sixteenth Century.* New York: Academic Press, 1974.

Ward, Philip, ed. *The Oxford Companion to Spanish Literature.* Oxford: Oxford University Press, 1978.

Weber, David J. *The Spanish Frontier in North America.* New Haven: Yale University Press, 1992.

Wheatcroft, Andrew. *The Hapsburgs: Embodying Empire.* London: Viking, 1995.

Whetstone, George. *The English Myrror.* 1586. Facsimile edition. New York: Da Capo Press, 1973.

Whigham, Frank. "Ideology and Class Conduct in *The Merchant of Venice*." *Renaissance Drama* 10 (1979): 93–115.

White, Hayden. *Metahistory: The Historical Imagination in Nineteenth-Century Europe.* Baltimore: Johns Hopkins University Press, 1973.

White, Peter. *A Discoverie of the Jesuitical Opinion of Justification, Guilefully Uttered by Sherwin at the Time of his Execution.* London, 1582. STC 25401.

Whittled, Christopher. "Sir Lewis Lewkenor and *The Merchant of Venice*: A Suggested Connection." *Notes and Queries*, n.s., 11 (1964): 123–33.

Wikipedia, s.v. "Peters, Ralph," at http://en.wikipedia.org/wiki/Ralph_Peters (accessed December 1, 2007).

William of Orange [ascribed to Pierre Loyseleur]. *An Apologie, or Defence of, My Lord the Prince of Orange.* Delft, 1580. STC 15208.

Williams, Deanne. *The French Fetish from Chaucer to Shakespeare.* Cambridge: Cambridge University Press, 2004.

Williams, Raymond. *Keywords: A Vocabulary of Culture and Society.* New York: Oxford University Press, 1983.

————. *Marxism and Literature*. Oxford: Oxford University Press, 1977.

Wills, Garry. *Venice: Lion City, The Religion of Empire*. New York: Washington Square Press, 2001.

Wilson, Edward M. "A Hispanist Looks at *Othello*." In *Spanish and English Literature of the 16th and 17th Centuries*. Cambridge: Cambridge University Press, 1980.

Wilson, Robert. *The Three Lords and Three Ladies of London*. 1590. Facsimile edition. Ed. John S. Farmer. London: Tudor Facsimile Texts, 1912.

Wilson, Thomas. *A Christian Dictionarie: opening the signification of the chiefe wordes of the Old and New Testament*. London, 1612. STC 25786.

————. *A Christian Dictionarie*. Third edition. London, 1615. STC 25788.

Winstanley, Lilian. *"Othello" as the Tragedy of Italy: showing that Shakespeare's Italian contemporaries interpreted the story of the Moor and the Lady of Venice as symbolizing the tragedy of their country in the grip of Spain*. London: T. F. Unwin, 1924.

Wolf, Eric R. *Europe and the People Without History*. Berkeley: University of California Press, 1982.

Wooden, Warren W. *John Foxe*. Boston: Twayne, 1983.

Woodfield, Denis B. *Surreptitious Printing in England*. New York: Bibliographical Society of America, 1971.

Wright, Louis B. "Propaganda Against James I's 'Appeasement' of Spain." *Huntington Library Quarterly* 6 (1942–43): 149–72.

Yates, Frances A. *Astraea: The Imperial Theme in the Sixteenth Century*. London: Routledge and Kegan Paul, 1975.

INDEX

ACKNOWLEDGMENTS

A BOOK THIS long in gestation accrues many debts. I owe Jerry Singerman special thanks for seeing the value in my initial proposal, and for working with me to bring the manuscript to fruition as a book. Penn's two anonymous readers, who helped make the end result more solid than it would otherwise have been, also have my sincere thanks.

I am especially grateful to three colleagues whose work I have much admired, and whose support at various stages of my career has been crucial. Huston Diehl has made the most graceful transition imaginable from instructor, to mentor, to friend and confidant; all these years on, I still imagine her my ideal reader. Emily Bartels took an interest in my early publications, which led to several joint conference presentations; I remain inspired by the common interests and occasional exchanges we share. Similar offers from Barbara Fuchs helped to put me on the scholarly map; more recently, Barbara's invitation to join her Folger Institute seminar "The Spanish Connection" introduced me to a growing network of Anglo-Hispanists with whom I continue to enjoy dialogue and fellowship.

As early portions of this book were presented at various meetings of the Shakespeare Association of America, the Renaissance Society of America, the Modern Language Association, and the Sixteenth-Century Studies Conference, I benefited from the comments of more scholars than I can remember. Among the many, Roland Greene, Jacques Lezra, Alan Rosen, Cyndia Clegg, Gary Taylor, Olga Valbuena, Imtiaz Habib, and especially Jonathan Burton (who graciously added Pittsburgh hospitality to the mix) have my deep appreciation.

Over the years, the Folger Shakespeare Library has been an indispensable resource and refuge. Alongside Robert Appelbaum, John Sweet, and Pompa Banerjee, I participated in Karen Kupperman's 2000 symposium, "Texts of Imagination and Empire: The Founding of Jamestown in Its Atlantic Context," which helped sharpen my imperial focus. Bob Appelbaum, in particular, lent me generous suggestions and his writerly ear. Dan Vitkus, in whose seminar (co-led by Arthur Little) at the 1996 World Shakespeare Congress I presented my first Othello-Santiago musings, Brian Lockey, for whom I presented a paper at the RSA meetings in Cambridge in 2005, and Edmund Campos, who has several times pointed me toward texts I had overlooked and with whom I was a copresenter in a paper session (organized by Barbara Fuchs) at the 2000 SAA meetings in Montreal, have been *compadres* at the Folger and elsewhere. While Kathleen Lynch made me feel at home in the Library from the moment of my first visit, Georgianna Zeigler, who continues to field my research queries, graciously helped to acquaint me with the Folger's resources and Washington, D.C. In the course of several trips to Washington, as well as one to England, I have found inspiration while breaking bread and sharing conversation with Gerard Kilroy.

I acknowledge also the enduring contributions of Alan Nagel, Alvin Snider, and Garrett Stewart, along with Laurie Graham, Francisco Sánchez, Katy Stavreva, Kate Moncrief, Pat Ryan, Kim Smith, Mary Janell Metzger, Robert Morey, Nancy Hayes, and the late Elizabeth Dietz, all of whom gave generously and repeatedly of their time and intellect during several phases of this effort. I credit, too, my undergraduate instructors at Pomona College—Arden Reed, Paul Mann, Tom Pinney, Howard Young, Bob Mezey, the late Dick Barnes, and my Shakespeare teacher, Martha Andresen—for having inspired me to join the profession. Among all my early influences, though, I owe most profound thanks to Samuel H. Mayo, dean and professor emeritus of Los Angeles Valley College, in whose courses on the history of the Americas and the history of Mexico I first began to confront *la leyenda negra*. The support of Harvey Cohen, my LAVC *carnal* and Sephardic interlocutor since the early 1980s, and Lorina Quartarone, who continues to avail me of her considerable Latin language expertise, I regard as having been vital.

Since arriving at Millsaps College in 1998 I have benefited from the support of the National Endowment for the Humanities, the E. B. Stewart Family Endowment, the Hearin Foundation, and a series of Faculty Development Grants. I am grateful to our dean, Richard Smith, who has supported faculty research and conference travel at a level uncommon among institutions of our size and financial resources. I am thankful, too, for the continuing fellowship of colleagues in the Millsaps Departments of English, History, Philosophy, Art, and Modern Languages, and to our librarians, who have entertained my incessant interlibrary loan requests. I recognize especially the intellectual exchange and camaraderie of our "New College" dean of International Education, George Bey, my Department of Sociology-Anthropology friends, Mike Galaty and Julian Murchison, and our associate at Kaxil Kiuic, Yucatán, Tomás Gallareta Negrón, from whom I continue to learn during our annual team-teaching adventures. And I am thankful as well for the former Millsaps students—including Lauren Garrett, Judith Coleman, Ashley Nichols, Michael Pickard, Kenneth Townsend, Matthew Luter, Richie Caldwell, and John Yargo—who have graced my years in Mississippi.

Early versions of several chapters have appeared in print. A portion of Chapter 1 was published as "From Etho*s* to Ethnos: Hispanizing 'the Spaniard' in the Old World and the New," *CR: The New Centennial Review* 2, no. 1 (Spring 2002), with added matter coming in part from "The Specter of Spain in John Smith's Colonial Writing," in *Envisioning an English Empire: Jamestown and the Making of the North Atlantic World*, edited by Robert Appelbaum and John Wood Sweet, pp. 111–34 (Philadelphia: University of Pennsylvania Press), 2005. In somewhat different form, Chapter 3 was published in *English Literary Renaissance* 31, no. 2 (Spring 2001), as "Ethos, Empire, and the Valiant Acts of Thomas Kyd's Tragedy of 'The Spains,'" with additional passages coming from "Nationalism, the Black Legend, and the Revised *Spanish Tragedy*," *English Literary Renaissance* 39, no. 2 (Spring 2009); similarly, a less developed version of Chapter 6 was published in *Representations* 62 (Spring 1998) as "Un-sainting James: *Othello* and the 'Spanish Spirits' of Shakespeare's Globe" (copyright © The Regents of the University of California). Material from each of these essays is reprinted by permission, with special thanks to Stephen Greenblatt and Arthur Kinney for their comments on the *Representations* and *ELR* essays, respectively.

Finally, I thank my wife, Kathi, for her love, perseverance, proofreading, and occasional rhetorical challenges, my stepdaughter, Karin, for her bibliographic aid and for bringing Charles Henry into our lives, and our extended Griffin-Rasmussen clan for emotional buttressing, good humor, and cold beer.